Poor Relief in England, 1350–1600

Between the mid fourteenth century and the Poor Laws of 1598 and 1601, English poor relief moved towards a more coherent and comprehensive network of support. Marjorie McIntosh's study, the first to trace developments across that time span, focuses on three types of assistance: licensed begging and the solicitation of charitable alms; hospitals and almshouses for the bedridden and elderly; and the aid given by parishes. It explores changing conceptions of poverty and charity and altered roles for the church, state, and private organizations in the provision of relief. The study highlights the creativity of local people in responding to poverty, cooperation between national and lower levels of government, the problems of fraud and negligence, and mounting concern with proper supervision and accounting. This ground-breaking work challenges existing accounts of the Poor Laws, showing that they addressed problems with forms of aid already in use rather than creating a new system of relief.

Marjorie Keniston McIntosh is Distinguished Professor of History Emerita, University of Colorado at Boulder. Her previous publications include *Controlling Misbehavior in England, 1370–1600* (Cambridge, 1998), *Working Women in English Society, 1300–1620* (Cambridge, 2005), and two books about African women in the nineteenth and twentieth centuries.

Poor Relief in England, 1350–1600

Marjorie Keniston McIntosh

University of Colorado at Boulder

CAMBRIDGE
UNIVERSITY PRESS

CAMBRIDGE
UNIVERSITY PRESS

The Edinburgh Building, Cambridge CB2 8RU, UK

Published in the United States of America by Cambridge University Press, New York

Cambridge University Press is part of the University of Cambridge.

It furthers the University's mission by disseminating knowledge in the pursuit of education, learning and research at the highest international levels of excellence.

www.cambridge.org
Information on this title: www.cambridge.org/9781107634534

© Marjorie Keniston McIntosh 2012

First published 2012
First paperback edition 2013

A catalogue record for this publication is available from the British Library

ISBN 978-1-107-01508-1 Hardback
ISBN 978-1-107-63453-4 Paperback

Contents

*Online appendices in website maintained by Cambridge University
Press (cited in text as "CUP Online Apps."):
www.cambridge.org/mcintosh/appendices*

Acknowledgements

Writing this book has heightened my gratitude to the many teachers who helped me become a social historian. David Riesman and Erik Erikson guided my initial independent studies on the relation between history, sociology, and psychology in 1960–1; Myron Gilmore supervised my attempt to utilize those approaches in an undergraduate honors thesis on the late medieval Dance of Death. During my first year in graduate school at Harvard, I focused on African history. But shortly before classes started the following September, the History Department decided that Africa was not a suitable field for Ph.D. work, because its history relied so heavily on oral sources. I therefore signed up at the last minute for a seminar on the reign of Edward VI of England. Led by W. K. Jordan, who was writing his two-volume study of the reign of the boy king, our discussions were structured around a series of interpretive questions. Each student was given a document to analyze and present weekly, an experience from which I gained an affection and respect for primary sources that has lasted ever since. Professor Jordan then supervised my Ph.D. thesis on the Cooke family of Gidea Hall with his usual gentlemanly courtesy. Joel Hurstfield provided valuable suggestions and friendship while I was doing thesis research in England, as did Michael Postan and Geoffrey Elton during the next decade. After Professor Jordan suffered an incapacitating stroke, Giles Constable kindly stepped in to offer advice and encouragement. To all of them, I am deeply indebted.

Because the sources for early poor relief are disparate in nature and scattered among many different collections, research for this study stretched over several decades. The book pulls together manuscript material from more than 70 archives, joined by information from printed primary sources and secondary studies. Most of the research in local record offices was done while I was working simultaneously on two earlier projects (*Controlling Misbehavior in England, 1370–1600* and *Working Women in English Society, 1300–1620*). The extended period of travel, analysis, and writing that finally resulted in this book was generously supported by a Research Fellowship from the National Endowment for

viii

the Humanities and the Visiting Research Fellowship in the Arts at Newnham College, Cambridge, 1983–4; a Visiting Research Fellowship at the Borthwick Institute for Historical Research, University of York, summer 1992; a Fellowship from the John Simon Guggenheim Memorial Foundation, 1995–6; and multiple grants from the Committee on Research and Creative Work, the Graduate Committee on the Arts and Humanities, and the Distinguished Professor program at the University of Colorado at Boulder, 1984–2010.

Notes on conventions and online resources

Several conventions need explanation. The 125 churchwardens' accounts or other church books used to analyze parish activity are cited in notes as CWA followed by a number (for example, CWA #52). The CWAs are listed numerically, with archival/bibliographic information, in part 1 of the References. In recent years I gained some information through the online entries in Access to Archives. That material is cited with a reference to the archival source, as "used through A2A," to make clear that I did not consult the original document. When a second reference is provided at the end of a given note with the wording "For below, see . . ." it refers to the following sentence. Money is given in the system of pounds ($\pounds$), shillings (s.), and pence (d.) in use at the time, in which 12d. = 1s. and 20s. = $\pounds$1. When an accounting year spans more than a single calendar year, the date is shown in the format 1576–7. I have modernized the spelling of place names, personal first names, and direct quotations from English manuscripts or early printed sources; Latin quotations are translated into modern English. Manuscript citations give fol. or p. before the folio or page number, with r indicating the front of a folio and v the back. The index includes all places mentioned in the text, but personal names appear only for major entries. Hospitals and almshouses are indexed under their location, not the name of the institution.

To lessen the mass of this book, ten of its detailed methodological and quantitative appendices have been posted on a permanent, open access website maintained by Cambridge University Press. They are cited in the notes as "CUP Online Apps." and are numbered, to distinguish them from the appendices included in the printed volume, which are labeled with letters. The web address for the supplementary appendices is: www.cambridge.org/mcintosh/appendices under the "resources" tab.

Abbreviations

A2A	Access to Archives, an online catalogue of document listings from many county and national collections
APC	*Acts of the Privy Council of England*
Beds&LA	Bedfordshire and Luton Archives, Bedford
BerksRO	Berkshire Record Office, Reading
BIA	Borthwick Institute for Archives, University of York
BodlL	Bodleian Library, University of Oxford
BristolRO	Bristol Record Office
BritL	British Library, London
B-u-TwRO	Berwick-upon-Tweed Record Office
CalB&EMSS	Calendar of the Bridgewater and Ellesmere MSS, Dockets, section 8 (an unpublished list of items in Huntington Library EL 3044–5609)
CambsA	Cambridgeshire Archives, Cambridge
CambUL	Cambridge University Library, Department of Manuscripts
CantCA	Canterbury Cathedral Archives
CBucksS	Centre for Buckinghamshire Studies, Aylesbury
CHAbing	Christ's Hospital, Abingdon, Berkshire
ChChRO	Cheshire and Chester Record Office, Chester
CKentS	Centre for Kentish Studies, Maidstone
CornwRO	Cornwall Record Office, Truro
CorpCCC	Corpus Christi College, Cambridge
CPR	*Calendar of the Patent Rolls*
CSPD	*Calendar of the State Papers, Domestic Series, 1547–1625*
CumbAS-C	Cumbria Archive Service, Carlisle
CWA	Churchwardens' accounts or parish books (see References, part 1)
DerbRO	Derbyshire Record Office, Matlock
DevonRO	Devon Record Office, Exeter
DoncA	Doncaster Archives

DorsetHC	Dorset History Centre, Dorchester
DurhUL	Durham University Library, Special Collections, Palace Green Library
ERYoAS-B	East Riding of Yorkshire Archives Service, Beverley
EssexRO-Ch	Essex Record Office, Chelmsford
EssexRO-Colch	Essex Record Office, Colchester
ESussRO	East Sussex Record Office, Lewes
GloucsA	Gloucestershire Archives, Gloucester
GuLLond	Guildhall Library, London, all of whose MSS are now at the LondMA
HadlTR	Hadleigh, Suffolk, town records
HampsRO	Hampshire Record Office, Winchester
HarvUA	Harvard University Archives, Cambridge, Mass.
HerefRO	Herefordshire Record Office, Hereford
HertsA	Hertfordshire Archives, Hertford
HMC	Historical Manuscripts Commission
HullCA	Hull City Archives, Kingston upon Hull
HuntL	Huntington Library, San Marino, Calif.
HuntsA	Huntingtonshire Archives, Huntington
JP	Justice of the Peace
LambA	Lambeth Archives, Minet Library, London
LambPL	Lambeth Palace Library, London
LancsRO	Lancashire Record Office, Preston
L&IS	List and Index Society
L&P	*Calendar of Letters and Papers, Foreign and Domestic, of the Reign of Henry VIII*
LichfRO	Lichfield Record Office, Lichfield
LincsA	Lincolnshire Archives, Lincoln
LondMA	London Metropolitan Archives, Clerkenwell, London
MS or MSS	Manuscript or manuscripts
NELA	North East Lincolnshire Archives, Grimsby
NewCO	New College, Oxford, Archives
NoDevRO	North Devon Record Office, Barnstaple
NorfRO	Norfolk Record Office, Norwich
NorthantsRO	Northamptonshire Record Office, Northampton
NottsA	Nottinghamshire Archives, Nottingham
N-u-TrMus	Newark-upon-Trent Museum
NYksRO	North Yorkshire County Record Office, Northallerton
OED	*Oxford English Dictionary*

OxfdsRO	Oxfordshire Record Office, Oxford
ROLeics	The Record Office for Leicestershire, Wigston Magna
ShakespCLA	Shakespeare Centre Library & Archive, Stratford-upon-Avon
ShropsA	Shropshire Archives, Shrewsbury
SomstRO	Somerset Record Office, Taunton
SouthCA	Southampton City Archives
SR	*The Statutes of the Realm*
StaffsRO	Staffordshire Record Office, Stafford
StGeoCh	St. George's Chapel, Windsor Castle
SuffRO-BSE	Suffolk Record Office, Bury St. Edmunds
SuffRO-I	Suffolk Record Office, Ipswich
SurreyHC	Surrey History Centre, Woking
T&WAS	Tyne and Wear Archives Service, Newcastle upon Tyne
TNA-PRO	The National Archives, Public Record Office, Kew
TRP	*Tudor Royal Proclamations*
ULondL	University of London Library, Archives and Manuscripts
UNottL	University of Nottingham Library, Manuscripts and Special Collections
VAI	*Visitation Articles and Injunctions of the Period of the Reformation*
VCH	Victoria County History (= *The Victoria History of the County of . . .*)
W&FM	Wisbech and Fenland Museum, Wisbech
WarwsRO	Warwickshire Record Office, Warwick
Wilts&SA	Wiltshire and Swindon Archives, Chippenham
WorcsRO	Worcestershire Record Office, Worcester
WSussRO	West Sussex Record Office, Chichester
WYksAS-L	West Yorkshire Archive Service, Leeds
YorkCA	York City Archives

1 Introduction

Between 1350 and 1600, poor relief in England moved from a complex array of diverse kinds of assistance towards a more coherent and comprehensive network of support. The first century after the massive outbreak of bubonic plague in 1348–9 was marked by low population and relatively mild problems with poverty, but unstable economic and demographic conditions in the later fifteenth and early sixteenth centuries rendered more people vulnerable to short-term hardship. Throughout those years most aid was awarded only occasionally, typically to individuals struck by some particular misfortune. Between around 1530 and 1553, poverty intensified and the forms of relief changed significantly. Whereas attitudes towards the poor and almsgiving had been shaped by Catholic beliefs during the later medieval years, the new patterns were influenced by humanist or "commonwealth" ideas about the responsibilities of a Christian state and by early Protestant theology. The most important development, initiated by the central government, was the introduction of parish-based aid, financed by regular payments made by wealthier members of the community. During the second half of the sixteenth century, as need continued to mount, local communities and generous individuals experimented with how best to provide assistance. The elderly and chronically poor now qualified for help, sometimes receiving ongoing support. The bad harvests of the later 1580s and 1590s increased the suffering and heightened public concern about poverty, leading to the massive Poor Laws of 1598 and 1601.

This book examines three main forms of poor relief across those centuries: licensed begging by individuals and gathering for charitable institutions; the free housing and sometimes other benefits offered by hospitals and almshouses; and aid given through or by parishes. Other kinds of aid receive only peripheral attention here, including the essential help provided by friends, relatives, and neighbors.[1] Although many people drew upon informal support, it is seldom documented in writing prior to the

---

[1] For these kinds of aid, see ch. 1.4 below.

seventeenth century and hence cannot be examined in any detail. The three kinds of semi-institutionalized aid, by contrast, found their way into the records, enabling us to trace their history over time.

I argue that the development of poor relief between the mid fourteenth and the late sixteenth centuries was molded by three main factors: major transitions in the material context, stemming from demographic and economic factors; the changing ideology of poverty and charity; and altered patterns of government, primarily the increasing legislative activity of Parliament, the initiative and energy of the royal Privy Council, the new authority of county Justices of the Peace (JPs), and the expanding roles of parishes in their secular capacity. My account emphasizes the originality of the statutes formulated at a national level and the creativity of the practices tried out at local levels during the middle and later sixteenth century. It highlights also the importance for poor people of access to predictable assistance during a period of need and in some cases to ongoing relief, through admittance to a residential institution or parish support.

This book offers a different analytical perspective from the many fine studies of late medieval and early modern poor relief written during the past century.[2] The pioneer scholars of English poor relief focused on the Poor Laws of 1598 and 1601.[3] Their interest in earlier developments rarely extended beyond the kinds of assistance found in sixteenth-century cities and the role of Parliament and the Privy Council in devising and enforcing policy. The legislation of 1598 and 1601 was presented as significant in two respects: it contained some unusual features, principally its use of the parish as the basic institution for administering aid and its reliance upon local taxes to pay for the needy; and it ushered in a new era of parish-based relief that continued – with some adjustment during the 1660s and the 1790s – until 1834. That era became known as "the Old Poor Law."

I show that the 1598 and 1601 laws did not create a new system of poor relief. With regard to parish aid, they offered corrections to certain features of the foundational statute of 1552, as modified slightly in 1563. If one wished to assign a birth date to the Old Poor Law's system of parish-based relief, the mid sixteenth century would be a better choice than 1598 and 1601. The late Elizabethan legislation also recognized that authorized begging and gathering were crippled by irremediable problems, and it

---

[2] For the historiography of this full span, see McIntosh, "Local Responses"; for the medieval period see also Horden, "Small Beer?" and Fideler, *Social Welfare*, chs. 1–2; for the sixteenth century, see also Fideler, "Introduction."

[3] E.g., Leonard, *Early History*, and Webb and Webb, *English Poor Law History, Part I*.

improved the functioning of residential institutions for the poor. The statutes created a more secure legal status for charitable activities and a new legal process through which proper performance of their functions could be demanded. The 1598 and 1601 laws thus enhanced the loosely connected network of relief that was already in operation in many parts of the country. That pattern, which has been described for a later period as "the mixed economy of welfare," combined parish-based assistance, private charities, and informal help.[4] The multiple kinds of potential aid – usually occasional – that had been available prior to the ending of Catholic institutions had thus been narrowed into a somewhat more coherent system.

In the past few decades, historians of poverty have broadened our horizons. We now have some excellent surveys of the early modern period. Paul Slack's *Poverty and Policy in Tudor and Stuart England* provides a concise and thoughtful overview that includes discussion of the legislation that preceded the late Elizabethan poor laws; the earlier sections of Steve Hindle's *On the Parish?: The Micro-Politics of Poor Relief in Rural England, c. 1550–1750* integrate political, economic, and social factors in investigating responses to poverty.[5] Other scholars have examined the lives and agency of the poor themselves, in rural as well as urban settings, at various times between the later sixteenth and the eighteenth centuries.[6] Medievalists have mined their own documents to see what can be extracted about needy people and aid to them, and we have several preliminary accounts of broader patterns of assistance.[7] Certain kinds of informal support have been described as fully as the sources permit.[8]

By the early twenty-first century, the pendulum of historical assessment concerning the relation between medieval and Elizabethan patterns had swung to the opposite extreme. Whereas the period before 1530 had previously been largely ignored, some medievalists now claimed that aspects of poor relief considered distinctive by early modernists were in place by the fourteenth or fifteenth centuries. Late medieval villages, they

---

[4] Innes, "'Mixed Economy'."

[5] Certain aspects of Slack's study were expanded later in his *From Reformation to Improvement*. Fideler's *Social Welfare* is unusual in discussing sub-periods between 1350 and 1610 as well as later ones.

[6] E.g., Hitchcock et al., eds., *Chronicling Poverty*, Schen, *Charity*, Botelho, *Old Age*, Hitchcock, *Down and Out*, Ottaway, *Decline of Life*, Ben-Amos, *Culture of Giving*, and Snell, *Parish and Belonging*.

[7] E.g., Rubin, *Charity and Community*, Cullum, "And Hir Name was Charite," Cullum and Goldberg, "Charitable Provision," and Clark, "Charitable Bequests." For valuable surveys, see Dyer, *Standards of Living*, ch. 9, and Horden, "Small Beer?"

[8] E.g., Clark, "Social Welfare," and Ben-Amos, "Gifts and Favors" and her *Culture of Giving*.

proposed, were already doing much of what had been seen as novel about Tudor legislation and local practice, including a linkage between taxation and assistance to the poor, use of a special box in the church to collect donations, and the particular techniques used to raise funds for parishioners who needed help.[9]

The evidence presented in this book shows that although many forms of aid were indeed present during the later medieval years, the range and predictability of institutionalized assistance were limited as compared to what began to develop during Edward's reign. Over the rest of the sixteenth century, authorized begging was extended to a wider range of people, while almshouses and hospitals continued to move towards sheltering the elderly poor. Many parishes went beyond the earlier pattern of handing out a little food or money from bequests or at funerals in favor of regular collections from their more prosperous members, using the income to help local people who could not work to support themselves. Some parishes imposed fixed, obligatory assessments on those who were able to pay and gave weekly sums to those who needed relief. Late Elizabethan assistance was different in intensity and scope from what had been present before around 1530. This chapter introduces some essential concepts and lays out the three types of aid to be analyzed below, together with some analytic questions and the sources used. After summarizing the ideological and practical context within which poor relief developed, we look briefly at some additional forms of help that will not be explored fully in this study.

1.1   Poverty, charity, and three forms of relief

Late medieval and early modern English people wrestled with complex issues concerning poverty and poor relief. What circumstances led to undeserved need, and how could the various types of poverty be defined? What forms of aid were available, and how should they be awarded? In deciding which sorts of poor people warranted assistance, should officials impose residency requirements or behavioral conditions? How could relief be structured so as to lessen the possibility of fraud on the part of those requesting relief and of dishonesty or incompetence on the part of those administering it? Was helping the poor primarily a religious and moral obligation, or were there more functional reasons for awarding

---

[9] Dyer, "English Medieval Village," esp. 415–16, his *An Age of Transition?*, 240 and 248, Smith, "Charity, Self-Interest," esp. 32, Bennett, "Conviviality and Charity," and see ch. 4 below.

assistance? The way in which these questions were framed and the answers to them were unstable between 1350 and 1600, due to changes in attitudes and the material environment. Ideas and approaches that worked well in one generation might not be useful in the next, as the nature and depth of poverty shifted, as religious, social, and political thought moved in new directions, and as institutions assumed different forms. Leaders of the church and state attempted to develop appropriate conceptual frameworks and national policies, while local officers made their own day-to-day decisions about how to respond. People making policy decisions and administering poor relief in Europe and North America in the twenty-first century struggle with similar problems.

Before investigating how those questions were addressed during the later medieval and Tudor periods, we need to consider who was included within the category of "the poor." The largest subset within that broad and diverse concept consisted of lay people who lacked sufficient resources to provide for themselves, usually because they were unable to work for their own support. Such dependence frequently stemmed from "life-cycle" problems, affecting people only at certain ages or stages. Among them were orphaned babies and young children below the age at which they could be placed as servants or apprentices, widows with youngsters at home, and the infirm elderly. Because most English households were small (containing just a nuclear family and perhaps some young servants, as was characteristic of the northwest European marriage pattern), needy people might not have the option of being taken in by an extended household of their relatives (as was more common in southern Europe). Physically or developmentally disabled people generally qualified for help too, as did those who had been injured or were temporarily or chronically ill. Another kind of poverty consisted of individuals who had previously enjoyed adequate means but had fallen into "accidental need" through some specific misfortune, such as a fire, shipwreck, or being forced to pay ransom after being captured by foreign enemies or pirates. Prior to the Reformation, members of religious orders who had accepted voluntary poverty and begging as a spiritual obligation were also viewed as legitimate recipients of alms, although they will not be discussed here. Poverty had a social component as well. People who faced extreme hardship were often isolated, lacking emotional and economic support from friends or kin.

Other kinds of poverty caused more anxiety. Leaders at all levels agreed that anyone who was physically capable of labor but chose not to do so, preferring to beg or resort to illegal means to make ends meet, should not be helped. Such people were especially worrying when they left home to wander around the country. A series of Parliamentary acts ordered that they be put in the stocks, whipped, or receive other forms of punishment. It was not clear, however, how to define people who were able and willing to labor but could not find sufficient work to support their families. Between 1350 and at least the 1460s (in some areas the 1520s), virtually everyone who sought employment could find it. By the later sixteenth century, however, the problem of people who could not obtain work – or enough work to provide for their households – had become far more severe. Although many of them faced real need, they rarely received assistance, because trying to support them all would have added enormously to the cost of relief.

The terminology of aid to the poor likewise needs explanation. The term "charity" grew out of the Latin word *caritas* as used in the Vulgate edition of the Bible to describe Christian love: both the love experienced between humans and God, and the way in which people should relate to their neighbors.[10] Every compassionate act was a reflection of that duality in the Pauline conception of love. Charity on earth could be expressed through kindness, affection, and generosity in one's dealings with others, sometimes termed "good neighborliness." Those meanings underlay the requirement of the late medieval Catholic church and the sixteenth-century Protestant one that people wishing to receive communion must be "in charity" – on good terms – with their fellow parishioners.[11] Gradually, however, "charity" gained the additional and more specific sense of benevolence to the poor.

Almsgiving was an essential form of charity in both Catholic and Protestant belief. The word "alms" derives ultimately from a Greek word meaning mercy or compassion. Alms could be bestowed during one's lifetime and through bequests after death. The medieval Catholic Church instructed testators to divide their movable goods into three parts, leaving one-third as religious or charitable alms to be distributed "for the good of their soul." Pious donations might take diverse forms. Some were expressly religious, such as gifts to one's parish church or members of the religious orders (monks, nuns, and friars), while others served a public function, such as maintaining roads, bridges, and piers. Increasingly, however, almsgiving focused on relief of the poor or assistance to prisoners. Contributions to individuals or institutions were sometimes promoted by indulgences awarded by the Catholic Church that granted spiritual rewards to donors. Uncertainty about what exactly was meant by the word "alms" contributes to the difficulty of tracing the extent to which testators and parishes directed charitable aid specifically towards needy people.

Many poor people who needed assistance solicited alms, obtained a place in a hospital or almshouse, or received help from their parishes.

---

[10] *OED* for this and "alms," below.   [11] McIntosh, *Controlling Misbehavior*, 188–9.

Charitable alms constituted the earliest and most frequent type of aid to the poor and the institutions that served them. Many thousands of laymen and a smaller number of women moved along England's pathways, roads, and urban streets between 1350 and 1600 to solicit donations. Some people asked for help within their own communities, either privately or in public, while others traveled away from home to request assistance. Another group consisted of people who had been granted licenses to solicit alms due to some special need. Most had experienced a loss through misfortune, while others were students, soldiers, mariners, or pilgrims en route to approved destinations. A final set of alms seekers consisted of the gatherers appointed by hospitals, almshouses, and other charitable projects to collect money on their behalf. Beginning in the 1530s, worry about people who traveled around requesting contributions increased greatly. The nature of their need also covered a wider range, for local Justices of the Peace were henceforth allowed to grant permission to chronically poor people to ask for help outside their own areas. For county initiatives concerning poverty and vagrancy and for large public projects, voluntary alms proved unable to bring in sufficient funds in a timely manner. Elizabeth's government therefore experimented with ways of requiring parishes to contribute, supervised usually by JPs. Fraudulent begging licenses or letters of protection were in common use.

Residential institutions provided long-term benefits for those people fortunate enough to gain a place. Most late medieval and early modern hospitals offered accommodation and simple bedside care for poor people unable to live on their own: because they were bedridden, old, disabled, and/or suffered from a debilitating disease. Almshouses usually served the elderly poor, providing permanent free housing and sometimes food, clothing, fuel, or a weekly cash stipend. During the fifteenth and sixteenth centuries, almshouses were founded far more frequently than hospitals, but generally had fewer residents. Of the institutions included in a database of information I have assembled, about 1,005 hospitals and almshouses that operated sometime between 1350 and 1600, the number in existence rose gradually to a peak of 617 in the 1520s.[12] At that time the institutions probably sheltered around 4,900 to 6,400 people. Across the next three decades, nearly half of those institutions were closed due to royal and Parliamentary policies that dissolved or appropriated resources from the religious bodies that had previously operated them. Although new foundations attempted to fill the gap, only two-thirds as many residential institutions were functioning in the 1560s as in the 1520s. Even in

---

[12] For the database, see ch. 3.1 below.

the 1590s, the number of houses in the database (slightly under 500) had merely reached the level seen around 1400, providing places for around 3,000 to 5,300 people. Especially in those almshouses founded in the later fifteenth and sixteenth centuries, residents might be required to meet defined religious and behavioral expectations. Whereas many earlier medieval foundations had been operated by monastic houses or were entirely self-governing, with no outside supervision, later institutions were usually placed under the control either of a group of feoffees who managed a landed endowment or of an existing lay-run body such as a town, merchant/craft guild, or parish.[13] Many founders now laid down stringent requirements to ensure careful management of finances and personnel and good external oversight for their houses.

The third type of aid considered here was provided through or by parishes. Although these units, which spanned the entire country, initially filled primarily religious roles – responsible for maintaining the fabric of the church, providing supplies for services, and sometimes hiring auxiliary staff – from the mid sixteenth century onwards they were assigned additional, secular duties by Parliamentary legislation.[14] In those respects they served in effect as arms of the state. Prior to the end of Henry VIII's reign, if churchwardens gave alms to the poor, they were usually handing out gifts or bequests from private donors. During the brief Edwardian period, however, parishes quite suddenly began to assume a far more active role in poor relief. A series of royal injunctions, Parliamentary statutes, and instructions from the new Protestant church ordered parishes to appoint specialized officers (Collectors for the Poor) who were to gather regular payments from those parishioners able to contribute and distribute the income to their less fortunate neighbors. Anyone who refused to help was to be sent to the bishop for correction. An act of 1563 authorized Justices of the Peace to punish people who were unwilling to contribute. The commonly misread statutes of 1572 and 1576 introduced several additional institutions for the poor at the county level, but did not change the parish-based system. To follow the changes over time in the activity of churchwardens and parishes with regard to the poor, I have used accounts from 125 parishes in 32 counties plus the cities of London and York, together with other ecclesiastical and governmental records.[15] Whereas Collectors for the Poor are rarely mentioned in earlier historical studies,

---

[13] Feoffees held property on behalf of and for the use of another person, project, or institution, like later trustees.

[14] See ch. 8.1 below.

[15] The regional distribution of the parishes is: north/northwest: 16 = 13%; southwest/west: 34 = 27%; Midlands/east central: 31 = 25%; and East Anglia/the southeast: 44 = 35%.

this study demonstrates that they were appointed in hundreds of parishes in the decades after 1552, moving in some churches towards regular relief for a subset of needy parishioners.

The late Elizabethan Poor Laws are viewed in a new light as we examine how they attempted to resolve the problems that were currently obstructing efficient charitable activity. Individual begging and traditional forms of institutional gathering were deemed so flawed that Parliament abolished them almost entirely while permitting newer forms of collection for large projects to continue. The statutes also simplified the procedures for endowing and incorporating hospitals and almshouses and improved their financial stability. The legislation clarified and offered minor corrections to the statutes of 1552 and 1563 concerning the system of parish-based relief, confirming that wealthier people were required to pay "rates" (local taxes) to assist their legitimately needy neighbors. The statutes also addressed some specific features of the parish approach that had proved unworkable or inadequate, such as re-casting the former Collectors for the Poor as Overseers of the Poor. More generally, the Elizabethan measures tackled several underlying legal weaknesses that had hindered the founding or operation of diverse sorts of projects for the poor. The acts recognized the existence of charitable trusts and defined their scope, replacing the earlier feoffees whose legal standing had been unclear. They created a new process that improved access to the law for people concerned about the malfunctioning of a charitable activity, especially smaller and informal ones. Local Commissions for Charitable Uses, appointed by the Lord Chancellor, were empowered to investigate allegations of wrongdoing by projects intended for the poor or the misuse of their resources by private people. Using cases from 1598 to 1603, we will see how these Commissions operated and why they were so popular.

1.2   Analytic questions and sources

In the course of tracing this history, we will explore a number of broader interpretive questions. Some have been discussed by previous scholars – although I suggest they have often been framed in unhelpful ways – while others open up new avenues of inquiry. One set of issues concerns changes in people's attitudes and responses to the poor. Earlier discussions have frequently been hampered by two implicit but questionable assumptions. The first is that negative ideas about the poor presented in

The distribution by type of community is: city – 11 = 9%; town – 18 = 14%; market center – 36 = 29%; and village – 60 = 48%. For the definition of those categories, see ch. 3, n. 42 below, and CUP Online App. 1, pt. 6.

certain theological or literary texts and the sometimes harsh policies of Parliament reflected widespread fear and hostility that were manifested also in the responses of people on the ground. This study shows that local households and officials made their own decisions about which people to assist and which to punish, quite apart from what the law required. Many poor wanderers, for example, who might have been put into the stocks or whipped in accordance with the statutes about begging and vagrancy, were instead given shelter and a little money and allowed to go on their way.

A second common assumption is that at some time in the past, aid to the poor had been awarded casually, without attention to the particular needs of those being assisted or the reasons for their poverty, whereas in the period studied by that author, donors began to discriminate about which people should be helped. Such a transition has been suggested in the wake of the 1348–9 plague, early in the Protestant era, and among the reformed Protestants known as puritans. Some medievalists have proposed that a new distinction was made after the plague between people who were incapable of labor or had fallen on hard times (who deserved help) and idle beggars or the law-breaking poor.[16] But Barbara Harvey, in her meticulous examination of the extensive charity distributed by Westminster Abbey between 1100 and 1540, found that from a very early date the monks themselves evinced "a preference for systematic arrangements, which they administered with a marked degree of discrimination."[17] Like some other early religious houses, Westminster's monks had converted their charitable obligations away from feeding whichever hungry poor came to their gates to caring for a small group of needy but respectable people on a regular basis. When the monks handed out casual doles to all the poor who attended funerals and commemorative services, they did so not by choice, but rather because lay benefactors and the executors of wills "sought in this way to spread the good work of prayers for their souls as widely as possible."

Influenced by Michel Mollat's work on poverty in medieval France, which described an outpouring of charity during the thirteenth and earlier fourteenth centuries followed by a decline in donations after the plague, Miri Rubin and Christopher Dyer described a similar hardening of attitudes in England.[18] The later fourteenth century was marked by increasing hostility and "a moral panic" with regard to the poor, especially mobile

---

[16] Rubin, *Charity and Community*, ch. 3, and Dyer, *Standards of Living*, 238–9.

[17] Harvey, *Living and Dying*, ch. 1, esp. 33, for this and the quotation later in the paragraph.

[18] Mollat, *Les Pauvres*, Rubin, *Charity and Community*, 50–3, and Dyer, *Standards of Living*, ch. 9.

people, "not unlike the hysterical reactions to Jews, lepers and heretics in earlier times."[19] Hospitals were criticized for assisting "lazy shirkers." That assessment too has been questioned. P. H. Cullum noted that a large body of evidence documents "a considerable upsurge in the foundation of small hospitals, alms-houses and maisons-Dieu in the years after the Black Death."[20] Most of the new institutions accommodated fewer residents and had more modest landed endowments than the great hospitals of earlier centuries, but the number of additional houses was significant.

Early modernists have sometimes proposed that Protestantism or puritanism led to an increase in the selectivity of poor relief. W. K. Jordan argued that whereas Catholic beliefs about almsgiving had led to casual assistance to all comers, the more rational approach to philanthropy promoted by Protestantism caused both careful judgments about which people should be assisted and a preference for support provided by institutions like parishes and almshouses in which lay officials could determine how resources were allocated.[21] More recent work indicates that Jordan exaggerated the extent of that transition. Some late medieval testators were already specifying which kinds of people were to receive aid, excluding the undeserving poor, whereas some Protestant testators as late as the 1580s and 1590s left generic doles to be handed out to all those who attended their funerals and joined in the prayers.[22] The decades around 1600 have likewise been described as a time when puritan values rendered some potential benefactors unwilling to assist people who were in any way responsible for their own need.[23] That attitude has been linked to studies documenting increasing social/cultural distinctions between the poor and those above them and attempts to regulate social misbehavior.[24] This book traces changes in the concepts of poverty and charity and in responses to the poor, but it argues that local people at all times made selective choices about which of the needy warranted assistance. Setting

---

[19] Dyer, *Standards of Living*, 238–9. For below, see Rubin, "Development and Change," esp. 53.

[20] Cullum, "Poverty and Charity," 140, and see her "For Pore People Harberles" and Phillips, "Charitable Institutions," Graph A.

[21] Jordan, *Philanthropy in England*, 146–79.

[22] Brigden, "Religion and Social Obligation" and Archer, *Pursuit of Stability*, 163–4, citing Thomson, "Piety and Charity," 182–3, and Beier, "Social Problems," 69–73.

[23] E.g., Hill, "Puritans and the Poor," and his *Society and Puritanism*, Wrightson and Levine, *Poverty and Piety*, Hunt, *Puritan Moment*, and Underdown, *Fire from Heaven*. Such attitudes could be coupled with vigorous attempts to help the deserving poor.

[24] E.g., the references cited in McIntosh, *Controlling Misbehavior*, 3–5, although that analysis does not argue that social regulation was tied to a more discriminating approach to charitable aid.

aside the unproductive question of whether discrimination abruptly increased, it explores instead which particular kinds of adults and children were chosen for aid in various periods and settings, and why.

A second set of interpretive themes deals with the mechanisms through which assistance to the poor was given. Whereas the forms of relief have generally been presented in dichotomous terms, as either one option or another, the evidence presented here indicates that apparently contradictory types were intertwined in practice. It is a historical truism that responsibility for charity lay primarily with the church in the later medieval period, but came under the control of the state in the early modern era. At some level, the changes described below do support that generalization, especially if one accepts that when sixteenth-century parishes collected and gave assistance to the poor by order of Parliament, they were acting as agents of the state. While growing governmental participation may have been influenced in part by a Foucauldian desire for information and control, it is more likely to have derived from a functional practical consideration: in the post-Reformation period, only those institutions that carried the authority of the state were capable of organizing and administering forms of poor relief on a sufficiently large scale. My book emphasizes the cooperation between the church and the state after 1547 in devising and enforcing forms of assistance.

Two other kinds of charity, voluntary and obligatory, should likewise not be regarded as mutually exclusive. Until the mid sixteenth century, all assistance to the poor was in some sense optional. Yet Catholic theology provided strong pressure and incentives to do so, as did clergymen throughout the late medieval and Tudor periods, both in their sermons and when helping people to write their wills.[25] If a collection for the poor was taken within a given church, the priest or minister and churchwardens may have used vigorous means to promote generous contributions. Compulsory payments for the poor as mandated by the government were indeed an increasingly important feature of the second half of the sixteenth century. Introduced in many cities and some parishes, they were required also for certain projects at the county or national level. Yet donations made entirely by choice (in the form of gifts by living people and bequests) continued to increase as well.[26] Within local communities, the two types of aid worked together in trying to meet deepening need.

---

[25] In an earlier paper, I offered a less nuanced discussion of the distinction between voluntary and compulsory support ("Local Responses"). Conversations with Clive Burgess and Peregrine Horden have persuaded me of the force of the medieval church's stance about charitable giving.

[26] E.g., Ben-Amos, *Culture of Giving*, chs. 3–4.

That issue is closely tied to the question of how much was contributed by private as compared to publicly funded relief. Although some earlier historians thought that private charity was largely displaced by provision of aid at the parish level, that assessment is now questioned.[27] Even when money based upon fixed assessments was collected by parish or civic bodies, it was intended to supplement the income derived from current gifts, bequests, and earlier endowments managed by those organizations. Ian Archer's analysis shows that in the early 1570s, private charity contributed 52 percent of all resources for the poor in London; in the mid-1590s, when need was greater, private aid yielded 67 percent.[28] Only in the early seventeenth century did the balance in London shift in favor of public provision. In Colchester, however, the roughly £120 generated annually by the public poor rate in the 1580s surpassed the £80 that came from private sources.[29] At the national level, figures offered by Slack suggest that formal poor rates generated about 40 percent of all money available for relief even as late as 1610. This study will not employ a public/private distinction, for the categories too often overlapped. While face-to-face donations between two people were clearly private and compulsory rates were clearly public, how should we classify a bequest of land from an individual to a parish, with its rents to be distributed to poor people by churchwardens or Collectors for the Poor in perpetuity? Forcing that aid into either a private or a public box distorts reality. We will, however, examine the benefits for the poor of having a predictable source of financial assistance within their own parishes thanks to required donations by their wealthier neighbors.

Some additional topics contribute to a more complex picture of poor relief. A recurring theme in this book is dishonesty: fraud with regard to begging, and greed or laxity on the part of those who operated or provided funds for charitable activities. Problems in those areas heightened already mounting concern with the governance of projects for the poor, seen with regard to almshouses/hospitals and parish activity, and they intensified demands for precise accounting. We explore identities, for beggars and recipients of poor relief, for benefactors, and for those who operated charitable projects, and we draw attention to gender factors. To look more closely at the settings of poor relief, we will frequently break down quantitative evidence by region of the country and type of community.

---

[27] E.g., Hill, *Society and Puritanism*, 259–97 and 483–7, Thomas, *Religion and the Decline of Magic*, 260–79, and Stone, *Family, Sex and Marriage*, 651–6, all as cited and challenged by Ben-Amos, *Culture of Giving*, 83–4.

[28] Archer, "Charity of Early Modern Londoners."

[29] Goose, "Rise and Decline." For below, see Slack, *Poverty and Policy*, 171–2. In English usage, a "rate" is a compulsory local tax of some kind.

Another question concerns the relationship between attitudes and policies at the national level (involving the crown and its advisors, Parliament, and the upper episcopacy) and what was happening locally. In this area we encounter the significance of the particular structure of English government and law: the involvement of members of Parliament and the Privy Council in formulating policies, the role of the Justices of the Peace who functioned as an intermediate layer within counties or smaller units, and the increasingly diverse contributions of parish officers. All of those features were essential to the development across the second half of the sixteenth century of the English system of formalized poor relief, mandated by the central government and implemented within parishes. That development occurred several centuries before equivalent programs began to function on the continent.[30]

This study draws upon a wide array of sources, including manuscript material from more than seventy archives plus printed texts and secondary studies. Because of the diverse nature and quantity of the evidence, the approach taken in individual chapters varies. For some topics, we have information that lends itself to a descriptive presentation, while for others we can pursue quantified analyses as well. Begging, gathering, and the introduction of new forms of collecting are documented in Parliamentary and royal records and in urban policies and practices, joined by the licenses granted to people soliciting alms for themselves or charitable institutions and by churchwardens' accounts. Popular works of (semi-) fiction shed light on attitudes towards the poor and the possibility of fraudulent claims. Hospitals and almshouses are described in the foundation documents, statutes, and financial accounts of the institutions themselves, augmented by town and parish records and the retrospective reports of nineteenth-century Charity Commissioners. We learn about the changing roles of the parish largely through the accounts kept by churchwardens and Collectors for the Poor; they are supplemented by visitation records and act books of the church courts and material produced by Justices of the Peace. Analysis of the Poor Laws of 1598 and 1601 sets that legislation against the kinds of problems illuminated in previous chapters, while the detailed documentation preserved by Commissions for Charitable Uses enables us to observe how the new legal process functioned.

---

[30] When discussing why England alone among early modern European countries produced a large and complicated system of social welfare so early, Slack highlighted its "political habits and structure of government" (*English Poor Law*, 57; see also ibid., 17, and his *Poverty and Policy*, 206). For the argument that the distinctive English system of government-run poor relief resulted from the class structure of its agricultural economy, see, most recently, Patriquin, "Agrarian Capitalism."

1.3   The changing practical and ideological context

Although poverty was a feature of English life throughout the later medieval and early modern periods, the proportion of poor people unable to provide for their own needs changed over time due to demographic and economic factors. During the first century after the 1348–9 plague, England's economy experienced a series of contrasting phases, ending with the recession of the mid fifteenth century.[31] In most sub-periods and regions of the country, however, poverty was relatively mild. The population was small in comparison with its early fourteenth-century peak, and land and housing were plentiful.[32] The demand for labor – whether on a regular or occasional basis – was high, and prices were low. Although mortality was elevated, with recurring outbreaks of disease contributing to further decline in the population, many of the peasants and wage earners who survived experienced a rising standard of living, able to dress, eat, and house themselves more comfortably than before 1348.[33]

Late medieval responses to the poor were affected by fluid and sometimes conflicting attitudes about the poor, charity, and social order. The core beliefs of Catholicism validated poverty and a system based upon almsgiving. God had created a world that contained poor people as well as those of more comfortable means, and serious misfortune could strike anyone at any time. Hence needy people who asked for assistance and those who provided help were both filling their designated place in God's plan. The image of a Christ-like beggar still carried some resonance. The seven "corporal works of mercy," which rested upon the idea that people who helped the less fortunate also served the Christ among them, included assisting people who lacked food, drink, shelter, or clothing, burying the dead, caring for the sick, and visiting prisoners.[34]

---

[31] Hatcher, "Great Slump," Britnell, "English Agricultural Output," and Campbell, "Grain Yields." For below, see McIntosh, "Local Responses" and Fideler, *Social Welfare*, ch. 1.

[32] Although historians disagree about the size of the total population during the later medieval years, we have some recent estimated figures (Broadberry et al., "English Medieval Population," but see also Smith, "Putting Benedictine Monks in Context"). The population was probably around 1.7 million in 1086 and 4.75 million by 1290. It dropped 12% due to high mortality from famine during the 1310s, but recovered to 4.81 million by 1348. It then dropped 46% by 1351 and continued to decline slowly thereafter. By 1377 it was around 2.5 million and reached a low point of 1.9 million in 1450. I am grateful to Bruce Campbell and Richard Smith for letting me have copies of their unpublished papers.

[33] Dyer, *Standards of Living*, esp. chs. 5–8.

[34] For a fuller discussion of medieval attitudes, see, e.g., Tierney, *Medieval Poor Law*, esp. chs. 1 and 3, and Clark, "Institutional and Legal Responses to Begging." For an early sixteenth-century image of Christ standing among the hungry poor being given bread by a charitable man and woman, see the cover to this book.

Contributing to hospitals, almshouses, and prisons was an acceptable substitute for the latter two. Priests and friars exhorted the laity to help the poor, both during their lifetimes and when preparing their wills. Early Franciscans produced powerful justifications for a religious life marked by voluntary poverty, although intra-clerical opposition to that order contributed to an argument that choosing to become poor and sustain oneself by begging instead of working were signs not of Christian sanctity but rather of idleness and sin.[35] The conception of charity began to change after the mid fourteenth century, becoming more inclusive to accommodate the widening interests of donors.[36] When the character "Truth" in William Langland's *Piers Plowman* wrote to wealthy merchants encouraging them to use their resources in acts of charity, he mentioned the following kinds of assistance: giving food to paupers and prisoners, helping miserable folk, endowing hospitals, providing poor girls with dowries for marriage or fees to enter convents, helping poor boys to attend school or learn a trade, assisting people in religious orders, and repairing roads and bridges.

In Catholic theology, people who provided help to the less fortunate gained spiritual benefits for themselves. When God assesses the quality of a person's life on the Day of Last Judgment, He will pay attention to good works, looking more favorably upon those who have been charitable. Benefactors mentioned by the poor in prayers for their souls gained a particular blessing, for it was believed that voices of the disadvantaged were heard with special clarity by God. The church's official stance was that donors were not obliged to limit their aid to needy people who seemed especially deserving, nor did they need to address the causes of poverty. In practice, however, late medieval and early modern donors appear to have made their own value judgments about which suppliants deserved assistance. I have found no evidence that aid was awarded indiscriminately by lay people except at funerals and "obits" (commemorative services held a month or year after a death), where the goal was to attract as many poor people as possible to pray for the deceased person. Almsgiving was promoted by more direct spiritual incentives as well. Indulgences could be granted by the Pope, bishops, and abbots to support fundraising by individuals or charitable institutions.[37] These awards stated that if donors had acknowledged and confessed their sins, the amount of time they

---

[35] E.g., FitzRalph, "Defensio Curatorum," esp. 71, 80, and 87–9, and Crassons, *Claims of Poverty*, 6–8.

[36] Horden, "Discipline of Relevance" and Rubin, "Imagining Medieval Hospitals." For below, see Langland, *The Vision of Piers Plowman* [B-text], passus 7, ll. 23–33, a work written sometime between 1360 and 1387.

[37] Swanson, *Indulgences*, esp. ch. 1.

would need to spend after their death doing penance in Purgatory would be reduced by a specified number of days, weeks, or even years.

Alongside those positive valuations of charitable giving and solicitation of alms, however, lay worry about geographic and social mobility and idleness among the poor. As peasants began to leave their manors after the plague to seek better opportunities elsewhere, their departure intensified the drop in income suffered by many manorial lords and weakened control over the remaining tenants. Peasants who remained on their home manors might gradually acquire additional property, elevating their status and becoming leaders within their villages and parishes. People who chose not to work regularly could usually find enough casual employment to get by. The uprising of 1381 heightened fear among the elite that all forms of hierarchy were at risk.

These developments contributed to a negative response to casual charitable giving among people of higher social levels. In 1357 Richard FitzRalph, Archbishop of Armagh, preached the extreme position that because God taught the merits of physical labor and legitimized wealth, the poor – especially beggars – should be hated by their neighbors.[38] William Langland expressed considerable ambivalence in *Piers Plowman* about older conceptions of poverty and charity as opposed to a sense that public beggars were deeply troubling, bringing shame to themselves and society. The friars evoked an increasingly hostile reaction in the later fourteenth and fifteenth centuries, due to their own reliance upon begging and questionable adherence to true poverty. A series of Parliamentary ordinances and statutes between 1349 and 1388 prohibited begging and said that those who gave alms were subject to punishment.[39] Although anxiety about poverty evidently decreased between around 1390 and 1460, the conflict between notions of Christian charity and these negative attitudes made it difficult to formulate and enforce consistent policies about aid to the poor.

Agricultural conditions worsened during the second half of the fifteenth century and the opening decades of the sixteenth. Due to changing weather patterns, crop yields were exceptionally variable from one year to the next, but on average were lower than in previous decades.[40] Bad harvests, including runs of poor years in the 1470s, 1480s, and the early sixteenth century, caused higher grain prices and lowered the purchasing

---

[38] FitzRalph, "Defensio Curatorum," 71 and 80–9, a view that derived from his antagonism towards the Franciscans, but was presented as a general recommendation that applied to everyone. For below, see Aers, *"Piers Plowman,"* and Shepherd, "Poverty in *Piers Plowman.*"

[39] See ch. 2.1 below.

[40] Campbell, "Grain Yields," and his "Physical Shocks" for this and below.

power of wages.[41] But because the previous standard of living had been fairly comfortable, crop failures brought dearth and greater poverty, but did not cause famine and mounting deaths. Some regions of the country were experiencing further changes due to new forms of agricultural production, enclosure of common land, and selective expansion of trade, manufacturing, transport, and retailing.[42]

Demographic conditions were likewise unsettled. The frequency and intensity of mortality crises (years with an exceptionally large number of deaths) rose after around 1450 as the result of outbreaks of plague and other diseases. Studies of demographic patterns among monks in Canterbury, Westminster Abbey, and Durham show many crisis peaks during the second half of the fifteenth and early sixteenth centuries, some found in two or three of those places (suggesting a wider epidemic), others found only locally.[43] As a result, life expectancy among the monks declined sharply after 1450. Other studies likewise show variable but generally high death rates and a decline in life expectancy during the second half of the fifteenth century.[44] Geographic mobility appears to have increased after around 1460, with net migration into the southeast and some mid-sized towns and market centers.[45] It is not clear for how long after 1450 England's total population continued its long-term decline and when it began to rise, moving towards the higher level proposed for the 1520s and the definite evidence of growth thereafter.[46]

This unstable environment increased the possibility of at least temporary hardship for many families and intensified concern about the behavior of the poor.[47] As people found themselves unable to weather periods of

[41] Campbell, "Four Famines." For below, see ibid. and his "Grain Yields."
[42] McIntosh, "Local Change."
[43] Hatcher, "Mortality," Harvey, *Living and Dying*, ch. 4, and Hatcher et al., "Monastic Mortality."
[44] Smith, "Putting Benedictine Monks in Context," and Hatcher, "Understanding The Population History."
[45] McIntosh, "Local Responses." Rigby's analysis shows that large communities experienced net population decline between 1377 and 1524 relative to their surrounding counties, whereas towns of intermediate size and market centers increased their proportions; the share of England's total taxable population living in provincial towns in 1524 was at best no larger than in 1377 and may have been slightly lower ("Urban Population").
[46] By the early 1520s the total population is estimated to have recovered to around 2.35 million; by 1541 it had reached 2.83 million (Broadberry et al., "English Medieval Population"). For recent arguments for ongoing decline, see Hatcher et al., "Monastic Mortality"; for possible net growth (based upon stagnant or declining levels in eastern England and the East Midlands, but vigorous expansion in the southwest, northwest, and immediate environs of London), see Broadberry et al., "English Medieval Population." For earlier work, see the references in McIntosh, "Local Responses," n. 45.
[47] Campbell, "Grain Yields," and McIntosh, "Local Responses," for this and below. Years of hardship worsened both the background level of "structural poverty" (need found under normal circumstances in a particular place and period) and "conjunctural poverty"

crisis without help, or if they felt they were at greater risk, they may have sought ways to obtain socio-economic insurance, such as joining religious fraternities or craft guilds that assisted their own members when in need. For some wealthier benefactors, founding an almshouse seemed a useful contribution to the poor of their community. At the same time, however, the crown, Parliament, and local leaders alike became more worried about disorder and vagrancy.[48] The percentage of lesser courts that reported people for sexual misconduct, alehouse offences, being "badly governed" or "of suspicious life," being a vagabond, or living idly rose sharply in the 1460s and 1470s, continuing to mount into the 1520s and 1530s.

Between 1530 and the late 1550s, objective problems with poverty became more severe and were distributed more widely throughout the country. The number of poor people and their visibility rose as they moved about in search of work or assistance. When contemporaries attempted to explain these problems, they commonly blamed avaricious men for such practices as enclosing into private holdings the common property formerly used by all manorial residents; the rural poor might be unable to live on their resulting smallholdings, while the larger units were often used to raise sheep for wool rather than growing food.[49] Former monks, nuns, and friars who could not manage on their small pensions after the Dissolution and ex-inmates of closed hospitals were also thought to contribute to vagrancy. Historians now believe that the major causes of greater poverty were renewed population growth and inflation, exacerbated by bad harvests in the 1520s and 1555–6, heavy taxation, and changes in the currency.[50] A sense of insecurity was heightened by swings in the official religion, the Pilgrimage of Grace of 1536, the two rebellions of 1549, and uncertainty about the royal succession. Many forms of assistance to the poor were lost between 1536 and 1553 as secondary consequences of the closure of the monasteries and convents, the lay religious fraternities, and the chantries that provided masses for the dead. The crown confiscated the property of those institutions as well as

---

[48] (resulting from particular crises that deepened the need of people who were already poor and forced others who were normally self-sufficient to seek aid): see, e.g., Slack, *Poverty and Policy*, 38–9.

[48] For concern at national and urban levels, see ch. 2.1 below. For below, see McIntosh, *Controlling Misbehavior*, 68–93.

[49] Enclosures had been criticized in the 1510s by Thomas More and others, but the attack on "rapacious landlords" sharpened during the 1540s (*Utopia*, 18–19, Yates, "Between Fact and Fiction," and Jordan, *Edward VI: The Young King*, 387–9 and 410–26). Modern analysis indicates that enclosures for grazing had occurred gradually across the later fourteenth and fifteenth centuries (Dyer, "Deserted Medieval Villages" and Blanchard, "Population Change").

[50] For the latter, see Campbell, "Four Famines."

much of the land and goods owned by parishes, leaving only enough to support a simple Protestant service. But at the same time, Parliament was becoming more active, passing legislation on a wide range of economic as well as religious and political issues. The statutes of 1547 and 1552 that established a parish-based system of relief attempted to fill the gap in charitable provision.

Poverty continued to worsen during the Elizabethan years.[51] Rapid population growth that outran economic expansion, ongoing inflation, boom-and-bust cycles in the leading industries, especially woolen cloth manufacture, and crop failures all contributed to the problem.[52] By the 1580s, a higher fraction of the population was poor and the depth of their need had intensified. Although private charitable giving and parish and urban aid were all rising, legitimate requests for assistance far outran available resources. When crop yields dropped severely due to bad weather during the later 1580s and 1590s, grain prices rose, hunger mounted, and deaths ensued in isolated regions of the country. Acute poverty was now recognized as a potential threat to the stability of local and national political institutions, for if poor people became desperate, they might deny the authority of local leaders, break down fences around private fields, or raid the storehouses of farmers and merchants for grain.

The ideological context too shifted in several respects beginning in the 1530s.[53] Early Protestant thinkers strove vigorously to marshal strong arguments in favor of almsgiving, for they were eager to demonstrate that their new church could promote Christian charity at least as effectively as its doctrinally flawed and functionally corrupt predecessor. Although the Protestant church no longer taught that one could earn salvation through good works or gain the benefit of indulgences, and although it did not believe in the efficacy of prayers for the souls of the dead, it insisted that God required almsgiving as part of the religious life of all Christians. A society that based its morality upon Jesus's teachings must not allow helpless poor people to suffer because their more fortunate fellows withheld assistance. Helping the needy also provided donors with the satisfaction of complying with God's instructions and in some cases offered spiritual gratification, including "an intensely felt piety."[54] Equally important, generous aid to the poor was advocated as a demonstration of

---

[51] E.g., Slack, *Poverty and Policy*, ch. 3.

[52] The national population, around 2.83 million in 1541, had risen to 4.16 million by 1601, an increase of 47% (Wrigley et al., *English Population History*, 614–15). Because food prices quadrupled between 1500 and 1600 whereas wages rose far more slowly, the purchasing power of wages in 1600 was less than half of what it had been in 1500.

[53] E.g., Fideler, "Poverty, Policy," and his *Social Welfare*, chs. 2–3.

[54] Sweetinburgh, "The Poor" and Ben-Amos, "Gifts and Favors," esp. 324.

the spiritual merits of the donor, a reflection of the faith that brought salvation. Thus, it suggested both to benefactors and to those who observed them that God had chosen the donor to be saved. Influenced by those attitudes, the leaders of the government and church promoted charitable giving with all means at their disposal.

Such concerns worked hand in hand with the humanist or "commonwealth" beliefs held by a few late Henrician and many Edwardian and Elizabethan leaders. Combining features of what are often described in continental contexts as civic humanism with Christian or Northern humanism, this approach argued that one of the central responsibilities of a well-ordered Christian state was to promote the wellbeing of the entire community.[55] A society in which the incapacitated poor were neglected did not meet the requirements of a just commonwealth. Because humanist theory stressed education, exhortation, and rhetoric – persuading people to do what was right so they would accept their obligations willingly, rather than forcing them into it – royal advisors and leaders of Parliament and the church under Edward and Elizabeth used their injunctions, statutes, homilies, and sermons to explain why both individual generosity and public action on behalf of the poor were essential. Although few village leaders had direct contact with humanist texts, the lessons learned from those public messages may well have affected their thinking.[56] The willingness of many churchwardens to implement Edwardian orders on behalf of the poor suggests that some of them were thinking about their Christian and community responsibilities in new ways.

Yet Protestant opposition to the Catholic theology of good works proved difficult to articulate persuasively and was slow to affect popular thought.[57] The Second Book of Homilies, published in 1563, which reprinted twelve official sermons prepared under Edward and added some new ones, included "An Homilie of Alms deeds, and mercifulness toward the poor and needy."[58] That homily, henceforth read aloud in parish churches every year, presents familiar encouragement "to help and succor the poor, hungry, and naked Christ, that cometh to your doors a begging."

---

[55] E.g., Slack, *From Reformation to Improvement*, ch. 1, and Withington, *Politics of Commonwealth*. Bishop Edwin Sandys exclaimed in a sermon preached in Parliament, "O, what shame is this [lack of relief for the poor] to a Christian commonwealth, in a reformed country!" (*Sermons*, 51).

[56] This assessment revises my statement in 1988 that the ideas of Christian humanism were not of much importance within the local setting, where traditional Christian morality and pragmatic concerns carried more weight ("Local Responses," 212). Conversations with Phil Withington led to my altered opinion.

[57] Wooding, "Charity, Community" and Heal, "Concepts of Generosity."

[58] *Certaine Sermons*, 154–66. For below, see ibid., 164.

A similarly traditional conception underlay orders from the Privy Council and the church during periods of food shortage late in Elizabeth's reign, urging the laity to fast during one meal each week, converting the resulting savings into alms for the poor.[59] But the homily on alms deeds also describes in more specifically Calvinist terms the benefits received by donors. Charitable Christians, "by their obedience unto God's holy will, and by their mercifulness and tender pity (wherein they show themselves to be like unto God, who is the fountain and spring of all mercy) ... declare openly and manifestly unto the sight of men, that they are the sons of God, and elect of him into salvation."[60]

As Protestantism took firmer root in England, some preachers taught that almsgiving should not merely perpetuate the poverty – much less the idleness – of recipients. Because labor was highly valued in Protestant thought, failure to work and reliance upon begging might be regarded as abhorrent to God. While that concern was especially strong among puritans, it was not limited to them.[61] The tension between compassion and disapproval is illustrated by the will of John Amie of Maidstone, Kent, from 1595.[62] Amie left £100 to provide raw materials with which the unemployed poor could be set to work, explaining that there now lived in Maidstone "an exceeding number of very aged, lame, and poor people, who through their great wants have not wherewith to set them nor their children in work, whereby they might relieve their extreme necessities." They were therefore "forced to become beggars from door to door." That sympathetic statement is followed, however, by the observation that once the poor have become accustomed to begging, they will never labor again. Instead they resort to "whoredoms, robberies, and all other profaneness, to the great offence of almighty God who hath expressly said that there shall be no beggars in the land."

Several recent analyses have concluded that by the late sixteenth century the Protestant church was more successful than its predecessor in linking aid to the poor with a desirable spirituality, in part because "the Protestant message" broadened the language of charitable giving and encouraged alternative modes of support.[63] Donors devoted an increasingly high percentage of their resources to poor relief, away from expressly

---

[59] Hindle, "Dearth, Fasting and Alms." Such orders were made first in 1587 and strengthened in 1596–7.

[60] *Certaine Sermons*, 161.

[61] E.g., Todd, *Christian Humanism*, esp. ch. 5, and Collinson, "Puritanism and the Poor."

[62] *Records of Maidstone*, 40–4, esp. 41.

[63] Archer, "Charity of Early Modern Londoners," who notes that charity became "a badge of protestant identity" as well as an agent of national integration (237), and Ben-Amos, *Culture of Giving*, 377.

religious ends. Jordan, in one of the first large-scale quantitative historical studies, analyzed the particular kinds of charity to which around 35,000 donors in ten sample counties made contributions between 1480 and 1600, through either life-time endowments or bequests.[64] Between 1480 and 1540, 53 percent of all charitable donations went to specifically religious causes (mainly prayers, church repairs or building, and maintenance of the clergy), while only 13 percent was given to poor relief.[65] Between 1540 and 1560, however, just 15 percent of the total went to religious causes, but 27 percent to poor relief; between 1561 and 1600, the figures reached 7 percent for religion and 39 percent to the poor, despite the endowment of some puritan lectureships.

Why were people willing to give to the poor? Contemporaries rarely described their reasons explicitly, but we can point to a number of probable factors. Human compassion and religious teachings must have carried great weight in promoting generosity, and some bequests may have

---

[64] Jordan did research in England during the 1950s, using wills, accounts, and many other local records; he and his assistant then analyzed the material, without the help of computers. They broke down and discussed their figures by gender, an interest rare in that generation. The larger analytical categories employed are religion, the poor, education, "social rehabilitation," and "municipal betterments," each of which is subdivided into more specific headings. The sub-groupings for poor relief are outright relief (gifts/bequests directly to the poor), almshouses and hospitals, help for the aged, and general charity. Some later scholars have found these categories unhelpful. Jordan's findings were published in *Philanthropy in England* plus a series of regional studies: *The Charities of London, The Charities of Rural England, Social Institutions in Kent, The Social Institutions of Lancashire, The Forming of the Charitable Institutions of the West of England*, and two unpublished essays, "The Charities of Worcestershire" and "The Charities of Hampshire."

[65] Jordan, *Philanthropy in England*, 368, for this and below. While Jordan's basic figures have rarely been challenged, his interpretations of the numbers have rightly been criticized on many fronts. An important problem concerns inflation. Although he provided a logical explanation for why he decided not to attempt to correct values to reflect the changing purchasing power of money (ibid., 34–6, in a section on "Frailties of the Method"), he seems to have forgotten about inflation as he wrote his enthusiastic descriptions of the great increase in charitable giving, especially after 1600. It was at first suggested by later scholars that if one corrected Jordan's figures through use of a price-wage series, his numbers showed no rise in philanthropy at all during the Elizabethan period as compared with the late fifteenth century (Bittle and Lane, "Inflation and Philanthropy"). Subsequent analyses, which take into account the growth of previous endowments as well as the value of new ones, suggest that there was some increase under Elizabeth, although it was only in the 1580s that private endowments reached a level that compensated for the loss in monastic charity (Hadwin, "Deflating Philanthropy," Gould, "Bittle and Lane on Charity," and Slack, *Poverty and Policy*, 162–4). Although Jordan discussed the great demographic increase across his period, he did not attempt to calculate the value of charitable donations as compared to the total population. He also exaggerated the contrast between late medieval and post-Reformation charitable giving because it is impossible to determine the actual recipients or assign a money value to residual bequests in Catholic wills "for the good of my soul."

attempted to compensate for neglect that troubled the dying person's conscience. As poverty intensified over the course of the sixteenth century, benefactors probably felt that the harmony and security of their communities would be strengthened if needy people were spared from desperate poverty.

Further, the names and generosity of donors might remain known after their death. The creation of charitable memory was promoted in many parishes and towns by the annual public "reading of the bede roll," a list of all those who had previously given any money or property to support the organization's activities, including assistance to the poor. Reading the roll thus maintained a link with the past while at the same time encouraging the living to give now for the future. A concern with one's ongoing reputation is reflected in the common practice of naming activities after their donor and henceforth referring to them in that way: Lady Cecil's loan fund for the poor, Roger Reede's almshouse, Lord Leicester's hospital. Visual means might also be used to recognize and promote charity, as was common among the London livery companies.[66] When the Duchess of Suffolk granted a manor in Yorkshire to the Carthusian house of St. Michael in (Kingston upon) Hull in 1462, in part to support regular distributions to local alms people, the prior agreed to have statues made of the Duke and Duchess, showing them handing out bread and ale. For founders of hospitals or almshouses, the buildings formed a continuous physical reminder of their charity. Their residents might be required to wear a distinctive robe when away from the house, thus functioning as walking billboards, pointing out to people throughout the community that an act of generosity to the poor could result in long-term recognition.

Helping to run or supervise a project for the poor offered other benefits. Charitable service often increased one's local standing and provided opportunities for patronage.[67] Some men may have hoped that they could gain selfishly, perhaps by appropriating income or property to their own use. When urban bodies, parishes, or merchant guilds operated effective forms of assistance, they gained favorable notice and a collective identity that combined generosity with astute financial practices. In some Elizabethan towns, a shared concern with poverty may have provided a unifying focus at a time when its leaders were divided over matters of religious policy.[68] The men who handled charitable endowments or

---

[66] Archer, "Arts and Acts," and see Cavallo, "Motivations of Benefactors." For below, see HMC, *Eighth Report*, Appendix, "MSS of Ewelme Almshouse," 628.

[67] E.g., Ben-Amos, *Culture of Giving*, 186–90. For below, see ch. 9.2 below and McIntosh, "Negligence, Greed."

[68] E.g., in Hadleigh, Suff., McIntosh, "Poverty, Charity, and Coercion" and Craig, "Reformers, Conflict, and Revisionism."

supervised institutions for the poor during the latter part of Elizabeth's reign must also have been aware that increasing demand for relief was causing financial pressure on parishes and urban governments. If voluntary charity did not continue to provide substantial aid, and if existing forms of assistance were not well managed, the burden of compulsory payments would be proportionately greater. Spending some of one's material resources and/or time in helping the poor was therefore a good investment.

1.4   Additional kinds of aid

Although the three types of poor relief upon which this study focuses were significant in terms of the number of people they helped and/or the amount of aid given, and although they are unusually well documented, they were by no means the only assistance available. When in subsequent chapters we pull out for analysis these selected strands from within the loosely knit fabric of English relief, we must bear in mind that they formed part of a broader whole. The additional types of help – given by private individuals, religious bodies, and secular institutions – are summarized here.

Some support was provided on a personal basis among the poor themselves, in the form of food, drink, clothing, housing, money, and/or care given by friends, relatives, or neighbors.[69] Like most other English people, the poor were commonly embedded in networks of social capital within which they assisted others when they could, knowing that they could ask for help in turn when necessary. It is significant that local records and almshouse statutes refer more commonly to people who lacked support from *friends* than to those who had no *family* to help them. Some parishes relieved needy people even if they had more prosperous relatives living nearby who were unwilling to assist them.

Poor people might receive aid privately from better-off members of their community. The households of the country's elite were expected to be visibly charitable, distributing excess food and sometimes providing other kinds of hospitality or alms to the poor.[70] Medieval manorial lords sometimes assisted their tenants, part of an aristocratic ethic of responsibility for one's dependents. At lower levels, someone with an empty house could allow a few people to live in it rent-free or permit a barn to be used for temporary shelter. Witchcraft accusations sometimes grew out of

---

[69] E.g., Ben-Amos, "Gifts and Favors" and her *Culture of Giving*, esp. chs. 1–2 and 4. For below, see McIntosh, "Diversity of Social Capital."

[70] Heal, *Hospitality*, esp. ch. 2.

requests for food or other kinds of aid that were denied, violating the traditional assumption that known people who came to the door asking for help would be relieved.[71]

Individual charity could take the form of bequests of money, food, or clothing in wills. Some testators specified that their executors should give aid to particular individuals or institutions, while others asked parishes, religious fraternities, urban governments, or merchant guilds to decide how to distribute their legacies to the poor. Endowments of land, money, or animals could be left to hospitals and almshouses; charities with different primary functions, such as operating schools or maintaining key bridges over large rivers, might also give aid to needy people. We can rarely tell, however, how much if any of the generic "soul alms" left by medieval testators were awarded by their executors to the poor and how much to other religious or charitable causes.

Many late medieval testators instructed that alms be given to the poor who attended their funerals or "obits." This practice continued later too, although Protestant theology did not encourage it. In the 1550s and 1560s, 24 percent of London widows who left wills awarded small doles to those who came to their funerals, and even at the end of the sixteenth century, some will-makers awarded money to the poor at their burials.[72] While such bequests may have derived in part from charitable motives, the primary goal was usually to encourage the presence of many needy people at the service, ensuring especially powerful prayers for the good of the deceased person's soul (for Catholics) or thanks for his or her generosity (for Protestants).

Because many wills have survived for some places and periods, they can be analyzed quantitatively. The proportion of testators who left explicit bequests to the poor varied considerably.[73] About one-quarter of testators in York and Salisbury left something to the poor during the later medieval period, as did those residents of Bristol and London during the second half of the sixteenth century who were of intermediate economic level. Wealthier residents of Bristol and London in the Elizabethan period were more charitable, with just over half mentioning such bequests. Of rural residents of Yorkshire, only 10 percent gave bequests to the poor in the sixteenth and early seventeenth centuries, but 20 percent of country people in the southwest of the country left such legacies in the 1520s and 43 percent in the 1560s. In Archer's sample, the proportions of London testators leaving assistance to the poor reached their peak in

---

[71] E.g., Macfarlane, *Witchcraft*, 196–7.   [72] Archer, "Charity of London Widows."
[73] Figures below are taken from the summary in Ben-Amos, *Culture of Giving*, 117. See also, e.g., Phillips, "Charitable Institutions," 197–200, and ch. 5.3 below.

1570–73 (at levels of 72 percent for wealthier and 35 percent for less prosperous people), perhaps the result of continued Protestant exhortation for charity and increasing need.[74] The figures then declined somewhat to 65 and 24 percent in 1594–7, probably because the parish-based system of relief was becoming more effective.

The multiple arms of the pre-Reformation Catholic Church were heavily involved in helping the poor. When those forms of assistance were terminated in the mid sixteenth century, the total array of relief became less varied, offering fewer types of aid to people in need. Most monasteries and convents gave some alms to the poor; a smaller fraction provided short-term hospitality, took in needy children, gave gentle employment to disabled or elderly people, or operated hospitals.[75] The level of monastic aid was probably somewhat higher in the late fourteenth and fifteenth centuries than it was in the 1530s, when more than 800 houses reported that they gave a total of between £6,500 and £11,500 annually to the poor.[76] (Those figures are based upon the *Valor Ecclesiasticus* of 1536, supplemented by other information, although we cannot always take the nominal amounts at face value.[77]) With the dissolution of monastic houses in 1536 and 1539, that support ended and the church-run hospitals closed. The far less wealthy Protestant church continued to advocate charitable generosity and supported assistance through its courts, but it administered less relief of its own.

Other kinds of aid were based within local churches.[78] In addition to the activity of the parish itself, to be explored in later chapters, many late medieval churches contained fraternities or religious guilds. Devoted usually to the worship of a particular saint or element within the liturgy and containing a primarily or totally lay membership, these associations also filled social functions and sometimes helped people in need.[79]

---

[74] Archer, "Charity of Early Modern Londoners." Among London widows, 74–79% bequeathed something to the poor during the 1550s and 1560s (Archer, "Charity of London Widows").

[75] E.g., *Rites of Durham*, 91–2, Harvey, *Living and Dying*, ch. 1, and see ch. 3.4 below.

[76] The lower estimate is from Hadwin, "Deflating Philanthropy," and the higher from Beier, *Problem of the Poor*, 20, based on Savine, *English Monasteries*, Snape, *English Monastic Finances*, and Knowles, *Religious Orders*; for a more recent calculation that arrives at roughly the latter figure, see Rushton, "Monastic Charitable Provision."

[77] Rushton argued that additional poor relief not recorded in the *Valor* was provided through in-kind donations and sheltering poor children and paupers ("Monastic Charitable Provision"), but conversely a visitation of the abbey in Faversham, Kent in 1511–12 was told that the house's alms were sometimes given to the monks' friends rather than to the poor (*Kentish Visitations*, 34).

[78] For the elements contained within a parish, see Burgess, "Time and Place."

[79] E.g., Hanawalt, "Keepers of the Lights," Hanawalt and McRee, "Guilds of *Homo Prudens*," Barron, "Parish Fraternities," and Bainbridge, *Gilds*. For their charitable activities, see McRee, "Charity and Gild Solidarity" and Rubin, *Charity and Community*, 250–9.

Although we lack good information about the number and geographical distribution of parish fraternities and how they changed over time, in some parts of the country nearly every parish had one or more fraternities in the later fourteenth century, with further expansion by the 1540s. Their membership consisted of the male heads of most self-supporting families, sometimes joined by their wives. Some fraternities accepted or even solicited new admissions from outside their home parish, using membership fees to increase their revenues.

Some of these organizations offered help to the poor. In incomplete returns to a government survey of fraternities taken in 1389, 31 percent said they provided assistance to their own members in times of need: if they became poor through injury, sickness, or old age.[80] Such help was normally short term, given in the form of a weekly allowance of 4d. to 6d. In those parts of the country in which fraternities were common, their aid may have relieved a good deal of the life-cycle or misfortune-based poverty in the community. Ten percent of the fraternities offered aid to poor people outside their own membership, in addition to the small sums distributed as "soul alms" at burials or commemorative services. While help to outsiders was often largely symbolic, such as a penny given each to thirteen poor people on the feast day of the association's saint, some of the larger and wealthier fraternities awarded more substantial sums or administered endowed charitable bequests.

Another national survey of fraternities was taken between 1545 and 1549, when the crown was preparing to close them and appropriate their property. The returns are even less complete than the earlier ones, but of 166 fraternities for which information about charitable assistance was provided, 36 percent reported that they helped poor people who fell into poverty.[81] In some cases their assistance was more than just occasional. They might pay needy parishioners to perform easy work within the church, and a few operated or assisted in the running of almshouses.[82] Some historians have questioned the claims of assistance to the poor made in 1389 and the 1540s, for the few surviving accounts record little help. But the accounts may not reveal the full story, for fraternities sometimes instructed their members to give aid privately to their needy fellows, presumably to avoid shaming people who needed help.[83] Such assistance would not have appeared in the records.

---

[80] McIntosh, "Local Responses," for the rest of this paragraph.

[81] Ibid., with numbers recalculated for fraternities only.

[82] E.g., *London and Middlesex Chantry Certificates*, 51, ShakespCLA BRT1/2/527, 1/3/4, 1/3/20, and 1/3/56, all used through A2A, Phillips, "Charitable Institutions," 41–2, 131–2, and 155–7, and see ch. 3.4 below.

[83] E.g., DorsetHC DC/BTB CD56 and *History of Chesterfield*, 127.

After the abolition of the fraternities, we encounter occasional references to their earlier charitable activities. In Canewdon, Essex, five pieces of
land were held by feoffees on behalf of the parish fraternities of St. Anne
and St. Margaret during the later medieval period.[84] Although fraternities
were supposed to convey their property to the crown in the late 1540s, and
although inquiries were held in the 1560s into "concealed lands,"
Canewdon's feoffees managed to retain possession of what were thereafter
termed "the poor's lands." In 1590, the recipient of a big royal grant of
lands and urban premises that had formerly belonged to the guilds of the
Holy Trinity and St. George in Warwick was required to pay 34s. 8d.
annually to eight poor women, at the rate of 8d. per week, as had been
done when the fraternities were active.[85]

Many late medieval parish churches and cathedrals housed chantries.
These institutions supported one or more priests who received a stipend
to pray for the souls of the chantry's founders, their relatives, and all
Christians.[86] Wealthier chantries were often located in their own chapels
within the main church building. Supported usually by an endowment of
land or other property, chantry priests sometimes provided assistance to
the poor, said extra masses for the parishioners, or taught local children.[87]
Like the fraternities, chantries were surveyed in the late 1540s prior to
their suppression and royal confiscation of their property. In returns
from seventeen counties plus London, 107 chantries said they gave alms
to the poor.[88] A few operated hospitals, but their impact was probably
modest.[89]

Both before and after the Reformation, the secular clergy (those who
interacted with the laity, as opposed to members of the religious orders)
were expected to assist the poor. Priests and ministers, bishops and
archbishops, and the dean and chapter/canons of cathedrals were supposed to distribute alms, donate a certain fraction of the value of their livings
to the poor, and/or provide hospitality.[90] Prior to the 1530s, cathedrals

---

[84] Crowe, "Charity," for this and below.   [85] L&IS, *Cal. Pat. R.*, *32 Eliz.*, Pt. 1, 161.
[86] Kreider, *English Chantries*, ch. 1.
[87] E.g., HMC, *Cal. of MSS of the Dean and Chapter of Wells*, vol. 1, 456–8, and HMC, *Twelfth Report*, App. 4, 54.
[88] Calculated from the sources listed in McIntosh, "Local Responses."
[89] Of thirty-three hospitals run by late medieval chantries in the counties of Essex, Warwickshire, Wiltshire, and Yorkshire, at least ten had apparently ceased to perform any charitable functions by 1546; the remainder provided support for 163 aged, poor, or infirm lay people and for thirty-six priests (Kreider, *English Chantries*, 64–6).
[90] E.g., Rubin, *Charity and Community*, 238–44, A. Brown, *Popular Piety*, 194–6, Kümin, "Parish Finance," Heal, "Archbishops of Canterbury," and her *Hospitality*, 258–74. For the obligations of medieval incumbents, see Tierney, *Medieval Poor Law*, 106–9, 15 Richard II, c. 6, and 4 Henry IV, c. 2, *SR*, vol. 2, 80 and 137; for their failure to do so,

commonly received gifts of land or rents to support the poor, often in connection with commemorative services for the dead. Bishops played secondary roles as well, by exhorting the parishioners of their diocese to charity and promoting a policy of lenience to poor people brought before the church courts.[91] After the confiscation of religious property in the later 1530s, Henry VIII re-founded eight older cathedrals, created six new ones, and granted some additional endowments to the deans and chapters, specifying that they were to use the income to "distribute sums of money yearly among poor householders and other poor people" and to repair highways.[92] The fact that bishops, like other members of the clergy, could marry after the Reformation posed a potential challenge, for a desire to support one's family and to educate and pass along resources to one's heirs might stand in the way of charitable giving.

Other kinds of relief were offered by secular communities and lay officials. During the medieval period, although less so by the sixteenth century, manorial or village bodies sometimes assisted the rural poor. Manor courts might help in furnishing aid to orphaned children, widowed mothers, and physically or mentally disabled people.[93] Elderly peasants could set up maintenance contracts in which another person took over the use of their land in return for providing housing and food. Local customs about gleaning or the gathering of peas sometimes favored poor people, mainly those who were unable to work, women, and children.[94] Some manorial land or revenue was given to hospitals or almshouses or bequeathed to the use of the local poor, while rent payments or fines might be lowered or excused in the face of legitimate poverty.

In urban contexts, charitable aid was administered in several ways beyond the help given by parishes. Officials of some of the country's cities and larger towns began experimenting in the later fourteenth and fifteenth centuries with ways of assisting their own needy residents. In London,

---

see, e.g., *Visitations in the Diocese of Lincoln*, vol. 1, 62–4 and 78–80 (hospitality) and 45–7 and 132–6 (alms), and Ault, "Manor Court and Parish Church." The charitable obligations of Protestant clergymen are discussed in chs. 5.3 and 8.2.1 below.

[91] For the latter, see, e.g., *Life, Love and Death*, 87 and 169–70, and BIA HC.AB.10, fols. 24r and 25r.

[92] *CPR, Edw. VI*, vol. 5, 403, and see ibid., vol. 1, 232. For below, see, e.g., *CSPD*, vol. 7, 478.

[93] Clark, "Custody of Children," her "Mothers at Risk of Poverty," her "Charitable Bequests," and her "Social Welfare." For an important early study, see Page, "Customary Poor-Law." For below, see Clark, "Some Aspects of Social Security" and Smith, "Manorial Court."

[94] E.g., Ault, "By-Laws of Gleaning," NorthantsRO PDC.CR Bundle F, #69, and Groom, "Piety and Locality," 112–13. For below, see, e.g., LincsA Holywell 71/31 and CornwRO AR/2/644, used through A2A; Post, "Manorial Amercements," and NewCO MS 4060, for 1489.

where welfare had previously been offered mainly by the church or wealthy citizens responding to religious injunctions, two new patterns emerged in the late medieval period.[95] Provision of help became increasingly secular, and the city's governors assumed greater responsibility for the rising level of welfare provision. By around 1500, many larger communities were confronting unwanted immigration by the poor and an increase in begging. For the rest of the sixteenth century urban authorities struggled with how to achieve an appropriate balance between two conflicting responses: charitable assistance to legitimately needy people recognized as belonging to the community, supported often by local rates; and policies designed to maintain order and keep poor outsiders from moving in.[96]

Cities and towns provided more targeted help under certain circumstances. The orphaned children of men who had been admitted as citizens or freemen, together with the property bequeathed to them, were commonly taken under the supervision of civic authorities, who tried to ensure that the children were assigned to suitable guardians and that their inheritances remained intact until they came of age.[97] In the late Elizabethan years, some towns paid to have poor orphans or illegitimate children boarded while they were young and sent out later as servants or apprentices; others undertook training programs for children or adults, intended to teach them skills that would render them self-supporting. Urban officials might provide relief if plague or other contagious illnesses struck the town, sometimes coupling delivery of food or money to the poor with quarantine measures to keep the disease from spreading through begging.[98] In years of bad harvests and very high food prices, some urban governments bought grain elsewhere, transported it to their community, and sold it at a subsidized price to the local poor. Special local assessments might be imposed to pay for help at times of plague or food shortage.

Many of England's larger communities contained guilds or companies whose members worked in a given craft or were merchants specializing in a certain type of goods. Created primarily to regulate apprenticeships, working conditions, and prices for their members, as well as to develop a sense of brotherhood among them through activities like periodic feasts,

---

[95] Barron, *London*, 267–8.   [96] See chs. 2.1 and 6.1 below.

[97] E.g., Clark, "City Orphans" and Barron, *London*, 268–73. For below, see, e.g., ESussRO Rye 1/3, fols. 42v and 86r, *Minutes and Accounts*, vol. 5, 36, *Books of Examinations and Depositions* [of Southampton], 51, HullCA HCA BRB 2, fol. 299 (a transcript of which was kindly sent to me by Helen Good), and McIntosh, "Networks of Care."

[98] E.g., *York Civic Records*, vol. 4, 30, vol. 5, 33, 35, 57, and 68, and *Poor Relief in Eliz. Ipswich*, 110–18. For below, see Slack, *Poverty and Policy*, 146–7, and for a particularly detailed record, ShropsA MS 3365/728 for Shrewsbury in 1587.

some urban guilds assisted their own members if they became poor.[99] Because, however, they might require that such help be provided privately, outside the view of the association's accounts, we cannot ascertain how common it was. Especially in London, some companies helped needy outsiders as well. When the guilds were surveyed by the crown in 1548, only two of the thirty-four London companies whose returns survive said that they gave aid to their own members, but fifteen reported that they assisted others.[100] By the late Elizabethan period, the contribution of London's livery companies was very substantial: the Grocers, Clothworkers, and Goldsmiths alone provided £348 in poor relief annually around 1595.

The crown played both direct and indirect roles in the provision of aid to the poor, actions often implemented from the 1540s onwards by the Privy Council. Medieval and early modern rulers gave alms to the poor on a daily basis and on special occasions. In the early Tudor period, most donations were paid through the royal almoners or assigned to particular institutions (like Westminster Abbey or the city of London) for distribution, but smaller sums were still handed out by the sovereign in person.[101] In 1572 Queen Elizabeth augmented the money given to the High Almoner by adding all "deodands" (objects that had caused someone's death) and goods forfeited to the crown after a person committed suicide. During the latter part of the century, the queen and Privy Council issued Books of Orders concerning responses to the plague and provision of grain after bad harvests.[102]

The crown made some effort to preserve traditional charity for the poor from religious livings or properties. Prior to the Reformation, it sometimes demanded that monasteries or cathedral chapters that "appropriated" parishes continue to render alms.[103] Because rectors were obligated by ecclesiastical and secular law to make some provision for the poor of their

---

[99] E.g., M. Davies, "Tailors of London," *York Memorandum Book*, 279–80, Rexroth, *Deviance and Power*, 226–45, and *CPR, Eliz.*, vol. 8, 133. For below, see, e.g., *History of Chesterfield*, 169–70.

[100] *London and Middlesex Chantry Certificates*, 81–95, passim. For below, see Archer, *Pursuit of Stability*, 123.

[101] E.g., *L&P*, vol. 2, pt. 2, 1445, and *APC*, vol. 2, 174. For below, see *CPR, Eliz.*, vol. 5, 396 and 466.

[102] Slack, *Poverty and Policy*, 138–48.

[103] The appropriating institution became the rector of that parish, taking the profits from its tithes and any property it held but also responsible for maintaining part of the church building and appointing and supporting a vicar to carry out services. Between 1391 and 1406 and again in 1425 and 1432, Parliament discussed and in some cases passed measures requiring that when a parish church was appropriated, a diocesan official should specify how much was to be set aside henceforth for poor parishioners (Given-Wilson, "Service, Serfdom").

parishes, earlier crown grants sometimes stipulated how much the appropriator was required to contribute. By the late fifteenth century, however, awards usually said only that "a certain sum of money," "a competent sum," or "a yearly sum" be given to the poor.[104] Continuation of the charitable requirements imposed upon religious property became more difficult after the royal confiscations of the mid sixteenth century. As the crown proceeded to lease or sell those lands and rectories to new lay owners, many of its initial awards included a proviso that customary payments to the poor must still be rendered.[105] During the 1570s and 1580s, that obligation was mentioned in some but not all grants; by the 1590s, alms were required infrequently, and then usually only in sales of tithes or rectories.[106] The gradual disappearance of almsgiving from royal grants of ex-religious property must have caused a considerable drop in the funds available to the poor in many local communities.

Monarchs were involved with multiple facets of the founding and operation of hospitals and almshouses. Medieval kings commonly appointed masters or granted entire institutions to individuals; all through this span, the crown awarded licenses to set up new houses, acquire land to support existing ones, or re-found houses that were no longer functioning properly.[107] The monarch might name visitors in response to complaints about the maladministration of specific residential institutions, and several Tudor rulers created general commissions to survey the accounts of hospitals, almshouses, and cathedral churches with regard to their use of charitable funds.[108] Especially in the 1580s and 1590s, the crown sometimes incorporated the body of men responsible for an almshouse or its master and residents as a legally defined unit.

From the mid sixteenth century, the crown attempted to assist poor ex-soldiers, especially those who had been disabled in the wars. The usual method was to name them to the "alms rooms" provided by cathedrals and certain other religious and educational institutions. Alms rooms conferred generous stipends to their holders (usually amounting to

[104] E.g., *CPR, Hen. VII*, vol. 1, 81 and 117, and vol. 2, 175.
[105] See, for the early 1550s, *CPR, Edw. VI*, vol. 4, 5, 11, 116–19, 122, 146–9, 337–43, 345–6, and 439–40.
[106] E.g., *CPR, Eliz.*, vol. 7, 186–8 and 210–11, vol. 8, 155, vol. 9, 251–3, and NottsA DD/SR/234/75, used through A2A; L&IS, *Cal. Pat. R., 32 Eliz.*, Pt. 1, 160–1, 186, and 203–4, and ibid., *33 Eliz.*, 27 and 169.
[107] E.g., *CPR, Hen. VI*, vol. 6, 233–4, 251–2, 277, 283, 434–5, and 510, *CPR, Edw. IV and Hen. VI*, 113, 306, and 604, *CPR, Ph. and Mary*, vol. 3, 471–3 and 522–3, *CPR, Eliz.*, vol. 6, 297–8, vol. 7, 213–14, *CSPD*, vol. 3, 525, L&IS, *Cal. Pat. R., 39 Eliz.*, 130–1 and 216.
[108] E.g., *CPR, Hen. VI*, vol. 6, 303, *CPR, Edw. VI*, vol. 5, 403, and HMC, *Cal. of the MSS of the Marquis of Salisbury*, vol. 14, 145. For below, see, e.g., L&IS, *Cal. Pat. R., 33 Eliz.*, 51 and 137–8, and McIntosh, "Negligence, Greed."

between £4 10s. and £6 13s. 4d. annually) and normally offered a dwelling at that location.[109] Henry VIII had given resources to cathedrals to provide support for 124 almsmen, who were to be nominated by the crown but given a salary and sometimes housing by the deans and chapters. At first these positions were granted primarily to royal servants, but as former soldiers began to ask for help during Edward VI's reign, the Privy Council realized that it could award alms rooms to those men. After 1588, recipients of places were usually maimed soldiers.[110] The crown also began requiring institutions other than cathedral chapters to take in such men, expanding the number of positions available. During the 1590s, it sent poor and/or injured soldiers as almsmen to seven other bodies as well as to the cathedrals.[111] For less privileged ex-servicemen, the queen occasionally granted small pensions from royal funds, but more commonly the Privy Council preferred to shift the financial burden onto others.[112] They sent some maimed soldiers to hospitals, which had to take care of them at their own cost, or required parishes, hundreds, counties, or cities to support individual men or their widows.[113] After Parliamentary legislation in 1593 that required all counties to levy local payments to support "distressed soldiers and sailors," the Privy Council issued both general and individual instructions on how that money should be employed.[114]

Some of these additional forms of assistance will be mentioned at least in passing, but other issues are largely ignored. I do not attempt to measure in quantitative fashion how many poor people existed in various

---

[109] Atherton et al., "Pressed Down by Want," Lehmberg, *Reformation of Cathedrals*, 293–7, and Orme and Webster, *English Hospital*, 159. At first, almsmen did not have to be in actual residency at the church or college to receive their stipends, but as pressure on places intensified, the expectation that they would live in the institution became stronger (e.g., *Cal. State Papers Dom.*, *Edw. VI*, 304, and TNA-PRO SP 12/25, fol. 9, for Christ Church, Oxford). The most desirable places were provided by the College of St. George at Windsor Castle, but they were rarely awarded to poor men.

[110] *APC*, vol. 2, 313 and 376–409, passim. For below, see, e.g., *CSPD*, vol. 4, 399, vol. 5, 112, 197, and 244, *APC*, vol. 12, 344, vol. 14, 237 and 377, and vol. 24, 184.

[111] In addition to the cathedrals – in Bristol, Canterbury, Carlisle, Chester, Durham, Ely, Exeter, Gloucester, Leicester, Norwich, Oxford (Christ Church), Rochester, Winchester, and Worcester – the crown sent almsmen to the churches of St. Peter and St. Stephen in Westminster, a hospital in Ledbury run by the Dean and Chapter of Hereford, King's and Trinity Colleges in Cambridge, Thornton College in Lincolnshire, and the royal almshouse at Donnington, Berks. (BritL Lansdowne MS 65, no. 21, *CSPD*, vol. 4, 306 and 399, vol. 5, 197, 209, and 213, and *APC*, vols. 17–20, passim).

[112] E.g., *CSPD*, vol. 4, 9, vol. 5, 63 and 197, and L&IS, *Cal. Pat. R.*, *32 Eliz.*, Pt. 1, 208.

[113] *APC*, vol. 21, 151 and 389, vol. 18, 209, and vol. 22, 13, 28, 131, and 228. A "hundred" was a territorial and administrative sub-unit of a county, often consisting of around five to ten villages, market centers, or towns.

[114] E.g., *APC*, vol. 24, 178–80, vol. 25, 16–17, vol. 26, 343, vol. 28, 150 and 181, and see ch. 6.3 below.

periods and places or how much they needed to survive.[115] Because the forms of poor relief organized by many large urban centers have been studied by other scholars, they receive less notice here than market towns and villages.[116] Specialized forms of endowed assistance (for poor maidens' marriages, poor boys' apprenticeships, or loans to young craftsmen) are left aside, as are efforts to provide grain for needy people and rules about building cottages on small plots of land. Charitable activities that were not aimed directly at the poor – such as endowments for schools, support of a minister or lecturer, and maintenance of roads and bridges – are omitted entirely.

The structure of this book facilitates exploration of how the three main kinds of assistance changed between 1350 and 1600. The next three chapters consider begging and gathering, residential institutions, and parish activity during the later medieval years and the early sixteenth century. We turn then to the dramatic alterations of the years between 1530 and 1553, which had a profound impact upon each of these types of relief. Developments during the second half of the sixteenth century are explored in Chapters 6 to 8. The final section begins with a reassessment of the Poor Laws of 1598 and 1601 and a discussion of Commissions for Charitable Uses during the closing years of Elizabeth's reign, followed by a summary conclusion.

---

[115] Dyer, *Standards of Living*, 252–3, his "Did the Peasants Really Starve?," Slack, *Poverty and Piety*, ch. 4 and 173–82, and Archer, *Pursuit of Stability*, 190–7.

[116] Among the many important studies that discuss urban poor relief in the later sixteenth century are Beier, "Social Problems," Pelling, "Healing the Sick Poor," her "Old Age, Poverty, and Disability," Schen, *Charity*, and Archer, "Charity of Early Modern Londoners."

Part I

Late medieval and early Tudor patterns

2 Seeking alms

Requesting charitable alms was the oldest and probably the most common method whereby poor people obtained aid in late medieval England. Because the Catholic Church taught that the poor were an integral component of society and that assisting them was a spiritual obligation, and because charitable giving contributed to the donor's chances of salvation, especially when backed by an indulgence issued by church officials, asking for assistance and bestowing alms were accepted parts of life.[1] Some people solicited help for themselves – in the form of money, food, clothing, or overnight lodging – while others gathered contributions for another individual or a charitable institution or project. The relatively low level of poverty between 1350 and at least the mid fifteenth century meant that informal charitable assistance was able to take care of the needs of many people struck by misfortune. Apart from some heated rhetorical statements and Parliamentary legislation about the mobile poor and beggars in the wake of the 1348–9 plague and the 1381 uprising, alms seekers do not appear to have created any particular anxiety, nor do we often hear about problems with fraudulent licenses.

The lay people who solicited alms may be placed into several categories. Some men and women sought help within their own communities, going to the doors of friends and neighbors to ask for aid. Most did so only occasionally, at times of special hardship, but a few relied regularly on the generosity of others. People who were unable to support themselves were allowed by statute to seek assistance privately within their own communities, and normally they were not punished even if they solicited alms in public places near their homes. A petition to Parliament probably from the 1510s was said to have been written by desperate poor people who were driven by necessity to beg, calling out for alms in churches and churchyards, fairs, and markets.[2] Because some hospitals and most medieval

---

[1] See ch. 1.3 above.
[2] TNA-PRO E175/11/65, with the damaged opening lines filled in from BritL Add MS 24459, 157–60.

almshouses did not provide full support, it was common for their residents to ask for donations from people who lived near the institution or traveled past it. The poor might also receive alms at funerals or commemorative services. Around 1500, as the problem of urban poverty began to mount, some of the larger towns and cities experimented with licensing certain residents to request charity publicly, a favored group often denoted by some sort of badge.

Informal local requests for aid rarely appear in historical sources. The practice was not illegal, and help was often given in kind, not as money that might be listed in accounts. Limited evidence suggests, however, that women were included both among those who sought assistance and among those who gave it. A witness in a matrimonial case in York in 1355 described Maud Katersouth as "a poor little woman and needy, having nothing by which she is able to live, and not able to work for her livelihood, but daily obtains her food and ... necessities around her neighbours' houses"; another witness said that "for a little bread or a draught of ale she will fetch water [or do other small jobs] ... and thus she lives and is supported among her neighbours."[3] Assisting people one knew built and sustained networks of social capital, pools of goodwill into which members could dip when they themselves needed help.[4] Mutual assistance was part of a deeply embedded culture of giving that created "binding commitments and bonds of obligation" within social groups and communities: contributors received deference or an obligation to reciprocate from recipients while at the same time gaining honor and respect from other people.

A second cluster of alms seekers left their homes to solicit money or other forms of help elsewhere. Women were less likely than men to travel away from home, due to the practical dangers and potential moral disapproval they faced. Some needy people who were unable to gain adequate aid locally may have hoped to find greater generosity at private households, religious houses, and charitable institutions in wealthier areas. Or, if there was some stigma associated with asking for relief (although we cannot assume that there was), they may have preferred to seek help in a place where they were not known. Prior to the 1530s, no law prohibited them from doing so or insisted that they have official permission and carry a license. Strangers who appeared to have legitimate need – suffering from an incurable disease, a physical or mental disability, or some sudden misfortune – often received a sympathetic response from

---

[3] BIA CP.E.32. I am grateful to Jeremy Goldberg for this reference and transcript.
[4] McIntosh, "Diversity of Social Capital." For below, see Ben-Amos, *Culture of Giving*, esp. chs. 4 and 6 and 376–7.

private households and local officials. The assistance they gained, given to unknown outsiders, does not fit readily into a model based upon reciprocal gift-giving within defined social communities. This kind of generosity must instead have been fed by basic human kindness as nourished by Christian teachings. Poor people who sought assistance for acceptable reasons – those in our first two categories – were rarely described as beggars in any pejorative sense.[5]

Ordinances and statutes from 1349 onwards made a clear distinction between people who were unable to work for their own support and able-bodied vagrants who chose to move around the region or country living off alms. Although some of these wanderers took a little short-term employment as they went, they generally relied upon charity. Such people were nominally banned from asking for aid, and local constables were supposed to arrest and punish them in accordance with current laws before sending them back to their home communities. Anyone who provided assistance could be fined. But in practice it was often difficult to decide which travelers should be given a little help and which should be punished as vagrants. People on the ground made their own decisions, regardless of the requirements of the law, based upon some mixture of compassion, religious beliefs, and practical considerations. Private households, monasteries, and hospitals sometimes provided aid for needy strangers without asking awkward questions. From the perspective of local officials, even if a person seemed to fit the definition of a vagrant, it might be worth a few pennies in alms to ensure that he would just keep moving right out of the community, rather than forcing constables to spend time and money on the legally prescribed punishment.

An example of the lack of clarity concerning which people should be assisted – and of the many ways in which poor travelers might receive help – comes from an examination conducted by the Canterbury Quarter Sessions on December 21, 1530.[6] A man calling himself John Thomas, who had formerly worked as a wheelwright in Chelmsford, Essex, told the JPs that since the previous summer he had been unable to earn money by practising his trade "owing to trouble in his arms." He therefore decided to leave home, living first "on the alms of good men" in Chelmsford, Colchester, and Ipswich. He went next to London, where he stayed in St. Mary Spytyl (hospital) outside Bishopsgate for two or three nights. Then he traveled to Waltham and Ware, "lodging in an alms house," and on to

---

[5] The term "to beg" initially meant only to ask for alms or a charitable gift, on an occasional or regular basis; the negative associations of being "a beggar" did not become strong until the 1530s (*OED*).

[6] CantCA CC/JQ/330/v, used through A2A.

Puckeridge, where he slept at a hostelry called the Catherine Wheel. After that he went to Royston and Cambridge, and at the time of the recent snow he had crossed the Thames on the ferry at Tilbury, going to Gravesend and Deptford before reaching Canterbury and being arrested by a constable. Should Thomas be viewed as a poor man who deserved charitable assistance because he was physically incapacitated or as a vagrant who did not want to work and was enjoying the chance to see something of the country? While Canterbury's constables obviously believed the latter, some of Thomas's contemporaries – both individuals and institutions – had been willing to help him.

Whereas under normal circumstances it was illegal to give alms to physically capable people, there were exceptions. Two categories of people were allowed to travel while asking for charitable assistance. One group solicited alms for themselves or another individual. Most had formerly been able to support themselves but had suffered some calamity that reduced them to poverty. Students going to or from their place of study were supposed to carry a letter or testimonial explaining the reasons for their travel and need for alms, as were soldiers or mariners moving towards home from the place where they had been demobilized or ended their voyage. Pilgrims too might receive licenses. A second cluster included the gatherers named by hospitals and almshouses to request and gather funds on their behalf.[7] They were joined by the collectors sent out by some of the other institutions to which Catholic alms might be given for the good of one's soul: church buildings, religious organizations, and infrastructural features like bridges, roads, and harbors.

Everyone authorized to request alms was supposed to carry a written certificate or license, although some evidently did not. Such a document, issued by a secular or religious official, explained why the bearer was soliciting help and exhorted others to generosity. While modern cataloguers and historians often term their certificates "begging licenses," alms seekers like these were not described as beggars at the time. Their permissions instead used such phrases as "requesting Christian alms" or "soliciting charitable donations from good people." Authorized collection is not mentioned in any statutes and has received little historical attention even though it is better documented than solicitation without official approval.

This chapter focuses upon lay people who asked for aid with formal permission. We begin by summarizing late medieval statutes and urban responses. The discussion turns then to authorized solicitation by and for

---

[7] See ch. 3 below.

individuals, looking at who issued permissions and the reasons for which they were granted. A final section considers gathering for hospitals, almshouses, and the other activities seen as appropriate recipients of charitable alms.

2.1   Parliamentary and urban policies

Parliament's earliest contributions to the issue of alms collection were part of its attempts to limit the geographical mobility of the poor after 1348–9 and 1381. One way to keep peasants in their own communities was to define all able-bodied people who asked for assistance while moving about, regardless of why they were traveling, as illegal vagrants.[8] In 1349, the Statute of Labourers banned donations to beggars who were physically capable of labor.[9] A series of statutes starting in 1351 similarly prohibited begging while also restricting the mobility of the poor, requiring that they labor, and setting maximum wage rates. The conflict between sympathetic and hostile valuations of poverty and begging is reflected in the Statute of Cambridge of 1388, which stated expressly that needy people who were unable to work were allowed to request alms within their own communities.[10] If those places could not provide for them, the impotent poor were to go to other towns within their hundred or return to the place of their birth, where they were permitted to seek help.[11] But the measure also ordered that able-bodied people who left their home communities and asked for alms should be punished by time in the stocks. If a person claimed to have been captured outside the realm and needed money for ransom, or was a student or pilgrim, he was required to carry a testimonial documenting his circumstances.

After 1388, concern about mobile alms seekers lessened for several generations, but it reappeared in the later fifteenth century as one facet of the renewed attention to the poor that marked the period of economic and demographic uncertainty between 1460 and 1530.[12] Physically capable people who requested charity were now sometimes described in pejorative terms as beggars in Parliamentary and urban orders. A statute of 1495 reaffirmed that even people unable to work were not permitted to travel about begging: they could ask for aid only in the place where they

---

[8] Clark, "Institutional and Legal Responses."
[9] 23 Edward III, stat. 1, c. 7, *SR*, vol. 1, 308. For below, see Given-Wilson, "Service, Serfdom."
[10] 12 Richard II, c. 7, *SR*, vol. 2, 58.
[11] For the definition of a hundred, see ch. 1, n. 113 above.   [12] See ch. 1.3 above.

had most recently lived or where they were "best known" or born.[13] If they were found begging elsewhere, they were to be put into the stocks for three days and three nights, fed only bread and water. The measure also specified that those asking for alms on the grounds that they were students at one of the universities or were mariners or soldiers traveling homewards must have a letter from an appropriate authority granting permission for their movement and solicitation of aid. The provisions of that act were qualified slightly in 1504–5 and renewed in a royal proclamation of 1511 that dealt in part with beggars and vagabonds.[14] An extremely popular handbook for Justices of the Peace first published in 1506 reviewed the laws about beggars then in effect, including a reminder that anyone giving alms to a person able to labor was subject to punishment.

Urban areas were the first to feel the practical pressures resulting from a rising number of poor, as people in need left their rural homes and moved to larger communities. The ethical and spiritual ambivalence that surrounded the issue of begging contributed to multi-faceted responses.[15] Many towns and cities felt some responsibility for their own long-term residents who were unable to support themselves. In the later fourteenth and fifteenth centuries, some urban officials were involved in the administration of residential institutions or the distribution of occasional relief to the poor. The town keepers of Beverley, E. Yorks. granted places and expelled people from local hospitals in the 1390s and 1450s, and in the mid fifteenth century, bailiffs in Bridgwater, Som. paid for repairs to the town's almshouse and gave wine to the master and alms brothers living in the town's hospital.[16] But urban hospitals were occasionally criticized for their lack of selectivity. When a London merchant left a bequest to four London hospitals in 1479, he specified that his donation was for the truly needy, those who lacked "friendship, comfort, and help"; he excluded "common beggars going about all the day light and lying in [hospitals] the night time."[17]

By the early sixteenth century, many urban bodies were becoming concerned about the immigration of outside poor people who lived by soliciting alms. A common initial reaction was to assess the extent of the problem by examining beggars and non-local poor and expelling

---

[13] 11 Henry VII, c. 2, secs. 2–3, *SR*, vol. 2, 569.

[14] 19 Henry VII, c. 12, secs. 1–2, *SR*, vol. 2, 656, and *TRP*, vol. 1, 85–93. See also Cavill, "The Problem of Labour." For below, see *The boke of Justices of Peas*, a work reprinted at least twelve times by the end of the 1530s.

[15] See ch. 1.3 above.

[16] *Beverley Town Documents*, 41, HMC, *Report on MSS of the Corp. of Beverley*, 134, and SomstRO D/B/bw 1662 and 1667.

[17] Hanawalt, "Reading the Lives," esp. 1080.

undesirable people from the community. We see such responses in York in 1492 and 1503, Gloucester in 1504, Coventry in 1517, and Lincoln in 1518.[18] During the mid-1510s and 1520s, smaller boroughs too tried to exclude poor strangers, and we see early attempts to control begging by appointing a supervisor whose job was to discourage the arrival of unwanted newcomers and ensure order among those who remained.[19]

But how were longer-term residents with legitimate reasons for requesting alms to be assisted? An early urban technique was to license such people to seek help within the community, giving them a badge or other identifying mark. In Gloucester, three married couples, twelve men, and seventeen women were described in 1504 as "the poor people that been assigned to live of alms within the town of Gloucester that hath received the badge and the livery of the foresaid town."[20] York's officials ordered in 1515 that "every beggar that is not able to labour have a token upon his shoulder of his overmost garment that he may be known, and that all other beggars be punished according to the statutes"; Coventry instituted badging of approved beggars in 1521. But that mechanism was usually abandoned within a decade after its introduction in a given community. Badges were too readily transferable from one person to another, and town officials probably realized that if they gave permission to everyone who qualified for assistance, the community would be overwhelmed by people begging in the streets.

2.2   Licensed requests for alms due to special need

One would not know from Parliamentary and urban orders that some people who had been struck by misfortune were permitted to travel around the country asking for assistance.[21] The license or certificate that authorized alms seekers were supposed to carry with them could take many different forms, but they were generally prepared in the form of an open letter directed to "all Christian people to whom these letters testimonial shall come" or a similar audience. Written on parchment, which

---

[18] *York Civic Records*, vol. 2, 88 and 182, GloucsA GBR B2/1, fol. 20v, *Coventry Leet Book*, 652, and LincsA L 1/1/1/1/1, fol. 90b.

[19] E.g., Droitwich, Worcs. in 1516 (WorcsRO 261.4/31, BA 1006/#352), Morpeth, Northumb. in 1523 (Boyle, "Orders for the Town"), and Marlborough, Wilts. in 1524–5 (Wilts&SA G22/1/15, p. 18); Leicester named a "beadle for the poor" for each of the town's quarters in 1520 (*Records of the Borough of Leicester*, 13–14).

[20] GloucsA GBR B2/1, fol. 233v. For below, see *York Civic Records*, vol. 3, 46, and *Coventry Leet Book*, 677.

[21] The Statute of Cambridge is a partial exception, for it mentions the documents that were to be carried by men who said they had been taken captive by foreigners (12 Richard II, c. 8, *SR*, vol. 2, 58).

could be folded into a small square that was easy to put into a pocket or pouch but might be opened repeatedly without ripping along the crease, the document named the recipient and gave a brief explanation of why he, she, or they were allowed to gather alms; some stated for how long a term they were valid and in what hundreds, counties, or regions of England the bearer was permitted to request help. The authorization was then signed and sealed by an appropriate official. We cannot determine to what extent these documents carried weight simply because they were written and had a seal, as opposed to the impact of their specific words: many of the recipients, like many churchwardens and constables, were themselves not literate. Permits were usually issued directly to the individuals who would benefit from the money gathered, but if the recipients were physically unable to travel or were held captive, they might name agents to do the actual collection. Licenses could also be sub-contracted to other people, in return for a payment to the original grantee.[22] Gathering often occurred at parish services, where the priest could advocate charity and the churchwardens help to collect alms from worshippers, but bearers of licenses also approached private households, religious bodies, and urban authorities.

The haphazard system for obtaining authorization to solicit alms was heavily weighted in favor of suppliants with access to information and resources. Someone hoping to get a license needed to know who was allowed to grant such documents, have enough money to pay the required fees, and perhaps be in contact with an influential person who would advance his or her cause. It is therefore not surprising that so few late medieval permissions were granted to people who had always lived in poverty or to women.

Some of the most prestigious licenses were issued by the king or Lord Chancellor. In 1496, Henry VII issued a proclamation allowing Thomas Andrew of South Mimms, Middx., to gather alms throughout the country.[23] Andrew had lost his house, four stables, two barns, and his movable goods through a fire, falling thereby into "great and extreme poverty, having nothing left to succor and relieve himself, his wife, and his children." The king took Andrew and his men and servants under his protection, ordering all religious and lay officials to allow them to travel in safety and "to gather almsdeeds and charitable gifts." Around 1450, Walter Orpyngton petitioned the Chancellor for authorization to request alms.[24] Orpyngton explained that he had fought at the seige of Harfleur

---

[22] E.g., TNA-PRO C 1/127/45.   [23] *TRP*, vol. 1, 36.

[24] TNA-PRO C 1/19/499. An online database about medieval English soldiers lists Orpyngton as having been a man-at-arms in the field under the Duke of Bedford at the

and in many other places in Normandy and France during his 36 years of service. He had often been taken prisoner and lost his goods, and now he was "fall[en] in great age and poverty and little hath wherewith him to help and sustain." He therefore requested letters patent "by which he may ask and take the alms of the people in this realm of England there as he shall suppose most profitable and expedient for him toward the helping and relieving of his poor estate, for God's love and in way of charity." Permissions to solicit assistance for individuals were still granted by the crown or royal officials during the first part of the sixteenth century, although now more often as a license issued under the broad seal.

Religious leaders promoted almsgiving by issuing "letters of recommendation" or – prior to the mid-1530s – indulgences on behalf of people asking for charitable aid. In 1453–4, the abbot of St. Albans in Hertfordshire prepared a document for William Hoby, who claimed that he had been riding homewards from London when he was ambushed and robbed of his own goods and those he was carrying for others.[25] The ruffians cut his throat and ripped out his tongue, leaving him lying on the ground for the night amidst a storm. During that time, he made a vow that if he survived, he would go as a pilgrim on foot to various shrines in England. He did recover and longed to fulfill his vow, "but because of his extreme poverty and loss of his full faculties [his inability to speak], he could not manage the pilgrimage unless supported by alms." The abbot's letter appealed to the compassion of religious communities, urging them to assist Hoby from the goods God had given them and reminding them that He would amply reward them with spiritual benefits. Bishops of Ely granted many indulgences for individuals, especially people harmed by fire.[26]

Borough officials too gave certificates. The town customal of Faversham, Kent recorded a sample letter of commendation, undated but probably from the fifteenth century. It explained that its bearer, while aboard an English ship, had been wounded and captured "by our unspeakable Scotch enemies."[27] After being held prisoner for more than 6 months, he agreed to pay ransom of 20 marks (£13 6s. 8d.) within a year after his release. He was now free (probably on bond), but had no way of obtaining such a large sum on his own. "Wherefore we ask you all in

---

relief of Paris in 1429 and as a member of the garrisons at Pontorson in 1429 and Avranches in 1430 (www.medievalsoldier.org, accessed August 3, 2010). I am grateful to Adrian Bell for directing me to this database.

[25] Gransden, "Letter of Recommendation."

[26] Rubin, *Charity and Community*, 265–9, and CambUL Ely Diocesan Records F/5/35, fol. 171r–v.

[27] CKentS Fa/LC 1, fol. 19v.

friendship to deign in charity to help him as an honest beggar for these reasons when he comes and passes among you, that by your alms he may be speedily freed from the punishment of prison which he must endure for life unless he faithfully pays the twenty marks." In 1514, four former mayors of Northampton joined the prior of the monastery of St. Andrew, an esquire, two gentlemen, and six other men in preparing a written recommendation that charity be given to Robert Mabbis of Little Houghton.[28] Mabbis's large house was one of eleven destroyed by a fire in the village. Officials of the manorial lord from whom he held his property had ordered him to rebuild the house or face imprisonment, but he lacked the resources to do so.

As these examples have suggested, licenses fell into certain designated categories, indicating careful selection by grantors. Medieval recipients were almost never living in chronic poverty, but had instead experienced some kind of specific and severe misfortune, through no fault of their own.[29] Due to such losses, these formerly self-sufficient merchants, craftsmen, landholders, soldiers, or sailors either needed a large amount of money right away or had been so reduced economically that they could no longer support themselves and their families adequately. Poverty was thus seen as a relative matter, consisting of less wealth or power than the person had previously enjoyed. Yet in a period that offered no formal mechanisms for insurance, someone whose personal possessions and trading goods were located in his house, shop, or a ship might indeed drop within a few hours from a comfortable position to economic need through a single catastrophe.

Licenses or proclamations permitting people to seek alms after a fire were among the most common. A petition submitted to the Chancellor around 1540 by John Norton, a husbandman of Camberwell in Lambeth, Surrey, claimed that he had lost not only his house but all his goods, to the value of over £40, in a fire.[30] He asked for letters patent that would authorize him "to go, travel, and resort into all and every place and places within this realm of England there to ask, gather, levy, receive, and bear away the charitable alms and devotion of the king's true and loving subjects."

Other people received permission because they had been captured or their goods seized by foreign enemies. A person held for ransom could either be freed on some kind of bond to go home and gather up the money,

---

[28] NorthantsRO NPL 1071.

[29] Simple poverty was rarely cited as the reason for medieval authorizations to gather alms or indulgences. Thus, of 235 indulgences granted to individuals by bishops of Ely between 1388 and 1500, only 11 (5%) went to people described merely as poor (Rubin, *Charity and Community*, 266).

[30] TNA-PRO C 1/1039/48, and see *L&P*, vol. 3, pt. 2, 973 (#12).

or he could appoint others to collect on his behalf while he remained in captivity. When the whole crew of a ship was taken, a few of its members might be released to request funds while the rest remained as sureties. John Colman of Bristol appealed to Chancery in the early 1460s, saying that he was one of a group of soldiers who had been returning home by sea after serving at the king's castle at Tenby in Wales when they were captured by Bretons and taken as prisoners to St. Malo.[31] He and one of the others were released to gather money in England to pay for the ransom of themselves and their fellows. They had obtained letters patent from the king authorizing them to do so, but when they came to Bristol, they were arrested – apparently for debt – and had now been incarcerated for 5 weeks. The few medieval women authorized to seek alms were generally soliciting funds with which to release their imprisoned husbands.[32]

In the pre-Reformation period, collections for ransom were sometimes supported by indulgences.[33] Such awards were usually made by English churchmen, but occasionally were given by the Pope or Roman cardinals to well-placed individuals. Indulgences were issued especially when ransom was being collected for people captured by the Barbary pirates or the Turks, enemies of the Christian faith.[34] Some of the recipients were English sailors. In 1511, the Lord Chancellor was told to grant a license to Thomas Sprakeling of the Isle of Thanet, Kent.[35] Sprakeling had been taken by the Moors while sailing along the Barbary coast and imprisoned in Fez until Ralph Alarde paid his ransom of £14. Sprakeling had now been released and wanted to gather alms in all of the parish churches in the diocese of London plus the counties of Kent and Sussex in order to reimburse Alarde. John Forget was licensed in 1512 to seek alms with which to ransom his brother and uncle, "taken prisoners in battle against the Turks and Saracens" in 1509.[36] Their captors demanded 2,000 "ducats de Camera," which had to be paid within the next 12 months. Henry VIII's award noted that "twelve cardinals of Rome have, out of the treasure of the Church, conferred on all who help the said John herein great indulgences, viz., each of them release of 100 days of enjoined penance."

Continental Europeans and members of Eastern Orthodox churches were sometimes permitted to gather the ransom demanded by Muslims.[37]

---

[31] TNA-PRO C 1/28/420.   [32] E.g., *L&P*, vol. 4, pt. 2, 1386.   [33] Swanson, "Tales."

[34] Henry VIII shared this view, joining the Pope in offering protection in 1518 to John Sargy, who was gathering funds "toward the redemption and deliverance" of certain prisoners "from the servitude and thralldom of the ... Turks, enemies to the name and religion of Christ" (*TRP*, vol. 1, 130).

[35] *L&P*, vol. 1, pt. 1, 396 (#18).   [36] *L&P*, vol. 1, pt. 1, 523 (#19).

[37] E.g., ibid., 352 (#3), and vol. 4, pt. 3, 2350 (#20). For below, see ibid., vol. 1, pt. 1, 164 (#23).

A Greek woman described as the Countess of Sarrinalle received a license in 1510 to ask alms for the liberation of her two sons from the Turks. She had a papal bull confirming that her husband had been slain by the Turks in Greece and her daughters taken prisoner but then ransomed with the help of Isabella, Queen of Castile; her sons remained in captivity. The following year, a Greek man and woman were arrested while collecting alms in Lincolnshire for the redemption of the woman's husband and children, "prisoners with the Grand Turk."[38] They claimed in a petition to Chancery that they had obtained letters patent from the English king for their collection, but officials of the city of Lincoln had nonetheless seized "their money and writing" and put them in prison, with no cause given.

Sir John Pyllet, a Knight of the Holy Sepulcher of Christ, was unusually effective in obtaining multiple backers for his efforts to repay ransom. As announced in a royal proclamation early in Henry VIII's reign, Pyllet had been on his way back from Jerusalem when he was captured by "the Moors and infidels" and through "great torments and threatenings of death was compelled either to [abjure Christ's] faith and to follow and observe their most damnable sect and laws, or [promise] unto them many millions of ducats of gold."[39] Pyllet chose the latter, arranging with some Venetians to pay the sum demanded by the Moors and binding himself in the sum of 2,000 ducats to repay them. He then obtained support from the church. The pope granted an indulgence of 15 years and 15 Lents of penance to those who assisted Pyllet; the archbishop of Canterbury gave 40 days of pardon; and three bishops each awarded 40 days. Together these indulgences totaled 7,500 days of pardon. Following their good example, Henry VIII issued letters patent that required all officials to "gather the alms deeds of every charitable and well-disposed person" and deliver the money to the collectors named by Pyllet.

Several other kinds of people occasionally received licenses to solicit alms. Merchants who had suffered losses at sea or been robbed were joined as mobile solicitors by a few poor ex-soldiers, especially those who had been maimed through loss of a limb or eye.[40] Some did so legally, occasionally even backed by an indulgence like that granted in 1521 by the bishop of Exeter to Ralph Pudsey, wounded in the king's wars. Yet former fighting men who traveled about while requesting charity were often feared: they might have enlisted in order to obtain a pardon for a previous offence, or they might convert their experience in military violence into crimes against civilians at home.[41] Other people were allowed to seek alms

---

[38] TNA-PRO C 1/1507/31.   [39] *TRP*, vol. 1, 132–3.
[40] CKentS Fa/LC 1, fol. 19r–v, and Orme, "Indulgences," for this and below.
[41] Hewitt, *Organization of War*, 172–5, and 34 Edward III, c.1, *SR*, vol. 1, 364–5. I am grateful to Mark Ormrod for suggesting these sources.

because of a physical disability. Bishop Fordham of Ely awarded indulgences on behalf of blind, disabled, or injured people during the decades around 1400.[42]

Although charity awarded at the doors or gatehouses of private households is sparsely documented, a few accounts suggest that individual donors were prepared to help not only the kinds of licensed alms seekers described above, but also other unknown poor people. Written documentation is not always mentioned and was probably not required: individuals were prepared to make their own decisions about the legitimacy of seekers' need. The head of the Willoughby family of Wollaton, Notts. gave 4d. to a woman from Leicestershire "that went with a testimonial for burning of her house," and the household of Edmund Mortimer, Earl of March, helped to raise a total of £6 13s. 4d. for the ransom of a soldier called Bosco de Caleys in 1413.[43] In 1463–4, Isabella, Lady Morley, living in Norfolk at the time, gave the substantial sum of 3s. 4d. to a man from Dunwich, Suff. who was gathering money with royal letters patent "for preparing 1 boat," presumably after a former ship had been lost. In 1521, the Willoughby household gave 1d. to 4d. each to a person collecting for "a man that lies bedridden," "a poor man that was robbed," two scholars, and two "poor men that come from Rome."[44] A household account for Robert Waterton of Methley, N. Yorks. for 1416–17 includes alms of 3d. to 5d. each given to three unnamed women and one man, all from villages located within about 20 kilometers from Methley.

Prior to the 1530s, references to fraudulent begging or misused licenses on behalf of individuals are rare. In London, civic courts convicted several men during the second half of the fourteenth century for falsely seeking alms by posing as invalids, war veterans, or returning pilgrims; two others wrongly claimed that they had been robbed and their tongues cut out.[45] The records of Fordwich, Kent contain a purported license to gather alms throughout the realm awarded by Henry VII to Elizabeth Holte, widow of Sir John Holte, knight, who had died while a prisoner in Normandy. The

---

[42] Rubin, *Charity and Community*, 268, and see CambUL Ely Diocesan Records F/5/35, fols. 173v–174r, for a 1516 grant to Ralph Pudsey, probably the same man mentioned above.

[43] HMC, *Report on MSS of Lord Middleton*, 391 (from 1543), and *Household Accounts*, 596. For below, see *Household Accounts*, 578.

[44] HMC, *Report on MSS of Lord Middleton*, 333–6. These gifts were in addition to the almsmen supported by the family on a regular basis (ibid., 339–47). For below, see *Household Accounts*, 512–13.

[45] Barron, *London*, 277. The reasons for pretending that one could not speak were presumably not only to evoke pity, but also to avoid close questioning and so that the bearer's local or regional accent could not be compared with his nominal home. For below, see HMC, *Fifth Report*, "MSS of the Corp. of Fordwich," 608, and CantCA U/4/17/1, used through A2A.

document was apparently impounded by borough officials who either doubted its validity or thought that the person using it was an imposter.

2.3   Gathering for hospitals and other charitable causes

Gathering was widely used to obtain charitable money or in-kind donations for late medieval hospitals and almshouses, religious buildings and organizations, and certain public projects involving infrastructural units like bridges and harbors. The scope of such collection varied greatly. Some gathering was done by single individuals within the local community. The almshouses in Saffron Walden, Essex were supported in part by the efforts of their male keeper, who was humbly to seek alms for the sick poor each week at the houses of healthy people.[46] The fifteenth-century master of St. John's Hospital in Stafford solicited contributions from gentlemen who came into the town; a collector for Exeter's lepers went through the city every Tuesday and Thursday asking for contributions and entered the cathedral choir each month to request alms from the canons; and the hospital of St. Mary's Bethlehem regularly sent two collecting boxes around London.[47]

Most gatherers, however, were appointed to seek charity while traveling about a given region or the whole country. Commonly termed proctors or procurators, these men or the deputies they appointed were supposed to carry written authorization for their collection plus documentation for any indulgences they said had been granted to their institution.[48] In addition to asking for contributions from the living, they often requested priests to encourage people writing their wills to bequeath alms to their house. Some clerical proctors gave sermons at the churches they visited, increasing the disruption of the normal service already caused by the presence of an outsider soliciting money.[49]

Gatherers for hospitals and almshouses could be appointed by diverse people. The master or warden of the house often chose its proctor(s), and in 1529, an alms collector for the Hospital of the Blessed Virgin Mary, located outside Augustine's Gates in St. Clement at Fyebridge, Norwich, was named by the brothers and sisters of the institution.[50] The lay patrons

[46] Steer, "Statutes," 166–7.   [47] Orme and Webster, *English Hospital*, 98 and 180.

[48] "Proctor" in this usage has a more specific meaning than when it merely denotes a proxy, often someone who appeared on behalf of another in a legal context. "Procurations" were the sums of money paid to the church courts for the costs of men and horses at the time of a visitation, not the sums collected by charitable procurators.

[49] Owst, *Preaching*, 100–3.

[50] NorfRO DN/MSC1/5, used through A2A. For below, see, e.g., DorsetHC DC/BTB AB46–47.

of an institution could authorize gatherers or at least add their approval to such grants. Hospital officials might enlist the support of urban leaders in granting licenses. In 1430, the sub-warden of the Hospital of the Holy Trinity in Salisbury, acting with the approval of the mayor (who was also the warden of the hospital), named Richard Savtell as his "true and legitimate proctor, agent, negotiator, and attorney" in collecting and receiving "throughout all of England ... the alms and subsidies made, bequeathed, or otherwise assigned to the hospital."[51] A generation later, the mayor of Salisbury and warden of that hospital joined with its lay confraternity in appointing a man to collect and receive charitable payments in the counties of Wiltshire, Berkshire, and Dorset.

Medieval monarchs occasionally confirmed or offered their protection to proctors named by others. Richard II issued letters patent conveying protection to the master, brethren, and procurators who collected alms for the Hospitals of St. Mary Magdalene and St. Anthony in Allington, Bridport, Dorset, which already had extensive ecclesiastical backing.[52] Noting that the Bridport hospitals "do not have enough to support themselves except by the charity of faithful Christians obtained by their attorneys or procurators sent to divers parts of the kingdom to collect alms for their sustenance," the king called upon "you men of the church" to receive the hospital's representatives kindly and to seek alms for them; he told bailiffs and others to "take care that they suffer no molestation." In 1509 Henry VIII authorized Roger Tole to collect alms for the hospital of lepers in Dartford, Kent, although the award was countersigned by Robert Blagge, its patron.[53] A document of protection issued by Henry VIII and Wolsey commanded all prelates and other ecclesiastical people to allow the proctor or his deputy to come into their churches to ask and fetch the alms of all charitable people.

Gathering for hospitals and almshouses was sometimes reinforced by indulgences. Bishops of Exeter granted indulgences on behalf of at least twenty-three hospitals between 1350 and 1450, plus a few before and after that time.[54] In 1379, the Archbishop of Canterbury and eleven bishops issued an indulgence of 40 days to those who gave charitable aid to Trinity Hospital in Salisbury, founded by Agnes Bottenham for support of the

---

[51] Wilts&SA 1446/58. For below, see ibid. 1446/73, from 1469, used through A2A.

[52] DorsetHC DC/BTB AB45. When Roger Page was named as procurator for that hospital in 1532, his grant carefully laid out the total number of days of indulgence awarded by previous benefactors (ibid., AB47).

[53] *L&P*, vol. I, pt. 1, 107. For below, see Aydelotte, *Elizabethan Rogues*, 24–5, which does not name the institution and must be incorrect in dating the letter as 1544.

[54] Orme, "Indulgences." For below, where the sum of all its indulgences came to 5 years, see Wilts&SA 1446/34.

poor, weak, and destitute. Bishop Skirlaw of Durham granted a similar indulgence in 1391 on behalf of St. Mary Magdalene Hospital in Durham, and the Hospital of Sts. Wolstan and Godwal in the city of Worcester received an indulgence of 40 days from the bishop of Hereford in 1419.[55] A few fortunate institutions possessed holy relics, receiving extra donations from pilgrims who came to receive spiritual blessings from them.[56] Because hospitals were competing for charitable alms, some of their claims for the indulgences they had been granted "strained the truth."

Indulgences appear to have been used even more frequently in the early sixteenth century, publicized at times by new techniques for mass circulation. In 1515, the Hospital of St. Thomas of Acon in London (which did not in fact care for the sick) arranged for the printing of a broadside with woodblock illustrations describing the indulgences it had been granted, validated by Pope Leo X and Henry VIII.[57] Gatherers carried copies of that paper document, although it was presumably less robust than traditional parchment authorizations. Between 1517 and 1534, the hospital's receipts from indulgences came to the quite staggering sum of around £550, although the annual amounts were gradually declining.[58]

Although people who solicited funds for hospitals were recompensed in various ways, appointment as a proctor was clearly seen as a way to gain personal income, not merely as a charitable position. Occasionally someone received a salary from the institution and was required to return to the house all of the money or in-kind payments collected. In 1407–8, a woman was paid 6d. per week by Trinity Hospital in Salisbury for gathering alms within the city.[59] In 1522, that hospital received 24s. 4d. in money collected by its (male) proctor for Wiltshire, Berkshire, and Dorset plus 14s. 10d. from the sale of wool donated the previous year. More commonly, however, proctors made an annual payment to obtain the right of collection, but were then allowed to keep the proceeds for themselves, a system that resembled tax farming. Thus, when Robert

---

[55] *Memorials of St. Giles's*, 238–9, and Owst, *Preaching*, 102. See also *Register of the Guild of Corpus Christi*, 254 and 258–9, Wilts&SA 9/15/54, used through A2A, and Phillips, "Charitable Institutions," 34.

[56] Phillips, "Charitable Institutions," 36–7. For below, see Orme and Webster, *English Hospital*, 98.

[57] BodlL Arch. A.b.8 (3), reproduced in Orme and Webster, *English Hospital*, 60–1, and see Swanson, *Indulgences*, 371–3. Anne Sutton thinks that the money was probably used by John Young, its master, to help sort out the house's finances (personal communication).

[58] Swanson, *Indulgences*, 372.

[59] Wilts&SA 1446/Box of Trinity Hospital Accounts, 1407–11 (T1). For below, see ibid., 1522 (T48). The only other female gatherer encountered in this study was Sister Mariana Swetman, authorized to collect alms on behalf of St. John's Hospital, Canterbury in 1465 (Clay, *Mediaeval Hospitals*, 153).

Cokke was named in 1451 as procurator for the poor house of St. Trinity next to Crossbridge in Beverley for a period of four years, he was to pay 20s. annually to the hospital.[60] The hospital apparently decided that those terms had been too generous, for when it later appointed William Waleys to the office, he was required to render 26s. 8d. annually if operating on his own and 33s. if joined by another man. Permission to solicit funds within a given territory was sometimes re-granted by the recipient to various deputies within sub-areas of the award, for an appropriate fee to the initial proctor.

One of the most highly developed systems for collecting money was organized by London's St. Anthony's Hospital during the fifteenth and early sixteenth centuries. That prosperous house, which provided comfortable livings for its master and clerical staff but supported only a dozen almsmen and some schoolboys, divided England and Wales into many regions, based usually on dioceses, and then named one or more proctors for each area.[61] The gatherers had to give bond that they would render a stated sum to the hospital each year for the designated length of their grant. In the early fifteenth century, most of the individual collectors named by the hospital brought in sums of between £5 and £15 each year; together their collection constituted the great majority of the hospital's annual income of roughly £580. In 1478–9, the first year after the appropriation of St. Anthony's by the College of St. George at Windsor Castle, the college received a total of £540 from its proctors.[62] Of that amount, the college used £351 (65 percent) for the hospital's expenses, but kept the rest for itself, forming a nice supplement to its other sources of income. In 1497–8, only £280 of the £477 received from proctors (57 percent) went to the hospital.[63] Because the gatherers were presumably soliciting alms on behalf of the hospital's poor residents, not for the already well-endowed members of the college, this discrepancy is troubling. Further, the cost of operating the hospital included lavish food for its master and other staff, with more modest rations for its almsmen.[64]

Even St. Anthony's, however, was not always able to extract the designated sums from its proctors. In 1501–2, £73 due from such payments had not been rendered.[65] Sometime after 1500, Margaret Morton, widow of the procurator named for the county of Kent, complained to Chancery against the master of the hospital and the dean and canons of Windsor, its

---

[60] HMC, *Report on MSS of the Corp. of Beverley*, 135, for this and below.
[61] StGeoCh XV.37.4, for this and below.   [62] Ibid., XV.37.15.   [63] Ibid., XV.37.22.
[64] See ch. 3.3 below.
[65] StGeoCh XV.37.25. For below, see TNA-PRO C 1/338/53. The jubilee year mentioned in that petition was probably 1500.

legal proprietors. She said that her late husband Richard and another man acting as surety had given bond of £40 to the college, guaranteeing that Richard would pay £24 13s. 4d. annually to the hospital for 5 years out of the alms he gathered. When, however, the pope declared a year of jubilee, all other types of collection were banned for 12 months, by both papal and royal orders. Because Richard was unable to gather any money that year, he did not deliver the required amount to the dean and canons. They had nevertheless brought legal action against him for non-payment of the full bonded amount.

Whereas asking for and giving alms to institutions were acceptable Catholic practices, late medieval moralists – especially Wycliffites – occasionally drew attention to the problems that could result from inadequately supervised charitable solicitation or to the theological flaws with indulgences.[66] Proctors for hospitals might display the same faults ascribed to pardoners who carried holy relics, such as claiming indulgences beyond those actually issued to their institutions.[67] A complaint submitted to Parliament probably in the early 1510s about malfeasance by the masters of hospitals alleged that they appointed proctors to travel about "with seals and images," falsely collecting money by persuading people to join the brotherhoods associated with their houses to gain spiritual benefits even though no masses or prayers were actually being said.[68] The proctor could himself be fraudulent, pretending to be an authorized collector but then pocketing the donations. A laborer arrested in London in 1412 while claiming to be an official alms gatherer for Bethlehem Hospital outside Bishopsgate was found to have a tidy sum inside his iron-bound collecting box.[69]

Gathering was used for some additional projects that fell within the scope of the Catholic definition of charitable alms. Among these were churches that needed extra funds to repair or add to their buildings, projects often backed by indulgences.[70] In order to publicize the rewards of giving, the recipient church might hire professional pardoners to carry its indulgence to other communities, preach about it, and collect donations. Less commonly, the crown awarded licenses to gather for religious ends. Henry VII granted letters patent to the Prior of Easton, Wilts. in

---

[66] Owst, *Preaching*, 103–7, and Swanson, *Indulgences*, ch. 7, esp. 346–8.

[67] Chaucer's Pardoner, hardly an exemplar of religious virtue, was said to be "of Rouncivale" (i.e. the Hospital of St. Mary Rounceval in London): *Canterbury Tales*, General Prologue, ll. 671–2.

[68] TNA-PRO E175/11/65.   [69] Barron, *London*, 277.

[70] For 138 indulgences for religious buildings in Exeter, 1301–1536, see Orme, "Indulgences"; for those issued by bishops of Ely, see Rubin, *Charity and Community*, 266. For below, see Orme, "Indulgences."

1493, authorizing him to appoint "proctors and nuncios to go round the kingdom" asking for alms with which to rebuild the priory church and other buildings that had been destroyed by fire.[71] The young Henry VIII similarly granted permission in 1511 after the Abbey of Sts. Peter and Paul in Kirkeby on Wrethik, Leics. was hit by fire and when the churchwardens of Dadlington, Leics. wanted to gather funds to build a commemorative chapel for those slain on Bosworth field.

Some of the larger religious fraternities employed collectors to gather funds. These associations commonly offered prayers for the souls of people who had given alms or signed up as non-resident members. In the early sixteenth century, the guild of St. Clement in the church of St. Clement Danes, London obtained royal letters patent for its collectors, who were appointed for individual counties, while deputies for the Guild of the Virgin Mary and St. George in St. George's church, Southwark received royal protection while they solicited contributions and new recruits throughout the country.[72] A case of broken covenant heard in Crossgate, Durham in 1506 concerned the right to collect in eight parishes and their dependent chapels for the East Anglian fraternity of Our Lady on the Sea, a sub-contract granted by Nicholas Blakehaa to Thomas Gyffurth but later withdrawn.

Expensive public projects that provided essential infrastructure might also receive support. In the diocese of Exeter between 1351 and 1536, bishops granted indulgences to donors who assisted in the repair of at least sixty-nine bridges, harbors, roads, and town walls; various bishops of Ely similarly backed bridges, causeways, and highways.[73] Repairs to Rochester bridge in Kent were supported by a papal bull of 1409 and an archiepiscopal indulgence of 1489, and in 1527, Cardinal Wolsey – with characteristic largesse – granted pardon of 10 years and 10 Lents to encourage contributions for the rebuilding of York's bridges.[74] Secular authorities too promoted gathering for public works. The borough of Bridport authorized John Greyve to seek alms in the fairly distant counties of Kent and Essex in 1447–8 for rebuilding its harbor.[75] In 1456 Henry VI confirmed previous letters patent and protection for four proctors on

---

[71] Wilts&SA 9/15/54, used through A2A. For below, see *L&P*, vol. 1, pt. 1, 473 (#2) and 454 (#18).

[72] TNA-PRO C 1/359/55 and *L&P*, vol. 1, pt. 1, 445 (#54). For below, see *Records of the Borough of Crossgate*, 143–8, passim. I am grateful to Richard Britnell for this reference.

[73] Orme, "Indulgences"; Rubin, *Charity and Community*, 267, and CambUL Ely Diocesan Records F/5/35, fols. 171v–172r.

[74] Swanson, *Indulgences*, 382–3 and 34. The latter was one of several exceptionally generous indulgences issued by Wolsey that "pushed at the formal boundaries of his powers."

[75] DorsetHC DC/BTB/N10, used through A2A. Greyve carried a written list of the alms and indulgences obtained by the town in support of the project.

behalf of St. Bartholomew's Hospital in Gloucester who were "journeying through the realm" to gather alms for repair of the town's bridge.[76] When the bridge over the river Eden in Carlisle needed rebuilding in 1516, the mayor, aldermen, and bailiffs of the town, joined by the Lord Warden of the Scottish Marches of England and the prior of the cathedral church in Carlisle, appointed one esquire, two gentlemen, and the former bailiff of Carlisle as official procurators to request and receive alms for that purpose.

Requesting alms, in some cases with formal permission, was thus a well-established practice in late medieval and early Tudor England, one relevant to many of the themes that recur in this study. Within the Catholic system of belief, providing charitable assistance filled an important social function, while at the same time increasing the donor's chances of salvation. While contributors were probably pleased to be seen as charitable people, there is no indication that those who received aid – whether local poor or outsiders – were identified as part of a recognizable category of beggars, nor did they cause more than occasional concern. Although women seldom moved about the country in pursuit of alms, they obtained help within local communities and occasionally sought ransom money for their husbands. It is striking that statutes and urban policies make no mention of those people who were granted licenses to request alms because of some calamity, nor do they refer to gatherers for institutions. Donations were nominally voluntary, although generosity was sometimes encouraged by priests, churchwardens, and collectors. Whereas Parliamentary policies and certain theological and literary works became more negative about the mobile, able-bodied poor in the aftermath of the plague of 1348–9 and the uprising of 1381, grantors of licenses seem always to have discriminated carefully between the various people who sought permits. Potential donors made their own decisions about which suppliants deserved help, and they did not always demand that alms seekers display written authorization. During these years, references to fraud among people requesting donations were scant. Significant changes in both attitudes and practices were, however, to start appearing in the 1530s and 1540s.

---

[76] *CPR, Henry VI*, vol. 6, 289. For additional examples, see NoDevRO B1/594, used through A2A, and Bewes, *Church Briefs*, 63–4. For below, see CumbAS-C Ca/2/380, used through A2A. Four cardinals had also granted pardons to people who contributed to the work.

3   Late medieval hospitals and almshouses

A privileged sub-group of needy English men and women, probably numbering more than 5,000 to 6,000 people in the 1520s, were assisted in residential institutions. Hospitals and almshouses served a variety of inmates, stemming from the multiple and changing definitions of what kind of people were considered "poor" and deserving of help. Some residents had been incapacitated by a chronic illness (including leprosy), an injury, or a physical or emotional disability, while a growing proportion were elderly. Other institutions focused upon travelers, old priests, or the retired servants of particular families. Hospitals usually provided meals and at least simple care for their residents, many of whom were bedridden, while almshouses generally offered only housing and perhaps a few other benefits. The advantages and obligations of the residents reflected the two roles of such houses. While they were intended to provide a social service, most of them also functioned as centers of prayer. Some institutions were operated by a religious house or civic body, but many were independent or had a landed endowment held by feoffees.[1] A rising number of almshouses were intended for female residents, and women were essential to the creation of many institutions: founding houses themselves, setting up institutions envisioned by their husbands, or supervising projects initiated by other deceased relatives.[2]

Examination of these institutions and their residents is closely linked to alms seeking and charitable gathering. Regardless of their financial structure, all houses hoped to receive donations and bequests from the faithful. Such charity was promoted by the church, for visiting the sick and giving shelter to the homeless (or – vicariously – assisting an institution that looked after them) were among the seven corporal works of mercy.

---

[1] Feoffees, like later trustees, held property on behalf of and for the use of another person, project, or institution.

[2] See the regionally specific works by Jordan as listed in the bibliography, Phillips, "Charitable Institutions," esp. 21 and 128, Cullum, "For Pore People Harberles," and B. Harris, "The Fabric of Piety."

Most leper hospitals relied heavily on begging by their own residents, while some institutions sent out gatherers to solicit contributions.[3] Because few almshouses provided full support, those residents who were mobile might need to ask individually for help to supplement whatever donations they received as unsolicited gifts and bequests.[4] No legislation prohibited institutional dwellers from requesting aid in their own communities or required that they have a license.

In considering late medieval hospitals and almshouses, this account will not retrace the valuable research already undertaken by other scholars. A careful summary is provided in the first part of Nicholas Orme's and Margaret Webster's *The English Hospital, 1070–1570*.[5] In addition to some other broadly based works, hundreds of books, articles, and pamphlets lay out the histories of individual institutions.[6] Through such studies we know a good deal about the founders and patrons of hospitals and almshouses, how the houses were supported economically, and the architecture of their buildings, which are among the oldest surviving structures in many English towns and villages.

This chapter examines selected topics that have previously received limited attention within the period between around 1350 and the late 1530s, prior to the full force of the English Reformation. We begin by defining hospitals and almshouses and looking at their living arrangements. After considering how many of these institutions were founded, closed, and in existence per decade, the discussion turns to their residents: who they were and how many of them found places, the benefits they

---

[3] Rawcliffe, *Leprosy*, 308–9.

[4] E.g., Alice de Bridford, a widow who died in 1390, left 1d. to every infirm poor person living in York's almshouses who was unable to beg (Cullum, "For Pore People Harberles"), and the poor men of St. John's Hospital in Shaftesbury, Dorset were wholly dependent upon "alms of the town" (Orme and Webster, *English Hospital*, 99). Robert Copland included "bedrid folk and such as cannot crave ... relief" among those accepted by a hospital in London, probably St. Bartholomew's (*The Hye Way to the Spyttell Hous*, in *Elizabethan Underworld*, 1–25, esp. 5).

[5] Chapters 1–8, written by Orme, discuss the origins of hospitals, their nature, location, functions, organization, resources, and inmates, as well as changes in the later Middle Ages and Reformation period (1–166).

[6] For general studies, see, e.g., Clay, *Mediaeval Hospitals*, Jordan, *Philanthropy in England*, Tobriner, "Almshouses," Bailey, *Almshouses*, Prescott, *English Medieval Hospital*, Howson, *Houses of Noble Poverty*, Rawcliffe, *Leprosy*, Watson, "Origins," Resl, "Hospitals," Archer, "Hospitals," and Goose, "English Almshouse." An important addition will be Patricia Cullum's forthcoming *Hospitals and Charitable Provisions*. For architecture, see Godfrey, *English Almshouse*. A few examples of newer studies of hospitals and almshouses in particular communities or regions are Rubin, *Charity and Community*, Rawcliffe, *Hospitals of Medieval Norwich*, Orme and Webster, *English Hospital*, pt. 2, Phillips, "Charitable Institutions," and Sweetinburgh, *Role of the Hospital*. Accounts of specific houses are too numerous to list, although some will be cited in subsequent references.

received, and their obligations. In conclusion, we look at the way in which the houses were governed. The chapter integrates three types of information: descriptive material from primary sources, most of them unpublished manuscripts in local archives that have not commonly been used in studies of residential institutions; quantitative evidence from a database of 1,005 houses that existed at some time between 1350 and 1599; and some secondary studies. Developments during the rest of the century will be considered in Chapters 5 and 7 below, which highlight the contrasts with the late medieval period in both the number and the nature of residential institutions. This account argues that although medieval hospitals and almshouses supported relatively few people, they performed a useful function in a period of low population and limited poverty. In some houses, the benefits received by residents in addition to free housing were accompanied by responsibility for an extended round of daily prayers and in a few cases by good behavior. Problems with the operation of hospitals and almshouses led to alterations in the form of governance prescribed by late medieval founders for the institutions they were creating.

3.1   Hospitals, almshouses, and living arrangements

In this analysis, we will often distinguish between institutions called "hospitals" (a hospice or place that offered hospitality to those in need, sometimes known as a Spital or Spittle house) and those called "almshouses" (a dwelling for the poor, supported by the alms or charitable gifts/bequests of others). In practice, however, neither category was clearly defined in the later medieval and early modern periods, nor was the distinction between them sharp. Hospitals might resemble or be absorbed by institutions with a more narrowly religious function. Some of the small, early hospitals gradually merged with priories, while religious colleges sometimes provided care similar to that offered by hospitals.[7] Institutions might change nature, as when a hospital founded initially for lepers shifted to care of other kinds of people as leprosy diminished in England after the mid fourteenth century.[8] In some cases, hospitals that had originally included both infirm residents and clerics to pray with/for them gradually reduced the number of poor residents, eventually becoming "free chapels" or chantries, where priests prayed for the souls of the dead. The "hospitals" founded by the crusading orders did not always offer assistance to sick or poor people or

---

[7] Cullum, "Medieval Colleges."   [8] E.g., Rawcliffe, *Leprosy*, 350–1.

travelers.[9] Certain wealthy hospitals turned into what were in effect retirement homes for those who could afford to make the payment required to obtain a place in them. By the fifteenth and especially the sixteenth centuries, some new foundations that were termed hospitals did not offer any care for their residents, but were instead almshouses operating under a more glorified name. Simple classification is made more difficult by institutions that functioned like almshouses but were labeled a "maison dieu" or "domus dei" (a God's house) or a "bede-house" (an institution that featured prayer). Despite the fluidity of terminology, however, we can draw some broad distinctions between the two main categories of houses.

Most English hospitals provided long-term accommodation and care for people who were unable to look after themselves, employing women to cook for and if necessary feed the residents, wash them and their bedding, and do housekeeping. Very few offered trained medical services for people suffering from an illness or injury. Some earlier medieval institutions were for lepers, who were not supposed to live with the rest of the population, but many houses refused to accept anyone who had a communicable or physically loathsome disease.[10] Hospitals did not always specify that they were for the poor, but in most cases that was understood: wealthier people could pay for more comfortable and individualized attention within their own homes. The poor of St. Leonard's Hospital in York were described in the early sixteenth century as "blind, lame, bedridden, and very old bodies," many of whom lay "continually in their beds both day and night."[11] Examination of thousands of skeletons from the medieval cemetery of St. Mary Spital in London found that many of the residents had suffered from severe physical disabilities that prevented them from living independently. Other institutions took in poor travelers for a few nights (some of whom would have been among the alms seekers and gatherers discussed above) or accepted unmarried women about to give birth or abandoned or orphaned children.[12] An occasional hospital had

---

[9] E.g., the Hospital of St. Thomas of Acre of London, which in the fifteenth century consisted of "a small group of secular canons and an impressively large church," but no poor inmates (Sutton, "Hospital," 199).

[10] E.g., statutes for Heytesbury Hospital in Wiltshire from the 1470s say that no leper was to be admitted into the house; if a current resident acquired leprosy or "any long sickness . . . grievous or noyous [bothersome]" to the other inmates, he was to be removed by the keeper and sent to some other place ("Ancient Statutes"). See also Goodall, *God's House*, 249, and BerksRO D/Q1 Q7/15.

[11] Cullum, "Cremetts and Corrodies," 13. For below, see White, "Excavations at St Mary Spital."

[12] Orme and Webster, *English Hospital*, 109–12, Cullum, "Cremetts and Corrodies," 28–9, White, "Excavations at St Mary Spital," and Copland, *The Hye Way to the Spyttell Hous*, in *Elizabethan Underworld*, 5.

educational functions as well: its clerical members might maintain a library or train young scholars, or the house could be part of a joint foundation with a school. Commonly supported by a landed endowment, many institutions had their own seals that validated documents, including licenses to the proctors who solicited alms on their behalf.

Most hospitals – not only those linked to a monastic organization – had a religious component.[13] A spiritual orientation is suggested by their names. Of the institutions in my database founded before 1350, 90 percent were given religious designations, usually the names of one or more saints, Our Lady, the Holy Cross, or the Holy Trinity.[14] Among the hospitals founded between 1350 and 1539, however, only 65 percent had religious names, with another fifth designated either by the name of the founder or the location of the house and the rest given diverse titles. Spiritual activities were intended in part to promote the health of the residents.[15] The clerical staff attached to most hospitals provided a regular sequence of masses, prayers, chants, and readings which the inmates at least observed and sometimes participated in. That regime together with housing and food provided a soothing environment conducive to mental and spiritual as well as physical health and to the atonement for any sins that may have contributed to the inmates' problems. In many institutions, the masses said by their clerics and the prayers of their inmates served the interests of founders and benefactors as well. Because prayers for the dead by poor people were thought to reach God's ear with special efficacy, many donors required residents not only to hear certain masses and/or say a certain round of prayers each day, but also to beseech God's favor for their souls and those of other designated people as well as for Christians more generally.[16] Such houses thus functioned at least partially as de facto chantries, intended to produce a substantial number of prayers in perpetuity.

Almshouses, by contrast, offered free housing and sometimes a cash stipend or other benefits to their residents, but they did not normally provide assistance with daily living. Their dwellers, usually elderly poor people, were expected to take care of themselves. Like many hospitals, almshouses guaranteed shelter for the rest of their lives to those they admitted (unless expelled due to misconduct), providing considerable

---

[13] For a thoughtful discussion, see Phillips, "Charitable Institutions," 1–53.

[14] For the database, see below.

[15] Rawcliffe, "Medicine for the Soul," for this and below.

[16] See pt. 4 below. As Rawcliffe has noted: "Put crudely, charitable institutions gave medieval benefactors a unique opportunity to kill two birds with one stone: in return for charity to the sick poor of Christ they could purchase a place in heaven, rendered additionally secure through intercessionary prayers and masses offered both in their own lifetimes and for the welfare of their souls after death" ("A Word," 168).

security and peace of mind. These institutions became popular with late medieval founders, set up either during their lifetimes or through bequests.[17] Generally smaller than hospitals, almshouses were less expensive to establish and run, although in turn less likely to survive for more than a few generations. These houses had a weaker religious identity than hospitals. Of the almshouses founded between 1350 and 1539, only 9 percent were given a religious name, as opposed to 40 percent named after the founder, 13 percent labeled by location, and the rest described in various ways. A few houses had their own chapels where the inmates were required to pray, but most assumed that their residents would be sufficiently mobile to worship at their parish church. Group prayer in almshouses was more likely to focus specifically on the souls of the donors rather than on general prayers for the dead.[18] While the line separating hospitals from the larger almshouses that offered additional benefits is often fuzzy, we encounter different problems at the bottom end of the range when trying to distinguish almshouses from ordinary private dwellings bequeathed to a named poor person for life or leased out at low rent by a parish.

In discussing the physical layout and living arrangements of these institutions, we can draw upon visual as well as textual material. But because some of that information comes from drawings and photographs of buildings that were still standing in the nineteenth and twentieth centuries, we are at risk of gaining a distorted picture. Such images normally show wealthy and longer-lived hospitals and the relatively few almshouses that were sufficiently well endowed to last for hundreds of years. Many hospitals and most almshouses occupied far less commodious and sturdy buildings. Some had started their lives as private residences. A charitable person might arrange for a few poor people to live rent-free in a house during his or her own lifetime, or donors could indicate in their wills that a particular building was henceforth to shelter needy people. While almshouses like those presumably resembled other dwellings of their period, we cannot examine them carefully, for the structure and utilization of space within simple dwellings built of wattle and daub or other local construction materials were not described in contemporary sources, and they rarely survived for more than a century in the absence of regular maintenance.

---

[17] Cullum, "For Pore People Harberles."

[18] Sweetinburgh distinguishes between two types of almshouses: bedehouses, where the residents were expected to fill a major intercessory function like people living in hospitals, and maisons dieu, smaller and less formal houses where residents received free housing and might need to beg for their support, but had no obligation to pray (*Role of the Hospital*, 102–5). Those two categories were often not clearly separated in practice.

Those hospitals and almshouses that lasted into the modern period were usually purpose-built structures, designed and erected to house the sick and/or poor. Most hospitals founded prior to 1350 were set up for communal care, with multiple beds located in one or more large rooms or dormitories, plus latrines, a kitchen, and often some kind of space for doing laundry. A common pattern featured a large shared infirmary hall (sometimes one for each sex) with an interior chapel adjoining at the east end so bedridden residents could hear and see the mass. Later, some hospitals featured a private sleeping area for each resident, although it is usually impossible to be sure exactly when these changes occurred. We can trace the re-working of interior space in the Hospital of Sts. John the Baptist and the Evangelist in Sherborne, Dorset, a two-storied building that originally contained open dormitories of roughly 19 by 6 meters on each floor.[19] Later, the institution, now known as Sherborne Almshouse, divided the upper hall into rooms occupied by women and converted the lower hall into rooms for men. A similar process is visible at St. Mary Magdalene's Hospital in Glastonbury, Som., where the original infirmary hall was separated into eleven self-contained, two-storey dwellings, each accessible from a central corridor.[20] The transition towards private spaces for residents in charitable institutions mirrors a similar change in the use of space within monasteries and convents and in higher status secular houses.[21]

Nearly all almshouses offered private living quarters for their residents, usually one room, occasionally two. Buildings constructed specifically to house the poor were commonly laid out in one of two patterns: either a row of rooms, often with a covered walkway (a "cloister" or "gallery") connecting them; or a square arrangement of chambers around an inner courtyard. When the Hospital of the Holy Cross in Stratford-upon-Avon, Warws. was rebuilt as almshouses around 1427, the new structure provided individual accommodations for ten poor people in a row of dwellings some 46 meters long, facing directly onto the street; each unit was two storeys high.[22] The row of almshouses in the Whitefriars' precinct of London built by Margaret, Countess of Kent shortly before 1538

---

[19] Godfrey, *English Almshouse*, plate 12(b) and p. 39 for this and below, and see DorsetHC D/SHA D24.

[20] Howson, *Houses of Noble Poverty*, Fig. 18 and p. 43.

[21] See, e.g., Gilchrist, *Gender and Material Culture*, 122–3. An important influence, as Caroline Barron kindly pointed out to me, may have been the layout of the London Charterhouse, a Carthusian monastery founded in 1371, in which individual cells for the monks surrounded a central cloister.

[22] Prescott, *English Medieval Hospital*, 44. For below, see *London Surveys of Ralph Treswell*, Survey 44, 129–30 (written description and floor plan).

consisted of ten single rooms, five on the ground floor and five above them, with a gallery alongside, reached by a stair at one end. Each room was about 4 meters on a side, with its own fireplace, chimney, and privy. In 1486, the College of Tattersall, Lincs. contracted with a local carpenter to build a bedehouse next to the parish cemetery.[23] This structure, 52 by 6 meters, was to contain thirteen chambers for the almsmen plus some additional common rooms. Each bedeman's chamber was to have two windows with two lights of "a competent height," and some of the public rooms were to have fireplaces and chimneys. When Hosyer's Almshouses were constructed in Ludlow, Shrops. in 1486, the thirty-three rooms all had their own wall fireplaces.[24]

God's House at Ewelme, Oxfds. illustrates the central courtyard pattern, in an exceptionally comfortable and aesthetically pleasing manner.[25] Constructed of brick (one of the first almshouses to use that material), the individual dwellings of the thirteen poor men, each with a second room upstairs, lay around a sunny and sheltered courtyard. The unit also had a well for common use, a kitchen, and a hall. The almsmen had immediate access to the adjoining parish church (although they had to climb a steep flight of steps to reach it), where they prayed in St. John's Chapel in one corner of the church, separated from the rest of the building by the elaborate tombs of the founders.

Many hospitals and some of the major almshouses included secondary buildings as well. To create some privacy and protection for the residents, as well as to display the collective identity of the institution and sometimes the generosity of the donor, houses might have gatehouses, porches, or entryways that set them off from the streets they faced.[26] In a few of the wealthiest almshouses, the inmates who were too frail to walk to their parish church could worship in a small chapel within their compound, summoned to prayers by its bell. Late medieval institutions often provided separate and more comfortable living quarters for their master or warden and any clerical staff. The new bedehouse in Tattersall was to contain a chamber for the man who supervised the residence and for the parish priest.[27] The already ample lodgings of the master of St. Anthony's Hospital in

---

[23] HMC, *Report on the MSS of Lord de L'Isle and Dudley*, vol. 1, 175–6. The building was to include a hall and chapel, both with high ceilings and two windows, a buttery, garner, and various passageways and galleries.

[24] Bailey, *Almshouses*, 70.

[25] God's House was founded in 1437 by William de la Pole, later Duke of Suffolk, and his wife Alice, a granddaughter of Geoffrey Chaucer (Goodall, *God's House*, chs. 2–3).

[26] E.g., Greenway's Almshouse in Tiverton, Dorset, founded around 1517 (Bailey, *Almshouses*, 76), and see Rawcliffe, "A Word."

[27] HMC, *Report on the MSS of Lord de L'Isle and Dudley*, vol. 1, 175–6. For below, see StGeoCh XV.37.25.

London, operated by the College of St. George at Windsor Castle, were made more pleasant in 1501–2 by the addition of a glass window featuring a picture and coat of arms. While rural institutions might have vegetable gardens, urban houses usually had to confine themselves to a more limited space.[28] Ford's Hospital in Coventry, built in 1529, had only a narrow interior courtyard.

Some foundations expected that their residents would cook and/or eat as a group. An unusually full description of shared cooking comes from an early fourteenth-century customal of St. Bartholomew's Hospital in Sandwich, Kent. In addition to eating bread, cheese, and butter made by the female residents of the house, the sixteen alms people gathered in the kitchen to prepare their food together, assisted by a cook.[29] Each day a porridge of beans, peas, or other vegetables was readied for communal use, "and every person may put his or her meat into the common pot, and the cook shall return it, when sufficiently boiled, with a basin of porridge. But no one shall be permitted to make use of a separate pot on the common fire." The residents of the hospital were also to drink a jug of ale together every Sunday after midday dinner, "to promote brotherly affection." Although shared cooking and eating were less frequently prescribed for later institutions, the statutes of Heytesbury Hospital in Wiltshire from 1471 say that the poor men and women were to take their meals together unless infirmity prevented them.[30] Some degree of common cooking and eating is suggested also by inventories of institutions' possessions. In 1472–3, Sherborne Almshouse contained twenty-eight platters, sixteen saucers, nine porringers, thirteen candlesticks, and various pots, pans, and lamps.[31]

To supplement the qualitative picture offered by manuscripts and secondary studies, I prepared – with excellent help from two research assistants – a database of information about many of the institutions that operated at some time between 1350 and 1599.[32] Using material from sources that provide at least some coverage for the whole country, the database also records founding and closing dates for houses that had

[28] For gardens, see Richmond, "Victorian Values" (Henry Chichele's bedehouse at Higham Ferrers, Northants.), and Orme and Webster, *English Hospital*, 122. For below, see Godfrey, *English Almshouse*, plate 11.

[29] *Collections for An History of Sandwich*, 17–19.

[30] "Ancient Statutes." At John Isbury's almshouses in Lambourn, Berks., however, the alms people were expressly told to eat in their own chambers (BerksRO D/Q1 Q7/15).

[31] DorsetHC D/SHA A29.

[32] Margaret Freel did much of the initial work of assembling information at the Cambridge University Library in 1983–4; Prof. Carol Loats, then a graduate student at the University of Colorado at Boulder, did the first round of data entry during the later 1980s. The database uses the Statistical Package for the Social Sciences.

already ceased to function by 1350.[33] For purposes of analysis, I have divided late medieval institutions into two chronological groups: those set up before 1350 but still functioning thereafter, and those established between 1350 and 1539. The database excludes institutions for which testators left founding instructions in their wills, but we have no confirmation that they were ever actually set up, and it does not utilize information from secondary descriptions of specific local areas, so as not to distort the regional distribution in favor of better-studied communities or regions.[34]

While the database is useful as a reflection of general trends, it does not claim to be a full listing or accurate in every detail. Because it certainly overlooks some institutions, it presents minimal total numbers. It is weighted in favor of larger and longer-lived houses supported by a landed endowment that are better documented in surviving records; it is most likely to undercount early hospitals and small almshouses that operated informally and briefly.[35] Dates of founding and closing are often recorded imprecisely in the sources. Although consistent techniques were employed to assign them to decades or centuries, some of the individual decisions may have been incorrect.[36] Nor is the geographical coverage provided by the sources entirely uniform. Fewer records survive from the north than from other regions of the country, and the volumes published by the Victoria County Histories do not provide consistent depth. But the

---

[33] The sources are: (1) the listing of institutions in David Knowles and R. N. Hadcock, *Medieval Religious Houses, England and Wales*, which relies heavily on Rotha M. Clay, *The Mediaeval Hospitals of England*, plus some additional information provided by Clay for their study; (2) all volumes of the Victoria County Histories as published through early 2009; and (3) the *Reports of the Charity Commissioners for England and Wales* published in forty-four volumes as part of the Parliamentary Papers between 1819 and 1842, arranged by county, hundred, and place. The latter attempted to document all previous and current charities, including ones that had long since died out, based upon testimony by local juries as well as written sources. For discussion of the problems in Knowles and Hadcock's list when compared with fuller local data, see Orme and Webster, *English Hospital*, 10–11.

[34] Groom, for example, identified a total of fourteen actual or intended almshouses in Surrey for the period before 1560 through his study of wills and other local records, whereas the standard sources noted only three ("Piety and Locality," 95–6); Phillips found that 128 hospitals and almshouses were established or planned in Norfolk and Suffolk prior to 1549, whereas Knowles and Hadcock list only 79 ("Charitable Institutions," iv).

[35] Orme and Webster conducted a thorough search of all local records for the counties of Cornwall and Devon, including wills, looking for hospitals and almshouses that operated some time between 1350 and 1540 (*English Hospital*, 173 and 186–266). Of the forty institutions they identified, my database includes thirty-three. Most of the remaining seven were either small leper hospitals that ceased operation in the early fifteenth century or almshouses without landed property that functioned only briefly.

[36] See CUP Online App. 1 for the methodology employed and CUP Online App. 2 for the numbers that resulted.

material in the database nevertheless helps us to identify some interesting patterns and significant shifts over time.

We may begin with an overview of the numbers.

Institutions founded before 1350 but also closed before 1350   242[37]
Institutions founded before 1350, continued after 1350   462
Institutions founded between 1350 and 1539   333
Institutions founded between 1540 and 1599   210
Total number in existence sometime between 1350 and 1599 1,005

Of the institutions established before 1350 that still operated after that date whose type was described, all were termed hospitals of some kind (see Appendix A). Two-fifths of these early hospitals were said at the time of their founding to have been for lepers. Among later medieval foundations, however, hospitals were less common. Only 40 percent of the institutions set up between 1350 and 1539 were described as hospitals of any kind, and a mere 9 percent were for lepers. The rest were almshouses.

We can count the number of hospitals and almshouses in the database that were founded, closed, and – for those that operated after 1350 – in existence during each decade. Appendix B displays the date of founding or first reference, distinguishing those that ceased to function before 1350 from ones that continued later.[38] It shows a rise in new creations through a peak in the 1210s, followed by an irregular decline through the first decade of the 1300s. Between the 1310s and 1360s, the number of new houses dropped further still. Foundings then rose unevenly through the 1520s, apart from a trough in the 1460s. The graph provides little support for the suggestion of a negative response to the poor in the generation after the 1348–9 plague: the lowered numbers for the 1350s and 1360s are evidently later stages within the period of decreasing foundations that began in the 1310s. That extended decline was probably due largely to demographic and economic problems, as was the drop in the 1460s.

Appendix C presents the number of institutions that closed or ceased to function as hospitals or almshouses per decade. It shows a rise in the 1310s to 1340s, another likely sign of economic hardship, but then relatively little variation in most decades between the 1350s and the 1520s, until the drastic impact of the government's religious policies in the 1530s

---

[37] Includes five institutions said to have been founded prior to 1050 that Orme and Webster believe were not yet independent, free-standing hospitals.

[38] For the numbers displayed in this and the other graphs, see CUP Online App. 2. Orme's estimate of the number of hospital foundations within half-century periods is as follows: 1080–1150, 68; 1151–1200, 191; 1201–50, 164; 1251–1300, 152; 1301–50, 101; 1351–1400, 71; 1401–50, 69; 1451–1500, 69; 1501–30, 67 (Orme and Webster, *English Hospital*, 11).

to 1550s.[39] Of 777 hospitals and almshouses that functioned at some time between 1350 and 1529, 180 (23 percent) ceased operation within that span. The closures did not stem primarily from a declining need for leper hospitals: only one-third of the houses that shut down or changed nature in those years had been for such people.[40] The number of institutions in existence during each decade from 1350 onwards may also be calculated.[41] As Appendix D shows, the figure rose gradually through the 1520s, when 617 of these houses were in operation.

Although the number of hospitals and almshouses per county varied widely, their distribution by region of England reveals some interesting chronological developments.[42] The largest group of hospitals founded prior to 1350 was located in East Anglia/the southeast, with lower but fairly even levels in the other areas (north/northwest, southwest/west, and Midlands/east central). Among houses founded between 1350 and 1539, hospitals and institutions of unspecified type again included a cluster in the north/northwest as well as additional houses in East Anglia/the southeast.[43] But very few of the almshouses were situated in the north/northwest, with the highest proportion in East Anglia/the southeast and a secondary group in the southwest/west.

When considering the location of these institutions within different types of communities, we find a decrease after 1350 in the fraction located in villages, as compared with cities, towns, and market centers.[44] The early

---

[39] See ch. 5.2 below.

[40] Another sixty-one hospitals initially said to be for lepers closed later in the sixteenth century, while the remaining forty-eight continued to function after 1600, but presumably served different kinds of residents.

[41] The dates of founding and closing for early houses are so often imprecise that a decadal calculation is not useful prior to the mid fourteenth century. Orme presents the following estimates for the number of houses in existence within 50-year periods: 1080–1150, 68; 1151–1200, 252; 1201–50, 389; 1251–1300, 496; 1301–50, 541; 1351–1400, 508; 1401–50, 513; 1451–1500, 552; 1501–30, 585 (Orme and Webster, *The English Hospital*, 11). Bailey's figure of "no less than 700" hospitals and almshouses in England by the end of the fourteenth century is probably too high (*Almshouses*, 53).

[42] See CUP Online App. 3. The regions used are: north/northwest = Ches., Cumb., Durham, Lancs., Northumb., Westml., Yorks. East Riding, Yorks. North Riding, and Yorks. West Riding; southwest/west = Corn., Devon, Dorset, Gloucs., Heref., Shrops., Som., Staffs., Wilts., and Worcs.; the Midlands/east central = Beds., Bucks., Derby., Hunts., Leices., Lincs., Northants., Notts., Oxfds., Rutl., and Warws.; East Anglia/the southeast = Berks., Cambs., Essex, Hamps., Herts., Kent, Middlx., Norf., Suff., Surrey, and Sussex plus London.

[43] Two-thirds of the houses founded in the north/northwest, 1350–1539, lay in the city of York or elsewhere in Yorkshire.

[44] See CUP Online App. 1, pt. 6 for definition of communities and CUP Online App. 3 for the numbers. For fuller discussions of the location of hospitals, see Orme and Webster, *English Hospital*, 41–8, and Rawcliffe, "Earthly and Spiritual Topography." For below, see Rawcliffe, *Leprosy*, 308–9.

hospitals, especially those for lepers, were commonly situated outside the walls of large communities, due to concern with contagion and because a site adjacent to a road or bridge used by travelers made it easier for the residents to beg for alms. Later hospitals and almshouses were frequently placed in the midst of urban areas. The proportion of institutions founded after 1350 that were situated in market communities was larger than the contribution of those places to the country's total population would have suggested. Market centers, which generally contained around 500 to 3,000 people and functioned as centers of local trade, displayed some disparity in wealth during the later medieval period: they might have a considerable number of elderly or otherwise disabled poor, but also at least a few successful residents who had the resources with which to establish a residential institution for their needy neighbors. Urban governments of all sizes may have been well aware of the publicity value of hospitals and almshouses, demonstrating to visitors that theirs was a prosperous, charitable, and well-run community.

3.2   The residents of hospitals and almshouses

We know something about the kinds of people who lived in these houses, how many of them there were, who appointed them, and what they had to do to gain entry. Although most institutions were for the poor, that broad term could be applied in diverse ways. Many residents had previously been self-supporting, but fell into need through a misfortune, usually illness or an injury, or due to old age. Relatively few medieval places went to people who had always lived in poverty. Of the hospitals founded before 1350 included in the database whose nature was specified, nearly three-quarters said they were intended for sick people, including lepers, some of whom were also described as poor (see Appendix A). Another quarter of the hospitals did not mention illness, but noted only that they were for the poor, presumably bedridden or physically disabled people who needed care.

During the later medieval period, however, newly founded houses had a very different character. Only one-sixth of the hospitals established between 1350 and 1539 were for sick people, whereas the poor, often described now as elderly, were the intended residents of nearly one-quarter of the hospitals and almost all of the almshouses. The ordinances of the town almshouse at Saffron Walden, Essex, from 1400, said that its thirteen residents were to be chosen from among the neediest local people, those who were "lame, crooked, blind, and bedridden."[45] When

---

[45] Steer, "Statutes," 172–3. The institution was also to give alms to incapacitated people living in their own homes within 5 miles of Walden (ibid., 174–5). For below, see *Ilchester Almshouse*, 117.

Robert Veel founded his almshouse in Ilchester, Som. in 1426, he said that its five to seven residents should be "poor men, infirm, broken down with old age, and unable to work." William Wyggeston (or Wigston), who established a hospital in Leicester in the 1510s, wanted his institution to serve twelve poor men, defined either as "blind, lame, decrepit, paralytic or maimed in their limbs" or as "idiots" who lacked "their natural senses ... [if] they be peaceable."[46] Those admitted to the almshouse run by the Holy Trinity Guild in Wisbech, Isle of Ely, in 1512 were to be "persons of the greatest weakness."

In terms of the sexual distribution of residents as seen in the database, nearly all houses set up prior to 1350 accepted only men or both men and women, whereas two-fifths of later medieval foundations were for women only.[47] (These figures, available for a minority of all institutions, are based largely on founding documents, not reflecting possible changes in the subsequent distribution of inmates.) Many late medieval houses did not specify the marital situation of prospective residents, but those that did usually said they should be unmarried.[48] A few institutions, however, allowed married couples to share a room and stipend. At Ford's Hospital in Coventry, founded initially in 1509 for five old men and one woman and changed later to six men aged 60 or more plus their wives, new statutes prepared around 1530 said that five of the rooms were to be for married couples. But because many old people are "not well able to keep themselves in good honest order and clean of their bodies," the sixth place was to go to a poor but respectable woman of the town, aged between 40 and 50 years, to help the others with washing and cooking.[49]

Some houses served a more specific clientele. Prior to 1350, one-fifth of the institutions in the database for which we have information accepted priests or other clerics, but virtually all late medieval foundations were for lay people only.[50] Among the latter, there might be further limitations. The Hospital of St. Giles outside Lincoln was said at the time of Bishop Alnwick's visitation in 1437 to have been founded specially for servants of the canons of Lincoln Cathedral.[51] Former servants of the Hungerford

---

[46] Slack, *From Reformation to Improvement*, 25. For below, see W&FM Wisbech Guild Book, p. 512.

[47] See CUP Online App. 4.

[48] E.g., Browne's Hospital in Stamford, Lincs., which ordered in 1495 that its ten poor men and two women be single (Wright, *Story of the "Domus Dei,"* 31).

[49] *So Long as the World Shall Endure*, 14–15 and 45. I am grateful to Angela Nicholls for suggesting this source.

[50] See the lower part of CUP Online App. 4. For the former, see Orme, "Medieval Almshouse," and Barron, *London*, 300.

[51] *Chapter Acts of the Cathedral Church of St. Mary of Lincoln*, 14. For below, see "Ancient Statutes" and Hicks, "St Katherine's Hospital."

family were given first priority at Heytesbury Hospital, which functioned as a fairly pleasant retirement home; tenants of the family's lands came next, followed by "such well disposed persons as be known and fall into poverty and have not wherewithall for to live." When Cardinal Beaufort founded his almshouse of noble poverty in Winchester in 1443, its thirty-eight lay residents were to be either gentlefolk who could no longer support themselves or former members of Beaufort's household.[52]

Other institutions were confined to the residents of the community or parish in which they were located or to members of designated fraternities or urban guilds. The first set of houses built at Christ's Hospital, Abingdon, Berks. in the 1440s was intended for seven poor men and six poor women of that town only; people born in the town or parish of Wokingham, Berks. were given preference for admission to Westende's Almshouses, founded in 1451.[53] The foundation deed for Hosyer's Almshouse in Ludlow, dated 1486, said that the institution was for brothers and sisters of the Fraternity of St. John Evangelist in Ludlow who had fallen into poverty. The very first almshouse in London, built from money bequeathed to the Tailors' Company in 1413, was for seven old men of that guild.[54] The influential house established by Richard Whittington in London after 1424 was intended for poor, enfeebled "yeomen" who worked in mercery, not the more successful men who had attained the livery of the Mercers' Company.

Especially in the earlier medieval years, another cluster of institutions provided temporary accommodation for people on the road.[55] Sixty institutions in the database created before 1350 were for travelers, as compared to just five such houses between 1350 and 1539. The founding document of Trinity Hospital in Salisbury said in 1379 that the seven works of mercy were to be fulfilled through provision of a total of thirty beds.[56] Twelve resident poor people were to be supported for life, but the hospital was also to offer food and shelter to eighteen needy strangers for three days and nights each. When Brackley Hospital in Northamptonshire was reorganized in 1425, Archbishop Chicheley's ordinances reduced the number of people to be assisted by the institution, due to insufficient revenues, but the house was still to provide four to six bedsteads "for the

---

[52] Belfield, "Cardinal Beaufort's Almshouse," and Hopewell, *Saint Cross*, ch. 6.
[53] CHAbing Minutes, March 1577/8–1694, fols. 1r–6r; BerksRO D/QWo 35/1/1. For below, see ShropsA 356/315.
[54] Barron, *London*, 298–9. For below, see Rawcliffe, "Dives Redeemed?"
[55] Carlin defined hospices for poor wayfarers and pilgrims as one of the four types of medieval hospitals, along with leper houses, institutions that cared for the sick poor, and almshouses ("Medieval English Hospitals").
[56] Wilts&SA 1446/34.

gratuitous relief of poor travelers for one night, or longer if necessary."[57] A tiny hospital with only two beds founded in 1506 by John Brunskill in Brough, Westml., a sparsely populated region, was intended mainly for travelers crossing the Pennines into Yorkshire.[58] Houses for transients were, however, difficult to run and might attract undesirable people into the community. Hence, they often died out or changed nature over time.

A less clearly defined element within some houses were its "brethren/ brothers" or "sisters." In earlier foundations, those terms usually referred to the clerical members of the establishment or to the staff who looked after the poor or attended to the hospital's practical affairs. The Hospital of St. Giles (or Kepier Hospital) on the outskirts of Durham had a master and thirteen brethren as well as at least thirteen long-term inmates (old men) and probably at least thirteen travelers or pilgrims every night.[59] Six of the brethren were chaplains who prayed for the souls of the founders, while the others were lay brothers who managed the operation of the house. In 1364, the staff of St. Leonard's Hospital in York included thirteen chaplain brothers who lived according to the Augustinian rule and eight sisters who cared for around 200 sick and infirm inmates.[60] Brothers and sisters could also be wealthier people who had paid to enter an institution and enjoyed a more privileged standard of living.[61] By the late medieval period, however, the terms sometimes referred to the poor residents themselves. At the Hospital of St. Nicholas in Salisbury, the brethren and sisters received payments as inmates in 1478.[62] In 1540–1, Magdalen Hospital in Exeter housed eight residents, people later described as "the leprous brothers and sisters of the hospital."

For some hospitals and almshouses in the database, we have information about how many people they were meant to house at the time of their foundation. Here we must distinguish between the mean number of people per institution (the average) and the median number (the middle number in the array if all values are laid out from smallest to largest). Because a few houses with very large or very small numbers can skew the average value, the median is probably a more representative figure.

[57] HMC, *Fourth Report*, "MSS of Magdalene College, Oxford," 459. The hospital was annexed to the college in 1484–5 due to its neglect of hospitality.

[58] Bailey, *Almshouses*, 71–3. For below, see, e.g., McIntosh, *Autonomy and Community*, 238–9.

[59] Meade, "The Hospital of Saint Giles."

[60] Cullum, "Cremetts and Corrodies." Other staff members were the lay brothers and/or maidservants who assisted in tending the sick, four secular chaplains employed in the church and chapels, and many lay servants who performed the practical work of the house.

[61] E.g., CKentS U270/Q5.

[62] Prescott, *English Medieval Hospital*, 46, and see DurhUL PK DCD Almoner's Rental, 1501–3, fols. 14v–15r. For below, see DevonRO Exeter City Archives G1/N2–4, for 1540–41 and 1594–5.

Among houses established prior to 1350, hospitals for lepers and other sick people were supposed to serve an average of nineteen residents, with an average of thirteen inhabitants in hospitals for the poor.[63] The median number for all types of hospitals was thirteen, a figure with biblical significance. The ambitions of later medieval founders were more modest. Even for hospitals, the average and median had dropped slightly, while almshouses were intended for an average of only eight inhabitants and a median of six-and-a-half.

Because, however, some institutions never housed as many people as their founders envisioned, while others shrank in size as their income diminished or their goals changed, it would be more useful to know how many people were actually living in hospitals and almshouses in various periods. That information has been obtained from accounts and other detailed records for 157 houses in operation at some point during the first half of the sixteenth century. Hospitals housed an average of thirteen people and a median of eight-and-a-half, while almshouses sheltered an average of eight and a median of seven.[64]

The average and median number of actual residents in those hospitals and almshouses for which we have information can be used together with the number of houses in existence in a given decade to provide a very rough estimate of the total number of people living in the institutions included in the database. If we carry out that calculation for the 1520s, the decade with the largest number of houses in operation (multiplying the 617 existing houses in the database by the average and median numbers per house), we obtain totals of around 4,900 to 6,400 residents.[65] Those figures can in turn be set against the estimated total population of England, which in the early 1520s was probably around 2.35 million.[66] That comparison suggests that the hospitals and almshouses in this study offered one place for every 370 to 480 people. On average, these houses would have provided between one-half and three-quarters of a place for each of the country's roughly 9,000 parishes, but in practice, the uneven geographical distribution of institutions and their specific requirements for admission meant that some people had a far better chance of finding an opening than others.

Residents of hospitals and almshouses were appointed by a variety of individuals or officers. Founders and patrons often valued the power that derived from being able to fill requests from potential inmates. Donors sometimes reserved the nomination for themselves or their heirs, at least

---

[63] See CUP Online App. 5.   [64] See CUP Online App. 6.
[65] See CUP Online App. 7.
[66] Broadberry et al., "English Medieval Population." See CUP Online App. 7.

initially. In his 1398 will, John Ake assigned the right to fill vacancies among the twenty poor people living in God's House at Crossbridge in Beverley, E. Yorks. to his wife Ellen during her lifetime; the inmates of Heytesbury Hospital were named by the founder's family in the 1470s.[67] If appointment was assigned to a patron or the feoffees who ran some later medieval houses, the vicar or rector of the parish was sometimes named as a back-up.

Town officials or urban guilds frequently chose residents for the institutions they operated or that lay within their area. When John Easterfield, a merchant and former mayor of Bristol, re-endowed Forster's Almshouse in 1504, he ordered that seven of the eight poor men were to be nominated by the mayor of Bristol and four of the five women by the mayor's wife; the other man and woman were appointees of the master of St. Mark's Hospital.[68] The town officers of Wilton, Wilts. awarded a place in St. Giles Hospital in 1535. In 1430, four mercers representing the Company of Merchant Adventurers in York granted to a clerk (probably in return for a payment) the right to name a person to the second "bed of the poor folks" that became available in the Hospital of the Trinity at Fossegate, run by the company.[69]

Some houses expected new residents to make a financial contribution, either to obtain a place or upon entering the institution, suggesting that their members were not the utterly indigent poor. An episcopal visitation of Newark College at Leicester in 1525 revealed that some inmates of the college's hospital had given money or fowls to obtain their positions.[70] A complaint lodged against St. Paul's Hospital (sometimes called Norman's Hospital) in Norwich at a visitation in 1492 was that to become a sister of the institution one had to pay an entrance fee of at least 10 marks (£6 13s. 4d.). In the almshouse or college at Tong, Shrops., an early sixteenth-century report said that by tradition, every new bedeman was supposed to give to the house "such certain sum of money or other substance as he might easily bear," to form a stock for maintenance of the house.[71] Institutions usually asked entering inmates to bring their own clothing, bedding, and eating utensils if possible. Possessions left in the

---

[67] HMC, *Report on MSS of the Corp. of Beverley*, 145–6; Wilts&SA 251/50. For below, see, e.g., ROLeics DE 1782/2, and HertsA D/P 105 25/1, E.

[68] *Cartulary of St. Mark's Hospital*, 287. For below, see Wilts&SA G25/1/21, 131.

[69] BIA Company of Merchant Adventurers, Trinity Hospital Administration #14. His appointee was to receive all of the alms and other benefits associated with that bed.

[70] *Visitations in the Diocese of Lincoln*, vol. 3, 230–8. For below, see Tanner, *The Church in Late Medieval Norwich*, 133–4.

[71] E.g., TNA-PRO C 1/364/22. For below, see, e.g., *Cartulary of God's House*, lxxxi, and "Ancient Statutes."

room of a deceased resident were appropriated by the house, which kept the bedding for future arrivals who had none of their own.[72]

Some of the large medieval hospitals and a few of the most desirable almshouses – like many monasteries and convents – offered "corrodies." Granted in return for an advance payment of money or land, a corrody guaranteed that an individual or married couple would receive specified food, clothing, and occasionally cash sums for life, as well as residence in the institution. The amount to be demanded for a corrody was especially difficult to calculate when purchased by a couple. The crown had the right to present one or two corrody holders to every house founded by a previous monarch. The institution was then required to support the person named (often a minor member of the royal household) for the rest of his – or occasionally her – life. Corrodies could be joined by less complete forms of support, requiring smaller advance payments, such as a "livery" that granted certain food or money to people who did not necessarily live in the institution.

People invested in the purchase of corrody, or the promise of one in the future, in hopes of acquiring a secure place for themselves or a relative when old or disabled. The corrody granted to Philip Wem, rector of a church in Kent, by the House of God in Ospringe in 1397 specified that he (and presumably his servants) were to have a chamber beside the gate of the hospital's garden plus fourteen loaves of white bread and seven loaves of black bread weekly, 7 gallons of the best ale and 3.5 gallons of lesser ale weekly, a daily allowance of meat, fish, and pottage, an annual livery of good quality woolen cloth, two cartloads of wood for fuel, and 6 lbs. of candles for his chamber each year.[73] Aden Berysford of Fenny Bentley, Derby. complained to Chancery around 1510 against the master of St. John's Hospital, Coventry for his refusal to admit Berysford's daughter as a sister of the hospital.[74] Berysford had agreed with the previous master that if he paid 10 marks (£6 13s. 4d.), his daughter would be accepted into the house. He had already given 8 marks before the old master died, but the incoming head refused to honor the agreement or to acknowledge Berysford's earlier payments.

Serious problems could result from the use of corrodies. While this practice provided a nice boost to current income for the house or its master, the institution might have trouble delivering the promised benefits if the recipient lived for many years or if the financial calculation of the amount of the payment as compared to future costs had been erroneous.

---

[72] E.g., DorsetHC D/SHA D24, statutes.   [73] Frohnsdorff, "Maison Dieu," 35.
[74] TNA-PRO C 1/286/11.

In 1399, St. Leonard's Hospital in York was found to be burdened by debt.[75] Its difficulty resulted largely from the sale of forty-four corrodies and seventy-two liveries by three previous masters within a 15-year period: the heads had apparently pocketed much of the money, possibly using some of it for repairs to the building, but leaving no additional income to support the new arrivals. During the later fifteenth and earlier sixteenth centuries, St. Bartholomew's Hospital in Sandwich offered corrodies in return for a cash payment to the mayor or one of the urban jurats who ran the institution.[76] Borough officials made several attempts to control the corruption and financial shortfalls that arose from such payments. A common assembly in 1480 limited the number of corrodies to be given (to eight brethren, five sisters, and two priests) and prohibited their use for married couples.

A few houses during the second half of the fifteenth and the early sixteenth centuries imposed a different requirement for admission, specifying that potential residents were to be well regarded by their peers. The foundation document of Westende's Almshouses in Wokingham said that those admitted must be "of good repute, behavior, and honesty."[77] Candidates for William Pykenham's almshouse in Hadleigh, Suff., set up in 1497 by a former rector, had to be known within the community as of "good and honest conversation and living and by fortune fall[en] to extreme poverty." Entrants to John Isbury's almshouses in Lambourn, Berks. (1501–2) were to be "courteous, humble, and meek in words and mind."[78] Religious stipulations were occasionally added. A person considered for Browne's Hospital in Stamford, Lincs. in 1495 must be "lowly, devout and poor and ... [know] thoroughly the Lord's Prayer, the Angelic Salutation, and the Apostles' Creed."[79]

3.3   Benefits and obligations

The benefits received by the residents of medieval hospitals and almshouses varied greatly.[80] In addition to whatever sociability and informal support came from living as a member of a group, all residents enjoyed free housing. While trained medical services were rare, the staff or hired servants of most hospitals and a few wealthy almshouses provided basic

---

[75] Cullum, "Cremetts and Corrodies."
[76] *Collections for An History of Sandwich*, 22, for the rest of this paragraph.
[77] BerksRO D/QWo 35/1/1. For below, see HadlTR MS 25/29.
[78] BerksRO D/Q1 Q7/15.   [79] Wright, *Story of the "Domus Dei,"* 37.
[80] Here again we must remind ourselves that information is skewed in favor of large, well-funded, and long-lasting institutions whose records are more likely to have survived.

bedside care.[81] Knolles Almshouses in Pontefract, W. Yorks., founded in 1391, were to employ two servants to look after the thirteen poor people, the master, and eight priests and clerks.[82] The almshouse in Saffron Walden paid annual wages to a female keeper or "dame" for looking after and washing the residents, making pottage for them, and keeping the house clean. Some almshouses expected healthier inmates to look after those who were sick or feeble, but a few hired a woman or even a medical professional to look after a poor resident suffering from a temporary illness.[83] Residents might be supplied with vessels in which they could do their own laundry, and a handful hired women to wash the hospital's clothes and bedding. Some houses paid barbers to shave the beards of male residents, and many provided a decent burial for those residents whose personal possessions were insufficient to cover the cost.[84]

A minority of institutions offered some kind of regular cash stipend or salary to help residents buy essential items. At the lower (and probably more characteristic) end of the scale, each of the fifteen poor women and men who lived in the almshouse run by the Drapers' Company of Shrewsbury received a penny per week between 1490 and 1530.[85] The thirteen poor people living in the maison dieu built by Joan Gregg in Hull, E. Yorks. shortly before her death in 1438 were to share 24d. per week, while the eight sisters in the Hospital of St. James outside the walls of Canterbury each received 3d. weekly in 1450–1 for "their livery in money." In 1540–1 the eight brothers and sisters of Magdalen Hospital in Exeter were paid 6d. per week per person.[86] At the top of the range were the poor men of God's House, Ewelme, who enjoyed 13d. per week each in 1499–1500. Houses that offered a stipend usually required regular prayers from their inmates.

Several problems hampered these cash payments. Because the awards were generally fixed in amount, their purchasing power declined as inflation

---

[81] By 1535, only thirty-nine hospitals seem to have provided regular medical care (Archer, "Hospitals"). Among them was St. Leonard's Hospital in York, which cared for at least some people who subsequently recovered from their affliction and were able to leave the institution (Cullum, "Cremetts and Corrodies").

[82] BIA CP.E 266. For below, see Steer, "Statutes," 172–3, and EssexRO-Ch T/A 401/1.

[83] E.g., "Ancient Statutes," UNottL MS Mi 6/179/18, BerksRO D/Q1 Q7/15, and DorsetHC D/SHA D24, statutes. For below, see, e.g., ROLeics 1 D 50/II/1 and 15, StGeoCh XV.37.25, and *Kent Chantries*, 65.

[84] For barbers, see, e.g., *Fifteenth Century Cartulary*, lxii, StGeoCh XV.37.25, and DorsetHC D/SHA A46; for burials, see, e.g., Steer, "Statutes," 172–5, and DorsetHC D/SHA A29.

[85] "Earliest Book," 198–220. For below, see Heath, "Urban Piety," and CKentS Studies U270/Q5.

[86] DevonRO Exeter City Archives G1/N2–4. For below, see BodlL MS D.D. Ewelme.c.2, E.A.1, first account.

began to rise, especially after around 1500. Nor were they always delivered as intended. A memorandum in the city of York's records from 1490 notes that 2s. 6d. from the rent of an urban tenement was supposed to go to the almswomen of the maison dieu at Ousbridge, but for the past 18 years that sum had not been paid to them.[87] After the tenement was sold and razed, the city negotiated a new agreement with the current tenant whereby he was to give 20s. to the almswomen for sums due in the past and 12d. annually to them in the future. While that compromise secured some income for the poor women, it was considerably less than they had previously received.

Although most institutions expected their residents to feed themselves out of their own resources, some provided basic foodstuffs. This practice was most common in houses in which the inmates cooked and ate together. Accounts reveal that the staple food was a porridge made of grains and/or peas. Some houses that bought no other food paid for oatmeal and salt, perhaps joined by candles or oil for lamps.[88] The almshouse in Saffron Walden offered a little more variety, purchasing oatmeal, wheatmeal, wheat, peas, and butter, plus salt and candles. A few institutions furnished ale and other kinds of food as well, at least for special occasions. Sherborne Almshouse bought wheat and hired a baker to make bread for the poor on a regular basis in 1472–3 and in some years added ale and meat at Christmas, Easter, and Pentecost.[89]

We know more about the food provided at Salisbury's unusually comfortable Trinity Hospital. The fifteenth-century accounts are, however, somewhat misleading, for they record in combined manner the food purchased for the higher status staff of the hospital (including a sub-keeper and a chaplain) and for the poor residents. In 1452, the accountant listed payments for oatmeal, peas, bread, and salt for ordinary meals, but added ale, cheese, eggs, several kinds of meat, and fresh and salted fish on religious holidays.[90] In 1481, the hospital supplemented those purchases with a pig for bacon, milk, and butter. In November and December, 1522, a period for which we have records of almost daily purchases, the hospital paid for beef, mutton, pork, veal, a cony (rabbit), herring, fresh fish, salt or stock fish, eels, a salted conger (a type of eel), oats, ale, eggs, and butter.[91]

[87] *York Memorandum Book*, 291–2, for this and below.
[88] E.g., BristolRO 33041 BMC/1/4 and ROLeics 1 D 50/II/1 and 15. For below, see EssexRO-Ch T/A 401/1.
[89] DorsetHC D/SHA A29, A13, and A19. The house's foundation statutes say that the master was to spend 10s. each week for food and drink for the sixteen poor men and women (ibid., D/SHA D24).
[90] Wilts&SA 1446/Box of Trinity Hospital Accounts, 1452 (T4). For below, see ibid., 1481 (T9).
[91] Ibid., accounts for 1522 (T48).

As Christmas approached, the house bought an ox and had it slaughtered and dressed, as well as paying 6d. to have pies made and baked.

The fullest kitchen accounts come from St. Anthony's Hospital in London during the late fifteenth and early sixteenth centuries, when it was operated by the College of St. George at Windsor Castle.[92] At this atypically luxurious institution, listings of daily or weekly expenses for food, which extend for years on end, usually distinguish between purchases for three groups: the twelve almsmen who ate together in the hospital; the hall (where the staff had their meals); and the master (who was served in his own quarters). In 1494–5, St. Anthony's almsmen ate some of the usual cooked oatmeal, but it was occasionally replaced by a porridge made of peas and onions or by a stew with flounder.[93] Their staple fare was augmented by mutton, pork, red and white herring, plaice, salted salmon, haddock, fried stock fish, mussels, and – in the spring – herbs for salads. As a beverage, they drank weak ale. The hall enjoyed a more varied menu. Purchases for the staff included chicken, more desirable kinds of fish (gurnards, sturgeons, bream, and brets), lamprey and conger eels, crabs, oysters, apples, and pears, plus red and "bastard" wine at dinner and supper. The master, meanwhile, was feasting on such additional items as larks, conies, fresh salmon, turbot, a pike, shrimp, and damson plums. Around Christmas, the level of opulence rose even higher. All of the house enjoyed beef, pork, mutton, and geese as well as fowls baked into pies; with their meals they drank Malmsey, red wine, and claret spiced with sugar, pepper, currants, ginger, cinnamon, raisins, dates, cloves, mace, saffron, and almonds; afterwards they sucked on sweet candies, made probably with nuts. The hall added mallards to its celebration of the Christmas season, while the master had three dozen larks, plovers, conies, crabs, custard, and curd.[94] When reading such accounts, we must remember that the almsmen in St. Anthony's were eating at a level far above that enjoyed by residents of other institutions that provided food and in a different league entirely from poor people who were fending for themselves. We may also feel some indignation that so much of the money collected for the hospital by its network of gatherers, nominally for its poor inmates, was in fact being used to support an aristocratic standard of living among the few who supervised or provided religious services for the institution.[95]

---

[92] StGeoCh, e.g., XV.37.8, 37.21, and 37.25. The children of the song school ate either with the poor, in which case they were given additional eggs, milk, cheese, and/or butter, or in the hall.

[93] Ibid., XV.37.21 and XV.37.8.

[94] For similar patterns in 1501–2, see ibid., XV.37.25.   [95] See ch. 2.3 above.

Wood or coals were offered by some institutions, to be used for cooking or heating. Sometime in the late fifteenth century, Hugh Chesenale, a former rector, bequeathed £6 13s. 4d. to the abbot of the monastery at Kenilworth, Warws.; income from loaning the money was to provide 20 quarters (160 bushels) of coal for the poor in the almshouse at Stratford-upon-Avon each year at Christmas.[96] In 1496–7, the abbot of Kenilworth agreed with the Guild of the Holy Cross that the latter would assume responsibility for Chesenale's endowment and deliver the coal to residents of the almshouse and other poor people in the town. Recipients were instructed to pray especially for the soul of the donor who "ordained these alms of coals yearly to be distributed among you poor people to warm you with this cold winter." The almshouse in Shrewsbury run by the Drapers' Company provided loads of fuel for its poor people in the decades around 1500.[97] The lessee of some land in Kent was allowed 20d. off his annual rent in 1521 for carrying three loads of wood to the almshouse in Hawkhurst, and Wyggeston's Hospital in Leicester paid for firewood and charcoal in 1521/2 and 1541/2.

Wealthy institutions might provide clothing for their residents. The founding statutes of Sherborne Almshouse stipulate that the master of the house should spend 8 marks (£5 6s. 8d.) annually for clothes, linen, woolen hose, shoes, and other necessities for the house's sixteen poor men and women; the earliest accounts of the house include annual payments for those items.[98] At a more modest level, the foundation charter for John Isbury's almshouses in Lambourn from 1501/2 said that once every two years each poor man was to receive frieze cloth with which to make a gown.[99] St. Peter's Hospital in Bury St. Edmunds had a special little fund for buying shoes for its inmates.

A small number of the most self-conscious houses gave their residents uniform robes or gowns with a distinctive marker that defined them as alms people of that particular institution. The inmates were then required to wear their robes when they left the house, especially when going to church. The poor men of God's House, Ewelme had gowns with a red cross sewn on them, as well as hoods and tabards that they had to wear when entering the church.[100] At Heytesbury Hospital, the residents received gowns and hoods of white wool, with "Jhu. Xrt." set in black

---

[96] ShakespCLA BRT1/2/527, used through A2A.

[97] "Earliest Book," 165–212, passim. For below, see ESussRO FRE/7031, used through A2A, and ROLeics 1 D 50/II/1 and 15.

[98] DorsetHC D/SHA D24 and A1–2. See also "Ancient Statutes."

[99] BerksRO D/Q1 Q7/15. For below, see Rowe, "Medieval Hospitals."

[100] UNottL MS Mi 6/179/18. Each of the poor men and women at Sherborne Almshouse was to receive every Christmas a white woolen robe with a hood, marked on the right breast with a bishop's mitre and on the left with an escutcheon of the arms of St. George (DorsetHC D/SHA D24, statutes).

letters upon their breasts and shoulders, every two or three years.[101] Cardinal Beaufort wanted the residents of his almshouse in Winchester to wear cloaks of a deep red fabric, with a cardinal's hat embroidered on them. Inmates of the Hospital of St. George and St. Christopher the Martyrs, founded in Yeovil, Som. in 1477, were to wear red crosses on their breasts in honor of St. George, described as "patron of the house of alms."[102] A special "livery" not only encouraged a sense of shared identity among the residents, it made them visible as a group in the eyes of others, making it easier to monitor their behavior when away from the institution and drawing attention to the generosity of founders.

Residents benefited also from charitable bequests in wills or other occasional gifts, although such donations might go to the institution collectively to augment its stock.[103] Some testators – especially women – left clothing or bedding to people in hospitals or almshouses.[104] More than one-third of 615 lay testators in Norwich, 1370 to 1532, left small bequests to one or more of the five city hospitals that now functioned as almshouses for old and sick men; contributions were usually between 6d. and 1s. 8d. per house, or 1d. to 4d. to each inmate.[105] In a sample of Sussex wills between 1380 and 1546, ninety-nine testators left bequests to designated hospitals or their individual inhabitants.[106] Thirteen hospitals were named, receiving between one and twenty-two gifts each. Many of the bequests were small (a few pence or a little clothing or bedding), but three hospitals in Chichester and one in Arundel gained over £2 each. When Thomas Cromwell fell from power in 1540, the twenty-six people living in two hospitals in Southover, outside Lewes, Sussex, each received the substantial gift of 13s. 4d. from his property.[107] Some donations suggest a personal relationship with the recipients.[108] During four months

---

[101] "Ancient Statutes." For below, see Belfield, "Cardinal Beaufort's Almshouse."

[102] Bailey, *Almshouses*, 68.

[103] Andrew Brown found that 13 percent of surviving wills from Salisbury, 1270–1349, left bequests to hospitals, as did 21 percent of wills from elsewhere in Wiltshire, Berkshire, and Dorset; for 1350–1499, the figures were 11–31 percent for Salisbury and 8–16 percent for the other regions; for 1500–1547, they were 22 and 4 percent (*Popular Piety*, 188).

[104] E.g., Cicely Hussey bequeathed a mattress, a pair of sheets, and an old white coverlet to the almshouse in Kingston on Thames, Surrey in 1509 for "the relieving of poor people" (Groom, "Piety and Locality," 90). See also HMC, *Report on MSS of the Corp. of Beverley*, 146, Sweetinburgh, "Clothing the Naked," and Cullum, "For Pore People Harberles." For below, see, e.g., CKentS Ch 10J A1, from 1506–7, and DorsetHC D/SHA A29.

[105] Tanner, *The Church in Late Medieval Norwich*, 133 and 223.

[106] See CUP Online App. 8 for the sample and its sources.

[107] TNA-PRO SC 6/Edward VI/453, a reference kindly suggested by Judith Breck.

[108] Cullum and Goldberg, "Charitable Provision." For below, see HMC, *Report on MSS of Lord Middleton*, 339–47.

in 1522, Sir Henry Willoughby of Wollaton Hall, Notts., who spent a good deal of his money betting on card games, gave 9s. 8d. to "his" bedesmen or almsmen.

In return for these benefits, the residents of hospitals and those almshouses that offered assistance beyond simple free housing were expected to fulfill certain obligations. The more generous the stipend or additional services provided by the house, the more extensive the duties and behavioral responsibilities of the inmates. While receiving rent-free housing and perhaps other forms of help were economically desirable, some potential alms people may have hesitated before accepting the religiously focused schedule, limited mobility, and demands for moral conduct that accompanied some institutional places.

The most important and common requirement was prayer and/or attendance at masses.[109] Trinity Hospital in Salisbury noted in 1379 that its poor residents (both permanent and overnight guests) were to say the Psalter of the Virgin daily and to pray for the benefactors and confraternity of the hospital, resulting in a yearly total of 26,280 psalters.[110] The poor men and women in Hosyer's almshouse in Ludlow were to pray twice daily in the institution's chapel for the souls of the founders ("which of their proper [own] costs have builded this chapel and almshouse") and for the brothers and sisters of the Fraternity of St. John the Evangelist of Palmers in that town. The Latin ordinances for the almshouse at Saffron Walden from 1400 were more open-ended. They said that the poor people were to be "duly urged and highly enjoined that daily, when they are well or can conveniently manage it, they shall not desist from coming together at the due hours to church, there piously to pray for the healthy condition of the brothers and sisters and of all the benefactors of the said work."[111]

Some almshouses had very specific requirements for prayer.[112] In 1407, the first statutes of the institution founded by John Ake in Beverley said that its twenty poor residents were to be summoned to the chapel twice each day by a bell run for 15 minutes, at 6 o'clock in the morning and 6 in

---

[109] Jordan described almshouses in London as devoted to "the intensely secular purpose of offering permanent haven – and withdrawal – from a now complex society to the invincibly poor and incompetent" (*Charities of London*, 135). He apparently overlooked the importance of the prayers offered by alms people, a focus that continued in some post-Reformation foundations too. Yet unlike other medieval institutions devoted to prayer, such as chantries and monasteries, the reciters here were lay people, not priests or members of a clerical order.

[110] Wilts&SA 1446/34. For below, see ShropsA 356/315.

[111] Steer, "Statutes," 166–9.

[112] For the exceptionally elaborate prayers at God's House, Ewelme, see UNottL MS Mi 6/179/18.

the evening daily.[113] Those inmates able to rise from their beds were to attend mass and vespers on bended knees. One of the inmates was to urge them to pray for the founders' souls and lead them in saying one Creed, three Lord's Prayers, three Angelic Salutations, and a third of the Psalm of the Blessed Virgin. They were to say the rest of the psalm for the Virgin by themselves, at convenient times during the day. A poor man admitted to St. Giles Hospital in Wilton in 1535 was to say every day before noon 100 Pater Nosters, 100 Aves, and 15 Creeds on behalf of the king, queen, the mayor of Wilton and his brethren, and the abbess and convent with which the hospital was associated.[114]

Later foundations – even small local ones – were especially likely to require prayers for the souls of the founders, thus functioning in effect as lay chantries. All the residents of Terumber's almshouse for six poor men or women in Trowbridge, Wilts. were to assemble when a bell in the yard was rung at 7 or 8 o'clock in the morning and again at 5 or 6 in the afternoon.[115] The most respected member of the house was then to say, in a loud voice: "We shall specially pray for the souls of James Terumber, Joan and Alice his wives, our founders, and of all the other benefactors." After each of those gatherings, the poor people were to go to the parish church and say "one whole Psalter of our Lady St. Mary." When Thomas Stokk refounded Browne's Hospital in Stamford in 1485, he wrote that in addition to a daily schedule of prayers, the senior man among the poor was to say "openly in English" at an assembly of all residents each morning and evening, "God have mercy upon the souls of William Browne of Stamford, and Dame Margaret his wife, and (after my death), on the soul of Mr. Thomas Stokk, founder of this almshouse, the souls of their fathers and mothers, and all Christian souls."[116] The rest of the poor were to answer, "Amen." In 1501 Stephen Hellard required the poor folks living in his almshouse in Stevenage, Herts. to "say daily, in the name of the holy trinity . . . 'Have mercy and pity upon the soul of Master Stephen Hellard and all Christian souls.'"[117] That plea was to be accompanied by three Pater Nosters, three Ave Marias, and one Creed. The ongoing role of the founder was made even more physically explicit at John Isbury's almshouse in Lambourn, where the residents were to pray twice daily while kneeling around his tomb in one of the chapels in the parish church.[118]

---

[113] HMC, *Report on MSS of the Corp. of Beverley*, 147–8.
[114] Wilts&SA G25/1/21, p. 131.   [115] "Terumber's Chantry," from 1483, esp. 250.
[116] Wright, *Story of the "Domus Dei*," 41.   [117] HertsA D/P 105 25/1, E.
[118] BerksRO D/Q1 Q7/15.

Some foundation documents from the late fifteenth and early sixteenth centuries distinguished between the religious requirements of literate and illiterate residents. This again suggests that inmates of hospitals and almshouses were not necessarily the chronically poor who lacked all education, and it may possibly reflect a rising level of basic literacy. People who could not read often had to say a larger number of short prayers, which they had memorized, whereas literate ones might be obliged to pursue some of the daily round of masses as recited within monasteries and cathedrals. Statutes for Heytesbury Hospital laid out a fairly lengthy regimen of daily prayers for all of the residents, but then prescribed additional requirements for those who were "lettered."[119] At St. Nicholas's Hospital in Salisbury in 1478, entrants who were not lettered were to say the Psalter of Our Lady twice daily (adding up to 100 Aves, with ten Pater Nosters interspersed); those who could read the services of Placebo and Dirige were to recite them daily.[120] When Pykenham founded his almshouses in Hadleigh, he issued detailed instructions for attendance at church and the prayers to be said by all of the inhabitants. Those able to read were to say additionally Matins, Prime, the Hours of Our Lady, and the Psalm of De Profundis each day, as well as the Seven (Penitential) Psalms, the Litany, Placebo, and Dirige once each week.

In addition to the paramount obligation to pray, residents of a few late medieval almshouses had to conform to certain behavioral requirements.[121] While good conduct was valued for social reasons, making the inmates more congenial and reliable members of the institution and the community around it, founders may also have thought that "God would incline his ear more readily to the prayers of the righteous."[122] So that residents could fulfill their religious duties and maintain proper morality, they were commonly required to remain in the house, not wandering about the town or elsewhere. At God's House, Ewelme, residents were not to be away from the house or church for more than an hour and were never to walk about in the parish; those who left the institution for more than a day were fined a small amount.[123] (Judging by the large number of fines recorded in the early sixteenth century, however, some people were willing to pay for the freedom to be away.) Apart from the limited number

---

[119] "Ancient Statutes." Residents who were not literate were to be taught the necessary prayers by the keeper and examined once each year for their ability to recite them. If an inmate failed to learn the prayers, he was to be punished by fasting or in other ways.

[120] *Fifteenth Century Cartulary*, 2. For below, see Had!TR MS 25/29.

[121] See McIntosh, *Controlling Misbehavior*, 116–19, for further discussion.

[122] Rawcliffe, "Medicine for the Soul," esp. 331.

[123] UNottL MS Mi 6/179/18. For below, see, e.g., accounts for 1499–1500, 1511–12, and 1512–13 (BodlL MS D.D. Ewelme.c.2, E.A.1).

of houses that admitted married couples, the inhabitants were not to allow members of the opposite sex into their rooms. They were forbidden to haunt alehouses or play illegal betting games, and within the house, they were often told not to spread malicious gossip or quarrel with their fellows. Residents of Saffron Walden's almhouse were to be "of good and honourable intercourse, not ribald nor inebriate nor immoderate nor quarrelsome nor chiding one another."[124] The statutes of Browne's Hospital specify that a resident should not be "a provoker of hatred, anger, discord, envy, contumely, strife, brawling, or quarrels of any kind," not engage in open fornication or adultery, and not frequent taverns or keep hawks and hounds.[125]

The founders or re-founders of an occasional late medieval institution were unwilling to accept begging on the part of their residents.[126] That policy meant that the house needed a sufficiently large endowment and/or adequate income from ongoing charitable contributions to cover all the needs of the inmates, and it accentuated the desirability of having residents wear a special badge or livery when leaving the institution. The statutes of St. Nicholas's Hospital in Salisbury from 1478 instructed the master to "not permit or allow any of the brothers and sisters to go begging through the streets or parishes."[127] The five poor men housed at Holy Trinity almshouse in Dartford, Kent, endowed by William Milett in 1500, were to receive 4d. per week provided they did not beg. Normally, however, institutions assumed that some fraction of their residents' support would come through individual solicitation of alms. Nor was there any expectation that inmates would work to help support themselves. On the contrary, the statutes of Browne's Hospital state that none of the residents "shall occupy himself or herself in any servile manual or labouring work, or in any manner carry on the same publicly or privately, save when they are so engaged for the repairing and mending their own necessaries; and even that let it be done secretly in their own rooms at especially fitting times."[128] Inmates might, however, be expected to keep their own rooms and the public spaces of the house swept and clean, to prevent infection.

---

[124] Steer, "Statutes," 168–9. If residents continued in such behavior after three warnings, they were to be expelled.

[125] Wright, Story of the "Domus Dei," 36. For below, see, e.g., BerksRO D/Q1 Q7/15 and UNottL MS Mi 6/179/18.

[126] E.g., Orme and Webster, English Hospital, 99, and UNottL MS Mi 6/179/18. Sherborne Almshouse's statutes said that if the master and supporting brotherhood obtained enough income to fill all obligations, the residents were not to beg in the town or elsewhere (DorsetHC D/SHA D24).

[127] Fifteenth Century Cartulary, 7. For below, see Sweetinburgh, Role of the Hospital, 103.

[128] Wright, Story of the "Domus Dei," 36–7, and see also "Ancient Statutes."

Institutional statutes indicate that masters were allowed a good deal of latitude in dealing with misconduct by inmates. At Salisbury's Hospital of St. Nicholas, any brother or sister who was "a frequent stirrer of strife" and did not improve after being twice warned by the master was to be expelled from the house.[129] According to the foundation deed of Hosyer's almshouse in Ludlow, a poor man or woman who was "obstinate, debateful, or of any other evil condition and will not be reformed" by the warden or his deputy was to be removed. The head of God's House, Ewelme could withhold the stipend of any member who was rebellious "in deed or in word" against his correction.[130]

Residents occasionally committed more serious offences. At the hospital of St. John the Baptist in Northampton, the construction of individual chambers for the inmates led to reports of "extravagances of food and clothing": they were warned by the bishop in 1381 to "abstain from revelling and drinking parties" in their own rooms.[131] A poor man belonging to the house of St. Trinity next to Crossbridge in Beverley was expelled from his place in 1449 for fornication and keeping a concubine. The "visitor" (outside supervisor) who inspected the Hospital of St. John the Baptist in Bridgwater, Som. in 1463 found that the brothers of the house were so badly behaved that he ordered that a dungeon be prepared, "fitted with stocks and fetters," for their correction.[132] At Ipswich's Sessions of the Peace around 1510, Alice Cavel of the borough's almshouse was reported for receiving suspicious items that had probably been stolen by thieves and for traveling around the countryside to sell them.

We can observe how the various categories of benefits and obligations might be linked in practice through the foundation document of a small and fairly informal institution, Roger Reede's almshouse in Romford, Essex. Reede's will, written in 1483, indicates that his institution (for which he had already erected a special building) was intended for five local men who were "no blasphemers of the name of almighty God" and "no common beggars but such as have been of good governance and be fallen in poverty."[133] They had their own rooms, but were to use the great hall as a common area, provided that they stayed on good terms with each other. In return for free housing, a stipend of 6d. weekly, and a load of wood each year, the almsmen had to pray daily, either in their own dwellings or in the parish church; they were to attend divine services

[129] *Fifteenth Century Cartulary*, 7. For below, see ShropsA 356/315.
[130] UNottL MS Mi 6/179/18.
[131] Prescott, *English Medieval Hospital*, 47. For below, see HMC, *Report on MSS of the Corp. of Beverley*, 134.
[132] *Bridgwater Borough Archives*, xiv–xv. For below, see SuffRO-I C 8/4/1, fol. 29.
[133] EssexRO-Ch D/Q 26, for the rest of this paragraph.

every Sunday and holy day, and when they came to church, they were to gather around Reede's tomb, praying for his soul and those of his wife and "all [his] good friends." The inmates were also obligated to come to Reede's commemorative services, losing a week's wages if they were not present at the beginning and ending of those masses. The almshouse had no staff, but if any of the residents fell sick, the others were to take care of him. The residents were required also to accept the authority of the man named by the feoffees who held the house's property as its "ruler," the most serious and wise of their membership. They could not leave the institution for more than a day and night without the ruler's permission. Although they were not to marry after entering the almshouse, if already wed their wife might join them; widows of almsmen could retain their places and a reduced annual salary of 6s. 8d. if they were older than 50 years and well behaved.

3.4   The governance of institutions

The founder of a medieval hospital or almshouse had to decide how the institution was to be governed. A master (or warden or keeper), often a member of the clergy, could be named to handle the day-to-day administration of the house, but who would supervise its operations, make policy decisions, and – if it had a landed endowment – hold its property? Marked changes between periods are visible in the type of governance put in place by founders, although the form of control was sometimes altered later. Information from the database indicates that of hospitals founded prior to 1350 but still in existence after that time, more than half were to be run by a religious house (see Appendix E). Some of these institutions had been set up by monasteries or convents themselves, while others were created by outsiders who designated a religious house as overseer and custodian of land. Another third of the pre-1350 foundations were entirely self-governing. The house held its own property and was subject to no external supervision at all. Although a few of these institutions had been formally incorporated, thereby allowed to hold property collectively and to plead as a personage in the courts, they were particularly vulnerable to loss of income, the appointment of unsuitable candidates, and internal disputes. Only one-tenth of the early foundations were governed by any kind of existing lay-run institution, private lay feoffees, or other bodies.

The later medieval years, however, saw a major shift. Only 15 percent of all institutions founded between 1350 and 1539 for which we have information were assigned to monastic houses. This seems surprising, as there was no reason to foresee the impermanence of religious bodies that was to have such devastating consequences in the 1530s. Donors may have come to feel that religious houses had so many concerns – including, in some cases, properties spread over several counties – that they did not take personal interest in the wellbeing of a single charitable institution and hence did not supervise it adequately or protect its property fully. They may also have worried about misuse of funds by ecclesiastical bodies. As Caroline Barron has suggested for late medieval London, when monastic officials "who, if not deliberately dishonest, were clearly incompetent stewards," failed to care for the secular properties assigned to religious houses, potential donors must have been discouraged from "entrusting their hard-won fortunes to those who were incapable of conserving them."[134] Further, although the proportion of hospitals that were entirely self-governing rose slightly, only 3 percent of almshouse founders chose to have no external oversight. After 1350 we see instead a substantial increase in the proportion of houses whose governance was assigned to an existing organization run by lay people: a town, parish, fraternity, urban guild, or school.[135] A quarter of the new hospitals and nearly half of the almshouses were placed under the supervision of one of those bodies. Their members, experienced at dealing with finances and people, were presumably thought likely to provide more knowledgeable and effective local control over the institution.

Cities and towns played an important role.[136] When John Ake described his new house for twenty poor people, he stipulated that the Twelve Keepers of Beverley should hold the land that provided income for the institution and name its residents after the death of his wife.[137] In 1426, Robert Veel granted the property that supported his new almshouse in Ilchester to twenty feoffees initially, but he ordered that in 50 years their successors should obtain the necessary license to amortize the land and convey it and

---

[134] *London*, 267–8. London merchants commonly assigned their bequests for the poor to the newly incorporated city companies instead.

[135] Although some religious fraternities included clerical members, they were generally dominated by lay people; although parishes performed both religious and secular functions, lay churchwardens were responsible for practical matters.

[136] Some towns provided part of the support for residential institutions or maintained their buildings without assuming full governance: e.g., HampsRO W/H1/19, SomstRO D/B/ bw/1662 and 1667, and *Henley Borough Records*, 214. In other cases, townspeople contributed to the founding or maintenance of an almshouse. In 1437–8, 145 residents of Sherborne plus eight outsiders contributed a total of £75 5s. towards the construction of Sherborne Almshouse. Their donations were recorded street by street within the ten neighborhoods of the town, with most gifts ranging between 4d. and 20s. (DorsetHC D/ SHA A11). For the association of hospitals and boroughs in the twelfth and thirteenth centuries, see Cullum, "Leperhouses" and Watson, "City as Charter."

[137] HMC, *Report on MSS of the Corp. of Beverley*, 147. For below, see *Ilchester Almshouse*, 111–12. For the costs of obtaining that license, totaling £81, see ibid., 131–4; for transfer to the bailiffs and burgesses in 1477, see ibid., 136–9.

supervision of the house to the bailiffs of the town of Ilchester in perpetuity. The almshouse in Saffron Walden was governed by twenty-four leading townsmen on behalf of the community, according to its statutes of 1400.[138] After the death of Bishop Bubwith, his executors reached an agreement in 1437 with officials of the town of Wells, Som. concerning construction of the almshouse he had endowed and selection of its members. The re-organization of Sherborne Almshouse in 1437–8 included creating a lay fraternity of twenty town leaders who were henceforth to govern the institution.[139] The chamberlain of Hull paid weekly stipends to the poor people of John Gregg's new maison dieu in 1464–5, and town officials in Grimsby, Lincs. appointed the head of its spittlehouse in 1517.[140] A convocation in Salisbury noted in 1534 that a local man had bequeathed to the city five almshouses, to be administered by the mayor and his brethren, plus two other houses whose rents were to support the charitable dwellings.

By the early sixteenth century, a limited number of institutions were operated and supervised by parishes or their churchwardens.[141] Because almshouses rarely had their own priests, altars, and burial grounds, they did not pose the same kind of threat to parish rights as had earlier hospitals. One of the first foundations to have the term "almshouse" in its title, Trinity Almshouse in Dartford, for which a royal charter was granted in 1453, was to be governed by the vicar and churchwardens of the town.[142] In Lambeth, Surrey, the parson and eight parishioners agreed in 1518 that the church-wardens were henceforth to have the right to appoint "feeble people" into the almshouse, to expel them for unreasonable offences, and to use the value of any goods left by the residents after their deaths towards repair of the house. Peter Edgcumbe of Drewsteignton, Devon bequeathed to the parish in 1546 a little house made of granite, adjoining the lychgate into the churchyard, to be used as an almshouse.[143]

Other late medieval hospitals and almshouses were controlled by religiously focused fraternities composed mainly of lay members or by craft or merchant guilds in the towns.[144] The Guild of the Holy Cross in Stratford-

---

[138] Steer, "Statutes," 180–3. Day-to-day administration was to be carried out by a male and a female keeper. For below, see HMC, *Eighth Report*, Appendix, "MSS of Bishop Bubwith's Almshouses," 639.
[139] Dyer, *Standards of Living*, 245–6. The governors also appointed the residents, who appear in some cases to have been their own relatives.
[140] *Selected Rentals*, 96, and NELA 1/102/1, fol. 169r. For below, see Wilts&SA G23/1/2, fol. 278r.
[141] See also ch. 4.2.2 below.
[142] Bailey, *Almshouses*, 65–6. For below, see CWA #94, pt. 1, 24–5.
[143] Bailey, *Almshouses*, 90.
[144] Rawcliffe has identified a minimum of fifty such almshouses between 1348–9 and 1547 ("Dives Redeemed?").

upon-Avon provided much of the funding for the town's almshouses in the fifteenth and early sixteenth centuries and handled the distribution of stipends and bequests to them.[145] Governance of the Hospital of St. Thomas outside Micklegate Bar in York was transferred in 1478 from the members of the house themselves to the master of the Guild of Corpus Christi in York and its wardens, brothers, and sisters. In London, incorporation of the guilds enabled them to become "the repositories of charitable trusts," in some cases administering large estates that supported almshouses among other activities.[146] Thus, the Vintners' Company was bequeathed property in 1446 to support an almshouse for thirteen poor men and women. The Drapers' Company of Shrewsbury ran an almshouse from 1480 onwards, spending money for repairs of the building, wood for the poor residents, and – in some years – cash payments or food for them.[147]

In a pattern that was to become even more marked after 1540, an eighth of the late medieval hospitals and two-fifths of the almshouses were to be governed by private lay feoffees, a body of men who held the institution's property and provided oversight. (See Appendix E.) Roger Reede's almshouse in Romford was to be supervised initially by five feoffees, local men to whom Reede had previously granted the property that would support the house; when they died, sixteen highly respected community leaders were to replace them.[148] In 1530, Sir William Fitzwilliam, Chancellor of the Duchy of Lancaster, arranged that a parcel of land in Guildford, Surrey, "upon which is newly erected a certain Alms House," should be conveyed to eight men, several of them knights or esquires, apparently the first feoffees of the institution he was founding.

Because the practical operation of a late medieval hospital or almshouse was fraught with potential problems, including the negligence or greed of those responsible for it, Parliament at several times during the fifteenth and earlier sixteenth centuries discussed possible remedies for such maladministration.[149] A bill drafted by several Lollard knights and submitted to Parliament in 1407 or 1410 offered the radical proposal that some of the temporal properties (land and other sources of non-spiritual income) of bishops, abbots, and priors be seized by the crown and converted to

---

[145] E.g., ShakespCLA BRT1/3/20, BRT1/3/56, and BRT1/3/113, all used through A2A. For below, see *Register of the Guild of Corpus Christi*, 270–3.
[146] Barron, *London*, 225, for this and below.   [147] "Earliest Book," 164–220, passim.
[148] EssexRO-Ch D/Q 26. The feoffees were also to have the right to appoint the residents. For below, see WSussRO SAS-BA/8, used through A2A.
[149] For the obstacles faced by these institutions, see Chs. 9.1.2 and 9.2 below and McIntosh, "Negligence, Greed."

charitable uses.[150] Because priests and other religious men had "full nigh destroyed all the houses of alms within the realm," one of the goals of this disendowment bill was to found 100 new almshouses, each of which would receive land worth 100 marks (£66 13s. 4d.) annually; the houses would be overseen by "good and true scholars." A less dramatic but successful measure introduced by the Commons in 1414 commented that many English hospitals were at that time decayed, their goods and profits misappropriated by both churchmen and lay people; as a result, numerous poor men and women "have died in great misery for default of aid."[151] Parliament therefore instructed certain ecclesiastical officials to inspect those hospitals founded by previous monarchs or under royal patronage and to submit a report to Chancery; the visitors were themselves to order necessary reforms for all other hospitals. A petition submitted to Parliament probably in the 1510s was written nominally by "the poor, blind, lame, sore, miserable, and impotent people of this land" who were forced to beg and starve because of the failings of masters of hospitals, but it also reflected the interests of the heirs of founders.[152]

Such measures did not stop the gradual withering away of some residential institutions. During the later medieval years, many houses took in fewer inmates, stopped serving the poor, or provided fewer benefits, even if they did not close entirely. The Hospital of Sts. James and John in Brackley, Northants., founded around 1150, was said in 1423 to contain no inmates and no religious rule, due to insufficient revenues.[153] Two years later it was merged with the former leper hospital of St. Leonard's and re-constituted, but now the combined unit provided only a weekly loaf of bread to six local poor people plus one night of free housing for needy travelers. When John Plumptre obtained a license in 1392 to found a hospital in Nottingham, he said the house was to consist of thirteen old and poor widows and two chaplains (one of whom was to act as master).[154] A few decades later, the house contained seven widows, but by

---

[150] *Selections from English Wycliffite Writings*, 135–7 and notes. I am grateful to Paul Cavill for this reference and those in the next two notes. That draft echoes Piers Plowman's complaint from the second half of the fourteenth century that whereas in the past Charity had spent time with bishops and archbishops, who shared Christ's patrimony with the poor, now Avarice keeps the keys to the church's wealth, which is handed over to the children, kinsmen, servants, and heirs of its leaders (Langland, *The Vision of Piers Plowman* [B-Text], Passus 15, ll. 244–8).

[151] 2 Henry V, stat. 1, c. 1, *SR*, vol. 2, 175.

[152] TNA-PRO E175/11/65, with damaged words supplied by BritL Add MS 24459, 157–60.

[153] *VCH Northamptonshire*, vol. 2, 151–3, and HMC, *Fourth Report*, "MSS of Magdalen College, Oxford," 459, for this and below.

[154] NottsA M 13,044 and 13,046 for this and below.

1545 it housed only the two priests and was described as a chantry. St. John's Hospital in Calne, Wilts. contained no poor people in the later 1540s: its annual income of 66s. 5d. went to the master alone.[155]

Although residential institutions were thus performing a useful service, their impact was limited. The number of houses was modest in comparison to the population as a whole, they harbored some people we would not consider to be poor, and they were unevenly distributed within the country and between types of communities. Yet during a period when poverty was generally mild, a place in a hospital or almshouse for one person from every one-and-a-half to two parishes may have made a real contribution to the support of the bedridden, disabled, and elderly poor.

This material sheds light on broader questions too. Catholic teachings about tending the sick, assisting the poor, and prayer together with a culture of gift-giving and deference encouraged donors to found or contribute to hospitals and almshouses and their residents. The shift after 1350 in the nature of intended residents – away from clerics, travelers, and people who were ill in favor of the local elderly poor, including women – stemmed from different priorities about which particular kinds of people warranted assistance, not from increased discrimination between deserving and undeserving recipients of aid. The evidence presented here shows a decline in new foundations between the 1310s and the 1360s, but does not indicate a hardening of attitudes towards the poor in the wake of the plague. Houses established during the later medieval years had a weaker religious definition than earlier ones, and the infrequent use of distinguishing clothing suggests limited concern with the group identity of the residents. In geographic terms, the concentration of late medieval institutions – especially almshouses – in East Anglia and the southeast, with a secondary cluster of hospitals in the north and northwest, implies that founders were responding to alterations in the distribution of population and wealth. The importance of market centers as the location of later houses parallels their importance in other respects.[156] Appointment of residents and enforcement of behavioral rules created new opportunities for patronage and the exercise of authority for founders and governors of institutions. Many features of later medieval institutions, including the increased preference among founders for lay rather than religious governance, dislike of begging, and requirements for good behavior on the part of residents, were to be magnified later in the sixteenth century.

---

[155] Clay, *Mediaeval Hospitals*, 225.
[156] E.g., McIntosh, *Controlling Misbehavior*, chs. 6–7, her "Local Change," and see ch. 4.2.2 below.

4   Aid given through and by the parish

One of the institutions through which poor people sometimes received assistance during the later medieval and early Tudor periods was the parish. By the fourteenth century, its lay-elected officers, the churchwardens, were helping to maintain the church building and providing utensils for its services; later they gained additional religious and secular responsibilities. In the early fifteenth century we begin to have good runs of churchwardens' accounts. Although activity on behalf of the poor may not have been fully reported in their accounts, the records show that some wardens distributed alms donated by other people (gifts from the living or bequests from wills), and in at least a few settings they provided help from funds raised by their own parishes. Their aid joined whatever assistance was given by the chantries or lay religious fraternities housed within the church building and the alms that were sometimes handed out at funerals and commemorative services.[1]

This discussion engages with some recent scholarship arguing that late medieval communities were already carrying out forms of poor relief that earlier historians believed had emerged only with the late Elizabethan Poor Laws. Christopher Dyer linked assistance to the poor with the collection of subsidies, national taxes imposed usually on secular units called vills, but in a few instances on parishes.[2] Beginning in 1334, he noted, communities divided up responsibility for their total subsidy payment among their own members and gathered those sums, delivering them to royal officials. Certain testators in East Anglia made bequests to a "common box" for a fund from which tax payments levied on the vill were made; a few wills left sums specifically for taxes assessed on "the poor of the vill."[3] Dyer therefore proposed that "the association between tax payment and poor relief is likely to have emerged in the fourteenth

---

[1] For the former groups and their charitable functions, see ch. 1.4 above.

[2] Vills, small areas resembling modern townships, were the units upon which most subsidies were assessed.

[3] Dyer, "English Medieval Village Community," and his "Taxation and Communities."

century."[4] He implied that the activities of the vill were joined with those of the parish, that the common box of the former was the same as the box kept by churchwardens. He pointed out also that some parishes were building or acquiring almshouses in the second half of the fifteenth century and that church rates (local taxes) or "leys" were used as early as the 1520s in Prescot, Lancs.[5] In his Ford Lectures of 2001, Dyer made two further suggestions: in years when no subsidy was levied, income from land bequeathed for tax purposes was used to help the poor in other ways; and vills deliberately collected more for taxation than was needed, with the surplus available for distribution to the needy. Other areas of proposed continuity between late medieval and Tudor patterns concern the installation of a special box in the church to collect donations for the poor and some of the techniques used to raise funds for parishioners who needed help.[6]

To explore more fully the role of the medieval parish in poor relief, I have analyzed churchwardens' accounts or other records from fifty-eight parishes that survive for some period between 1404 and 1546, plus a few other ecclesiastical sources.[7] Nearly a quarter of these accounts said that the wardens distributed alms to needy individuals at some point. The assistance they gave, however, had often been bequeathed by other people and was in most cases occasional, unpredictable, and of low value (for example, a loaf of bread or a penny), not intended to provide regular support. Only a few parishes appear to have collected money specifically for the poor or to have provided ongoing help. This chapter first reviews the history of churchwardens and the techniques used to generate income for the parish as a whole. After noting the limitations of late medieval churchwardens' accounts, it describes what we know about how these officers functioned before 1547 as a conduit for aid to the poor as provided by others and how they raised or distributed help from their own funds.[8]

---

[4] Dyer, "English Medieval Village Community," 416. For below, see his *Standards of Living*, 256.

[5] Dyer, "English Medieval Village Community." For below, see his *An Age of Transition?*, 240, which cites his "English Medieval Village Community," 415–16, and his "Taxation and Communities," 187. Those pages refer to two wills that left money to help the poor pay taxes plus a will from 1434 that says that if no tax were imposed in a given year, the bequest should be used for ornaments for the church, but does not mention the poor.

[6] See ch. 4.2 below.

[7] The churchwardens' accounts or church/vestry books used are listed in pt. A of the References; they are cited in notes through the CWA # assigned to them there. For other sources, see the notes to App. F.

[8] The chapter does not describe the special situation of parishes linked to secular cathedrals, monastic-parochial churches, or chapels, for which see Lepine, "And Alle Oure Paresshens," Heale, "Monastic-Parochial Churches," and Orme, "Other Parish Churches."

4.1   Churchwardens and general fundraising activities

The parish emerged only gradually as a legally defined unit, able to hold property and act collectively in the courts. The office of churchwarden, described in various Latin and English terms, can be traced back to the thirteenth century as lay parishioners began to gain more authority within their neighborhood churches.[9] Most parishes had two wardens, but their number could go as high as four. Elected usually by the leading members of the parish, they served for one-year but renewable terms. By the sixteenth century, they were generally men of middling local rank: yeomen and prosperous husbandmen in rural communities, crafts people and smaller merchants in the towns.[10] Gentlemen rarely served as wardens, nor did those of lower status. Some men were happy to stay in office for several years at a time, while others sought to avoid the position.

The primary functions of the wardens were to take care of the church building and its contents (including keeping the nave in good repair) and to furnish equipment for divine services. By the late medieval years, some parishes carried out a range of activities designed to produce income for the church, provide sociability through religiously focused events, and organize commemorative services for those who had died. Wardens might also be charged with raising money with which to pay the salary of a parish clerk. In pre-Reformation Peterborough, Northants., the wardens "administered, bought, and sold property, organized collections on certain feasts, lent out money and various church goods, received testamentary bequests and contributions by local gilds, staged entertainments, and demanded fees for bell-ringing or burial, while spending money on church maintenance, ornaments, salaries, subsidies, bridge-building, legal matters, priests, and ceremonies."[11] Upon leaving office wardens were required to submit an oral and written account to their fellow parishioners of all income and expenditures, turning over any balance to their successors. Those annual accountings have been described as "a community-defining exercise that acknowledged the importance and uniqueness of a parish's own space, history and ritual."[12]

Wardens had further responsibilities that took them outside the parish. They were required to appear at the visitations held by their bishop or

---

[9] For convenient summaries, see Kümin, *Shaping of a Community*, ch. 2 and Burgess, "Time and Place."

[10] Houlbrooke, *Church Courts*, 151–2 and Craig, "Co-operation and Initiatives," for this and below. Most churchwardens were men, but for a few female wardens, see French, "Women Churchwardens."

[11] Kümin, *Shaping of a Community*, 23.

[12] Kümin, "Secular Legacy," 102, citing French, *People of the Parish*, 49.

archdeacon or his official. There they were given their "charge," articles of inquiry about religious and often social practices within their parish. That system of public reporting demanded that they describe any wrongdoing on the part of the local clergy and their lay neighbors. (We cannot assume, however, that all offenses were actually mentioned: wardens sometimes placed loyalty to their fellows above their duties as defined by the church and its courts.)[13] Wardens were also the legal representatives of the parish, able to sue and be sued on its behalf.[14]

To generate the money needed for their various functions, churchwardens during the fifteenth and first part of the sixteenth centuries engaged in a number of fundraising activities. Beat Kümin believes that when all of the types of income are added up, the annual amount brought in by pre-Reformation churchwardens normally exceeded the payments made to the Exchequer for subsidies and the money given to the clergy through tithes and other dues.[15] Most parishes solicited alms from their own members and sometimes outsiders to support their activities. Collections, taken usually at services, were nominally voluntary, although pressure to donate was presumably applied by the priest and wardens. The parish of Saffron Walden received the bulk of its income in 1439–40 from collections in the church.[16] Parishes might also impose obligatory rates on their members, at some fixed level of assessment.[17] Rates were typically employed for unusually costly projects, such as major repairs or improvements to the church. The "leys" assessed by churchwardens in Prescot on people living in the various sub-regions of that extensive parish in 1523–4 and the following year helped to cover the costs of casting and re-hanging new bells and repairs to the steeple; in 1529–30 another ley provided money for additional work on the bells and re-slating the church roof.[18] But Clive Burgess believes that by the 1460s and 1470s, some parishes were already using rates on a regular basis; as of 1480, punishments were

---

[13] Craig, "Co-operation and Initiatives."

[14] At least a few parishes had their own seals (New, "Signs of Community").

[15] Kümin, *Shaping of a Community*, 257. For below, see, e.g., French, "Parochial Fund-Raising," and her *People of the Parish*, ch. 4.

[16] CWA #38.

[17] For church rates, which were in use by the beginning of the fourteenth century and were usually based on the amount of land or number of animals a person held within the parish, see, e.g., Cannan, *History of Local Rates*, 14–16. Lists of rate payers were commonly recorded separately, not in the main churchwardens' accounts, and hence have not survived. Christopher Dyer has proposed that in collecting such rates, parishes extended the mechanism established for collecting subsidies in vills into a religious context ("Political Life").

[18] CWA #58, 2–9 and 12–14. There is no indication that these leys were used to assist the poor.

imposed on those who failed to contribute.[19] In 1520, Robert Hartwell of North Marston, Bucks. was called before the archdeacon's court for non-payment of 8d. annually in "alms" (or salary) for the parish clerk, an obligation said to be "of ancient custom."[20] Compulsory payments to the parish for specifically religious purposes were thus present at least as a concept a generation or more before Parliamentary legislation of the 1530s, 1540s, and 1550s required that they be used to support the poor.

Some churchwardens or lay groups within the parish used additional means to produce income. In Allhallows Church, London Wall in the later fifteenth and early sixteenth centuries, the wives of the parish, led by those married to the wardens, went door to door to request funds; in 1528–9 the parish received 24s. 8d. from the "gathering money of the wives." [21] That income supplemented what was received from regular collections in the church at communion services and from special gatherings at Christmas, the feasts associated with the Passion and Easter, and certain saints' days. In some parishes, contributions were made at plays, dances, or other rituals organized by associations or guilds within the parish as fundraising measures; the groups might be divided by marital status and sex, such as bachelors, maidens, and married women.[22] Hocktide, the second Monday and Tuesday after Easter, was particularly associated with revelries, often led by women, which produced money for church projects.

Further resources came through individual payments by the parishioners or others. Some were linked to the intercessory system, designed to obtain prayers for the dead.[23] Such income, unpredictable in timing and amount, included gifts or bequests to the parish; payments for burials, funerals, and the commemorative services known as obits, held a month or a year after a person's death; and donations when women were "purified" or "churched" after giving birth. In 1439 and 1440, churchwardens in Saffron Walden, Essex, received a total of £7 15s. from the bequests of seventeen people, four of them servants, plus 1d. each from fourteen women who came to the church to be purified.[24] Wardens of the suburban parish of Lambeth, Surrey accounted in 1515–16 for receipts of between 4d. and 3s. each for three "month's mind" services and 12d. for each of eleven "year's mind" obits. The parish was also paid for twenty-four burials, ranging from 2d. to 13s. 8d. each, depending upon the location of the grave.

[19] Personal communication.   [20] *Courts of the Archdeaconry of Buckingham*, 271.
[21] CWA #69, xix–xx; ibid., 60.
[22] E.g., French, *Good Women of the Parish*, esp. 120–32. For below, see ibid., 157–79.
[23] Burgess and Kümin, "Penitential Bequests," Burgess, "Benefactions of Mortality," his "London Parishioners," and his "Service for the Dead."
[24] CWA #38. For below, see CWA #94, pt. 1, 14–15.

Many parishes hosted "church ales." In this practice, a group within the parish used the church house or other large facility to brew a generous volume of ale, with supplies purchased by the parish. A cheerful evening of drinking ensued, held often within the church itself. The ale was sold, commonly accompanied by bread or cakes to keep the drinkers going, with all money received above expenses going for support of the church or some special project within it.[25] Church ales were popular throughout the country, for they simultaneously generated funds for the parish and promoted sociability and goodwill among the parishioners. In Bishop's Stortford, Herts., the churchwardens accounted in 1484 for expenses of 9s. 8d. for 9 bushels of malt and 4 bushels of wheat for an ale held at Hocktide, plus 21d. for brewing the ale and baking the bread.[26] In 1489, they recorded a net profit of 15s. from the "Hokking" ale, £4 6s. 8d. from "two drinkings called May Ales," and 11s. 2d. from "a drinking made by Sir John the Chantry Priest here and William Morse." The parish of Bassingbourn, Cambs. held nine ales in 1498, each yielding a net profit of between 5s. and 18s.[27]

A growing number of late medieval parishes maintained a stock of cash, animals, land, or houses that were then rented out to help support the church.[28] The stock was usually built up through bequests. In Allhallows parish, London Wall, churchwardens received 3s. 4d. in 1481–2 "for the loan of the church money," while St. Andrew Hubbard in London held several houses on long-term leases in 1454–6 that the wardens granted out for a few years at a time.[29] Thirteen parishes in Suffolk in 1524 had enough money in a church "box" to be taxed. In Wandsworth, Surrey, the churchwardens paid 15s. to each of four men in 1545–6 to buy cows for the parish stock; the cows were then rented out for 2s. 4d. annually, joining the urban tenements and land that the parish held and granted on short leases.[30] Stocks could also be operated by groups within the parish to help support their own projects, like maintaining a light in front of an image of their patron saint. In Chagford, Devon in the first half of the sixteenth century, a women's guild sold wool from its flock of sheep and rented out its brewing equipment.[31]

In order to secure the money belonging to the parish and its written records (churchwardens' accounts, deeds, inventories, and other documents), most churches had some kind of a chest or box in which valuable

[25] See, e.g., French, "Parochial Fund-Raising," and Bennett, "Conviviality and Charity."
[26] CWA #49b, 26. For below, see ibid., 20 and also 22.   [27] CWA #17.
[28] For bequests of land or animals to the church, see, e.g., Ault, "Village Church."
[29] CWA #69, 22, and CWA #70, 1–2. For below, see Dyer, "Political Life." Seven guilds or religious fraternities had similar "boxes," while sixty-one had stocks of other kinds.
[30] CWA #97, 83–4.   [31] French, *Good Women of the Parish*, 147–8.

items could be stored.[32] These chests usually had several locks, with the keys put into the separate keeping of the parish priest, the churchwardens, or an important parishioner. The chest was supposed to be opened only in the presence of all key-holders and other witnesses, to ensure that nothing was removed from it improperly. Church boxes appear in the records when they were built or needed repair, or when outgoing churchwardens rendered their accounts and new ones took over.[33] At St. Andrew Hubbard, London, churchwardens reported what they received "in the box when they came into office" in the 1450s, while wardens of St. Michael Spurriergate, York noted how much they were leaving "in the box" to their successors beginning in the mid-1530s.

4.2   Assistance to the poor within the late medieval parish

Some churchwardens in the fifteenth and first part of the sixteenth centuries distributed occasional aid to the poor. These alms had often been given by other individuals, with the wardens only handing them out, but in a few cases the money was generated within the parish itself. In awarding relief, churchwardens operated largely on their own, with little direction from higher levels of the church other than generic preaching in support of almsgiving and efforts to persuade testators to remember the poor. At least one bishop, however, tried to encourage more regular parish involvement with needy people. In an injunction to the churches in his diocese issued in 1451, Bishop Carpenter of Worcester reminded his audience that giving alms to the poor was one of the works of charity and that generosity would contribute to the remission of sins.[34] He then ordered the churchwardens of every parish to make a collection for the poor three times each year, backed by an indulgence of 40 days to each person who gave such alms.

Our understanding of the actual role of late medieval parishes and wardens in poor relief is, however, limited. Most of the evidence comes from churchwardens' accounts, which survive at least fragmentarily from several hundred late medieval parishes.[35] The difficulty is that some wardens may not have mentioned all of their activities in their accounts, especially matters that seemed peripheral to their central responsibilities for the church and its services. If, for example, they received and

---

[32] Kümin describes the chests as "archives and safes preserving the most cherished objects of communal heritage" ("Secular Legacy," 101).

[33] E.g., the parish of Wing, Bucks. paid 2d. to a smith in the mid-1530s for work on "the lock of the coffer" (CWA #16b, 316). For below, see CWA #70, 1–3, and CWA #118.

[34] Haines, "Bishop Carpenter's Injunctions."

[35] Kümin has identified 234 from *c.* 1300 to 1547 (*Shaping of a Community*, 265–9).

immediately distributed a bequest to needy people, or if they took a collection for the poor and delivered the money right away, they might not have bothered to record those actions. Therefore, one cannot argue that the absence of references to poor relief necessarily means that it was not occurring. The problem is most severe before around 1500, for many accounts become fuller thereafter; it largely disappears after 1547, when helping needy members became an explicit duty of parish officials. Another complication stems from the multiple and changing meanings of the words "alms" and "charity."[36] Just as the alms left by testators for the good of their soul could be devoted to diverse religious and charitable purposes, it is often impossible to be sure whether the offerings given to a parish church were intended to support its general religious and sociable activities or were intended more specifically for poor people.

I believe, however, that we can extract more information about aid to the poor from churchwardens' accounts than has usually been assumed. Some types of activity must have been recorded. If money was given to needy recipients out of normal parish funds, including alms collected for generic church purposes, the wardens would have needed to include those expenditures to balance their accounts. Further, even if some individual churchwardens did not record assistance to the poor, use of accounts from many different parishes enables us to describe in broad terms the kinds of activities in which wardens were engaged, while recognizing that our picture may be incomplete.[37]

Whereas the discussion of parochial involvement in poor relief in this and later chapters is primarily descriptive, I have also summarized the material in tabular, numerical form to facilitate comparison. The left side of Appendix F lists the various ways in which churchwardens obtained money for the poor and awarded it to needy recipients. Part A shows activities that acquired or protected such income, while Part B displays the forms of help given to the poor. The full chronological span from 1404 through 1598 is divided into four shorter periods, shown as separate columns, to highlight changes over time.[38] Two types of information are

---

[36] See ch. 1.1 above.

[37] Burgess has questioned whether it is useful to employ churchwardens' accounts in an attempt to determine wider patterns, as opposed to imbedding them within detailed studies of particular communities ("Pre-Reformation Churchwardens' Accounts" and his "The Broader Church?"), but see Kümin's response in "Late Medieval Churchwardens' Accounts," his *Shaping of a Community*, ch. 1, and French, *People of the Parish*, 44–67.

[38] Some of the churchwardens' accounts I examined survive for only part of the chronological spans employed (see pt. 1 of the References), and in a few cases I sampled particularly relevant sub-periods, focusing on the 1530s, 1547–53, the 1560s, and the 1590s.

provided within each period. The first sub-column notes the number of parishes that mention each activity based upon the churchwardens' accounts I used for that particular time span. For these numbers, a percentage can be provided since we know the total number of parishes under observation. The second sub-column indicates how many additional references I found in other sources. The last page gives the key to the symbols used and summarizes the sources.

4.2.1   A limited role in handling alms given or bequeathed by others

Although a substantial minority of testators left something for the poor, it appears that churchwardens were rarely asked to administer such bequests prior to 1547.[39] Normally the executors of wills, or in some cases the spouse of the deceased person, were charged with distributing alms. Thus, P. H. Cullum and Jeremy Goldberg found that about a quarter of 2,286 wills by lay testators in York during the fourteenth and fifteenth centuries left specific charitable bequests for money, food, drink, clothing, shoes, or fuel for needy people or dowries for poor maids' marriages, beyond the generic provision for "pious works."[40] But the authors saw no sign that churchwardens were expected to play a part in the distribution of these legacies.

A few statements in accounts and wills indicate, however, that at least occasionally churchwardens did allocate legacies to the poor. The wardens of St. Edmund's parish in Salisbury noted in 1500–1 that 4d. had been bequeathed for certain poor people living in "le bedridden row."[41] In 1532, Richard Collyer, a successful London mercer, left £3 annually for ten years to the churchwardens of Horsham, Norf. to buy herring or other salt fish during Lent for poor inhabitants of the parish. Informal participation by wardens in the distribution of bequests may have increased in the late fifteenth and early sixteenth centuries as more testators began to specify that their alms should go to the poor of a specific parish.[42] In such cases, the churchwardens or the priest may have been asked to recommend recipients. This study has not found evidence that late medieval parishes administered bequests that helped poor people to pay their taxes.[43]

---

[39] See ch. 1.4 above.
[40] Cullum and Goldberg, "Charitable Provision." For below, see ibid., and personal communication from Goldberg.
[41] CWA #106, 53. For below, see Willson, *History of Collyer's School*, 192–4. I am grateful to Beat Kümin for this reference.
[42] See, e.g., Fleming, "Charity, Faith."
[43] The few instances in which East Anglian testators left money to assist those for whom subsidies were a hardship were handled by secular officials, not by churchwardens. The two fifteenth-century bequests for this purpose cited by Dyer were granted to a town and a

Another form of aid came from the alms bestowed at funerals or obits. While these donations were a form of Christian charity, they also encouraged the presence and prayers of needy people whose intercession for the soul of the deceased was thought to be especially efficacious. No effort appears to have been made to limit recipients to the most deserving poor. Of testators in the city of Salisbury and other parts of Wiltshire, Berkshire, and Dorset who specified a funeral between 1270 and 1547, 54 to 58 percent referred to the presence of the poor.[44] But, as Miri Rubin concluded from her study of Cambridge, "giving [to the poor] at funerals seems to have been aimed at procuring a variety of benefits for the dead, not at alleviating the lot of intercessors."[45] Testators who left sums for obits might similarly instruct that something be awarded to the needy who came to pray for them. Poor people would have been alerted to these opportunities by the tolling of church bells or, in some urban settings, by a beadle or town crier who announced the services.[46]

We cannot be certain to what extent churchwardens were involved in these activities. At funerals, executors normally handled gifts to the poor. Wardens perhaps played a more direct role in awarding whatever alms were provided at obits: executors might convey all of the necessary funds to them after the testator's death for later distribution. Because it is generally impossible to determine whether it was executors or churchwardens who received and distributed bequests to the poor and gave out alms at funerals and memorial services, I did not attempt to quantify those actions in Appendix F, providing instead a rough verbal indication of the wardens' probable degree of involvement, under headings A1 and B1–2.

The value and impact of the alms given out at these services is likewise difficult to measure, for when churchwardens accounted for obits, they rarely specified how much had been given to the poor. In the wealthy parish of All Saints', Bristol, however, a few records from the late fifteenth century indicate that alms worth 12d. to 20d. were distributed to needy local people at obits, constituting an eighth to a quarter of the full amount expended.[47] In some communities in the later fifteenth and early sixteenth centuries, distributions to the poor who assiduously attended funerals and

vill, not to parishes ("English Medieval Village Community," 416); Alice Dixe's late medieval bequest, part of which was to pay the taxes assessed on poor parishioners in Icklingham, Suff., was likewise assigned to the town (SuffRO-BSE 1871/19–20).

[44] A. Brown, *Popular Piety*, 199. Christine Peters found that in the diocese of Worcester, 1509–47, women were more likely than men to specify that bequests to the poor were to be distributed at their funerals or obits (*Patterns of Piety*, 55–6).

[45] Rubin, *Charity and Community*, 262. Burgess notes that bread given to the poor at such services was commonly baked into small "farthing loaves" (i.e. quarter size) in order to oblige as many paupers as possible to pray for the deceased ("Service for the Dead").

[46] Burgess, "Service for the Dead," and CWA #40b, 135 (bis).

[47] E.g., CWA #40b, 135–6.

anniversaries may have provided a nice source of supplemental income.[48] Alan Kreider estimated that obits, lights in honor of saints, and other lesser intercessory institutions should together have provided about £90 annually to the poor in four sample counties in 1546 to 1548, but such almsgiving was not always carried out as intended.[49] Moreover, doles at funerals and obits were often distributed as small amounts of food or drink to be consumed on the spot. Of a sample of Sussex wills between 1500 and 1546, 46 percent of the testators who left alms for the poor at their services specified that it should be awarded in kind, rather than as cash.[50] For needy people, money that could be taken home and employed for whatever purposes they wished might have been preferable.

4.2.2 Obtaining and distributing money for the poor from the parish's resources

The left-most pair of chronological columns in Appendix F summarizes information about parishes' own activities for the poor between the early fifteenth century and the final years of Henry VIII's reign. Of the fifty-eight parishes whose accounts were used, sixteen (28 percent) recorded some kind of involvement in at least a single year. One cluster of active parishes was located in major cities or suburban villages (three in London, two in Bristol, one in York, and one in Lambeth, Surrey), while another group consisted of seven prosperous market centers or county towns.[51] Many of these smaller communities had a growing proportion of wealthy residents, thanks to the woolen cloth industry or their position as trading centers on main roads, as well as a group of poor people dependent upon wages. Just two of the parishes were in rural villages.[52] A modest level of parish engagement with the poor is consistent with relatively mild poverty until at least the 1460s and only gradually increasing problems until the 1530s and 1540s.

Churchwardens seem to have made little effort prior to 1547 to raise funds expressly for poor parishioners (see Part A of Appendix F). Only three parishes, all in London, recorded collection of alms that may have

---

[48] Horden, "Small Beer?." Barbara Harvey has suggested that some of the poor living in London and its environs had mastered the calendar of anniversaries at which Westminster Abbey distributed alms, enabling them to take full advantage of the pennies handed out on such occasions (*Living and Dying*, 29–30).

[49] Kreider, *English Chantries*, 67–9, for this and below. The counties were Essex, Warws., Wilts., and Yorks.

[50] See CUP Online App. 8.

[51] Saffron Walden, Mildenhall, Suff., Bishop's Stortford, Louth, Lincs., Sherborne, Dorset, Ashburton, Devon, and Cambridge.

[52] Wing, Bucks. and Childrey, Berks. For below, see ch. 1.3 above.

been intended for the poor. In 1459–60, the wardens of Allhallows Church, London Wall received 2s. 6d. from "the men and women of the parish for the charity pot."[53] That pot, which is not mentioned thereafter, could have contained either charitable offerings for the church as a whole or money gathered for poor people. Wardens of St. Andrew Hubbard reported in 1488–9 that they had received 43s. 8d. "of alms in the street," another ambiguous wording.[54] At St. Mary at Hill, two men were said in 1512 to 1513 to have in their hands certain moneys "gathered of the alms in the church which shall be . . . reserved toward burials of poor people and other deeds of charity"; a decade later, the churchwardens paid 11s. 5 1/2d. out of the alms money for 25 quarters of coal "for the poor people."[55] The latter descriptions suggest that alms were collected for the church's general purposes, from which some were assigned to the poor. Although other medieval wardens may have used parish money to provide occasional assistance at times of need, my project found no evidence of regular levies to support the poor or of stocks that were to be rented out with the income earmarked for needy folks.[56]

Another potential source of assistance came from the drinking sessions commonly known as "help-ales," used occasionally prior to 1547 to raise money for individuals who had suffered some particular loss.[57] These occasions provided aid for the same kinds of people who might have qualified for a license to solicit charitable alms, but they were held in one's own community and avoided the possible embarrassment of asking for charity. Help-ales do not appear, however, to have been organized for the chronically poor, nor were they normally sponsored by the church or its wardens (although parochial equipment might be rented for the purpose). Some drinking sessions were hosted by people who had themselves fallen into sudden need, who had to pay for the brewing but were then allowed to keep the sums paid by their guests for ale.[58] Alternatively, a

---

[53] CWA #69, 7. The parish had a box used for keeping church money and a "great chest" in the vestiary (ibid., e.g., 3, 7, and 8).

[54] CWA #70, 54.

[55] CWA #71, pt. I, 284; ibid., 318. The parish also received contributions to pay for the burials of poor men in 1491–2 and 1521–2 (ibid., 171 and 314).

[56] In a statement for which no reference is provided, Hampson said that at Great St. Mary's church in Cambridge, a customary collection on behalf of the poor was made after divine service in 1515 (*Treatment of Poverty*, 2). Although the gathering relied nominally on "every man's goodwill," each person evidently gave according to a prearranged rate, "by a certain roll." That date seems unlikely to be correct.

[57] Bennett, "Conviviality and Charity," for this paragraph.

[58] The most detailed example in Bennett's paper comes from a sixteenth-century ballad concerning a minstrel from Tamworth, Staffs. who had been robbed of £60 that he had collected to repay his debts; when his neighbors urged him to brew some ale and sell it, he raised the improbably large – and hence humorous – sum of £5 from their drinking (ibid., 19).

neighbor could put on a help-ale for someone else's benefit, as happened in the sprawling manor of Wakefield, W. Yorks. during the fifteenth century. In a few cases, "parishioners" or "the parish" organized or assisted with help-ales on behalf of named people, although the records do not say why the beneficiaries needed money.[59] Judith Bennett has claimed that "church-ales also directly benefited the poor, for in many parishes they raised funds for general poor relief."[60] In support of that statement, she cited a nostalgic comment by John Aubrey, written in the second half of the seventeenth century, about circumstances prior to the Reformation and enclosures.[61] The sources used for the present study did not reveal any help-ales or church ales that generated money for the poor of the parish prior to the Edwardian years.[62]

A key question is when parishes began to use a special box for collecting and storing money for the poor. Churchwardens who had no mechanism for keeping such alms separate from other parish income were more likely to grant them out immediately, as one-time gifts, whereas if they had some kind of designated container in which to reserve the funds, they could distribute assistance as needed over time. The presence of a collection box for the poor situated publicly in the church might also promote giving by the parishioners. In exploring this question, we must be careful not to conflate the generic church chests found in most parishes with boxes intended particularly for alms. The accounts of All Saints', Bristol include multiple references between 1437 and 1491 to boxes that stored deeds and other evidences and to a "treasure coffer" in which the parish's money was kept, but there is no mention of a box used for alms, despite the fact that Bishop Carpenter (who ordered trice-yearly collections for the poor) was directly involved in that parish.[63] Confusion may stem as well from

---

[59] Bennett cites two instances from Cratfield, Suff. in the 1490s, an undated reference from East Budleigh, Devon, and a final one without place-name or date (ibid., 28 and n. 29).

[60] Ibid., 27.

[61] Aubrey's reminiscence, from around 1659–70, does not provide unambiguous support for Bennett's statement. When describing in glowing terms the neighborly conditions that had formerly existed, Aubrey alleges that there were no rates for the poor even as late as his grandfather's day; other sources of income helped needy people. One of the earlier techniques was that every parish had a church house that hosted ales to raise funds for parish and charitable uses. In one parish, the church ale held at Easter was used to pay the parish clerk, while in another the Whitsuntide ale produced money for the poor (*Wiltshire*, 10–11).

[62] Katherine French, who has worked with many churchwardens' and guild accounts from the fifteenth and earlier sixteenth centuries, likewise encountered no parishes that sponsored ales to raise money for poor relief, although she noted that possibly they were not recorded in the accounts (personal communication).

[63] CWA #40b, 68–138, passim. Clive Burgess has found no evidence that the treasury chest was ever used by the churchwardens to provide charitable doles (personal communication).

occasional use of the term "alms chest" to refer to a stock of money donated by a benefactor, to be loaned to poor people.[64]

It has for some time been a commonplace among historians that a box for the poor was required by a statute of 1536. That is not, however, an entirely accurate reading. The 1536 measure, the primary intent of which was to clamp down on vagabonds and beggars by instituting a system of care for the poor within their own parishes, ordered civic officers and churchwardens to collect money for the poor on Sundays and holy days.[65] They were to gather up the money using some kind of box, perhaps so they could not be suspected of slipping it into their own pockets. Assistance was no longer to be given to the poor by individuals, but delivered only to these "common boxes and common gatherings." All alms collected by churchwardens were to be kept safely until spent, either placed into "the common coffer or box standing in the church of every parish" or given into the hands of a substantial and trusty parishioner. The common coffer evidently refers to the traditional parish chest, not to a special box for the poor. Moreover, the 1536 act remained in effect for no more than 6 months, and I know of only a single case in which a parish may possibly have set up an alms box in response to it.[66]

More recently, some scholars have claimed that boxes for the poor had been mandated much earlier. Dyer wrote: "By the mid-fifteenth century, church-wardens were keeping a parish box for donations, from which alms were distributed at their discretion."[67] The source cited for that statement is the injunctions issued by Bishop Carpenter of Worcester in 1451. Steve Hindle extended Dyer's statement slightly, noting that churchwardens had been required since the mid fifteenth century "to keep a parish 'poor box', usually kept in the church, into which donations might be made and from which alms were distributed."[68] My research suggests that such assertions are probably not correct. Bishop Carpenter's orders said that after churchwardens had collected alms for the poor, they

---

[64] *Gild of St. Mary, Lichfield*, 19. Childrey, Berks. received a bequest of £4 in 1530 from a former rector of the parish, to be loaned in small batches to poor people of the community (CWA #4, at back of book).

[65] 27 Henry VIII, c. 25, *SR*, vol. 3, 558–62, discussed more fully in ch. 5.3 below.

[66] St. Dunstan in the East, London had an alms box by summer, 1536, to which income from a bequest was assigned and into which the vestry ordered that fines for non-submission of parish accounts be paid. Neither reference says that the alms box was for the poor, nor do we know whether it had been present for some time or had recently been installed to conform to the new legislation (TNA-PRO PROB 11/25, fol. 40v, July 27, 1536, and LondMA P69/DUN1/B/001/MS04887 [ex-GuLLond], fol. 72, November 4, 1537). Jennifer Ledfords kindly sent me these references and a transcript of the latter.

[67] Dyer, *Standards of Living*, 248. For below, see Haines, "Bishop Carpenter's Injunctions."

[68] Hindle, *On the Parish?*, 231.

were to count the money immediately in the presence of the curate(s) of the parish and designate it for the poor.[69] With the clergyman and other parishioners observing, it was then to be either delivered back into the hands of the churchwardens for distribution or put into the "common box" (*communi pixide*), where it was to be kept until given to the poor of the parish, with the advice of the curate. The "common box" again appears to refer to the main church chest, not to a separate box used for alms. Nor is there any indication that the bishop intended the box to be used between collections to solicit individual contributions.[70] Further, Carpenter's injunctions applied to a single diocese, and we do not know how effectively they were enforced even in that region.

Alms boxes are documented in a few pre-Reformation churches, but whether they were used for contributions for the parish's general needs or for the poor is unclear. In the parish of St. Mary at Hill, London, a memorandum in the churchwardens' accounts in 1517–18 noted that 30s. 9d. had been taken "out of the alms box" and used to pay a carpenter, reflecting the multiple uses of such contributions.[71] Physical evidence is inconclusive due to the difficulty of dating objects precisely and the poor preservation of early church furnishings. The latest editions of the series of county volumes prepared initially by Nikolaus Pevsner document only four or five alms boxes in parish churches that definitely or probably pre-date 1547.[72] In their study of English church furniture, Cox and Harvey listed a total of eleven parish boxes that they say were intended to collect alms and that date to the late fifteenth or early sixteenth century.[73] But one of them, described as having three locks, was mentioned in churchwardens' accounts in 1553, suggesting that it was probably one of the many boxes for the poor introduced during Edward's reign. Because the next chronological unit in Cox and Harvey's analysis is Elizabethan, it is likely that most of the other boxes assigned to their earlier period were likewise set up only in the Edwardian years. It is significant that when designated containers for collecting and storing money for the needy were installed beginning in 1547, they were almost always called "poor men's

---

[69] Haines, "Bishop Carpenter's Injunctions," esp. 206.

[70] Caroline Litzenberger found no wills from Gloucestershire earlier than 1547 that left bequests for the poor to a box (personal communication).

[71] CWA #71, pt. I, 299. The following year, the wardens ordered that "the money of the alms box be made account of" (ibid., 304).

[72] In Ludham, Norf., Old Leake, Lincs., Kedington, Suff., Car Colston, Notts., and perhaps Steeple Bumpstead, Essex (Pevsner, *The Buildings of England*, and later editions written with or by other authors). The volumes were searched using Good, *Compendium of Pevsner's Buildings of England*. Four other early alms boxes were located in a cathedral, a priory church, a royal chapel, and a hospital.

[73] Cox and Harvey, *English Church Furniture*, 240–1.

boxes" or some other term that distinguished them from alms boxes for general donations to the church.

Turning now to churchwardens' role in awarding aid to the poor, we find that nearly a quarter of the parishes in this sample (fourteen, or 24 percent) recorded some involvement (see Part B of Appendix F). Because this fraction was much larger than the number that reported raising money, most of the income probably came from gifts and bequests being channeled through the parish. Assistance was usually given in very small amounts and on particular occasions. Kümin's careful analysis of long runs of churchwardens' accounts from four metropolitan parishes, four market centers, and two rural villages shows that four of the parishes handed out some alms to the poor before 1547, using income derived from a variety of sources, but in tiny amounts that together constituted just 0.1 to 0.3 percent of the total expenditures of those churches.[74]

Beginning in the late fifteenth century, a few parishes distributed small gifts of food, drink, or money to poor people. The parish of Holy Trinity, Cambridge gave bread "to poor folk of the parish" several times each year between 1504–5 and 1511–12, while wardens in Cratfield, Suff. spent 3d. "in alms for the relief of Kempe, his wife, and their children" in 1534.[75] Alms might be bestowed on special religious occasions, as when church-wardens in Wing, Bucks. accounted for 3s. 4d. "that us gave to poor folk for charity" on All Soul's Day in 1543–4. Churchwardens of St. Ewen's, Bristol paid for loaves of bread and ale for poor people between 1492–3 and the end of Henry VIII's reign, but always on days when far more lavish food was purchased as well, probably for a dinner after the annual render-ing of parish accounts.[76] Use of generic terms like "the poor" or "poor folk" should not be taken as evidence that churchwardens were unselec-tive about who received alms. Unlike funerals and obits, wardens presum-ably applied their own criteria of worthiness and need when deciding how to distribute other kinds of aid. But poor people gained little more than symbolic assistance from a loaf of bread or a penny now and then.

Two goals were accomplished simultaneously by hiring poor people to do necessary work for the church (extra income for them, at low cost to the parish). This was usually short-term employment. Holy Trinity parish in Cambridge paid poor men in 1517–18 for cleaning the gutter beside the

---

[74] Kümin, *Shaping of a Community*, 276–315, passim; explanations on 270–4. Kümin defined as poor relief all payments to the poor, orphans, and widows, but excluded general alms given at obits (273).

[75] CWA #18, P22/5/1, fols. 11v–86v, passim, and *Cratfield*, 49. For below, see CWA #16b, 318.

[76] CWA #41, 137–84, passim. For below, see, e.g., CWA #38, from 1457–8 and 1459–60, CWA #49b, 33, and ch. 2.2 above.

church wall and removing dust from the church.[77] In 1538, St. Michael Spurriergate, York gave a poor man 2d. to help a dauber make mortar and carry it for a day and a half; four years later it paid 2d. to another needy man for going to Tadcaster to fetch lime. Occasionally, however, the work was more regular. In the 1520s, St. Mary at Hill, London paid 2d. to three almsmen (probably the same bedesmen who received money each week from a chantry in the parish church) "when they do blow the organs" for services.[78] Sherborne parish in Dorset likewise made use of the labor of bedesmen in the 1530s. Either individually or as a group, they received small sums for carrying away a dung hill from the churchyard, cleaning out the church gutters, and keeping watch over the sepulcher at Easter.[79] In an entry that confirms the presence of needy people with some education, Saffron Walden paid a half-penny in 1470 to a poor man for writing up the churchwardens' annual account.

A few urban or suburban communities provided more substantial aid to a selected group of poor people who were granted places in almshouses partially supported by the parish or were helped with the cost of housing.[80] Residents of the parish almshouse of All Saints in Bristol are mentioned in bequests from 1509 and 1532.[81] Our Lady's Bede House in Louth was run mainly by the town, but the churchwardens of St. James, a parish closely associated with urban government, paid for repairs to its building in 1503–4.[82] When the churchwardens of St. Mary at Hill, London paid for tiling "the poor men's houses" in 1491–2, the beneficiaries may have been the three almsmen assisted by the chantry.[83] Some time before 1548, the parishioners of St. Clement Danes in London built a hall in the churchyard, granting the rooms underneath it to poor people without paying rent. At St. Michael Spurriergate in York, churchwardens in the 1540s excused all or part of the rents due from some of the people living in tenements owned by the parish, and they cancelled the 10s. of arrears owed by Miles Axby when he left his dwelling in 1545, "because he was a poor man and fallen in poverty."[84]

---

[77] CWA #18, P22/5/1, fols. 53v–54r. For below, see CWA #118, fols. 148r and 181r.
[78] CWA #71, pt. I, 328, and see 110–211, passim.
[79] DorsetHC Transcripts (of PE/SH CW 1/4–17), 260, 53. For below, see CWA #38.
[80] Twelve almshouses founded between 1350 and 1539 in my database were to be run or supervised by parishes: see App. E and ch. 3.4 above.
[81] *Pre-Reformation Records of All Saints' Church*, 47 and 52.
[82] CWA #65, 7/1, and see ibid., 7/2, fols. 7v–41v, passim.
[83] CWA #71, pt. I, 174. In 1494–5 the churchwardens paid for making a pew for the poor people; by 1502–3, a special bell was rung for them (ibid., 215, and 246). For below, see Barron, *London*, 299.
[84] CWA #118, fols. 193v–217r, passim, esp. 205v.

In the only instance encountered in these records of a practice that was later to expand greatly, churchwardens in Ashburton gave weekly alms to a few poor people in the mid-1540s. In 1543–4 and 1544–5, the wardens of this market town, made prosperous in the fifteenth and earlier sixteenth centuries by trade in tin and wool, laid out a total of 30s. 5d. to three men and a woman, each of whom received 1d. or 2d. every week.[85] For the poor, the predictability of such assistance must have provided far greater security than occasional doles.

The picture sketched here confirms that late medieval parishes had the capacity to gather and distribute money for the poor and that more than a quarter were starting to do so in some fashion. The active parishes were located almost entirely in major cities and market centers, concentrated in East Anglia and the southwest. Although poverty-related activities may have been incompletely recorded in early churchwardens' accounts, the observed pattern is that their contributions were confined to a fairly narrow range of functions: many of the types of fundraising and assistance shown in Appendix F emerged only after 1546. Further, the alms bestowed were usually of small economic value and were given only rarely: they were occasional acts of generosity that derived often from gifts or bequests from other individuals. Few parishes appear to have gathered and stored special funds for the poor that could be awarded as needed or attempted to provide ongoing assistance, through housing or regular cash payments. With the possible exception of a handful of churches in larger communities, there is thus little sign that late medieval parishes defined themselves as institutional centers for the provision of aid to needy people. Only in the first year of Edward VI's reign did massive change begin, laying the foundation for a formal system of poor relief based within the parishes.

---

[85] CWA #33, 112 and 115.

Part II

Profound change during the early Reformation period

5   New ideas and new policies, *c.* 1530–1553

The years between around 1530 and 1553, containing the early stages of the English Reformation, were marked by worsening poverty that demanded attention, new attitudes towards the poor, and experimental governmental policies about how they should be treated.[1] Many earlier forms of aid were eliminated during these years as secondary consequences of a series of royal and Parliamentary decisions based nominally upon spiritual factors but heavily influenced by economic and political considerations. The dissolution of the monasteries and convents in 1536 and 1539 was followed by the termination of chantries in 1545 and 1547 and of religious fraternities in 1548. The buildings, lands, and other property of these bodies were appropriated by the crown and usually sold eventually to lay owners, and the charitable projects they had run – including hospitals and almshouses – were closed. Within parishes, religious images and prayers for the dead were abolished, and after several years of advance warning, any stocks of money, animals, or land associated with proscribed Catholic practices were confiscated early in 1553, together with all goods beyond those needed for a simple Protestant service. Those changes eliminated the auxiliary religious organizations previously based in local churches as well as many of the activities and possessions that had helped to define parish identities.

The pressures caused by mounting poverty and decreasing assistance were addressed and to some extent mitigated by a cluster of new practices introduced by the government and church. They stemmed from three closely related forces: a desire among people influenced by humanist or "commonwealth" thinking to build just and equitable social and economic relationships, led by the state and based upon the labor of all of the country's residents; the idealistic commitment of early Protestant leaders to creating a more truly Christian and charitable community, one in which unfortunate people would not suffer from desperate hunger

---

[1] See ch. 1.3 above for the practical and ideological context for this paragraph and the next.

or the need to beg; and the heightened willingness of Parliament, often cooperating with royal advisors, to legislate about many aspects of English life.[2] Following preliminary attempts in the 1530s, the state and the new Protestant church worked hand in hand during Edward VI's short reign to tackle economic and social problems and formulate public measures to help the needy. While the decision to use parishes as the unit of implementation may perhaps have been influenced by their previous role in distributing alms, more powerful was the pragmatic consideration that parishes were the only still active administrative bodies that spanned the whole country.[3] For local churches and their officers, a required role in charitable assistance helped to counteract the damage to their prior self-image that resulted from religious closures and confiscations of property.

Substantial change is visible in each of the aspects of poor relief examined here. Attitudes towards begging and charitable donation shifted, providing the context for a series of Parliamentary statutes that introduced harsher measures against able-bodied alms seekers while at the same time promoting aid to the legitimately needy. The number of hospitals and almshouses dropped sharply, but Edwardian legislation provided some compensation by taking the first and most important steps towards a formal system based on obligatory payments that supported regular assistance within the parishes. This chapter examines the new ways of thinking and responding that emerged during the early Reformation era.

5.1   A flood of beggars and responses to them

During the 1530s and 1540s, the number and visibility of people requesting alms increased considerably, at least in urban centers. Poor immigrants may have hoped to benefit from the charitable institutions located in larger communities or thought that begging would be more profitable there. Town and city officials, fearing that existing provision for the poor was being overwhelmed by needy newcomers, attempted to assess the nature and magnitude of the problem and devise targeted responses to the various forms of alms seeking. Chester, Coventry, and Ipswich conducted surveys of the poor between 1539 and 1551; Oxford and King's Lynn, Norf. experimented in 1546 and 1548 with how to set some needy people

---

[2] E.g., Lever, "A Sermon Preached," Becon, "The Pathway unto Prayer," esp. 162–3, his "A Pleasant New Nosegay," esp. 226–8, and Jordan, *Edward VI: The Young King*, 386–438.

[3] The earlier vills and hundreds were now used primarily for assessing and collecting national subsidies. The temporary statute of 1536 had based almsgiving in parishes (see ch. 4.2.2 above), and several overtly secular duties were assigned to parishes in the 1550s and 1560s (see ch. 8.1 below). Even constables, technically officers appointed for hundreds, were sometimes given duties based upon parishes (see ch. 6.3 below).

to work.[4] Cambridge, Southampton, and Louth, Lincs. introduced badging of local beggars in 1536 to 1538, as did Nottingham, Lincoln, and
King's Lynn in 1540 to 1547. Supervision of alms seekers increased.
Southampton appointed a "controller over all beggars" in 1536, and
York ordered its chamberlain in 1541 to have gowns made for the "master
beggars" of the city's four wards.[5] These men were instructed to maintain
good rule among the poor, punish vagrants (with birch rods), and see that
no outside poor entered the city on major holy days, regarded as particularly favorable for begging. Policies like these could well have appeared
if England had remained fully Catholic and loyal to the Pope.

London tried out various approaches to the problems of poverty and
begging. The city first ordered in 1533 that charitable alms be collected in
all parishes; urban officials went on to impose in 1547 what has been
described as the country's first compulsory poor rate, to support the
residents of its hospitals.[6] Four years later the Court of Aldermen
instructed the city's chamberlain to prepare 600 bills authorizing impotent people to beg. After Bishop Nicholas Ridley of London delivered a
powerful sermon on charity in the presence of Edward VI in 1552, he
prevailed upon the lord mayor to appoint a committee to describe in detail
the categories of poor people and propose a response for each.[7] In addition to thriftless people, who did not warrant aid, the committee grouped
the deserving poor into two main categories: people who were "poor by
casualty" (including wounded soldiers, householders whose fortunes had
decayed, and people struck by serious illness), and those who were "poor
by impotency" (including "the fatherless or poor man's child," aged,
blind, and lame people, and those afflicted by crippling diseases).
Whereas such people had commonly been assisted in the past through
licenses to request alms, they were henceforth to be the primary beneficiaries of new forms of parish-based help.

Concern about begging was probably accentuated because people seeking help for themselves were joined by more aggressive solicitation of alms
for charitable institutions. As the system of gathering became yet more
complex, and as hospitals put greater pressure on their proctors to bring in

---

[4] Slack, *Poverty and Policy*, 123. For below, see Cooper, *Annals of Cambridge*, 385, *Third
Book of Remembrance of Southampton*, 52–3, LincsA Louth St. James parish 7/2, fol. 42r
(this parish functioned in effect as a town institution); *Records of the Borough of Nottingham*,
390, LincsA L 1/1/1/2, fol. 41r, and Phillips, "Charitable Institutions," 159.
[5] *Third Book of Remembrance of Southampton*, 53, and *York Civic Records*, vol. 4, 64, and see
also vol. 5, 115 and 158.
[6] Slack, *Poverty and Policy*, 118, and Pound, *Poverty and Vagrancy*, 107–8. For below, see
Aydelotte, *Elizabethan Rogues*, 26. London's chamberlain was also to make 200 passports
for vagabonds who had been whipped in the city and were being sent home.
[7] Grafton, *Chronicle*, 1320–2, for this and below.

specified sums every year, competition over territory and income mounted. One of a cluster of petitions concerning disputes between collectors submitted to the Courts of Chancery and Requests in the 1530s and 1540s came from John Berege of Barkby, Leics., who complained against Christopher Brampston, a baker of Lincoln, in the mid-1530s.[8] Berege claimed that he had purchased one-quarter of the proctorship granted by St. Anthony's Hospital in London to collect in a region that covered the capital city and eight counties, but Brampston was standing in his way as he attempted to exercise that office. Peter Mewtas, a gentleman of Henry VIII's Privy Chamber and master of Bethlehem Hospital in London, wrote to the Chancellor sometime around 1540 alleging embezzlement of money collected for the inmates of his institution by William Kyngstone of Foleshill, Warws.[9] Kyngstone, he claimed, had gathered "great sums of money" in Warwickshire over a period of four years, supposedly for "the relief and comfort of the poor people within the same hospital of Bethlehem," although without authority from Mewtas to do so. Further, Kyngstone had paid "never a penny to the nourishing and comforting of the said poor people," instead keeping the income for his own profit.

Collection for religious fraternities likewise intensified in the 1530s. The Brotherhood of Jesus that met in the crypt of St. Paul's in London awarded to various people the right to gather funds for the organization and to offer religious pardons within particular regions, such as the county of Kent or the province of York.[10] To obtain that right, an individual collector or a partnership made payment to the guild. York's powerful Corpus Christi Guild had six people out gathering support in 1534, each within specified territorial limits.[11] Fraudulent use of indulgences for fraternities and monasteries appears to have increased.[12]

In response to the barrage of individual and institutional collectors, local people were becoming more suspicious of the validity of alms seekers. Dennis Fyll, a priest, submitted a petition to the Chancellor

---

[8] TNA-PRO C 1/748/40. Berege also petitioned against Brampston and another man whom he described as his partners in that proctorship, who were behind in their share of payments to the hospital, leaving him responsible for the full amount owed (C 1/748/41).

[9] TNA-PRO C 1/1033/23–24. In his defense, Kyngstone said that he had been granted the proctorship "by the assent of the confreres of the same house and under their common seal," but because Mewtas awarded the position to someone else, Kyngstone had been unable to gather any money, which is why he had paid nothing to the hospital.

[10] TNA-PRO C 1/725/33 and C 1/1033/4.   [11] YorkCA C102:3.

[12] In a particularly ambitious scam, an indulgence crudely printed in York sometime in the 1530s recited the many thousand years of pardon granted by previous popes to those who visited the monastery of Langley in Kent, in multiple chunks of 18,000 to 28,000 years each (Swanson, *Indulgences*, 459–61). The problem was that no such monastery existed.

around 1540 asking for a license to request help.[13] Fyll said that he was so "extremely taken and vexed with the palsy that he can scarcely or never a whit speak," making it impossible for him to say mass or find employment. He had previously obtained permission to solicit alms, but because that document was not sufficiently explicit, "the curates nor churchwardens would say nor do nothing for him." Fyll requested that his new license state expressly that all ecclesiastical persons were commanded under penalty of contempt of the crown to exhort their parishioners to help him, and he asked that one of the churchwardens of his parish be appointed to go with him, to assist in traveling and to request and receive his alms.[14] When Miles Chamlett of St. John Bedwardine in Worcester received letters patent around 1540 to solicit alms after his house burned down, he sent out his servants to collect on his behalf.[15] Two of the men entered a church in Droitwich, where they delivered their authorization to a churchwarden, asking him to request alms from people at the service. But one of the parishioners, "a man of small charity," seized and inspected the document, declared it false, and refused to return it, leaving Chamlett unable to continue seeking help. John Crede was committed to the Marshalsea prison by the Privy Council in 1546 for falsely claiming that he was collecting alms for the "lazars at Guildford."[16]

Objective problems with begging and gathering added force to early Protestant critiques of existing forms of charitable solicitation. These attacks were based upon several factors: almsgiving was no longer thought to contribute directly to the donor's salvation, indulgences were based on an erroneous theological conception, Catholic charity had failed to provide adequately for the deserving poor, and unselective assistance might perpetuate poverty and fraud. Simon Fish's *A Supplicacyon for the Beggers*, published probably in 1529 on the continent and smuggled into England, claims to speak for deformed people, foul and unhappy lepers, and "other sore people, needy, impotent, blind, lame, and sick, that live only by alms."[17] The author alleges that "their number is daily so sore increased, that all the alms of all the well-disposed people of [the king's] realm is not half enough for to sustain them." Hence they are left to die of hunger. The cause of their suffering is the Roman Catholic Church, both the secular clergy and the monasteries, which do little to relieve the poor even though together they hold – by Fish's estimation – one-third of all the land in

---

[13] TNA-PRO C 1/984/57.

[14] This may be an example of a "guider," as discussed in ch. 6, n. 96 below.

[15] TNA-PRO C 1/970/20.

[16] *APC*, vol. 1, 515. The old leper hospital there was last mentioned in 1399: Groom, "Piety and Locality," 84–5.

[17] *Supplicacyon*, 1, for this and below.

England and one-half of the nation's wealth.[18] The tithes imposed by the church help to drive people of limited means into further want, while alms solicited for narrowly religious purposes stand in the way of assistance to the legitimate poor. Fish also attacks hospitals run by the church and the use of indulgences to promote almsgiving. His solution is that all able-bodied clergymen, monks, and friars ("holy idle thieves," some of whom gain their livings by "importunate begging") should be whipped naked at the cart's tail until they agree to labor for their own upkeep.[19] If that happened, the wealth of the common people would increase and all charitable aid could go to the poor, who would then have enough for their needs.

A successor tract from 1546, *A Supplication of the Poore Commons,* directs its animosity at Henry VIII.[20] Despite the closing of many religious institutions and the appropriation of their property by the crown, the king has failed to provide assistance to the poor. Referring back to Fish's work, the *Supplication* points out that "poor impotent creatures" had previously received at least some scraps from monasteries, "whereas now they have nothing. Then had they hospitals and almshouses to be lodged in, but now they lie and starve in the streets. Then was their number great, but now much greater." Henry Brinklow, a London mercer who wrote under an assumed name in the guise of an exiled former friar, similarly describes the innumerable poor people in the capital who are "forced to go from door to door, and to sit openly in the streets a begging ... and die for lack of aid of the rich, to the great shame of thee, oh London."[21]

Catholic charity was said to promote dishonesty, as described in the forerunner of what was to become a popular Elizabethan literary genre that describes the various types of beggars and rogues who made fraudulent claims about their need. *The Hye Way to the Spyttell Hous,* a poem published some time after 1531 by Robert Copland, takes the form of a dialogue between Copland and the porter of a charitable institution, probably St. Barthomew's Hospital in London.[22] It warns against the kinds of misbehavior, idleness, and folly that could lead an able-bodied person to vagabondage and begging. Some of the people described by the porter had sought temporary accommodation at the hospital due to legitimate poverty, but many attempted to gain lodging and alms through deceit. Although Copland expresses satisfaction that proctors and

---

[18] Ibid., 2 and 4.   [19] Ibid., 14, for this and below.   [20] *Supplication,* 79.

[21] Brinklow, writing as Roderigo Mors, "Lamentacyon of a Christen," 90, published in 1542 and publicly burnt in London in 1546. See Yates, "Between Fact and Fiction."

[22] *Elizabethan Underworld,* 1–25. The work probably drew upon Sebastian Brandt's *Shyp of Folys,* published in German in 1494 and in English in 1503, and the satirical poem, "Cocke Lorelles Bote," from around 1500 (Aydelotte, *Elizabethan Rogues,* 116–7).

pardoners, with their "false popery" and indulgences, have been over-thrown, he is careful to validate charity to the legitimately needy.[23] He emphasizes that "To despite poor folk is not my appetite, Nor such as live of very [true] alms' deed," and he exhorts those of his readers who "have enough, with grace, For the love of God to do your charity, and from the poor never turn your face."

Royal and Parliamentary policies concerning begging were multivalent, shaped by the necessity of addressing the practical problems that stemmed from mounting vagrancy and alms seeking as well as by the increasing influence of Protestant and humanist beliefs. The new policies frequently used the terms "beggar" and "begging" in a pejorative fashion. A royal proclamation of 1530, noting that the number of vagabonds and beggars was rising every day, ordered local officials to punish all vagrants and physically able beggars found outside of the hundreds where they were born or had last lived for a period of 3 years.[24] After being stripped naked from the waist upwards and "sharply beaten and scourged," they were to be given a letter or passport stating where they had been arrested and punished as a vagabond and then sent on their way to their home community.

A statute of 1531 had a similar tone, but prescribed a more measured and complex response.[25] Its preamble observed that throughout the country vagabonds and beggars:

daily do increase in great and excessive numbers by the occasion of idleness, mother and root of all vices, whereby hath insurged and sprung ... continual thefts, murders, and other heinous offences and great enormities to the high displeasure of God, the inquietation and damage of the King's people, and to the marvelous disturbance of the common weal of this realm.

The act instructed Justices of the Peace in every county to conduct regular inspections of "all aged, poor, and impotent persons which ... of necessity be compelled to live by alms of the charity of the people." In the first national-level authorization of licensed begging, the measure went on to say that the JPs were to decide and keep a record of which of the poor were to receive written permission to beg within stated regions other than their own communities.[26] A person allowed to seek alms with a certificate who was found begging outside his designated area was to be punished by spending two days and nights in the stocks, given only bread and water, before being sent back to his own turf.

[23] *Elizabethan Underworld*, 12. For below, see ibid., 1 and 3.
[24] *TRP*, vol. 1, 191–3. For hundreds, see ch. 1, n. 113 above.
[25] 22 Henry VIII, c. 12, *SR*, vol. 3, 328–32.
[26] I have found no examples of local licenses from this early period.

Anyone begging away from home without a license was to be arrested by local authorities and brought before a JP, high constable, or mayor. Legitimately needy offenders were to be whipped or placed in the stocks for three days and nights and then given a license to beg within a certain area. But if someone capable of labor was arrested as a beggar or vagrant, he was "to be tied to the end of a cart naked and be beaten with whips" throughout the community "til his body be bloody by reason of such whipping." Thereafter he was to be returned to his home community (defined as where he was born or had lived for three previous years) and forced to labor. Scholars, sailors, and others who traveled around begging without a letter of authorization similarly faced punishment as vagabonds, as did proctors and pardoners who lacked formal permission. The measure imposed a penalty of as much as 100s. or even imprisonment on anyone who gave money or lodging to "any beggars being strong and able in their bodies to work," but it exempted monastic almsgiving from the prohibition. An updated *Boke for a Justyce of Peace neverso wel and dylygently set forth,* published around 1538, added a new section on beggars.[27] After summarizing the opening of the 1531 statute insofar as it concerned the duties of JPs, the manual threw up its hands at the complexity of the requirements: "And because it is over long here to recite all that Justices of Peace are bound to do concerning aged, poor, impotent persons, and strong valiant beggars, I refer them to the statute in that case provided, anno 22 Henry 8, ca. 12." Because that act placed able-bodied alms seekers in considerable practical jeopardy (as well as reinforcing a negative identity for them), acquiring a license that permitted solicitation became far more important: it was henceforth worth a greater expenditure of time and money to obtain a document that freed the bearer from punishment as a vagrant. That impulse set the stage for production of fraudulent licenses.[28]

The mid 1530s saw further Parliamentary attempts to distinguish between various kinds of solicitation of aid and further experiments with responses to people who asked for help. The short-lived statute of 1536 said that the poor were not to "wander idly and go openly in begging," but they were not banned from asking privately for help.[29] In cities and towns, designated poor people were ordered to go around to every house several times each week to collect excess food and drink, which would be distributed to the rest of those in need. A significant weakening of the measure as originally submitted to Parliament reflects older attitudes

---

[27] Fols. 15v–16r (which provide another indication that the statute of 1536 did not remain in force), for this and below.
[28] See ch. 6.4 below.   [29] 27 Henry VIII, c. 25, *SR*, vol. 3, 558–62.

towards almsgiving. Exemptions to the prohibition of public begging added during debate covered not only friars, but also people who had been shipwrecked or lost their goods at sea; collectors for hospitals, almshouses, and prisons and the residents of those institutions; the poor within one's own parish, to whom food, money, or drink might be given; and any "lame, blind, or sick, aged, and impotent people" to whom travelers wished, as a matter of conscience or charity, to make a contribution. In far harsher terms, the statute ordered that able-bodied vagabonds and beggars who offended a second time were to be whipped and have part of their right ear cut off for future identification; if found idling thereafter, they were to be declared felons, subject ultimately to hanging. In a milder reflection of that same attitude, when Henry VIII's commissioners permitted the Hospital of St. Cross in Winchester to continue its tradition of providing daily meals for 100 non-resident poor people, they imposed the condition that food and drink be given only to those who made some effort to work for their own living, not to "strong, robust, and indolent mendicants, like so many that wander about such places, who ought rather to be driven away with staves, as drones and useless burdens upon the earth."[30]

At the start of Edward VI's reign, Parliament passed an exceptionally repressive measure against able-bodied alms seekers and idle wanderers. The act of 1547 included some fairly sympathetic language, describing the movement of "many maimed and otherwise lamed, sore, aged and impotent persons" into the cities and towns, thereby filling the streets with so many beggars that the urban communities could not support them all.[31] Because the legitimate poor "might easily be nourished" if they returned to their home areas, the statute provided instructions for how such people should be deported from urban areas and how they were to be supported or helped to work in their place of origin. But the 1547 statute also ordered startling new punishments for physically capable wanderers, implying some sense of Parliamentary desperation. If a vagrant who refused to work was reported to two JPs, they could order that the offender be branded on the chest with a V; thereafter, he or she was to be assigned to the informer for two years as a slave. Harsh treatment was suggested for these slaves, and if they ran away, they were to be enslaved for life. In a blow to very poor families, the statute ruled that beggars' children aged 4 to 5 years or more could be removed from their mothers by order of a JP and placed into service with a master willing to accept them, to remain there until they reached full adulthood. The decree for branding and enslavement seems not to have been enforced and was repealed in

---

[30] Bailey, *Almshouses*, 86–7, which does not indicate the original source.
[31] 1 Edward VI, c. 3, *SR*, vol. 4, 5–8, and see C. Davies, "Slavery and Protector Somerset."

1550.[32] The latter measure instead restored the punishments laid out in the act of 1531. Negative policies towards the idle poor formed the other side of legislation that introduced and developed a system of parish-based assistance for the deserving poor of the community.

While the climate of attitudes and policies was thus becoming less favorable to alms seeking, a change that may have had more directly harmful consequences was the collapse of indulgences in the 1530s. The statutes that terminated papal authority in England ended the validity of such grants from the Pope himself, and indulgences from religious figures within England quickly died out as well.[33] The puzzling ease with which indulgences disappeared and the lack of public concern about their absence may have stemmed in part from their association with unpopular or dishonest begging and gathering. While we cannot measure the extent to which late medieval Catholics had been inspired to greater charity by the promise of reduction of their time in Purgatory, that incentive must have been a factor for some donors. Because the Protestant church and state did not come up with an entirely satisfactory substitute to encourage voluntary charity, the ending of indulgences contributed to the gradual movement towards compulsory payments for needy people and projects.

5.2   The drastic impact of religious policies on hospitals and almshouses

In parallel with changing attitudes towards begging, Protestant moralists were deeply concerned about the shortage of places in hospitals and almshouses and the mismanagement of institutions run by Catholic organizations. William Tyndale began the attack on Catholic practices in his influential *The Obedyence of a Christian Man*, originally published in Antwerp in 1528, which claimed that monks were devouring the property given by charitable people that should have supported hospitals, parishes, and schools.[34] Fish's *Supplicacyon for the Beggers* rejected the idea that the way to assist the poor, sick, and lame was by creating new hospitals run by religious bodies: "the more the worse, for ever the fat [wealth] of the whole foundation hangeth on the priests' beards."[35] In his *The Hye Way to the Spyttell Hous*, Copland commented that he had "seen at sundry hospitals that many have lain dead without the walls, and for lack of succour have died wretchedly."

[32] 3 and 4 Edward VI, c. 16, *SR*, vol. 4, 115–17.
[33] 25 Henry VIII, c. 21 and 28 Henry VIII, c. 16, *SR*, vol. 3, 464–71 and 672–3, and Swanson, *Indulgences*, ch. 10, esp. 499–509.
[34] *Obedyence*, fol. 72v.   [35] *Supplicacyon*, 13. For below, see *Elizabethan Underworld*, 4.

The faults of the masters of institutions were emphasized. Because many houses did not insist that their heads be present in person, it was possible to hold the masterships of several institutions simultaneously or to combine those positions with additional offices.[36] Brinklow wrote, "I hear that the masters of your hospitals be so fat that the poor be kept lean and bare enough." He proposed that some of the wealth confiscated from the church be used to maintain houses in every community "to lodge and keep poor men in, such as be not able to labor, sick, sore, blind and lame." The residents were to have "wherewith to live," cared for by good women. At St. Thomas's Hospital in Southwark, Surrey, the many abuses committed or permitted by its master in the 1530s, Richard Mabot, were publicized through Archbishop Thomas Cranmer's visitation in the summer of 1536 and Thomas Cromwell's intervention in 1538.[37]

Objections to the administration of hospitals and almshouses operated by the church may have weakened protests against their closure. The statute of 1545 that permitted the dissolution and royal confiscation of the property of certain chantries, colleges, and religiously run hospitals offered as one of its justifications the malfunctioning of those institutions.[38] In a measure of 1547, however, termination of religious bodies and the charities they maintained was defended on theological grounds, because they were based upon false doctrine and superstitious errors. Their property could better be used for support of schools, universities, and "provision for the poor and needy," although in fact these aims were only minimally pursued.

The number of hospitals and almshouses functioning in England was substantially reduced during the 1530s, 1540s, and 1550s. The closures in my database are displayed in Appendix C, which makes clear the massive impact of the Henrician and Edwardian programs.[39] Between 1530 and 1559, 291 of these houses were shut down, constituting 47 percent of the 617 houses in existence in the 1520s. Most were hospitals, as almshouses had rarely been placed under the control of religious bodies. If we apply the average and median number of people actually living in hospitals and almshouses during the first half of the

---

[36] Rotha Clay believed that the decline in later medieval hospitals stemmed largely from the fact that many wardens were non-resident and/or pluralists (*Mediaeval Hospitals*, 220). For below, see Brinklow, "Complaynt of Roderyck Mors," 52.

[37] Robison, "The Bawdy Master." For below, see 37 Henry VIII, c. 4, *SR*, vol. 3, 988–93.

[38] 37 Henry VIII, c. 4, *SR*, vol. 3, 988–93. For below, see 1 Edward VI, c. 14, *SR*, vol. 4, 24–33.

[39] For discussion of these figures, see ch. 3.1 above and CUP Online App. 1. App. C may undercount the number of houses closed in the 1530s and exaggerate the number shut in the 1540s and 1550s, due to the way in which "last reference" dates were entered into the database (see CUP Online App. 1, pt. 3).

sixteenth century, we find that around 2,300 to 3,000 people – most of them the bedridden or elderly poor – were displaced through these closings.[40] Although some new houses were established in the 1530s and 1540s, followed by a larger number in the 1550s, they by no means compensated for the losses (see Appendices B and D).

The condition of the institutions that were ended varied greatly. Some were already badly decayed. The hospital in Well, N. Yorks. had housed twenty-four poor people at the time of its founding in the fourteenth century; by Edward VI's reign, it contained only fourteen poor folk.[41] The medieval Hospital of St. John the Baptist in Meer, Lincs. had supported thirteen poor people when it was established, whereas in the 1550s it had between one and three residents. But other houses were playing a sufficiently vital role within their local communities that urban governments or leading citizens moved to preserve them. In 1548, as many charitable activities run by chantries and fraternities were being closed, the mayor and brethren of the small town of High Wycombe, Bucks. took possession of the local Hospital of St. John's "for the use of the whole town and relief of the poor, according to the foundation thereof."[42] The burgesses of Poole, Dorset paid the crown in 1550 to acquire the hospital that had formerly been attached to the town's Corpus Christi Guild.

Among the new institutions founded (or re-founded) after the Dissolution, the most significant were the five royal hospitals in London, several of which served as models for subsequent houses elsewhere.[43] Between 1544 and 1557, St. Bartholomew's Hospital and St. Thomas's Hospital were reconstituted to take in and perhaps heal sick people and provide for the elderly poor; Bethlehem (or Bedlam) housed the insane; and Christ's Hospital received orphan and foundling children. The Bridewell initially functioned mainly as a workhouse and school to teach poor children employable skills, but increasingly it was used for whipping vagrants and "the temporary incarceration of the petty criminal fraternity of the capital," including prostitutes, gamblers, and pickpockets.[44] Although by around 1560 London's hospitals were admitting more than 1,400 people annually, they met only a fraction of the need, constantly renewed and gradually expanded by the arrival of poor newcomers into the city.

---

[40] See CUP Online App. 6. The smaller values, derived from the median number of people per house, are probably a better reflection of the true picture than the larger average figures.

[41] *Certificates of . . . Chantries . . . in County of York*, 110. For below, see TNA-PRO C 1/1312/60–1.

[42] *First Ledger Book of High Wycombe*, 76. For below, see Howson, *Houses of Noble Poverty*, 83.

[43] Slack, "Social Policy."   [44] Slack, *Poverty and Policy*, 70.

Appendix D shows the number of houses in existence per decade, based on the dataset. The figure dropped from its peak of 617 in the 1520s to a low of 422 in the 1560s, a decrease of 32 percent. Because a higher fraction of the large old hospitals run by religious organizations were closed, leaving proportionately more almshouses, and because most of the recent foundations were smaller than those that had been abolished, the institutions included in this study probably housed somewhere between 2,500 and 4,500 people in the 1560s, as compared with 5,000 to 6,400 in the 1520s.[45]

5.3   The introduction of parish-based poor relief under Edward VI

During the 1520s and 1530s, commonwealth thinking together with news of the provisions for the poor recently introduced into certain European cities, Catholic as well as Protestant, began to influence English leaders.[46] In response to the crop failures of the 1520s, some towns provided stocks of grain for needy people, and Cardinal Wolsey ordered local commissioners to search out all available grain and ensure that it was brought to markets. National projects to provide assistance and employment for the poor were proposed in 1530 and 1535, although neither was converted into Parliamentary legislation. Parish-based relief was first ordered in a statute of 1536.[47] That measure instructed the churchwardens (or two others) of every parish and the secular officers of urban communities to gather "such charitable and voluntary alms of the good Christian people within the same with boxes every Sunday, holy day and other festival day or otherwise among them selves, in such good and discreet wise as the poor, impotent, lame, feeble, sick and diseased people, being not able to work, may be provided, holpen and relieved." Collectors of Alms named by the parish were to distribute whatever money was given to the poor, and indiscriminate almsgiving was banned. The final version of the statute was, however, far weaker than the bill originally introduced, which was too radical for most members of Parliament. The measure as approved emphasized that giving within the parish or town was not compulsory, nor should set amounts be imposed: no one was to be "constrained to any such certain contribution but as their free wills and charities shall extend." Even after a series of provisos were tacked on to the bill to defend traditional almsgiving and the institutions that depended on it, the statute

---

[45] See CUP Online App. 7.   [46] Slack, *Poverty and Policy*, 115–19, for this and below.
[47] 27 Henry VIII, c. 25, *SR*, vol. 3, 558–62, and Elton, "Early Tudor Poor Law," for this and below.

remained unpopular. The second Parliament of 1536 did not confirm it, reinstating instead the act of 1531 against begging and vagabonds, and local records provide no indication that it was enforced within the parishes.[48]

By the early years of Edward VI's reign, a new intellectual and practical climate was developing, due to the spread of Protestant as well as commonwealth ideas about poor relief and the closings and confiscations that had ended much of the assistance formerly provided within local churches. The crown and Parliament, backed by the new church, formulated legislation that went beyond the statute of 1536 in instructing parish officials how to implement ongoing relief within their own communities. On July 31, 1547, shortly after becoming king, Edward (said to have been advised by Protector Somerset and the royal council) issued a set of royal injunctions for religious reform.[49] They included a more formal technique for encouraging donations for the poor, substituting them for some of the payments previously made to the Catholic church. Every parish was ordered to provide "a strong chest, with a hole in the upper part thereof," specifically for contributions to needy people. The box was to have three keys: one kept by the minister of the church and the other two by the churchwardens or men named by the parish. The injunctions ordered the parish clergy to "call upon, exhort, and move their neighbors to confer and give as they may well spare to the said chest," including when parishioners were writing their wills. The box was supposed to solicit as well as store contributions: it was to be set up "near unto the high altar, to the intent the parishioners should put into it their oblation and alms for their poor neighbors."

The injunctions' Protestant call for charity was reinforced by a reminder that the laity were no longer required to spend money upon "pardons, pilgrimages, trentals, decking of images, offering of candles, giving to friars, and upon other like blind devotions." The location of the box suggests that money given to the poor was seen as a substitute for the common bequest in Catholic wills of a small amount to the high altar of the testator's parish church for payments that had been forgotten or "negligently withheld." Income from church stocks or bequests that had previously supported "torches, lights, tapers, and lamps" was also to go into the box for the poor, as was a fine of 3s. 4d. imposed upon parishes that did not maintain a register book of christenings, weddings, and burials. The minister and churchwardens were instructed to remove

---

[48]   28 Henry VIII, c. 6, *SR*, vol. 3, 655. For a single possible exception, see ch. 4, n. 66 above.
[49]   *TRP*, vol. 1, 393–403, for this paragraph. The quotations are on 401.

"the alms and devotion of the people" from the box at convenient times and distribute them "to their most needy neighbors," in the presence of at least six members of the parish.

Those injunctions were backed by a statute of 1547 that ordered a collection of charitable alms for the poor at church services every Sunday and holy day.[50] After the reading of the Gospel, the minister was to give "a godly and brief exhortation to his parishioners, moving and exciting them to remember the poor people and the duty of Christian charity in relieving of them which be their brethren in Christ, born in the same parish and needing their helps." Aid was not to be given indiscriminately, however, but was to go to those who "are in unfeigned misery and to whom charity ought to be extended." Two years later, a statute emphasized that urban entities too, not just parishes, bore some responsibility for poor relief.[51]

The Parliamentary order for regular collection of aid for the poor was reinforced through detailed royal injunctions to the parishes. As instructions for Doncaster, W. Yorks. stated in 1548: "The church-wardens of every parish church shall, some one Sunday or other festival day every month, go about the church, and make request to every of the parish for their charitable contribution to the poor: and the same so collected shall be put in the chest of alms for that purpose provided."[52] The injunction also noted that since the parish clerk no longer had to carry his holy water around the community, he should instead "accompany the said church wardens, and in a book register the name and sum of any man that giveth anything to the poor." He was then to list those donations in a document that would be hung up in some open place in the church before the next day of collection, so that "the poor having knowledge thereby, by whose charity and alms they be relieved, may pray for the increase and prosperity of the same." Here we have an echo of prayers for the dead, a Protestant form of thanksgiving by poor people that will be seen also in almshouses and hospitals founded after the Reformation.

The requirements that parishes provide a poor men's box and that ministers promote contributions to it were stressed at episcopal visitations too. The visitation articles for the diocese of Canterbury in 1547, for example, inquired whether parishes had provided "a strong chest for the poor men's box," and whether they had "set and fastened the same near to

---

[50] 1 Edward VI, c. 3, sec. 12, *SR*, vol. 4, 8, for this and below. Old poor people capable of some labor were to be given work by their communities, in return for food and drink.
[51] 3 and 4 Edward VI, c. 16, sec. 4, *SR*, vol. 4, 116.
[52] *VAI*, vol. 2, 172–3. It is not clear why the orders required monthly rather than weekly collections.

their high altar."[53] The clergy were to remind their congregations that they should contribute to "the poor chest" the money they had previously bestowed upon now banned Catholic practices. In a stronger move, Bishop Ridley's injunctions for London Diocese in 1550 ordered that immediately after the offertory, the minister should say to those who hoped to receive the communion: "Now is the time, if it please you, to remember the poor men's chest with your charitable alms."[54]

Evidence from wills indicates that calls for generosity by the state and church did indeed have an effect upon the level of almsgiving. In Surrey, whereas 6 to 10 percent of testators in various sub-periods between 1521 and 1547 had made bequests for relief of the poor, including to hospitals and almshouses, between 1547 and 1553 that fraction rose to 34 percent.[55] In Gloucestershire, 8 percent of Henrician wills left something to the poor, but 27 percent of Edwardian wills did so. In Colchester, Essex, bequests to the poor increased from 15 percent of all testators between 1528 and 1537 to 38 percent between 1548 and 1553.[56] Among wealthier London testators, 58 percent left something to the poor in 1528 to 1530, compared with 69 percent in 1550 to 1553; among will-makers of more modest means, the comparable figures were 13 percent rising to 32 percent.[57]

An extremely important statute of 1552 provided detailed instructions for collection and distribution of alms.[58] This act was not repealed under either Mary or Elizabeth, despite the swings in official religious policy. It therefore provided the underpinning for the system of parish-based poor relief that came into practice during the second half of the century, and its general plan continued to function until the 1830s as transmitted by the Poor Laws of 1598 and 1601. The 1552 statute ordered that parish ministers and churchwardens (or, in boroughs and incorporated towns, appropriate urban officers) should first compile a register of all the inhabitants and householders in their area and of "all such impotent, aged and needy persons" who "are not able to live of themselves nor with their own labor." Then, after a church service, the leaders were to call all of the inhabitants together and choose from among them two or more "Gatherers and Collectors of the charitable alms of all the residue of the

---

[53] *Documentary Annals*, vol. 1, 55. See also GloucsA GDR 4, p. 10, from 1548.
[54] *VAI*, vol. 2, 244.
[55] Groom, "Piety and Locality," 247. For below, see Litzenberger, "Local Responses."
[56] Ward, "Reformation in Colchester." Goose found that 16–22% of Colchester's testators left bequests to the poor each decade between 1500 and 1549, a fraction that rose to 30% in the 1550s and 42% in the 1560s, before declining to 32%–36% for the rest of the century (Goose, "Rise and Decline").
[57] Archer, "Charity of Early Modern Londoners."
[58] 5 and 6 Edward VI, c. 2, *SR*, vol. 4, 131–2, for this and the quotations below.

people for the relief of the poor." On the Sunday following their appointment, "when the people is at the church and hath heard God's holy word," the Collectors "shall gently ask and demand of every man and woman what they of their charity will be contented to give weekly towards the relief of the poor; and the same to be written in the said register." Thereafter, the Collectors were each week to "justly gather and truly distribute the same charitable alms ... to the said poor and impotent persons." If anyone who was financially able to give to the poor refused to do so, the minister and churchwardens were to urge him to generosity. Should the recalcitrant person continue to withhold aid, he was to be reported to the bishop of the diocese, who would try to persuade him to contribute and if necessary "take order for the reformation thereof."

The Collectors were warned to be fair-minded in their decisions about who should be assisted, awarding relief "without fraud or covin [collusion], favor or affection," and they were to be selective, ensuring that "the more impotent may have the more help, and such as can get part of their living to have the less." No one was "to go or sit openly a begging," and the poor could be set to work. Chosen for one-year terms, Collectors were required to submit quarterly accounts to the minister and churchwardens of their parish, or, in urban areas, to the mayor and other head officers. A person chosen as Collector who refused to take up the office faced a fine of 20s., and a Collector who failed to turn in his accounts could be sent to the bishop. The Privy Council sent out letters to individual people in some counties, instructing them to put the measure into execution.[59]

Orders from above were implemented to a surprising degree by parish officials (churchwardens alone until 1552, joined thereafter in some parishes by Collectors for the Poor).[60] They also devised some new techniques of their own for raising and distributing funds. Although Edward's reign lasted for just six-and-a-half years, 52 percent of the sixty-two parishes whose accounts I examined reported some action on behalf of the poor in addition to any alms given out from bequests and at funerals and commemorative services (see Appendix F, the second set of chronological columns). The types of communities involved in poor relief had changed.[61] Whereas four-fifths of the active parishes in the earlier period had been located in cities, towns, or market centers, during Edward's reign nearly half lay in rural villages, indicating that charitable activity was

---

[59] *APC*, vol. 4, 161–2.
[60] A few parishes prior to 1552 had officers who dealt with donations to the poor, as in Chagford, Devon, where four men were chosen in 1551 as "receivers for the whole parish" of charitable gifts for the poor and repair of the church (DevonRO 1429 A-1/PW 1, used through A2A).
[61] See CUP Online App. 9, pt. 1.

spreading into smaller places.[62] Located in nineteen counties plus London and York, they were more evenly dispersed throughout the country than before, with 13 percent of the total in the north/northwest and 34 percent in the southwest/west and in East Anglia/the southeast.

Although some churchwardens presumably complied with demands to assist the poor simply because they feared punishment for refusal, such a strong response to mandates from the government and church suggests that certain parishes may have welcomed the new approach. Even if wardens did not share the theological/moral assumptions upon which it was based, they perhaps hoped that it would help to address the increasingly severe problems of poverty in their communities. We must remember that during Edward's reign parishes were also responding to (or in some cases seeking to avoid) orders to remove the physical manifestations of the Catholic faith, and many churchwardens were trying valiantly to protect their churches' stocks, landed property, and goods from impending confiscation by the crown. The use of parish funds to assist the poor may therefore have been seen as conversion of earlier fundraising practices for such purposes as hiring auxiliary clergy or beautification of the church, both of which were functionally ended by the Reformation, in favor of an alternative project that continued to fill religious as well as locally important social goals.

In looking more closely at parish activities, we may refer to the summary in Appendix F, which distinguishes between acquiring and protecting income for the poor (in Part A) and distributing it (in Part B). Some churchwardens may have gathered money for the poor each week as ordered in 1547 without recording it in their accounts, mentioning only familiar kinds of collections or rates used for general church purposes. But 31 percent of the sixty-two parishes whose accounts were examined here reported activities that produced money for their needy members. For this period and the rest of the sixteenth century, we can supplement information from parish documents with other sources: injunctions, proclamations, statutes, visitation materials, and the records of church courts and Justices of the Peace. In them I encountered references to aid to the poor in eleven additional parishes.

Of the parishes analyzed, 29 percent reported setting up a poor men's box and/or dealing with contributions to it. This was the highest fraction seen for any single activity in any of the four periods examined. Starting in 1547, parishes throughout the country paid for having a box built and installed within the church, sometimes accounting for necessary repairs

---

[62] For these regions, see ch. 3, n. 42 above.

thereafter; locks and keys were also purchased.[63] These early receptacles were given diverse names, but nearly all referred directly to the poor, thus distinguishing them from earlier church chests and general alms boxes. Churchwardens in Morebath, Devon paid 16d. "for making of the chest aliter the poor men box"; St. Michael's parish, Oxford laid out 18d. for locks and hinges "for poor men's coffer"; Ludlow, Shrops. paid for two bands of iron and nails for "the poor man's chest"; and Mildenhall, Suff. purchased two locks and two keys for "the hutch for the poor."[64] Nor was their use limited to parishes with a strong Reformed presence. When the two keepers of the light devoted to the blessed sacrament in the church of St. Michael Spurriergate, York rendered account in 1547 for £4 5s. 6d., they were told to put 4s. 8d. of that amount into the poor folk's chest.[65] Other sources refer to failure to install a box. At the bishop of Salisbury's visitation of 1550, for example, the parishioners of Monkton Farleigh, Wilts. "sayeth that there is no chest called the poor men's box."[66]

Charitable people quickly began using poor men's boxes at least for smaller donations. Of a sample of Sussex wills from Edward's reign, sixty-seven left sums to the poor men's box of their parish churches, as compared with thirty-nine that gave individual bequests to the poor.[67] The average amount bequeathed to the box in those wills was 2s. 3d., the median amount 12d. Churchwardens now commonly mentioned small sums given to, taken from, or left in the poor men's box at the end of their terms.[68]

The requirement for a special container with which to solicit and store alms for the poor had consequences for both parish officials and needy people. In administrative or accounting terms, having this box meant that money for the poor would be kept separate from other church funds. Funds collected regularly from the parish could be placed there until needed, as could any gifts or legacies for the poor that were assigned to churchwardens for distribution over a period of time. For recipients, it was of great benefit that money could now be reserved and awarded gradually, either on a regular basis or in response to their particular needs, rather than being handed out on the spot as soon as it was donated.

---

[63] I encountered references in Corn., Devon, Gloucs., Herts., Kent, London, Oxfds., Shrops., Suff., Surrey, Sussex, Lancs., Wilts., Worcs., and York. Although some wardens might possibly have been adding locks to an earlier alms box, I found no explicit references to that practice.
[64] CWA #35, 159 and see 161; CWA #78b, 214; CWA #85, 34; and CWA #92, 110/5/3.
[65] CWA #118, fol. 217v.   [66] Wilts&SA D1/43/1, fol. 19r.
[67] See CUP Online App. 8.
[68] E.g., CWA #25, p. 43, CWA #26, 322/1, fol. 32v, CWA #58, 29, and CWA #81, 55.

Knowing that the parish had assistance available in case of unusual hardship may have brought peace of mind to people living at subsistence level. To augment the income from required collections and other contributions to the box, Edwardian churchwardens experimented with some new means of raising money for their impoverished neighbors. One was to set up a stock of animals, cash, land, or goods whose rental income was earmarked for the poor. In Boxford, Suff., the plate belonging to the church was leased out to the use of the poor when not needed for parish functions. In 1550, after warden John Porter accounted for £3 13s. in cash from other sources plus 35s. from "plate money," he was told to bestow the full sum "among the poor people as he shall see need."[69] An occasional parish organized church ales to benefit the poor. A memorandum in the churchwardens' accounts for Winkfield, Berks. in 1551 noted that "we the inhabitants of the said parish hath made ale this year," using "the gains that we have by the said ale . . . to refresh our poor neighbors and mend our high ways."[70]

Some parishes began to enforce royal and ecclesiastical orders concerning the obligations of ministers who held a living that yielded £20 or more annually. A royal injunction of 1536 had instructed beneficed clergy to provide hospitality if they were resident in their cure or to distribute onefortieth of their income to the poor of their parish if they were not.[71] That order does not appear to have been noticed immediately by churchwardens or local diocesan officials. Edward's injunctions for religious reform commented sourly that "the goods of the Church are called the goods of the poor, [but] at these days nothing is less seen than the poor to be sustained with the same."[72] But an order in 1547 that repeated the Henrician injunction verbatim was reinforced by episcopal articles and interrogatories at visitations, leading to reports by churchwardens about non-resident ministers who were not assisting the poor. In 1550, the wardens of Stonehouse, Gloucs. presented at a visitation that "one Mr. Richard Browne, vicar there, doth not distribute the 40th part of his benefice to the poor, not these three years past."[73] That report was followed by a series of similar ones from other churches in the next few months. Several parishes told the bishop of Salisbury in 1550 either that their vicar "doth keep no hospitality and giveth no distribution to the poor people there, his benefice being worth 40 marks and above" or that their parsons do not

---

[69] CWA #89, 57.   [70] CWA #12, p. 31 of original.
[71] *VAI*, vol. 2, 10, and Houlbrooke, *Church Courts*, 156–7.
[72] *TRP*, vol. 1, 397. For below, see *VAI*, vol. 2, 121, 106, and 305, and GloucsA GDR 4, p. 8.
[73] GloucsA GDR 4, p. 29. For below, see ibid. and successive pages.

"distribute any of their revenues there amongst the poverty of the parish according to the king's injunctions."[74]

With their newly enlarged revenues for the poor, augmented in some cases by sale of goods before the anticipated royal appropriation of parish property, many Edwardian churchwardens expanded their activities on behalf of the needy. Of the accounts used in this project, 31 percent reported giving some kind of assistance to the poor from the parish's own funds. Beat Kümin's detailed analysis of churchwardens' accounts from ten parishes shows that eight gave assistance to the poor in the Edwardian years, double the previous number, and the amounts bestowed were much greater.[75] Six of his parishes devoted up to 5 percent of their total expenditures to the needy, and two spent 17 to 24 percent on that cause. Wardens occasionally distributed gifts and bequests from other people to the poor, although executors/-trices normally handled the latter, and a few may have given out alms at funerals.[76] Obits were prohibited, as they focused on prayers for the dead, and fewer Protestant testators left money for commemorative services. But Sussex wills indicate that when testators gave charitable legacies to the poor or stipulated that alms be distributed at their funerals, they were now more likely to give money, not just food or drink.[77] Cash awards, even if of equally low value, provided greater flexibility for the recipients.

Some of the forms of assistance awarded by parishes from their own funds had already been used in a few places before 1547. More churchwardens now reported small gifts of money, bread, or clothing to local people, especially on special religious days like Whitsontide, Lent, Good Friday, Easter, or Christmas.[78] Some payments were still unpredictable, depending upon the amount gathered at church services or donated/bequeathed to the poor men's box. Mildenhall's wardens noted that of the money collected on August 6, 1548, they gave sums of 3d. to 6d. each to one man, one married woman, four women described in their own names or as Mother, and one poor boy.[79] But they evidently stored some of their income, for later in the year they laid out more "to the poor people at times when they did call for it." Wardens might also contribute occasional alms to outside poor people who solicited assistance.[80]

---

[74] Wilts&SA D1/43/1, fols. 19v and 23v.
[75] Kümin, *Shaping of a Community*, 276–315, passim; explanations on 270–4.
[76] For executors, see, e.g., Sweetinburgh, "The Poor"; for churchwardens, see, e.g., *CPR, Edw. VI*, vol. 2, 172.
[77] See CUP Online App. 8.
[78] E.g., CWA #114, 25 and 30, CWA #68, fol. 1v, CWA #97, 103 and 106, and CWA #104, for 1550 and 1553.
[79] CWA #92, 110/5/3, and see CWA #87, 160–1.   [80] See ch. 2.2 above and ch. 6.2 below.

A few parishes were evidently moving towards a more regular system of payment even before the imposition of formal assessments in 1552. Churchwardens in Wandsworth, Surrey differentiated in their accounts for 1550 to 1552 between token gifts to the poor at Lent or Christmas and larger sums "paid to sustain poor folks of the parish"; aid to poor people in the parishes of St. James in Louth and St. John in Winchester may likewise have been ongoing.[81] Ashburton, Devon expanded its practice, already visible in the mid-1540s, of supporting some local people on an apparently regular basis, although we cannot tell whether the much greater annual expenses recorded in the Edwardian period resulted from giving more money to each person or from maintaining a larger number of people.[82]

We see in this period the beginnings of an activity that was to increase across the second half of the sixteenth century: paying for the temporary boarding or raising of poor children who had been orphaned or abandoned, sometimes because they were illegitimate.[83] By hiring needy local people, usually women, to provide such care, churchwardens filled two social needs at once. In Wing, Bucks., when a male baby was found in December 1548 "under a bush in Ascot field, neither father nor mother known," he was given to a married woman to be "kept of the charity of the town."[84] Wardens in Wandsworth paid 16d. per month first to William Speryng and later to "the butcher's wife" for keeping Woodsett's child, payments that continued for 12.5 months in 1550–1; the parish of St. John in Winchester laid out the exceptional sum of £6 14s. 9d. for the "nourishing" of four children in 1552 to 1554. Such assistance was not always given willingly. Churchwardens in Halesowen, Worcs. made no comment in 1548–9 about paying for "the nursing of John Lowys' child" and for care of "the child that was at the church door," but four years later they reported that they had spent 4s. for keeping another poor child "at the commandment of John Hydley, high bailiff" and others.[85] To some extent parishes may have been taking over a role that had previously been filled informally, by relatives or friends, but it seems likely that the number of children at risk was also starting to rise.

---

[81] CWA #97, 101, 103, and 106; CWA #65, 7/2, at back of the book, and CWA #45, from 1552–4.
[82] CWA #33, 121–8, passim.
[83] A survey of 2,100 people in London who needed relief in the early 1550s found that 300 were fatherless children (*John Howes' MS.*, 21).
[84] CWA #16b, n. 23. The baby died two weeks later, whereupon the churchwardens paid the sexton for preparing his grave (ibid., 319). For below, see CWA #97, 102 and 105, and CWA #45.
[85] CWA #111, 93–4 and 99. For below, see ch. 8.2.2 below.

Other kinds of help were provided as well. Some parishes furnished care or financial assistance to adults who were sick or injured.[86] Wardens in St. Martin Coney Street in York gave 7s. in 1552–3 to "Agnes that kept Tomson's house in the plague time," while Boxford's wardens reported 4d. "laid out to father Baker when he was sick" in 1547.[87] In 1547–8, the parish of St. Michael's in Bedwardine, Worcester delivered 12d. "to the poor sick woman next the parsonage" and paid 3s. 8d. to the person who kept Ankerett Bayly in her illness. Wardens might also cover burial costs. Lamb's wife received 12d. in 1548 "to bury her child" in Boxford.[88] Several parishes helped to maintain almshouses or paid for housing for the poor.

Some wardens were called upon to deal with the consequences of confiscation of religious property as it affected the poor. When a large conglomeration of land in Herefordshire that had formerly belonged to monasteries and chantries was granted out by the crown in 1553, the new owners – an esquire and yeoman – were required to pay 20s. annually to the wardens of three parishes for the use of poor inhabitants of those areas.[89] As Edward VI's government prepared to appropriate the excess property of parish churches, some churchwardens, seeing the handwriting on the wall, sold off part of their parish's possessions before the final orders were issued early in 1553. The income was generally used for repairs or improvements to the building or other religious or charitable ends, including aid to the poor. A report about such sales in the diocese of London indicated that eleven parishes had used part of the income to help needy people. In Essex, Great Bromley distributed £12 plus 30 yards of linen to the poor; Clavering spent 10s. in caring for a poor child; Great Bentley expended £1 6s. "in alms and on almshouses"; the prosperous market center of Saffron Walden devoted its £82 6s. 8d. to "relief of the poor, maintenance of the free school, and other charitable uses"; and the fishing village of Leigh spent 17s. 10d. "for redeeming men of the parish taken prisoner in France."[90]

In parishes where the statute of 1552 was implemented immediately, churchwardens were joined by Collectors for the Poor in the final year of Edward's reign. Although our ability to trace the presence of early Collectors is limited by poor survival of sources, it is clear that at least a

---

[86] In London, 200 of the people who required assistance in the early 1550s were described as "sore and sick," in addition to 400 aged persons (*John Howes' MS.*, 21).

[87] CWA #117, MCS 16, p. 5, and CWA #89, 52. For below, see CWA #114, 19 and 23.

[88] CWA #89, 53. For below, see, e.g., CWA #92, 110/5/3, for 1551–2 and 1552–3, and CWA #89, 55.

[89] *CPR, Edw. VI*, vol. 5, 126–9.   [90] *Cal. State Papers Dom., Edw. VI*, 75–9.

few places responded to the order right away.[91] I have encountered Collectors' accounts or references to these officers in 1552 or 1553 from New Windsor, Berks., the suburban London parishes of St. Saviour, Southwark and St. Mary's, Lambeth, and five parishes in Southampton. Three other references from that year do not mention Collectors per se, but indicate that the parishes were implementing a more regular system for assessing and/or distributing alms, suggesting that the new officers may have been at work.[92]

The years between 1530 and 1553 had both negative and positive repercussions for poor people and the assistance available to them. Practical demographic and economic pressures that increased the number of people seeking aid contributed to harsher attitudes towards beggars, and alms gathering – whether for individuals or institutions – became more difficult as indulgences were abolished. The crown's decision to close the monasteries and other Catholic institutions and confiscate their property led to the termination of many forms of local charity. These included the loss of several thousand places for sick, bedridden, or elderly poor people through the closing of hospitals and almshouses. But the social/moral emphases of humanist or commonwealth thinking and Protestant theology, which together formed the basis for a critique of earlier forms of aid to the poor, joined with Parliament's newfound legislative involvement to launch a more structured and regular form of parish-based support that was to continue developing across the rest of the sixteenth century. Whereas many of the changes of the early Reformation period weakened parishes by eliminating their subsidiary organizations and lessening their economic resources, the system of poor relief made possible an alternative identity as the primary locus of charitable assistance.

---

[91] For fuller discussion, see ch. 8.3 below. For below, see BerksRO D/XP 149/1/1, fol. 13, LondMA P92/SAV/1383, LambA P 2/33–4, used through A2A, and SouthCA SC/10/1.
[92] Wilts&SA D1/43/1, fol. 104 (Stoke), CWA #114, 32, and SuffRO-BSE FL 501/6/27 and 501/7/34 (Clare).

Part III

Intensified problems and altered approaches in the later sixteenth century

6 The burgeoning of begging, collection, and fraud

As the sixteenth century progressed and poverty intensified, begging and gathering blossomed. Rapid population rise that outpaced economic expansion increased both the breadth and the depth of need. The number of poor people seeking charitable alms for themselves was magnified by the closing of many hospitals and almshouses and the ending of support previously distributed by fraternities and chantries. Even if one's local parish offered regular support – and some did not – that aid could seldom keep up with the demand. The ending of indulgences probably reduced the level of contributions to people collecting for individuals and institutions alike, leading to efforts to exert pressure on donors in other ways. As in the past, people requesting assistance went to private households, parish churches during services, and urban officials, where they gained at best unpredictable help. Contributions were voluntary, and there was little if any external supervision over how the income was collected or employed.

The definitions of poverty and legitimate need continued to become more complex in response to changing realities. The vagrancy statute of 1572 excluded from its punishments itinerant harvest workers, people who had been robbed while traveling, and servants whose masters had sent them away or died.[1] A measure of 1576 eliminated the simple and familiar distinction between those capable of work and those who could not labor to support themselves, implicitly acknowledging for the first time that some able-bodied people who were willing to work could not find employment. In 1577 William Harrison described the categories of poor people in much the same terms used in London in 1552, explaining that those who qualified for relief had been affected by the various forms of "casualty" or "impotency."[2] Significantly, however, Harrison omitted from the earlier list the children of living poor men, a group that must

---

[1] 14 Elizabeth, c. 5, sec. 11, *SR*, vol. 4, 592. For below, see 18 Elizabeth, c. 3, sec. 4, *SR*, vol. 4, 611.
[2] W. Harrison, *Description of England*, 180, and see ch. 5.1 above.

now have been recognized as so numerous that attempting to assist them was impossible.

Each of the groups of alms seekers seen during the later medieval years expanded after 1553. Some people solicited donations privately within their own local communities, without formal authorization, as was still permitted by law. Everyone who asked for help away from home, however, was now expected to carry some sort of written permission, in accordance with the statute of 1531.[3] Following the late medieval pattern, some licenses were awarded to individuals who had suffered a specific misfortune, authorizing them to travel widely within a region or the whole country. By the 1580s and 1590s, however, they were joined by poor people said to be old, sick, disabled, feeble, and/or overburdened with children. Their permissions, issued usually by local Justices of the Peace (JPs), allowed them to request alms in hundreds near where they lived or while traveling to seek help from relatives or friends.[4] Other genuinely needy people who had not been granted licenses also sought aid away from home, despite the risk of being punished as a vagabond. Many of the remaining hospitals and some almshouses sent out proctors to solicit contributions on their behalf, and for larger projects, such as towns struck by fire or damaged harbors, the crown sometimes awarded briefs authorizing collection.[5]

Some able-bodied people too asked for charitable assistance, preferring the freedom and interest of travel, perhaps interrupted occasionally by casual employment, to staying at home with a regular job. These wanderers, commonly termed "sturdy beggars" or "rogues" in the statutes, were especially worrying when they traveled in groups, were former soldiers, or used dishonest or illegal means to supplement their incomes. For constables, responsible for the only form of policing, unknown strangers were far more difficult to control than their own neighbors; they might therefore be willing to apply to disruptive vagrants the physical punishments required by statute. Among both deserving and illegitimate alms seekers, women were mentioned more frequently than in the past, and they may have evoked particular concern. By the 1590s, local as well as national

---

[3] See ch. 5.1 above.   [4] For the definition of a hundred, see ch. 1, n. 113.
[5] Briefs as used for charitable purposes in the medieval period had usually been permissions to collect alms issued by a pope, archbishop, or bishop; with the break from Rome, any briefs obtained from the Pope were declared void and no new ones were to be requested. Thereafter, most charitable briefs were granted by the monarch, although similar documents were occasionally prepared by bishops of the English church (Bewes, *Church Briefs*, 6–13, and M. Harris, "Inky Blots"). A statute of 1547 permitted the issuance of briefs by the Chancellor or the Keeper of the Great Seal to people who had suffered damage from fire and unspecified other losses (1 Edward VI, c. 3, sec. 18, *SR*, vol. 4, 8); that practice was later applied more widely.

leaders felt that the country was swarming with beggars and gatherers of all kinds. While their anxiety was probably exaggerated, it seems clear that many thousands of people were indeed moving about while requesting aid, with or without a license.

The limitations of a form of relief based upon begging and gathering were becoming increasingly obvious. Not only did those approaches contribute to the number of alms seekers on the roads, the Parliamentary requirement that people must carry a valid license in order to receive aid was unenforceable. Although the 1531 measure had ordered severe punishment of healthy beggars who lacked formal permission and imposed a penalty on those who assisted them, local people commonly ignored the rules. If constables accepted a wanderer's reason for requesting alms, they would probably not put the outsider into the stocks or deliver a whipping. If churchwardens felt that a poor stranger warranted aid, they might well make a contribution regardless of whether or not the suppliant carried written documentation. Even if the wardens were themselves reluctant to give aid out of church funds, the parishioners sometimes intervened.[6] Human sympathy and ongoing teaching about Christian charity often won out over respect for the letter of the law.

Other problems undermined the utility of traditional gathering of funds for public projects. As new initiatives were introduced at the county level to address poverty and vagrancy, and when costly infrastructural work of national importance was needed, like repair of essential harbors, Parliament, the Privy Council, and the episcopacy gradually realized that solicitation of voluntary charitable alms could not produce sufficient funds on a predictable schedule. Further, because the amount of cash needed was in some cases substantial, careful supervision and accounting were essential. To create more effective ways to generate funds for public purposes, secular and religious leaders beginning in the 1570s tried out some new techniques. Most of these experiments imposed semi- or fully obligatory payments upon the parishes, monitored by JPs. Although some of the projects did not focus on the poor, the methods were important to the parallel development of assistance by parishes for their own needy people.

Yet another challenge to the older system of begging and gathering was fraud. Permissions to request alms for an individual or institution could be altered or carried by a person other than the one named on the document. Counterfeit begging licenses, some with seals that looked valid, were in use by the 1560s and were found throughout the country by the 1590s.

---

[6] E.g., churchwardens in Pattingham, Staffs. noted in 1591–2 that they gave 6d. "to a poor man in the church by the parishioners' commandment" (CWA #88, fol. 6v).

Almshouses, hospitals, and prisons contributed to the growing number and questionable legitimacy of people who solicited alms by issuing permissions to collect but not checking on how they were used. Even the crown was granting letters of protection to apparently non-existent institutions. The problem of dishonesty was so great that begging and traditional types of gathering were abolished by the Poor Laws of 1598 and 1601.[7] This chapter looks first at the kinds of people who were soliciting help between 1554 and the end of the century and at the urban and Parliamentary policies that related to them. The next section examines licensed begging and gathering, for individuals and institutions. After considering experiments with more forcible collection for public projects, we turn to the mounting problem of fraud.

6.1   Alms seekers and policies

Authorized alms seekers, those carrying some kind of license, became more common during the second half of the sixteenth century and reflected greater diversity of need. Some categories were familiar from the later medieval years: people who had suffered a calamitous misfortune, scholars, soldiers, and mariners; and proctors named by charitable institutions or public works. But now they were joined on the roads by several new types of licensed beggars. What was probably the largest cluster consisted of poor people whose home communities were unable to support them and who had been given a certificate by JPs to request alms elsewhere. Other travelers were impoverished immigrants who had been expelled from the towns or cities to which they had moved and sent back to their home communities, given passports that allowed them to beg while making the trip.[8]

More worrisome to local and national officials was an increase in the number of able-bodied, wandering beggars.[9] Constables and JPs feared that these vagrants would supplement the income they received from alms by theft or sharp activity at gaming tables, and they were thought to be prone to violence and sexual immorality. Even for vagabonds, however, compassion or a desire to get rid of them as easily as possible might overpower a strict application of the statutes. Churchwardens and

---

[7] See ch. 9.1 below.

[8] These documents authorized travel within the country, not abroad. For a sad little set of passports for a family shuttled from one place to another in 1598, see HuntL EL 2523.

[9] See, e.g., Beier, "Vagrants," and his *Masterless Men*, esp. ch. 2; for the seventeenth century, see, e.g., Slack, "Vagrants and Vagrancy," and Hindle, "Technologies of Identification." For the tendency to classify all poor people moving in search of employment as vagrants, see Fumerton, *Unsettled*, esp. ch. 3.

constables sometimes decided that giving an unknown stranger a few pennies and perhaps a night's lodging in an empty barn, coupled with instructions to move out of the area the next day, was quicker and less expensive than administering a whipping or keeping the person in the stocks, and then finding a local official to prepare the passport that authorized travel back to his or her home community by the most direct route.[10] Constables' accounts suggest that fewer than one-tenth of the migrants who came through an area were actually whipped and ordered to return to their own parishes. Most were handed a little money and sent on their way.

Private families provided help too. Of ninety-eight wandering people questioned in Warwick between 1580 and 1587, 59 percent said they had previously received food, drink, or lodging from households with which they had no previous connection, plus another 11 percent who had been sheltered by relatives or friends.[11] A 22-year-old man from Stratford-upon-Avon arrested as a vagabond in Warwick in 1581 said that while traveling about during the past year, "he had dwelled with no body but most commonly got his living by charity of good folks," going to "many gentlemen's and honest men's houses" to ask for their help.[12] The man with him, who had previously been employed as a swineherd in Wolverton but had been on the road for a year, confessed that although he had worked for a few days in each of a number of different places, "many times he got his living by begging."

Urban areas – now including some of the market towns – continued to bear the brunt of begging due to the immigration of poor people from rural areas. During the Elizabethan period, many civic bodies instituted multi-pronged strategies for dealing with the poor.[13] In a charitable vein, they tried out methods of identifying and providing support for their own long-term residents who could not work for their own living. Some assistance came through private almsgiving, but increasingly urban leaders took steps of their own. Cities and towns might continue the earlier practice of limiting begging by badging or licensing only certain people to

---

[10] During 12 months in 1598–9, the city of Salisbury issued passports to thirty-nine vagrant men, forty-eight women, seven couples, and nine children under 14 years of age, most of whom had been punished, but a few exempted. The register frequently described the bearer in such terms as "a vagrant and idle person and sturdy beggar" or "an idle wandering person and a rogue" (*Poverty in Early-Stuart Salisbury*, 17–23). For below, see Slack, *Poverty and Policy*, 92, referring apparently to the late sixteenth and early seventeenth centuries.
[11] Beier, *Masterless Men*, 223.   [12] *Book of John Fisher*, 29, for this and below.
[13] Examples are found in the records of virtually every town and city in the country; only a few illustrations are provided here.

seek alms locally.[14] These approaches were generally unsuccessful, however, and were soon abandoned. A growing number of large communities
began assessing payments upon inhabitants of middling or higher economic status to provide regular support for certain poor people.[15] Those
charges were often described initially as "benevolences" or voluntary
contributions, but eventually were admitted to be compulsory. In an
ambitious plan that proved too expensive to sustain, York ordered in
1588 that an assessment be made upon gentlemen and wealthy citizens
so that residents who were "aged, lame, and impotent, and past their
work" could receive an allowance of at least 1.5d. daily and would not
need to beg; those capable of labor were to be employed by the aldermen
and former chamberlains of the city.[16]

But even the institution of urban rates for the poor might not meet the
demand. In response, some authorities conducted surveys to determine in
more detail who was asking for alms, what their connection to the community was, and sometimes who provided housing for them. In Warwick,
the poor were surveyed in 1586 at the instigation of Rev. Thomas
Cartwright.[17] Cartwright, the recently appointed master of the Earl of
Leicester's Hospital in the town, was upset by the level of disorder and
begging he observed. Evidently to his surprise, the survey showed that
nearly all of Warwick's poor were local people and that children were
among those who asked for help. Norwich's "census of the poor" of 1570
had similarly found many children, but there few of the needy begged.[18]
When York's officials ordered designated "viewers" to go through the
city's wards in 1588, visiting the dwelling places of the poor, they were told
to classify residents into several categories.[19] Legitimately needy people
who did not qualify for York's assistance through birth or at least 3 years'
residence were to be sent back to the places from which they had come;
"rogues, vagabonds, strange beggars, and such as will not work" were
either to be forced to labor in Houses of Correction or banished from
the city.

---

[14] Badging was instituted in Beverley, E. Yorks. and Newcastle upon Tyne, Northumb. in
1558 and 1562, and one of Chester's parishes contributed 2s. in 1575 "to old Stockton's
wife" who had "a license to gather in the church from Mr. Mayor" (HMC, *Report on MSS
of the Corp. of Beverley*, 181, T&WAS 543/14, fol. 120r, and CWA #22).
[15] E.g., Hereford by 1555 (HerefRO Hereford City Documents, bound vol. 3, transcript,
10–11), Southampton by 1569 (*Court Leet Records [of Southampton]*, vol. 1, pt. 1, 51),
Ipswich by 1573 and perhaps by 1557 (*Poor Relief in Elizabethan Ipswich*, 18), and
Leicester by 1577 (*Records of the Borough of Leicester*, 167).
[16] *York Civic Records*, vol. 8, 157–8.   [17] *Book of John Fisher*, 165–72.
[18] *Norwich Census of the Poor*, e.g., 74, and see *Poor Relief in Elizabethan Ipswich*, 121–40.
[19] *York Civic Records*, vol. 8, 157–8, for this and below.

While town leaders were aware that failure to provide for needy local people demonstrated a lack of Christian charity and poor urban management, inadequately supervised generosity to the poor could introduce other difficulties. Berwick-upon-Tweed, Northumb. had been giving a "benevolence" to its poor for several years prior to 1588.[20] Intended to support widows and other needy residents, it had been distributed too casually, drawing great numbers of poor people into the community and increasing the number of beggars going from house to house. The town council therefore ordered that the benevolence henceforth be granted to more carefully selected residents by a committee consisting of the mayor, the town's preacher, and two of the churchwardens. Additional people deemed worthy to solicit alms were to be given a badge, and no one was to offer assistance at his door to a person who failed to display that marker.

Alongside efforts to assist at least some of the deserving poor, many towns attempted to limit the influx of vagrants and potential beggars. The two men appointed as "surveyors of beggars and vagabonds" in Newark-upon-Trent, Notts. were instructed to walk the streets at midday, making sure that any poor newcomers had passports authorizing their travel; if not, they were to be put in the stocks.[21] Doncaster, W. Yorks. named a "begle" in 1585 to enforce "good order amongst the poor people in the town" and hinder outside beggars from entering unless they were "lawfully authorized by two Justices of Peace." In Abingdon, Berks., a beadle received wages in 1590 from the master and governors of Christ's Hospital, "in consideration that no foreign beggar or idle person shall make their abode within this borough to the hindrance of the poor inhabitants within the same."[22]

Parliament and the crown likewise enacted a series of measures concerning begging and vagrancy. The only relevant Marian legislation, passed in 1555, confirmed the statute of 1531 but added some further provisions.[23] Acknowledging that a given parish or urban center might contain more genuinely needy people than the other inhabitants were able to support, the

---

[20] B-u-TwRO C.1/1, fol. 68r–v, for this and below.
[21] N-u-TrMus D6.75/HT 8, ink fols. 4r and 24r. In accounts for 1557–8, the office was termed "master of the beggars and cleaner of the market," an interesting pairing of dirty duties (D6.75/HT 2, fol. 221v). See also GloucsA TBR A1/1, fol. 11v, and T&WAS MS 543/18, fol. 1r. For below, see Calendar to the Records of Doncaster, 12.
[22] Carter and Smith, Give and Take, 6. I am grateful to the authors for a copy of this study, as well as for their assistance in obtaining permission to use the rich sources still preserved at the hospital.
[23] 2 & 3 Philip & Mary, c. 5, SR, vol. 4, 280–1. The provision for licensed begging does not appear to have stemmed from specifically Catholic attitudes towards almsgiving, however, for it was retained in the first Elizabethan act dealing with begging, from 1563 (5 Elizabeth, c. 3, SR, vol. 4, 411–14).

act permitted several leading members of such communities to certify to county JPs the names of those with whom they were "surcharged." The JPs could then grant licenses to "go abroad to beg, get, and receive the charitable alms of th'inhabitants" of the county as a whole. In a borrowing from urban practice, the statute ordered that those licensed to beg outside their home areas were to wear on the front and back of their outer garment "some notable badge or token" given to them by local authorities.

Official discomfort about beggars and those who assisted them increased across the Elizabethan years. During a Parliamentary debate in 1571, Thomas Wilson, the Master of Requests, pointed out that although Christ said that the "poor of necessity we must have," He also said that there should be no beggars amongst God's people.[24] The way to avoid the latter was to prohibit giving to strangers, thereby lessening the "looseness and lewdness" that were currently so pronounced. The statute that resulted from that discussion in 1572 said that sturdy beggars aged 15 years or older were to be committed to jail until trial and if found guilty of vagabondage were to be "grievously whipped, and burnt through the gristle of the right ear with a hot iron"; if convicted a second time, they were subject to death as felons.[25] Anyone who gave lodging, money, or any other relief to an able-bodied beggar or vagabond who did not have a license was to be punished by a fine imposed by the JPs. A further measure in 1576 stipulated that a person who was receiving relief from his or her home parish but was found wandering elsewhere, "loitering and begging," was to be whipped.[26] In response to the increasing problem of people who were willing to work but could not find employment, the act instructed civic bodies to purchase stocks of wool, hemp, flax, iron, and other raw materials with which the poor could labor instead of living in idleness and begging. When William Harrison described the weekly collections taken by parishes to support the legitimately poor, he explained that such help was needed so that even these deserving people "should not scatter abroad and, by begging here and there, annoy both town and country."[27]

6.2   Traditional forms of licensed begging and gathering

Some people seeking help for individuals, whether themselves or others, and some of the gatherers appointed by charitable institutions carried

---

[24] *Proceedings in the Parls. of Eliz.*, vol. 1, 219.
[25] 14 Elizabeth, c. 5, secs. 2–4, *SR*, vol. 4, 591–2. For below, see ibid., sec. 6, 592. This act was repealed in 1593, replaced by the old statute of 1531 (35 Elizabeth, c. 7, secs. 6–7, *SR*, vol. 4, 855).
[26] 18 Elizabeth, c. 3, *SR*, vol. 4, 610–13, for this and below.
[27] W. Harrison, *Description of England*, 181.

written authorization to request assistance. Although obtaining a license required contact with an appropriate official, time, and usually money, having formal permission offered several advantages. As the laws against vagrants and idle beggars became more stringent, possession of a document could make the difference between alms and punishment. A third-party description of why the bearer warranted charity might inspire potential donors to greater generosity and may have helped to compensate for the absence of indulgences.

6.2.1   Alms seeking for individuals

Although permission to request alms for individuals could take many different forms (licenses, letters patent, briefs, letters of recommendation, certificates, placards, or letters of protection), they all explained why, where, and for how long the bearer was allowed to seek assistance. Sheriffs, mayors, and constables were generally instructed to allow the recipient to pass through their areas without trouble, and local officials were sometimes asked to help poor travelers find lodging.[28] Some awards asked ministers to urge parishioners to charity and encouraged church-wardens to assist the bearer, a reflection of the common pattern of gathering at services. Usually granted to a specific person, licenses could be transferred by the recipient to others who would do the actual collection on his or her behalf.

We rarely learn how much money individual alms seekers received over time. At least a few, however, obtained more than the minimum required for their daily needs. Mother Arden of Norwich, "who used daily to go a begging the streets," had amassed more than £44 in a variety of coins when her earnings were inspected by the town's court in 1562.[29] A. L. Beier estimated that in the early seventeenth century a beggar carrying a license might gather around 6d. per day. That was more than local poor people received from their own parishes and as much as agricultural laborers were earning. Especially in urban areas, the total sums given by a parish to all those carrying warrants could be substantial. In St. Botolph Aldgate, London in the late sixteenth century, the amount contributed by parishioners to authorized collections came to around £8 per year, as compared with £40 generated by the poor rate in that parish.[30]

---

[28] E.g., ULondL MS 684, items 6–8 and 12 (described and partially transcribed in Clarke, "Norfolk Licenses to Beg") and SurreyHC BR/OC/2/4, item 6.
[29] Pound, *Poverty and Vagrancy*, 100. She was allowed to keep only 6s. 8d. of that sum. For below, see Beier, *Masterless Men*, 27.
[30] Archer, "Charity of Early Modern Londoners."

After the Reformation, nearly all permissions to seek charitable aid were granted by secular officials. The crown, Lord Chancellor, Privy Council, and top military men were key figures. In 1567, the government attempted to create a consolidated method of granting and documenting royal permits. A single official was henceforth to issue – under the Great Seal – and enroll "all grants, licences and protections authorising persons to collect alms whether for the poor of any hospital or for themselves as having sustained loss by casual mishap or fire."[31] No permissions were to be awarded by others, and the newly appointed officer was to receive all of the customary fees required of applicants. By the 1580s and 1590s, royal letters of protection had become especially common. We are fortunate in having a record of the documents granted under the Great Seal but awaiting enrollment in the docket books to people who were soliciting assistance for themselves or a charitable institution between May 1592 and February 1596.[32] Of the 371 people who received royal protection, 111 (30 percent) solicited assistance for individuals, while the rest gathered for institutions or communities. Churchwardens' accounts indicate that royal authorization evoked a positive response in at least some parishes. Poor people gathering "with the queen's seal" or "broad seal" were assisted in St. Albans, Herts. in 1573–4, in South Newington, Oxfds. in 1596, in Melton Mowbray, Leics. in 1596–7, and in Howden, E. Yorks. in 1597.[33]

Urban officers sometimes issued or requested permits for local residents to seek alms in other areas, a practice that must have been resented by communities already struggling with their own poor. In 1555, Hereford asked county JPs to authorize twenty-seven adults and their eleven children to beg throughout the county, and in 1576 the mayor of Exeter prepared a "letter of commendation" for a local man who wanted to travel with his wife and child in hopes of finding work.[34] Some of the people who requested alms at the parish church of St. Botolph Aldgate, London in the late sixteenth century had been

---

[31] *CPR, Eliz.*, vol. 4, 62.
[32] HuntL CalB&EMSS. A cataloguer described these as "begging licenses," although the documents themselves do not use that term. The letters were issued while Sir John Pickering was Lord Keeper, and through his successor, Sir Thomas Egerton, they ended up in the Ellesmere MSS acquired by the Huntington Library (W. J. Jones, short report on these docket items prepared for the HuntL probably in the 1960s). I am grateful to John Broad for mentioning this listing to me and to Mary Robertson for providing information about it.
[33] CWA #52a, fol. 4r, CWA #80, 36, CWA #59, 36/140/26, and CWA #120.
[34] HerefRO, Hereford City Documents, bound vol. 3, transcript, 8–9, and *Tudor Economic Documents*, 334. The latter ended up in the Chester records.

authorized by the lord mayor of London and aldermen to ask for help in wards other than their own.[35]

Especially in the later Elizabethan years, county JPs issued many permits to beg. In 1573, an Essex landowner wrote to the Quarter Sessions to request a license for Richard Denyson, "a poor aged man" of the parish of Roydon, to allow him "to gather the charitable alms of good people within such hundreds as the justices shall think convenient."[36] The justices of Hertfordshire meeting at Hatfield between 1590 and 1595 received petitions requesting licenses to beg on behalf of a man who had lost his house and goods in a fire, several men described only as poor, and a "very poor man [who] has lately been robbed of his possessions from his house and almost ruined." The Sessions for the West Riding of Yorkshire likewise ordered in 1598 that a Rothwell man should receive a license to beg.[37]

Two or three justices from a given sub-region of the county could also authorize alms seeking. Although the documents they provided were less formal and rarely survive, they may have been the most common of all. Among some altered or counterfeit licenses confiscated in Guildford, Surrey, in the 1560s were ones nominally issued by three JPs in Gloucestershire, three JPs in Devon (at the recommendation of the mayor of Plymouth), and three JPs in Cornwall plus the mayor of Truro.[38] A testimonial and passport for John Smith of Bocking, Essex, whose house was destroyed by fire in 1590, was issued by three JPs of his neighborhood. Three JPs in Kent granted licenses in 1594 to Alice Colston of Nonington, aged more than 60 years, to collect within a particular hundred for one year and to Anthony Wood of Stourmouth and his wife, who could collect in two hundreds.[39] The pairs of JPs in northeast Norfolk who issued begging permits in the later 1580s and 1590s were aware of the need to justify their authority, occasionally referring to the statute that granted them this right.[40] One of their permits was later voided because it authorized solicitation in hundreds that lay outside the division of the county within which those JPs were allowed to act.

---

[35] Archer, "Charity of Early Modern Londoners." Others had licenses from the crown, the lord admiral, the bishop of London, or local preachers.

[36] EssexRO-Ch Q/SR 46/15, and see Q/SR 46/85. For below, see HertsA HAT/SR 2/79 (a petition supported by the minister of the man's church and nine other people who had signed or put their marks on it), HAT/SR 4/20, and HAT/SR 7/155–156.

[37] *West Riding Sessions Rolls*, 75.

[38] SurreyHC BR/OC/2/4, items 2a, 3a, and 9. For below, see *Staffordshire Quarter Session Rolls*, 32–3.

[39] CKentS QM/SB 21.

[40] ULondL MS 684, esp. item 15. For below, see ibid., item 14 dorse.

After the disappearance of indulgences, leaders of the new English church appear to have made only limited use of their moral authority to promote charitable giving to individuals.[41] Although bishops of London issued some certificates to people requesting alms, most of their fellows acted only in their secular capacities.[42] Thus, five licenses authorizing poor people to seek assistance in 1591 or 1592 were co-signed by the bishop of Norwich, but in his role as a Norfolk JP.[43] In Howden, the churchwardens gave small sums in 1597 to four poor men who had licenses from "my Lord's grace and the council," probably referring to either the archbishop of York or the head of the Council of the North.

With written authorization in hand, the process of legal alms solicitation could begin. Some requests were made at private homes, although this practice is poorly recorded. When widow Marjory Russell petitioned the mayor and JPs of Chester around 1585, asking for assistance from the town, she said that after living in Chester for more than 80 years, she was now unable to support herself but was reluctant to "seek her relief from door to door."[44] Two of the licenses granted by Norfolk JPs said that the recipients were allowed to ask for alms "at the house or houses of inhabitants of every town and parish" within the hundreds listed.

We know more about the contributions made in parishes. Many alms seekers came to religious services in the places they visited, displaying their permit to the minister and churchwardens in hope that the former would encourage the worshippers to contribute and the latter to donate something from parish funds. Either the churchwardens or the bearer would then solicit alms individually from the parishioners. A license ostensibly issued by the Lord Lieutenant and three JPs of Devon and Cornwall in 1565 authorizing collection of alms after a fire that destroyed eighteen houses called upon "all parsons, vicars, and curates and all ecclesiastical persons" to declare "the great calamity and misfortune of these poor bearers" in church on Sundays and at other services.[45] The churchwardens, "or other honest men in their absence," were then to "collect and gather the charitable devotion of their parishioners, that they through your good help may the better be relieved and comforted."

---

[41] Ping, "Raising Funds."
[42] For London, see Aydelotte, *Elizabethan Rogues*, 24, and Archer, "Charity of Early Modern Londoners."
[43] ULondL MS 684, items 1, 6, 9, 10, and 15. For below, see CWA #120.
[44] ChChRO QSF/35, no. 66, used through A2A. For below, see ULondL MS 684, items 1 and 15.
[45] SurreyHC BR/OC/2/4, item 6. Although this license was later confiscated by constables in Guildford, perhaps because someone other than the named recipients was using it, the original document may have been valid.

Licensed people might have to compete with unlicensed ones at church services. Some strangers who lacked authorization were able to persuade the wardens and parishioners to help anyway, although perhaps without the minister's endorsement. But in what was probably a traditional pattern that was increasingly viewed as disruptive of good religious order and civic propriety, troublesome local beggars solicited assistance during or around the edges of services. In Liverpool, the mayor prohibited "the begging woman with 5 children following her" from wandering openly in the chapel during service time in 1573; the bishop of Durham's visitation in 1577 ordered that no beggar should ask publicly for assistance – whether sitting, lying, or standing – during divine services.[46] York's officials requested the masters of the Minster in 1588 to try to prohibit beggars from coming into the church and asked that the city be allowed to send officials to remove them.[47] The church of Ely St. Mary, Cambs. was so plagued by beggars in 1583 that even authorized solicitation of alms during services was banned. A rule made "by the consent of all the inhabitants of the said parish" ordered that beggars, whether or not they had licenses, were "not to trouble the congregation" individually. Instead, the churchwardens, with the consent of two senior parishioners, were to give them something out of parish funds.

The reasons for which permission to seek alms were granted expanded across the Elizabethan period. Some people had suffered a sudden calamity. The fire that led to the testimonial and passport received by John Smith of Bocking in 1590 had burned down his house, killed two of his children, and destroyed the tools he needed to work as a millwright.[48] "Burnings" were the most common reason for which poor women were granted licenses.[49] Of 111 letters of protection granted by the crown to individuals seeking alms between 1592 and 1596, eight went to women soliciting help after a fire, one of whom was suffering from sickness and extreme poverty as well. Fires could be especially devastating for the elderly. Several JPs in Norfolk issued a travel pass in 1583 to 86-year-old

---

[46] *Liverpool Town Books*, 97, and *Injunctions and Other Ecclesiastical Proceedings*, 24.

[47] *York Civic Records*, vol. 8, 159. For below, see CWA #19, 18.

[48] *Staffordshire Quarter Session Rolls*, vol. 1, 32–3. Although Smith's written authorization said that he, his wife, and surviving children were allowed to ask for "godly charities" from individuals and parishes as they traveled to Chester in the northwest of the country, where they planned to settle with one of his uncles, notes on the back of the license indicate that in fact the Smith family wandered around seven counties before their permit was confiscated in Stafford.

[49] E.g., CWA #11, first account, and CWA #3, 96. For below, see HuntL CalB&EMSS. Most of these letters went to women on their own, but one was joined by two male relatives.

Edmund Fuller and his 84-year-old wife Margery.[50] Although Margery was bedridden, the couple had previously managed to take care of themselves in the little house where they lived. But after it burned down, consuming their possessions and grain, "the said poor old creatures have not left them any thing for their relief in this, their old and impotent state." They were permitted to move to "their children, kinsfolks, and friends, by whom they hope to receive some comfort," reminding us of the dangers of isolation and the importance of personal ties in the provision of aid. Churchwardens' accounts indicate that many parishes provided aid in response to such disasters. Wardens in Pattingham gave 12d. in 1593 to "one Grene of Horburne having had his house burned," and the church in Melton Mowbray contributed to four poor men in 1596–7 who had lost homes in Worcestershire, Northamptonshire, and Lincolnshire.[51] Occasionally a license to collect was awarded to multiple people who had been struck by a given fire, thereby forming a link between individual certificates and grants to entire communities.[52]

When examining churchwardens' contributions because of a fire, we encounter a contradiction between the laws requiring a license to beg and actual practice. Whereas parish officers did sometimes assist people said to have displayed appropriate documentation, many payments to people harmed by fire (or other misfortunes) make no mention of any kind of formal authorization, even when other entries in the same account specify that recipients had licenses.[53] Although it is risky to argue from negative evidence, what seems to be the willingness of parish officers to ignore the rule about official permission is illustrated in accounts from all around the country. If a needy person was able to persuade the wardens that his or her loss was genuine, sympathy proved more powerful than Parliamentary statutes. The wardens may have recognized that obtaining authorization was difficult for poor people who lacked ready access to the officials who could provide such documents.

Gathering was also permitted for merchants or sailors who had suffered losses at sea, sometimes described as the result of storms or shipwreck. A mariner of Woodbridge, Suff. who had lost merchandise worth over £400 "by misfortune and great tempests on the seas" was allowed to seek alms in 1565; a license to solicit aid in London and three counties was granted in 1573 to a seaman of Ipswich after two ships laden with goods

---

[50] ULondL MS 684, item 12.   [51] CWA #88, fol. 8r, and CWA #59, 36/140/26.
[52] E.g., SurreyHC BR/OC/2/4, item 6, and *CPR, Eliz.*, vol. 7, 372.
[53] E.g., with no reference to licenses when giving after fires, CWA #26, 322/1, fols. 74 and 96, and CWA #31, fol. 20; with some entries mentioning a license and others not, CWA #59, 36/140/25 and 26.

were lost in a storm at Yarmouth, Norf.[54] John Gunbye of Maldon, Essex suffered a double misfortune. In May 1577, a ship of his carrying coals from Newcastle upon Tyne to Maldon was wrecked near Tilmouth, Northumb.; four months later, a second ship was wrecked while traveling from Staningborough, Lincs. towards Newcastle.[55] Other licenses were awarded to merchants or seamen from London, Devon, and Yorkshire, and some parishes responded favorably to such requests for alms.[56]

People might be allowed to ask for assistance after foreign adversaries or pirates had captured them or their relatives or taken their goods. In 1565, Thomas Otley, a mariner of Harwich, Essex, received permission to collect for himself and a fellow townsman.[57] They had been sailing from Ireland towards Yarmouth when they were taken by the French and carried to Calais. The other man was still a prisoner there, but Otley had been "licensed upon surety" to return to England to gather the £130 needed to secure their freedom. Capture by Barbary pirates, "Moors," or "Turks" was evidently a growing peril. In 1578 the widowed mother and the wife of John Wynter, a shipwright and merchant of Bristol being held by the Turks at la Roche, Barbary, obtained letters patent to request alms for his release; the following year two merchants of Bristol were licensed to collect alms for their fellows, still in captivity, who had been captured by Turks off the coast of Sardinia.[58] Especially in the late sixteenth century, the Spanish were sometimes named as enemies.[59] Two recipients of royal letters of protection in the early 1590s were women raising funds to ransom their husbands, held prisoner by Moors or Spaniards.

Eastern Orthodox Christians sometimes received permission to collect alms. George Habib, said to be a Chaldean born in the city of Babylon, was licensed in 1565 to gather money for the release of his son, sister, and two other kinsmen.[60] While trading in the city of "Nassebine" in Persia at the time the city was seized by the Great Turk, they and some other Christians had been taken captive. He and several of his relatives had escaped after being held for two years, but he could not obtain release of the others "without charity." A Christian man from Macedonia,

---

[54] *CPR, Eliz.*, vol. 3, 321; ibid., vol. 6, 56.
[55] Ibid., vol. 7, 539. For below, see ibid., vol. 3, 473, vol. 5, 8, and vol. 7, 63.
[56] CWA #93, KG 2/2/3, p. 157, and CWA #3, 97–8 (which do not mention licenses), and CWA #53, from 1595 (referring to a brief).
[57] *CPR, Eliz.*, vol. 3, 243.
[58] Ibid., vol. 7, 440; ibid., vol. 8, 33. See also ibid., vol. 8, 25, Wilts&SA A1/150/1, p. 138, and ShropsA 3365/2624.
[59] E.g., *CPR, Eliz.*, vol. 3, 393. For below, see HuntL CalB&EMSS.
[60] *CPR, Eliz.*, vol. 3, 233.

"despoiled and imprisoned by the Tartars and afterwards ransomed by certain Christians," was given permission to collect alms in an unusually large number of counties in 1582.[61] Elizabeth granted an interesting license in 1597 – published simultaneously in Greek – to Emmanuel Achilles for collection of alms towards the ransom of the sons of the former head of the church of Thessaloniki, murdered by the Turkish sultan.

Churchwardens' accounts show that local people were willing to give to people harmed by England's enemies and to foreign Christians, often making larger contributions than were common for other kinds of alms seekers.[62] By the late sixteenth century, however, the central government was starting to recognize that funds gathered for ransoms might need supervision to ensure that they reached their designated recipients. The Privy Council sent an "open placard" to all mayors and other officials in Devon and Cornwall in 1590 on behalf of two merchants of the West Country who were part of a group recently robbed at sea and taken prisoner by the Spanish.[63] Noting that the men were authorized to "collect the devotions of good disposed people in Cornwall and Devon for one year," the council instructed the Earl of Bath to see that the money was "employed as it is meant."

As the result of wars in Ireland and the Low Countries, followed by the Spanish Armada and subsequent fighting, a growing number of poor ex-soldiers solicited alms, often in a quasi-authorized fashion. Physically healthy soldiers discharged from service were supposed to carry a pass issued by the JPs of the port where they landed, describing the route to be taken while moving homewards and requiring them to cover a minimum of 12 miles per day.[64] While such certificates offered protection against punishment as a vagrant, they made no provision for travel expenses, leaving former soldiers reliant upon alms. The issue was more complex if the men had been wounded or become ill before being released from service. The costs of returning home might then fall on the shoulders of the communities where they landed. Dover's officials complained to Robert Cecil in 1597 about their "great charges" in relieving poor, sick, and lame soldiers who had recently returned from France, including furnishing money for their travel.[65] London faced a somewhat

---

[61] Ibid., vol. 9, 196. For below, see Vickers, "Elizabethan Contact with Greece."
[62] CWA #93, 2/2/3, p. 157, CWA #27, fol. 44, and CWA #117, MCS 17, fol. 33r.
[63] *APC*, vol. 19, 451–2. The men were required to pay ransom of £325, as surety for which two other members of their company remained "in durance."
[64] Cruickshank, *Elizabeth's Army*, 36–40.
[65] HMC, *Cal. of the MSS of the Marquis of Salisbury*, vol. 7, 156–7. For below, see Archer, *Pursuit of Stability*, 156, and *John Howes' MS.*, 4–5.

different problem, as maimed soldiers flocked into the city seeking relief in its hospitals.

To promote longer-term assistance for injured former soldiers, local officials as well as the central government issued licenses to seek alms, in some cases long after their service had ended. In 1566, a Carlisle man who had been "mutilated and maimed in his body in the Queens' Majesty's service" along the West Marches received a license from military, county, and urban officers in Cumberland to "travel and receive the devotion and charitable alms of well disposed people" at "churches and other convenient places of assembly."[66] The award was made because he was now "impotent and unable to labour for his living" as well as "destitute of able friends or other provision for his relief." Elizabeth granted a license in 1577 to a "very poor, aged, impotent, and almost blind" yeoman from Northiam, Sussex to gather in two counties for one year because of "his service to Henry VIII by sea and land in the wars."[67] It is not entirely clear, however, in what settings ex-soldiers were allowed to seek assistance. A bill discussed in Parliament in May 1572 but not passed said explicitly that soldiers and mariners traveling with passports were not to ask for alms "at anybody's door, but resort to such as keep the poor man's box at every town."[68] The Privy Council granted a license to a poor, crippled soldier in 1592 to collect "the devotion and benevolence of the inhabitants within the county of Suffolk" for six months in all places except "chapels, churches, and such like places of public assembly." Perhaps men who had fought were considered too rough to be encouraged to visit private houses and church services, or perhaps their competition with other alms seekers was unwelcome.

A more privileged set of former soldiers was allowed to solicit alms temporarily because they had received a royal grant of an "alms room" at one of the cathedral churches or other institutions.[69] Although alms rooms were intended to provide a secure living, the system sometimes contributed to begging, for many recipients were authorized to ask for alms while traveling to take up their places. Further, if the daily stipend were not sufficient, the cathedral might allow its almsmen to "go abroad for their better living."[70] By the 1590s, severe pressure on these places

---

[66] SurreyHC BR/OC/2/4, item 4. When the man carrying this authorization, which had been altered, was arrested in Guildford, Surrey, he was ordered to return to Carlisle within 30 days.

[67] *CPR, Eliz.*, vol. 7, 302.

[68] *Proceedings in the Parls. of Eliz.*, vol. 1, 344. The statute concerning vagabonds and relief of the poor passed in 1572 does not contain this requirement (14 Elizabeth, c. 5, *SR*, vol. 4, 590–8). For below, see *APC*, vol. 22, 534.

[69] See ch. 1.4 above. For below, see, e.g., *APC*, vol. 19, 103 and 165–6.

[70] Atherton et al., "Pressed Down by Want," 30, from Ely in the 1560s.

due to the rising number of incapacitated soldiers meant that most royal appointments were given in reversion, to be implemented after the death of the current tenant of the position and whatever people were ahead of the recipient in line. Because reversionary grants left new awardees with no form of support in the meantime, permission to solicit alms was commonly granted either for a designated period of time or until the place assigned to them became vacant.[71] Many licenses for prospective almsmen barred the recipient from soliciting alms at church services.

Whereas urban officials commonly objected to the arrival of former soldiers requesting alms, due in part to fear that they might have been vagrants conscripted from the streets or had kept their weapons after being disbanded, churchwardens and constables in smaller communities appear to have responded more sympathetically to men who said that they had fought in wars.[72] Especially in rural areas and particularly as appeals mounted after 1588, parish accounts suggest that they did not always carry proper authorization.[73] One soldier assisted in South Newington in 1580 was moving properly with a passport, but six others who received money from the parish in 1581, 1591, and 1592 evidently lacked official permission.[74] Pattingham contributed 8d. "to a soldier that had the queen's broad seal" in 1592–3 but gave the same amount to a man described simply as "a soldier in the church." In 1590, a constable of Scothorne, Lincs. brought to the churchwardens "a poor man being a soldier" and two other soldiers, each of whom received 3d.[75]

Another cluster of alms seekers received permission due to a physical disability or chronic illness. Although a few people had been allowed to seek alms for such reasons in previous centuries, their number was multiplied many-fold by the worsening of need. In some cases, the Protestant crown tried to fill the gap left by the collapse of indulgences. Elizabeth awarded a license to a man from Hertford "afflicted with the palsy" in 1565; the Privy Council gave a passport in 1590 to a Welshman described as "a poor impotent person possessed with a palsy over all his body and many other infirmities," permitting him to request alms as he traveled to the baths (a curative water source) in Somerset to seek healing for his ailments.[76]

---

[71] E.g., *APC*, vol. 20, 10–11, 51 (tris), 241 (bis), 249, and 296, and vol. 22, 75 and 117–18. For below, see ibid., vol. 20, 10–11, 51, and 296.
[72] Cruickshank, *Elizabeth's Army*, 36–40 and 125–6.
[73] E.g., CWA #84, 64, CWA #3, 86–7, and BritL Add. MSS 30,278, used through HarvUA 17729, Box 3, Somerset, Staplegrove, VI-C-1, 427.
[74] CWA #80, 14, 15, and 29–30. For below, see CWA #88, fol. 8r.
[75] CWA #67, fol. 3r–v.
[76] *CPR, Eliz.*, vol. 3, 320, and *APC*, vol. 20, 86. See also CKentS QM/SO/7 (from 1593/4, used through A2A) and HuntL CalB&EMSS.

Disabled people might receive certificates from county or local officials too. In 1590, the parson and five other inhabitants of Thundersley, Essex wrote to the Quarter Sessions to request that William Warner, "a very poor, lame, and impotent person no way able to get his living nor any part thereof," be allowed to "crave the devotion of well-disposed people."[77] JPs in northeast Norfolk granted licenses to solicit alms or passes to travel in the early 1590s to a blind man, a man with an infirmity in one of his arms and both legs who had a wife and five children to support, and a mariner from Cromer who needed money to pay a surgeon for cutting off his infected leg, injured while at sea.

Sick or disabled people frequently received aid from churchwardens. Wardens of St. Werburgh's parish, Bristol, gave a shilling in 1563 to "a poor lazar man [a leper, or someone with a skin disease] which had a license to beg in Bristow," and St. Mary's in Ely gave 6d. in 1581 to Elizabeth Mascall of Peterborough, "by license, being lame."[78] In 1584–5, the churchwardens of St. Martin Coney Street in York paid 16d. "to a poor man of Castlegate that had his leg broken" and 12d. "to a poor cripple." Between 1589 and 1596, Pattingham's churchwardens gave 6d. each to a blind man, "a poor lame maid," and a blind woman, all of whom were said to have come into the church asking for alms.[79]

Although some earlier licenses had mentioned old age or poverty as secondary factors, by the late Elizabethan period, permission might be granted simply because the poor recipient was elderly or enfeebled or the parent of a large number of children. That pattern was especially common in certificates granted by local JPs. Many of the licenses to poor people issued by JPs in northeast Norfolk explained that they had been issued at the request of the inhabitants of the recipient's home communities, which had more poverty-stricken people than they could relieve themselves.[80] Walter Fosse, who had lived for over 21 years in Horsford and Horsham St. Faith, was authorized to beg in 1591. During his younger years, he had "behaved him self honestly, painfully getting his living, with the sweat of his brows," but now, "by means of much pain, and other infirmities both in body and limbs," he was no longer able to work for his own support. Richard Alyson of Catfield was described that same year as a very poor

---

[77] EssexRO-Ch Q/SR 112/69. Three of the men marked rather than signed the petition. For below, see ULondL MS 684, items 15, 4, and 8.
[78] CWA #43 and CWA #19, 16. For below, see CWA #117, MCS 16, p. 190, and also SomstRO DD/SAS C795/CH 20, under 1590.
[79] CWA #88, fols. 5v, 10r, and 11r.
[80] ULondL MS 684, items 1, 2, 6, 9, and 14. That wording met the requirement of being "surcharged" by poor inhabitants as imposed by the statute of 1555. For below, see ibid., item 5.

man who "hath many poor young children depending upon him."[81] He had obtained a special license to erect a little dwelling in Catfield, but he needed money with which to construct it. His permit authorized him "to gather the benevolence of his good friends" living within six nearby hundreds.

In Elizabethan churchwardens' accounts, the largest group of outsiders who received alms were described merely as poor, with no further qualification. Some but not all displayed documentation that confirmed their legitimate need. Half a dozen poor men and women said to have carried testimonials received assistance in Camborne, Corn. between 1557 and 1593.[82] In Kilkhampton, near Bude, Corn., between 1570 and 1593 and in Ely St. Mary in 1584, churchwardens gave somewhat larger payments to poor people who were said to have "gathered," which may suggest some kind of certificate, than to those described merely as poor. In Shillington, Beds., four poor men "which had a license to gather in the church" received payments in 1581–2, but so did "a poor man" and "a poor man of Westoning," both of whom were given slightly larger sums despite the apparent absence of certificates.[83] In St. Martin Coney Street, York, eight men described as poor but bearing testimonials were assisted in 1584–5, but so were two poor men without documentation, who received similar amounts. Melton Mowbray's wardens gave small sums in 1595–6 to two poor men with licenses, to several others lacking authorization, and to a man who had requested alms in the church but received nothing.[84]

A few additional reasons appear occasionally as the justification for a license or donation. Theft was rarely mentioned, although Pattingham's churchwardens gave 8d. in 1591–2 to a "fellow that came with letters patents to gather for one that was robbed on the sea."[85] People could receive alms in connection with their educational or clerical status: scholars traveling to or from the university, ministers, or preachers. In Pitminster, Som., Thomas Por(bor), "being a dark man," received 4d.

[81] Ibid., item 10.
[82] CWA #26, 322/1, fols. 46–102, passim, and 322/2, fols. 113 and 129–30. For below, see CWA #27, fols. 24, 44, and 55, and CWA #19, 20–2.
[83] CWA #3, 75–6. For below, see CWA #117, MCS 16, pp. 189–91. In Pattingham, eighteen non-local poor people, many of whom were said to have requested alms in the church, were given 4–6d. each between 1588 and 1596, but only one was described as carrying a testimonial (CWA #88, fols. 4v–11r, passim).
[84] CWA #59, DG 36/140/25.
[85] CWA #88, fol. 6v. For below, see, e.g., CWA #80, 13 and 19, and CWA #88, fol. 10r. The Register of the University of Oxford lists fifteen travel licenses granted to students between 1551 and 1572 (Aydelotte, *Elizabethan Rogues*, 24).

in 1590.[86] In conservative communities, even someone found guilty of wrongdoing might evoke the churchwardens' sympathy, reflecting an older conception of charity. Camborne gave 12d. in 1570 for bread and shoes "for the poor woman in prisonage," while Kilkhampton's wardens paid 2d. in 1575–6 "for meat for a poor woman that was set in the stocks at the fair."[87]

While most of the examples cited here come from parish sources, similar reasons for bestowing alms – and a similar disregard for documentation – are visible in urban records. The detailed accounts of the chamberlains of Nottingham between 1574 and 1592 illustrate the pattern.[88] Natural disasters and capture by enemies were commonly mentioned. "A poor man dwelling in Southwell having a testimonial from the Justices that his house was burned" was given 6d. in 1578–9, but so was "a poor man that had his house burnt." "A poor Scotsman that lost his ship" was assisted in 1589–90. In 1585–6, the chamberlains contributed small sums to six poor mariners who had been taken prisoner; they gave a slightly larger amount to a poor sailor from Bristol who had written authorization from his captain to gather alms after being seized by pirates. In 1589–90, "a poor man which was taken captive by the Turk" received 4d., while a more generous contribution was given to "three Hungarians who had the Queen and Council's warrant to collect and gather the realm themselves as captives from the Turk." In 1574–5, three soldiers on their way from Oxford to Newcastle upon Tyne received small donations, and the town contributed to maimed soldiers, mainly men returning from Ireland (between 1577 and 1585) or France (in 1591). Nottingham's officials were charitably inclined towards those with physical disabilities. In 1578–9, they gave 12d. to "4 lame men coming from Kendall [in Westmoreland] going unto the bath in Leicester shire," and two years later they contributed 4d. to a poor woman likewise heading to a curative spring. The following year they paid 4d. "to a poor lame man which came forth of Ireland." The miscellaneous categories are represented too. "A poor man dwelling at Blyth who was robbed and had taken from him threescore pounds" received 4d. in 1587–8, and scholars of Cambridge and Oxford were awarded small sums in 1577–8, 1580–1, and 1591–2. Unlike the parishes, Nottingham's chamberlains rarely helped outsiders described

---

[86] SomstRO DD/SAS/C795/CH/20.
[87] CWA #26, 322/1, fol. 80, and CWA #27, fol. 24.
[88] *Records of the Borough of Nottingham*, vol. 4, 158–235, passim. Individual references will not be provided for the examples below. For similar payments in Beverley in the early 1570s, see ERYoAS-B DDBC/II/7/3, fols. 16r, 37r, and 48r.

simply as poor: the accountant usually added some additional feature, from the categories considered above, that justified the use of civic funds for unknown people who sought charitable assistance.

6.2.2   Gathering for hospitals, almshouses, and prisoners

Despite the opposition of early Protestant reformers to abuses in the utilization of proctors, that traditional method of gathering for hospitals and other charitable institutions was employed throughout the second half of the sixteenth century. Gatherers operated in much the same manner as people collecting for individuals, moving from one community to the next to solicit alms from potential donors. They went especially to churches at service times, in hopes of receiving donations from the worshippers as well as from the churchwardens out of parish funds.[89] Traveling within designated areas, they were allowed to deduct their own living expenses before delivering the remaining income to the house they represented. Especially during the 1580s and 1590s, many almshouses and hospitals whose expenses exceeded the income from their own endowments and whatever support was contributed by local people used gatherers for additional funds. Proctors were usually appointed by the institution itself. "William Umfries, having the seal of the hospital of Stamford" (Lincs.), received 6d. from the churchwardens of Melton Mowbray in 1597–8.[90] A few hospitals sent out their own residents to gather. Two JPs in Norfolk prepared a document in 1591 permitting Richard Ashe, one of sixteen men living in the poor house without St. Augustine's gates at Norwich, or his deputy, to gather alms throughout Norfolk.[91]

Royal support for institutional collection changed form over time. Although Elizabeth issued a proclamation in 1560 permitting gathering in Wales for the hospitals in London founded or re-founded during Edward's reign, there is no indication that she continued to use that mechanism to support fundraising for institutions.[92] Not until around

---

[89] In 1596–7, the wardens of Lambeth, Surrey paid for a paper book in which they could record "the proctors when they come with the broad seal to gather in the church" (CWA #94, pt. 2, 200).

[90] CWA #59, 36/140/26. For below, see, e.g., the "lazar men" or "poor men" who came to Bishop's Stortford, Herts. to collect for their hospitals in or near London, Colchester, and Waltham in 1566: HertsRO 12A/1, #5.

[91] ULondL MS 684, item 13. The justices were apparently uncertain as to whether they had the right to grant this permission, for the document says they have licensed Ashe to collect for the house "so far as in us lyeth."

[92] TRP, vol. 2, 161–2, supported by a brief (Bewes, Church Briefs, 64–5, and BritL "Pressmark c. 41.h.I," as reproduced in Aydelotte, Elizabethan Rogues, plate II, facing p. 25).

1570 did the crown begin to use its power in more vigorous fashion to help compensate at least in part for Protestantism's limited ability to encourage and reward charitable giving. For the rest of Elizabeth's reign, her government issued a growing number of briefs and letters of protection on behalf of people gathering for institutions. By 1587, so many organizations were receiving royal permission to solicit funds that Thomas Purfoote obtained the right from the Stationers' Company to print the briefs that authorized their collection.[93] The crown also made some effort to ensure that money gathered by proctors went to the institutions that authorized collection: in 1578 it demanded a bond of £5 from a man appointed to collect alms for the hospital at Highgate, Middx., subject to his accounting for the sums he gathered and delivery of his royal license to the governor of the hospital when it expired.[94]

We gain a valuable window into the volume and nature of royal letters of protection for institutional gatherers from the docket items preserved at the Huntington Library. Of the awards issued between May 1592 and February 1596, 252 were granted to individuals collecting for "poor houses" (a generic term that covered both hospitals and almshouses) located in or near a named place.[95] Some of the letters gave protection to men described as "proctors" for the houses, while other recipients were termed "guiders." The meaning of the latter term is uncertain, but because a guider was in some cases appointed at the same time as a proctor for the same institution and set of counties, the word probably refers here to a knowledgeable person who accompanied the proctor on his travels.[96]

---

[93] Kitching, "Fire Disasters." Despite a historiographical emphasis on the impact of printing, it is not clear that a brief that had been run off in multiple copies on paper would have appeared more official than a hand-written license on parchment with the issuer's seal impressed in wax.

[94] NottsA DD/4P/71/11, used through A2A.

[95] HuntL CalB&EMSS. A disproportionate number of the recipients had what appear to be Welsh names: were silver-tongued medieval pardoners replaced by equally eloquent Welshmen? The dockets for 1578–9 included letters of protection for ten poor houses, all of which were included in the later awards as well (Bewes, *Church Briefs*, 16).

[96] Although few other references to a "guider" were encountered in the records used for this project, the term appears to have had two possible meanings. In a usage like that in the dockets, a man arrested for traveling with a false license in 1581 was said to have been begging in various towns in Warwickshire, "having an other fellow with him to guide him" (*Book of John Fisher*, 77); a grant from two JPs of Norfolk in 1591 refers to a license to gather alms for a poor house in Norwich formerly issued to a "chief proctor or guider" (ULondL MS 684, item 13); and see ch. 5, n. 14 above. But the head of the lazar house at Augustine's gate in Norwich was referred to as the warden or guider in the 1560s, and Christ's Hospital in Ipswich described the man who supervised its poor as "the guider" during the later Elizabethan period (Phillips, "Charitable Institutions," 245, and *Poor Relief in Elizabethan Ipswich*, 15–16). The *OED*'s definition of "guider" as the chief officer of a charitable institution reflects only the second meaning.

Eighty-one houses are named in the docket letters, although sometimes titled in various ways, plus another eight that are imprecisely described and may refer to one of the named houses or to different ones. With the exception of four institutions in Yorkshire, all of the houses lay south and east of a line that stretched from Cornwall through Gloucester and Leicestershire and on to Lincolnshire in the east-central part of the country. Some houses received only a single award, but most received multiple licenses, either granted in different years or giving protection to people gathering in different counties at the same time. Ten houses received six to eleven grants each: six large hospitals outside London that served more than local residents – located in Enfield, Hammersmith, Highgate, Kingsland (in Hackney), Knightsbridge, and Mile End (in Stratford at Bow) – plus four others scattered around the central and southern parts of the country.[97] Usually the grant permitted collection in the county in which the house was located plus one adjacent county, but a few covered a wider range. Collectors for the six London-area hospitals were authorized to work in ten to eighteen counties.

Parish accounts indicate that churchwardens commonly contributed small amounts to these traveling representatives.[98] Some gatherers worked within counties near their house, where its name and functions would presumably have been known. In Cornwall during the late 1560s, wardens in St. Breock contributed to the poor house of St. Leonard in Launceston, to a lazar house probably in Liskeard, and to unnamed poor houses in Exeter and Tavistock, Devon.[99] In Ely St. Mary, churchwardens gave small sums between 1579 and 1587 to proctors for hospitals in Cambridge, Dunstable, Beds., Beccles and Ipswich in Suffolk, and Norwich and (Little) Walsingham in Norfolk. Other institutions sent their proctors further afield. During the 1580s and 1590s, men collecting for houses in Chichester and Worcester received alms in Kingston on Thames, Surrey, as did a proctor gathering for an institution in Tynemouth, Northumb. in Staplegrove, Som.[100] The most active over long distances, however, were the six large hospitals around London. Some parishes were visited by a

---

[97] In Dunstable, Beds., Waltham (or Walton) Cross, Herts., East Harnham (near Salisbury), Wilts., and Langport Westover, Som. It is not clear why these houses received special protection. The London-perimeter houses had originally served lepers, but were re-founded for the poor.

[98] For a few cases that mention "the Queen's letters" or "a license under her majesty's broad seal," see CWA #80, 36, and CWA #120, for 1597.

[99] CWA #31, fols. 20 ff., and Somerscales, "Lazar Houses in Cornwall." For below, see CWA #19, 12–13, 27, and 32–3.

[100] CWA #93, KG 2/2/3, p. 157, and BritL Add MSS 30,278, used through HarvUA 17729, Box 3, Somerset, Staplegrove, VI-C-1, 427. For below, see, e.g., CWA #19, 16, 21, 27–8, and 32–3, CWA #3, 84–5, and CWA #93, KG 2/2/3, p. 157.

stream of gatherers every year. Ely St. Mary, for example, contributed to twelve proctors in 1587; Kingston on Thames gave to six institutions in one year in the 1590s.[101] But parishioners were not compelled to contribute individually, nor was the presence of a collector always welcomed. Churchwardens in St. Albans paid a proctor to prevent him from gathering at a service on Sunday, July 19, 1590.[102]

Less clearly sanctioned and poorly supervised gatherers raised money for poor people detained in the prisons associated with the courts of the Marshalsea and King's (or Queen's) Bench. As late as 1596, a royal proclamation emphasized that inmates in the Marshalsea prison had no means of living unless they received alms from charitably disposed people.[103] During the late 1580s and most of the 1590s, nominal agents collected donations from churchwardens throughout the country for these prisoners.[104] A man who claimed to be a gatherer for the Marshalsea or King's Bench prison in 1590 carried a staff that he presented as a sign of his office. Among the few references to any kind of written permission in parish accounts is an entry from Great Paxton, Hunts. in 1593, where the churchwardens inspected "a brief brought & sent by Edward Sutton, collector in the same brief named for Huntingtonshire," before making a small contribution for the Marshalsea prison.[105] Most of these collectors were described in unspecific terms like "a poor man that did gather for the King's Bench." Whether the contributions they received found their way back to the prisons we do not know.

6.3   New techniques for county and national projects

Whereas medieval definitions continued to shape what were considered to be legitimate objects of charitable alms after the Reformation, including such activities as rebuilding damaged churches and paying for necessary but expensive infrastructure, it was becoming apparent by the 1570s that older methods of gathering voluntary alms did not produce enough money for big projects. Nor did they provide adequate supervision of the collectors who were now handling large sums. Leaders of the church together with Parliament and the Privy Council therefore experimented with some alternative techniques for raising money for county initiatives

---

[101] CWA #19, 32–3, and CWA #93, KG 2/2/3, p. 157.   [102] CWA #52a, fol. 32r.
[103] TRP, vol. 3, 168–9. This study does not consider assistance for people incarcerated in debtors' prisons.
[104] E.g., SomstRO DD/SAS C795/CH/20 and CWA #15, both from 1589. For below, see Records of the Borough of Leicester, 268. The man was arrested for cheating at cards.
[105] CWA #53, from 1593. For below, see CWA #3, 87, and also CWA #113, 5660/3, fol. 29v, and CWA #52a, fol. 33v.

that dealt with poverty and vagrancy as well as for public works of national importance. These methods represent a transition from voluntary to semi- or fully compulsory payments, imposed in most cases upon parishes.[106] Churchwardens or constables – the latter often treated in this context as if they were officers of parishes, not hundreds – were instructed to allocate individual amounts within their units and gather the funds. They were also to record the names of those who had paid, and how much they had given, before delivering the money to a designated agent of the project being supported and submitting their list of payers to a higher authority. External oversight, provided in early Elizabethan measures by bishops or urban authorities, was later assigned to JPs, usually a small group within each district. Those men wielded greater authority than churchwardens and constables, but were close enough to individual communities to respond to particular circumstances within them.

Experiments with obligatory levies to support external projects were important to the simultaneous development of poor relief within the parishes. The government was able to try out various methods of collection, supervision, and accounting, some of which were later applied to the system of parish support for locally needy people in the Poor Laws of 1598 and 1601. By the late 1590s, parishioners throughout the country were accustomed to making payments for assorted purposes located outside their immediate area, as well as to their own poor neighbors. Churchwardens too had gained experience in assessing and collecting charitable contributions, techniques that could be transferred to intra-parish efforts. It is possible that collection for county and national projects may even have lessened resistance to rendering parish dues. People who were initially reluctant to contribute to the local poor, as ordered in 1552 and 1563, may have come to feel that those donations were less objectionable than supporting vagrants and wounded ex-soldiers they had never met or paying for repair of a distant harbor they would never see. At least the level and the recipients of local rates were determined by their own churchwardens and Collectors for the Poor, and the parishioners could see for themselves whether the money was being collected fairly and used appropriately.

The first county-wide issue concerned prisoners in county jails.[107] Unlike people held in the Marshalsea and King's Bench prisons, those

---

[106] By semi-compulsory payments, I mean that parishes were required to contribute something, but the amount was not specified. Fully compulsory levies dictated how much each church had to render.

[107] County jails had been created pursuant to an act of 1531–2 that permitted JPs, with the agreement of the high constables or other officials of the hundreds, to impose a payment on wealthier members of the county to support these institutions (23 Henry VIII, c. 2, *SR*, vol. 3, 363–5).

detained at the county level had not been the object of regular collection. A statute of 1572 authorized JPs sitting in Quarter Sessions to impose a fixed payment of not more than 6d. to 8d. per week on every parish to support poor people in their county's jail.[108] Churchwardens were to rate their parishioners, collect the money, and deliver it quarterly to the high constable of their area.

A later effort tried to generate ongoing funds for maimed ex-soldiers, for whom previous options of licensed begging and alms rooms had proved insufficient. In 1593, Parliament passed a measure that created pensions at the county level for those who had fought for the crown but were now disabled or enfeebled.[109] The statute ordered that an assessment be levied in every parish for the relief of soldiers and sailors incapacitated by wounds or illness since 1588. Either the parishioners collectively or the churchwardens and constables were to allocate individual responsibility for paying the rate. If ex-soldiers who received a pension were found begging, they would lose their award and be subject to punishment as rogues. For the rest of the 1590s, churchwardens' accounts from throughout the country and some urban communities record quarterly deliveries, such as "paid to the high constable for the maimed soldiers and mariners at the Quarter Sessions after twelfthtide."[110] In 1593, churchwardens in St. Michael le Belfrey in York, which was required to render 4d. weekly (17s. 4d. annually), distributed its obligation among forty-five parishioners, assessed either by the week or the quarter.[111] That the levy was resented by some communities is suggested by the wording in the parish accounts of Wilmslow, Ches. in 1594–5: the churchwardens paid 17s. 4d. "unto the maimed soldiers, being imposed upon our parish by Statute."

The new plan did not serve its desired purpose of eliminating begging by individual former soldiers. In distributing the funds collected, county JPs chose, at least initially, to give substantial support – far more than was given to most poor people – to a limited number of men.[112] Because so few wounded soldiers were actually supported by the rate, individual

---

[108] 14 Elizabeth, c. 5, sec. 38, *SR*, vol. 4, 597. For implementation, see, e.g., *Wiltshire Co. Records: Mins. of Procs. in Sessions*, 29, and WYksAS-L NP/D1/5 (5).
[109] 35 Elizabeth, c. 4, *SR*, vol. 4, 847–9. No parish was to pay less than 1d. or more than 6d. weekly; the money was to be delivered to the high constable of each hundred, who would give it to a special treasurer named by the Quarter Sessions for distribution (Hudson, "Disabled Veterans").
[110] CWA #88, fol. 8v. See also CWA #13, fols. 28v–29r, CWA #58, 122 and 128, CWA #116, p. 134, CWA #121, from 1595–7, CWA #122, pp. 128–31c, SurreyHC LM 1023/ 29, and N-u-TrMus D6.75/HT 2, from 1597.
[111] BIA PR Y/MB 33, fol. 31r. For below, see CWA #24, fol. 35r.
[112] E.g., *Papers of Nathaniel Bacon*, 250, and CKentS QM/SB 35.

licenses to beg continued to be issued. In 1596–7, for instance, churchwardens in Melton Mowbray gave 6d. "to a poor man having the Queen's
broad seal, being a maimed person serving her majesty in diverse countries."[113] Some ex-servicemen were still authorized to seek alms by military or local officials. In 1595, Sir Francis Vere, chief commander of Her
Majesty's forces in the Low Countries, issued a certificate to John
Goodridge, who had been lamed when his left thigh was shot in battle.[114]
Because Goodridge was now "altogether unable of body for any service in
the field," Vere licensed him to return to England to seek alms for his relief
and maintenance. Although Goodridge used his license to collect 4s. 6d.
in the parish church in Lewisham, Kent, he later obtained a directive to
county JPs, instructing them to provide a regular stipend for him.[115]

Parliament introduced additional parish rates to support county-wide
correction for poor people who were chronically on the roads or refused to
work. A statute of 1572 initiated what was to become a system of work
houses for the poor.[116] Stressing that all needy people should have fixed
and adequate abodes where they received relief, rather than wandering
about and begging, the act ordered JPs to "make diligent search and
inquiry of all aged, poor, impotent and decayed persons" born in their
district or dwelling there for 3 years "which live or of necessity be compelled to live by alms of the charity of the people." After registering those
names, the JPs were to determine whether the parishes to which the people
belonged could provide for them. If not, the JPs were to appoint residences (termed "abiding places") in the county's various districts where poor
people would be housed and required to do whatever work they could.
These institutions were to be supported by a weekly payment owed by all
inhabitants of the district or sub-district, as imposed by the JPs; anyone
refusing to pay could be jailed by order of two JPs. The justices were
instructed to name special collectors to gather and distribute the
money, as well as overseers for the institutions. In practice, however,
although many cities had created their own "Bridewells" (after the
London model) even before 1575, only a quarter of the counties had
founded abiding/workhouses in smaller communities by the end of
Elizabeth's reign.[117]

---

[113] CWA #59, 36/140/26.   [114] CKentS QM/SB 63.
[115] Ibid., dorse, and QM/SB 86 and 97.
[116] 14 Elizabeth, c. 5, secs. 16–22, *SR*, vol. 4, 593–4, for this and below.
[117] Innes, "Prisons for the Poor." Slack commented that the first original contribution made
       by England to welfare strategies in Europe – and the most widely copied – was not
       compulsory taxation for the poor, but rather the workhouse ("Hospitals, Workhouses,"
       esp. 237).

Legislation of 1576 addressed the inadequacy of earlier laws against able-bodied vagrants.[118] Because the number of "rogues, vagabonds, and sturdy beggars" continued to rise, Parliament tried a harsher approach. The statute ordered that a residential House of Correction be established in every county to which people arrested as chronic vagrants should be brought and kept. After suitable punishment, inmates were to be set to work on a stock of supplies provided by the house. Run by overseers, the houses were supported by rates imposed within the county by JPs; payments were to be gathered by special collectors, who were required to submit their accounts to the JPs. Money was to be levied in the hundreds and probably sub-divided among the parishes, and those assessed for the tax who did not render their payments were to forfeit double the amount of the initial sum. Houses of Correction were subsequently erected by many counties, sometimes subsuming earlier Bridewells.[119]

New types of collection for certain public projects of national concern made use of the parish as the site for the collection of semi-obligatory payments. Requesting charitable alms for religious purposes was now limited to churches that needed repair or rebuilding, of which the most significant were the gatherings for St. Paul's Cathedral in London, damaged by fire in 1561, and for a central church in Bath, Som. starting in 1573.[120] Oversight as provided by the bishops for the latter was found to be inadequate, however, for collection was slow and the funds were not always returned; even by the end of the century, the body of the church in Bath was still bare. Protestant refugees or foreign churches were occasionally the subject of authorized gathering.[121]

More extensive experiments with compulsion and supervision were made for large secular projects like towns struck by fire. Officials in charge of the rebuilding needed a great deal of money, some of which had to be produced quickly, and they needed to know how much more would come in later and when. The crown still granted permission to solicit purely voluntary contributions, in the older style, for some communities

---

[118] 18 Elizabeth, c. 3, secs. 5–8, *SR*, vol. 4, 611–12. For implementation, see, e.g., Wilts&SA A1/150/1, p. 131, and BIA CP.G 2579.

[119] Van der Slice, "Elizabethan Houses of Correction," and Innes, "Prisons for the Poor."

[120] M. Harris, "'Inky Blots'," Bewes, *Church Briefs*, 66, *CPR, Eliz.*, vol. 6, 129, LincsA Lincoln Diocesan Records, Charities and Briefs, #8, and CambUL Ely Diocesan Records F/5/34, fols. 39 and 59. Traditional gathering was still used for smaller churches (e.g., *CPR, Eliz.*, vol. 9, 140, L&IS, *Cal. Pat. R., 32 Eliz.*, pt. 1, 208, and HuntL CalB&EMSS). For below, see *APC*, vol. 9, 163–4; Sir John Harrington, *Metamorphosis of Ajax* and his *Nugae Antiquae*, as quoted by Bewes, *Church Briefs*, 69.

[121] E.g., Bewes, *Church Briefs*, 57, LincsA Lincoln Diocesan Records, Charities and Briefs, #8, and Ben-Amos, *Culture of Giving*, 339.

damaged by fire.[122] But now bishops or secular authorities might be instructed to assist the gatherers or to offer financial backing themselves.[123] An intermediate stage between purely voluntary and obligatory contributions was seen in Portsmouth, a major military port, after severe losses from a fire in August 1579. The queen issued a proclamation and letters patent instructing the churchwardens and constables of every parish to organize a collection on behalf of Portsmouth.[124] They were to set down in writing the names of all of the parishioners and how much each contributed and deliver that list to the bishop of the diocese at his next visitation. Two men were appointed as official collectors of the contributions. These orders did bear fruit, although payments from most parishes were small.[125]

A movement towards more forcible collection is likewise seen with regard to collection of funds for infrastructure. For less expensive projects like repair of bridges or small piers, traditional gathering continued to be used, although now usually authorized by the crown, not by local officials as in the past.[126] But royal awards for some harbors – especially those that served an extended region of the coast – imposed more widespread and structured contributions. When the pier at St. Ives, Corn. needed work in 1575, royal letters patent authorized the inhabitants of the borough to gather in thirteen counties and cities for repair of their pier.[127] Solicitation was not to be handled by individual collectors, however, nor were donations entirely a matter of choice: JPs, mayors, and other officials were ordered to instruct "the constables within every parish" to gather funds and deliver the money to JPs of the county. In a similar manner,

---

[122] E.g., *CPR, Eliz.*, vol. 8, 225, CWA #75, fol. 57A, HuntL CalB&EMSS, and Kitching, "Fire Disasters."

[123] E.g., *CPR, Eliz.*, vol. 7, 440–1, and for Nantwich, Ches., hit by a terrible fire in 1583, Wilts&SA G23/1/3, fol. 79r, EssexRO-Ch D/Y 2/8, 225–6, HerefRO Hereford City Records, Tourn, 1558–97, transcript, p. 331, *Oxford Council Acts*, 7–8, TNA-PRO SP 12/184/22, Kitching, "Fire Disasters," and C. Harrison, "Great Fire," an unpublished paper kindly given to me by the author.

[124] *TRP*, vol. 2, 464–6, for this and below. Parishes were likewise required to prepare a list of contributors to a royally backed collection after Spaniards burned the towns of Penzance, Mousehole, and Newlin and the parish church of St. Paul in Cornwall in July 1595 (*TRP*, vol. 3, 151–3).

[125] In Worksop Priory, Notts., where the parish account book describes the payments as "the charitable benevolences and contributions of the inhabitants there to the town of Portsmouth," twenty-four people gave 1d. or 2d. each early in 1580; later that year, eighteen people paid 1/2 d. to 1d. (CWA #75, fols. 49B and 51A). In St. Saviour parish, Southwark, a total of 187 people paid in 1580, most giving less than a penny each, yielding a total of 26s. 4 3/4d. (LondMA P92/SAV/1932).

[126] E.g., for bridges, *CPR, Philip & Mary*, vol. 4, 312, ibid., *Eliz.*, vol. 4, 333, vol. 5, 208 and 324, vol. 6, 538–9, and vol. 7, 538–9; and for a pier, *CPR, Eliz.*, vol. 5, 20.

[127] *CPR, Eliz.*, vol. 6, 510, and *TRP*, vol. 2, 510–11.

churchwardens and constables were ordered to gather funds for repair of the sea mark at Selsey, Sussex in 1590.[128]

Greater supervision was imposed for the harbor at Colaton (or Colyton), near Seaton in Devon. Its decay left a long stretch of the coast extending from Exmouth, Devon to Lyme Regis, Dorset without a safe haven. The royal proclamation and letters patent of 1575 that licensed collection for the harbor began with a traditional appointment of two inhabitants of Colaton and two merchants of London, plus anyone who might be deputed by them, to collect charitable gifts and contributions anywhere in England for at least 12 years.[129] In language reminiscent of pre-Reformation practice, ministers and churchwardens were to exhort their parishioners to contribute liberally and remind "wealthy persons in time of sickness to further the works by way of their gifts and legacies." But the deputies who picked up contributions from the parishes were to submit and account for the funds to designated agents in London, turning in their lists of all donors, their dwelling places, and how much each had given. Proper use of the income to rebuild the harbor was overseen by a small group of knights and other local leaders, who had to report to the queen or Privy Council every 6 months about what work had been accomplished. Collection for Colaton haven at local churches was widespread and lengthy, extending from 1575 well into the 1580s.[130] For parishes situated far away from the south coast, the express royal order to contribute probably carried more weight than a generic sense of national duty. The churchwardens of Great Salkeld, Westml. grumbled in 1583: "We did also collect and gather for Collenton Haven as we were charged by Queen's letters patent – 13d."[131]

Even when contributors and donations were recorded, this kind of residually voluntary collection was problematic. If no fixed sum was assessed upon the parish, the amounts that people chose to contribute could be very small indeed. In an early form of "donor fatigue," the willingness of individual parishioners to give generously apparently waned during the later decades of Elizabeth's reign as the number of government-sponsored collections increased at the same time as

---

[128] *TRP*, vol. 3, 51–2. The Privy Council tried a different approach for the haven at Rye, Sussex in 1595. Urban officials were authorized to solicit contributions, but additional assistance was to be provided by the JPs of several maritime counties, who were to organize collections in their districts and give the money to Rye's officials (*Records of Maidstone*, 262–3).

[129] *CPR, Eliz.*, vol. 6, 463, which says 21 years; *TRP*, vol. 2, 387–9, says 12 years.

[130] CambrUL Ely Diocesan Records F/5/34, fols. 49 and 59, LondMA P92/SAV/1929, CWA #62, fol. 21r, and CWA #75, fols. 49B, 50A, 52A, 53r, and passim thereafter.

[131] CWA #103.

increasing numbers of individual and institutional gatherers flocked into parish churches. Churchwardens and constables may also have been unwilling to collect vigorously for other communities at a time when they were implementing the new system of providing for their own needy parishioners.

Yet fully obligatory payments were imposed only in the case of a few essential harbors used by the navy as well as by merchant shipping. To pay for repairs to the haven at Hastings, Sussex, one of the Cinque Ports facing France, the letters patent and proclamation authorizing collection in 1578 instructed JPs to appoint one churchwarden in every parish and one constable in every hundred who were to write down the names of all those able to contribute, with how much they ought to give, and then collect the money from them.[132] The JPs were to call any recalcitrant donors before them, and if they continued to object, send their names to the queen or Privy Council. This was the first time that individuals had been told in advance how much they had to pay for an outside project, as opposed to merely having the amount they had chosen to contribute recorded. We know that parish and urban officials did enforce the new rules.[133] For the strategically placed harbors and piers at Dover, Kent and Lyme Regis, Dorset, the government relied upon tonnage – a tax on merchandise that passed through ports or areas of shipping – from 1580 onwards.[134]

Collection for outside projects sometimes met at least passive resistance. A letter from the Privy Council to the Archbishop of York in 1591 concerning gathering for the town of Beccles, Suff., hit by a fire in 1586 shows that local officials might be unwilling to cooperate.[135] The queen had ordered that money be collected for Beccles in all parishes as soon as they received a copy of her authorizing brief; the income was to be returned to a designated gatherer within 20 days thereafter. But the man appointed by Beccles to receive money in the province of York had complained to the council that although he sent out the briefs and "continued his travels within your Province of York by the space of one year and a quarter," he had thus far received very little money. Many parishes had given him no contributions at all and had not returned their copy of the brief. The fault, the council commented pointedly, "must needs be in

---

[132] *CPR*, vol. 7, 438–9, and *TRP*, vol. 2, 426–30.
[133] E.g., LondMA P92/SAV/1930 and 1931, CWA #75, fol. 49D, *Records of the Borough of Leicester*, 179–80, and *Records of the Borough of Nottingham*, vol. 4, 194.
[134] E.g., 23 Elizabeth, c. 6, *SR*, vol. 4, 668, *Catalogue of the MSS in the Cottonian Library*, 556, *CSPD*, vol. 2, 106 and 238, BritL Lansdowne MS 66, no. 4, and *Proceedings in the Parls. of Eliz.*, vol. 1, 538–43, and vol. 3, 149–50.
[135] *APC*, vol. 22, 229, for this and below.

the ministers, churchwardens, and constables of the parish or some of them" who had failed to respond through negligence or contempt. Because the scant donations that Beccles's deputy for York had received thus far had all been consumed by his living expenses, the council required the archbishop to ensure that the provisions of the royal order henceforth be implemented.

6.4 The problem of fraud

During the second half of the sixteenth century, the legal obligation to carry a license when seeking alms created a vast pool of temptation and opportunity for producers and users of falsified documents. Some licenses were entirely counterfeit, created by a person who could make them appear to have been issued by a legitimate authorizing body, complete with signatures and seals. Alternatively, the names, places, and/or dates on a valid document could be scratched out and replaced by forged entries. Or an authentic license could be carried by someone who falsely claimed to be its designated recipient. Moreover, even if an institutional alms seeker had a valid permit, there was no assurance that the money collected would be delivered to the house that had issued the license. By the 1590s, national and local leaders clearly felt that dishonesty had undermined the entire system of charitable collection, leading to the drastic solution imposed by the Poor Laws of 1598 and 1601.

In the mid sixteenth century we start to encounter references to counterfeited authorizations as carried by individuals for their own benefit. A forged document licensing two men to beg was sent to the Privy Council in 1551 by the Lord Admiral: it purported to have been prepared by the admiral and Lord Russell, with their names subscribed.[136] The following decade, the council wrote to the lord mayor of London, enclosing the confession of a man who had produced counterfeit licenses to beg. The mayor was instructed to punish him severely, along with "others detected of this fault ... to the terror and example of others."

A lovely packet of nine small "beggars' licenses" confiscated by constables in Guildford between 1562 and 1567 is preserved in the borough records.[137] These little slips of parchment not only illustrate many of the possible forms of fraud among those requesting alms, but they are especially valuable because some have a note on the back describing why local officials decided that the license was invalid. One document granted

---

[136] *APC*, vol. 3, 389. The two men taken while begging with that license were sent to the pillory. For below, see ibid., vol. 7, 257, from 1565.
[137] SurreyHC BR/OC/2/4.

permission to Edward Browne and John Williams to request alms for 5 months.[138] They, together with twelve other men and a boy, had been on a ship of Cardiff, laden with merchandise to the value of £900 and headed for Bristol, when they were captured by pirates. Released at Milford Haven in Wales after losing all of their goods, they were authorized by local officials to seek charitable donations. The back of the document says that Browne and Williams were punished in Guildford because their names had been substituted for those originally written on the testimonial. "Neither be these persons any mariners, nor never lost any thing of nine hundred pounds specified in the testimonial, which they do confess to be false." Another license, alleging loss of a ship and goods at the hands of pirates near the Scilly Isles while sailing from Ireland towards London, was issued to two merchants.[139] When the man who carried it was arrested, Guildford's officials found notes on the back of the document saying that its bearer had previously been examined in the towns of Crewkerne, Som. (by a constable), and Romsey, Hants. (by the vicar), both of whom doubted that he was the person to whom the grant had been issued. Several other men were begging with a license that the constables thought was forged, but while they were trying to question one of its bearers, who claimed he could not speak English, his fellows ran away.[140] A man and woman asserted that they were traveling legitimately, on the basis of a certificate from their home parish. But the document they displayed, signed by the curate of Fakenham, Norf., and nine leading inhabitants, actually testified only that they had been married in Fakenham church on a stated day, not that they were authorized to seek alms while traveling.[141]

False authorizations to beg became an increasing problem as Elizabeth's reign progressed. Some of the documents had nominally been granted by the crown or Privy Council. In 1582, William Wright came into Winchelsea, Sussex carrying royal letters patent permitting him to "ask the devotion" of people in Kent and Sussex on the grounds that his tongue had been cut by his enemies in Lincolnshire.[142] When he was brought before the mayor and jurats for examination, he was found to be "a counterfeit rogue," whereupon he and his letters patent were sent off to the Lord Chancellor. Ralph Bower, a schoolmaster in Penrith, Cumb. confessed in 1596 that he had illegally prepared a passport for a vagrant that was used by its recipient to travel through at least six counties.[143] John

---

138 Ibid., item 2.   139 Ibid., item 9.   140 Ibid., item 3.   141 Ibid., item 5.
142 ESussRO Winchelsea 53, fol. 182v.
143 BritL Lansdowne MS 81, no. 64, and Aydelotte, *Elizabethan Rogues*, Plate III, after 40, showing the notations by local officers who had allowed him to pass.

Steele, a Northumberland man, was approved in 1597 to receive a begging license from the Privy Council on the grounds that he had been "burnt and wasted by the Scots," his goods and cattle carried away.[144] Subsequent inquiry by suspicious JPs in Nottinghamshire revealed, however, that the document he carried while "going up and down the country" had been counterfeited.

At least a few people were semi-professional producers of counterfeit licenses. A court book of Bethlehem Hospital in London describes a forger who could be found at the Griffin public house in Waltham (Holy) Cross, Essex in the mid-1570s.[145] For half a crown (2s. 6d.), he would produce a license that appeared to have been appropriately signed by Bethlehem's treasurer or keeper authorizing the bearer to beg. Robert Buck of Thaxsted, Essex was accused in 1597 of "very notable forgery and common counterfeiting [of] the Great Seal, the hands and seals of noblemen, Justices of the Peace, and other her Majesty's officers."[146] By such licenses he had authorized "vagrant and ill-disposed persons to range up and down the country abegging, to the great offence of her Majesty and extreme danger of the commonwealth." A woman who testified against Buck said she had seen in his house "so many counterfeit seals as would fill a hat" and that he had sold a copy of the Lord Admiral's seal to a beggar for 20s. Another witness said that Buck had counterfeited a passport with the seal of Dover for a man who henceforth sought alms as a lame soldier.

People might also be coerced into issuing certificates. In 1583, an official in Colchester, Essex confiscated a certificate with three seals at the bottom that appeared to be a passport for John Thynson to travel with his wife and children to seek his living with friends.[147] (It described him as "a poor, lame, impotent man and diseased and not able to work.") But above two of the seals, in the place of the normal signature, was written the phrase, "I dare not write no otherwise"; the third seal was signed only "I am he." It appears, therefore, that the bearer of the document had pushed the authors into preparing it, but was unable to read the statements that disavowed their support.

Particular suspicion was directed at men who requested aid due to military service or injuries incurred in battle. In Norwich, Edmund Abbot was picked up in 1561 for begging without written authorization

---

[144] HMC, *Cal. of the MSS of the Marquis of Salisbury*, vol. 7, 529–30 and 294–5, and *APC*, vol. 27, 295, for this and below.

[145] O'Donoghue, *Story of Bethlehem Hospital*, 128, which notes: "The governors do not seem to have ever issued any such licenses."

[146] HMC, *Seventh Report*, "MSS of G. A. Lowndes, Barrington Hall," 541, for the rest of this paragraph.

[147] EssexRO-Ch D/Y 2/5, 25.

and brought before the city court.[148] When he claimed that he had been hurt and his arm maimed "in the queen's affairs," doubting officials asked for details. How was he injured, where and when did the conflict occur, in which ship, and who was his captain? Constables and rural JPs were similarly careful in their inspection of the documents of supposed former soldiers. Sir William Brereton sent a letter to the Privy Council in June 1597 from his home in Cheshire.[149] He reported that a man had come to his house that day who claimed to have been born in Cumberland and to have served lately under Sir Paul Backes in Brabant. The alms seeker requested help "by virtue of a passport and license he pretended to have from certain of the Privy Council." After looking at the passport, however, Brereton thought it was probably counterfeit.

I therefore examined him, and he at the first said his name was William Fielding, allowed in the license to demand people's benevolence for the ransom of his brother. But afterwards he said his name was Thomas Swafield and showed a letter of deputation to beg in that name. Yet in the end he denied both those names and confessed for a truth that his name is William Wright, and that William Fielding, late a soldier with Sir Francis Vere, gave him the license and deputation a month ago at a tippling house, at the sign of The Holy Lamb in Shoreditch, and told him that with them he could beg all through England; and at the end he was to give Fielding 40s. for a recompense.

Brereton committed Wright to Chester Castle and sent the license and letter of deputation to the council.

The problem of fraudulent ex-soldiers intensified from the mid-1580s onwards due to the difficulty of distinguishing the increasing number of genuine soldiers returning from war from other disabled men who sought alms. The Privy Council wrote to the mayor of London and JPs of Middlesex in 1586, ordering them to examine all of the maimed people who were begging in the streets.[150] Those hurt in the wars were to be relieved by a general contribution and sent home to their own counties, while counterfeit ex-soldiers were to be severely punished. Three years later, the council required the JPs of Middlesex, Essex, and Surrey to work with the mayor of London and others to apprehend "such vagrant persons and masterless, as under color of having been used as soldiers in Her Majesty's services go about a begging on the high ways."[151] In 1589, the queen appointed a Provost Marshal for every county, with authority to

---

[148] *Records of the City of Norwich*, vol. 2, 180. I am grateful to Steven Gunn for this reference.
[149] HMC, *Cal. of the MSS of the Marquis of Salisbury*, vol. 7, 277, for the rest of this paragraph.
[150] *APC*, vol. 14, 253.   [151] Ibid., vol. 18, 214, and see also 222–3 and 236–8.

exercise martial law over both authentic and pretended ex-soldiers.[152] When "idle people and vagabonds" continued to "annoy the people by begging, on pretense of serving in the wars without relief," especially around London and the court, the queen instructed local officials in 1596 to designate certain days each month for searching and imprisoning such men; she would appoint a national Provost Marshal "with power to execute them upon the gallows without delay."

Even some of the men appointed to the highly desired alms rooms were not actually ex-soldiers. In April 1592, the Privy Council wrote to all of the cathedrals in response to complaints that "diverse persons that have received hurts or bruises and some lame and maimed that have never served in the wars" had been named to alms rooms.[153] Because such men had taken some of the places, soldiers who really had been injured in the wars "want that relief they ought to have and go up and down begging in pitiful manner." The council admitted that the queen herself had erroneously awarded places to some men due to "wrong suggestions to Her Majesty and undue means," but it believed that local institutions were similarly appointing improper almsmen. The deans and chapters were therefore ordered to send in reports about the holders of their places, describing "what hurts or maims they have, and where and under whose charge they received the same, either by their own report or to your knowledge, and in what places they have served, under whom."

As with individual begging licenses, certificates and letters of protection for those gathering for hospitals and almshouses could be counterfeited, altered, or used by an unauthorized person. William More of Loseley, Surrey wrote to Nicholas Bacon, the Lord Keeper, in 1574 to say that he had arrested a man who claimed to be a deputy to the governor of Moulsham Hospital in Essex, carrying what appeared to be a forged license for collecting alms in Surrey, Hampshire, and the Isle of Wight.[154] More forwarded the confiscated license and proof of deputation to Bacon, requesting further instructions. One of the licenses seized by constables in Guildford in the 1560s was nominally a grant from Queen Elizabeth to a proctor for the leper hospital of St. Mark and

---

[152] *TRP*, vol. 3, 46–8. For below, see TNA-PRO SP 12/261/70.
[153] *APC*, vol. 22, 382–3, for this paragraph.
[154] SurreyHC LM/COR/3/171, used through A2A. More seems to have been especially vigilant in dealing with proctors. In 1568 he had arrested Powell David, a proctor licensed to beg in Kent and Surrey for the hospital at Enfield, and given him "some correction" for choosing bad companions and abusing a constable (SurreyHC 6729/9/114, used through A2A).

St. Mary Magdalene in Dunstable.[155] A search of relevant records, however, reveals no indication of a hospital with either of those names operating in or near Dunstable after 1540. Proctors were held in such bad repute that some potential benefactors refused to assist them at all. The almshouse founded by Richard Watts in Rochester, Kent in 1579 was to provide one night's lodging, food, and 4d. for six poor travelers, so long as they were not "rogues or proctors."[156]

We have strongly suggestive evidence from the late Elizabethan period that some people were dishonestly obtaining royal letters of protection to gather alms for institutions. Of the Huntington Library's docket items from 1592 to 1596, seventy-three describe the "poor houses" for which collectors received protection in sufficient detail that we can identify both what they were called and where they were located.[157] I compared those institutions against several other sources: my database of hospitals and almshouses, Access to Archives, and various secondary studies. Of the seventy-three houses, just over half (thirty-seven) appear to have been functional during the 1590s. Even here, however, we cannot be sure that the person who received the letter of protection had in fact been authorized by that house to collect alms for it or that the money he gathered was taken back to the designated institution. The financial accounts of hospitals and almshouses from the Elizabethan period contain a conspicuous absence of references to income rendered by proctors.

The remaining houses whose collectors received royal protection are troubling. Slightly more than a quarter (nineteen) had operated at some time in the past but are said to have closed before 1592, many of them in the 1530s and 1540s.[158] For another fifteen houses, I found no evidence that they had ever existed at all. The major hospitals in urban areas that gained protection were active in the 1590s, but many of the doubtful ones were located in smaller communities away from the capital where only a person from that specific area would have known whether the supposed institution was real. For example, the dockets indicate that a surprising total of thirteen letters of protection were issued to people gathering for poor houses in or near Dunstable (four specifically named institutions and

---

[155] SurreyHC BR/OC/2/4, item 8, a damaged document dated November 1563 or 1564. I found no references to a Hospital of St. Mark at all. The Hospital of St. Mary Magdalene in Dunstable was last mentioned in 1338, and even if it had continued beyond that time, it was highly unlikely to have survived the Dissolution, as it was a dependant of Dunstable Priory. A Hospital of St. Mary Magdalene in Stopsley, on the far side of Luton, had closed by 1540.
[156] Howson, *Houses of Noble Poverty*, 91.
[157] HuntL CalB&EMSS. For the database, below, see ch. 3.1 above.
[158] Two other houses might possibly have existed at the time of their license, but probably did not.

seven others), a higher number of awards than for any other community or for any of the large London hospitals.[159] A license for the poor house of St. Mark probably referred to the same institution mentioned in the confiscated document from the 1560s, which was evidently defunct. The others (the houses of St. James, St. Leonard's, and Our Saviour) do not appear in any records.[160] Indeed, my project shows no hospitals at all operating in Dunstable or within five miles around it between 1540 and the end of the century. It is of course possible that some of the houses I was unable to identify were valid, just small and informal; a few institutions that had apparently ceased to function may have survived for a longer time. But it seems likely that even modest or struggling houses would have been mentioned in at least one of the sources consulted.

This analysis implies that clever but unscrupulous people had found ways of obtaining royal letters of protection to gather money for non-existent institutions. The cluster of references to houses in Dunstable further suggests that as news spread within a given community that one person had succeeded in this approach, others may have followed suit. With a royal license, a proctor could travel in the designated region for a year or two, free from fear of being arrested and punished as a vagrant. The contributions received, supposedly for the house, could stay in his own pocket. For someone who preferred being on the road to the constraints of a regular job and fixed abode, the system of charitable gathering offered excellent opportunities.

One wonders how fraudulent letters of protection from the crown might have been obtained. Perhaps the petitioner brought in a counterfeit document nominally from the head of a non-existent institution stating that he had been authorized as its proctor. In that case, central government officials need not have been aware of a problem (just as the Privy Council said that the queen had been fooled by people wrongly claiming to be maimed soldiers). Alternatively, since fees had to be paid by anyone obtaining a document under the Great Seal, a potential gatherer may simply have increased the amount given to one or more clerks within the issuing office in return for a letter of protection that had not demanded

---

[159] The seven institutions designated only by place might refer to any of the named ones.
[160] None of those houses is mentioned in any of the standard medieval sources for Bedfordshire and Dunstable, although those works do refer to a hospital or almonry run by the Fraternity of St. John during the second half of the fifteenth and early part of the sixteenth centuries (e.g., Evans, *Dunstable*). The only other house in Bedfordshire with a designation like these was the Hospital of St. Leonard in Bedford, which was probably closed in the 1530s; its property was certainly in private hands by 1556. I am grateful to Sue Evans, Senior Archivist at the Bedfordshire and Luton Archives and Record Service for her assistance with this query.

proof of the applicant's credentials. If that happened, people acting on behalf of the crown were complicit in the practice.

Similar problems are visible with regard to collectors for prisoners in the Marshalsea and King's Bench prisons. Because at least some churchwardens were prepared to make contributions even in the absence of a license, and because the prisons themselves exercised little if any supervision over the gatherers they appointed, the system was ripe for deceit. In 1581, Edmond Dakyns from Hartshorne, Derby., who was traveling under the name of Thomas Page, was arrested for vagrancy in Warwick.[161] Using a license to beg for alms for the Marshalsea prison issued to Page, Dakyns had gone "abroad begging in diverse towns in Warwickshire." When questioned by the town's bailiff, he claimed that Page, who lived in Westminster, had named him as one of the many men to whom he had sub-contracted the right to collect alms. To obtain Page's permission, Dakyns had left 30s. with him and was obligated to pay £3 in total. Close examination, however, revealed that Dakyns carried only "an old license of the Marshalsea expired three years since which was to beg in Leicestershire." He was therefore punished for a day and night, probably in the town stocks, and then set free.

Parliament and the crown tried to crack down on producers and bearers of false licenses. When defining the category of "rogues, vagabonds, and study beggars," a statute of 1572 listed various types of illegal alms gatherers, among them, "counterfeiters of licenses, passports and all users of the same, knowing the same to be counterfeit," and people "that be or utter themselves to be Proctors or Procurators, going in or about any country or countries within this realm, without sufficient authority" derived from the queen.[162] A royal proclamation of 1596 strengthened the hand of local authorities in dealing with illegitimate beggars. It referred to the many vagrants who either prepared themselves or acquired from someone else "counterfeit passports ... and licenses to beg and gather alms, pretending that they have been hurt and maimed in her majesty's service, or received some other great loss or hindrance by casualty." To add apparent authenticity to their documents, they forged the signatures and seals of members of the Privy Council, JPs, or military officers. The proclamation ordered ministers, churchwardens, and other local officers who interviewed such people to inspect their licenses carefully. If they had reason to doubt the authenticity of the documents, they should send them and their bearers to a nearby JP for further examination. If the latter was likewise suspicious, he was ordered to commit the

---

[161] *The Book of John Fisher*, 77–8, for the rest of this paragraph.
[162] 14 Elizabeth, c. 5, sec. 5, *SR*, vol. 4, 591–2. For below, see *TRP*, vol. 3, 159–62.

vagabond to prison until it could be established whether the names subscribed to the licenses were valid. Letters patent drafted in 1596 for a
collection in Kent and the Cinque Ports for prisoners in the Marshalsea
prison attempted to restrain abuses by ordering the arrest of any unauthorized collectors.[163]

The evidence presented here offers a new perspective on Elizabethan
literary works about rogues and vagabonds. This lively genre of tracts and
ballads, popular from the early 1560s into the early seventeenth century,
presented colorful accounts of various classifications of roaming beggars
and confidence men, each of which was said to have its own slang name
and share a special vocabulary.[164] Among the dishonest characters
described by John Awdeley in his work of 1561, *The Fraternity of
Vagabonds*, are people whose attributes resonate with the material we
have already seen. The "Whip-Jack" uses a counterfeit license "to beg
like a mariner," and the "Ruffler" travels with a weapon, "saying that he
hath been a servitor in the wars, and beggeth for his relief."[165] "Fraters" go
about with forged licenses to beg for a hospital, while literate "Jarkmen,"
some of whom know Latin, prepare false licenses, complete with seals.
Many of the men in all categories stole when they had a chance. Awdeley
mentions women in two roles: "Kitchen Morts" (girls who are brought
into the trade when they are young, evidently acting as servants); and
"Doxies" (adult women who work as petty thieves after being "broken" by
an "Upright-man," the chief among his particular group of wanderers,
who is able to command the services of its women).

The various categories of rogues and dissembling beggars – together
with their distinctive "canting" terminology and the amusing tales they
told – were portrayed in greater detail in Thomas Harman's influential
work, *A Caveat or Warning for Common Cursitors, Vulgarly Called
Vagabonds*.[166] First published in 1566 but reprinted several times thereafter, the *Caveat* claims to be based upon Harman's own experience as a
landholder in Kent who, while housebound during an illness, interviewed
the beggars who came by his home. He dedicated his work to Elizabeth,
Countess of Shrewsbury, as a warning: she was known for giving alms not
only to "the poor, indigent, and feeble" people of her own parish, but also
to "all such as cometh for relief unto your luckly gates."[167] Harman

---

[163] Bewes, *Church Briefs*, 89.
[164] The major texts are printed in *Elizabethan Underworld*.
[165] Ibid., 51–60, esp. 53–5, for the rest of this paragraph. The work was republished in
1575.
[166] Ibid., 60–118. The *Caveat* was reprinted four times in 1567–8, with a revised edition in
1573.
[167] Ibid., 61.

emphasized that she was pouring out her "ardent and bountiful charity" upon those who "through great hypocrisy do win and gain great alms in all places where they wilily wander," feigning "great misery, diseases, and other innumerable calamities." He encouraged the countess instead to reserve her mercy for "all such poor householders, both sick and sore, as neither can nor may walk abroad for relief and comfort."

The editor of the first modern edition of the *Caveat* wrote in 1930 that Harman was a virtual sociologist who had "no axe to grind" and whose account may be accepted as "genuine and in most particulars correct," but subsequent scholars have questioned that assessment.[168] Although Harman was apparently not a JP for Kent, he was an esquire and held other local offices, so he probably reflected the anxiety about vagrants shared by many of the country's elite.[169] The *Caveat*, sometimes described as related to the "role-playing" performed on the early modern stage or as a kind of "jest book," contains negative assumptions about poor people who sought alms while on the road (for example, that they were idle by choice and often traveled in large, organized groups) and offers troubling suggestions that legitimate peddlers and itinerant laborers seeking employment were sometimes labeled – and punished – as vagrants.[170]

Although Harman was most concerned about those wanderers who stole or used violence, he painted vivid pictures of some kinds of beggars we have met before. He labeled as "Fresh-Water Mariners" the "Whipjacks" who claimed to have suffered losses at sea but whose "ships were drowned in the plain of Salisbury" (i.e., far from any coast).[171] Carrying counterfeit licenses supposedly written by four or five important men that described either shipwreck or despoiling by pirates off the coast of Cornwall or Devon, these men commonly came from the West Country or Ireland. They were careful not to beg near the places of their supposed losses, waiting until they had reached the southeast of the country. (Harman's description accords almost verbatim with several of the documents confiscated in Guildford that same decade.)[172] He said that he had often impounded from such men their licenses and the money they had gathered, distributing the latter to poor people who lived near him. But in any town, he complained, they would be able to get a new license, sometimes even with a counterfeit seal from the Admiralty. "Once with much threatening and fair promises, I required to know of one

[168] Ibid., 495.   [169] Beier, "On the Boundaries."
[170] E.g., Woodbridge, "Jest Books," Fumerton, "Making Vagrancy (In)Visible," and the studies cited there.
[171] *Elizabethan Underworld*, 84.   [172] SurreyHC BR/OC/2/4, items 2, 3, and 6.

company, who made their license? And they swear that they bought the same at Portsmouth of a mariner there, and it cost them two shillings."[173] The "Rufflers" who claimed to have been injured in warfare might display a wound actually obtained in a drunken fray. "Fraters" sometimes carried "black boxes at their girdle, wherein they have a [counterfeit] brief of the Queen's Majesty's letters patents, given to such a poor spital-house for the relief of the poor there."[174] Harman recommended that "the founders of every such house, or the chief of the parish where they be . . . see unto these proctors, that they might do their duty."

Women are highly visible in the *Caveat*. In addition to a fuller description of "Doxies," who are now said more explicitly to have been raped by an "Upright Man," Harman introduces "Demanders for Glimmer."[175] These women travel with:

feigned licenses and counterfeited writings, having the hands and seals of such gentlemen as dwelleth near to the place where they feign themselves to have been burnt, and their goods consumed with fire. They will most lamentably demand your charity, and will quickly shed salt tears, they be so tender-hearted. They will never beg in that shire where their losses (as they say) was.

"Bawdy-baskets" went about with small domestic items for sale, seeking help from maidservants and engaging in petty theft; "Autem-Morts" and "Walking Morts" were married or unmarried women or widows who asked for alms while stealing whatever came to their hands.[176] While this literature was certainly exaggerated for dramatic effect, it may have been so well liked in part because its often unjustifiably hostile assumptions were intermingled not only with lively stories, but also with fairly accurate descriptions of some of the people who were fraudulently begging in Elizabethan England.

By the 1590s, English people were not only besieged with requests for alms from the individual beggars and institutional gatherers who came to their houses and churches, some of whom were dishonest, they were obliged also to respond to a variety of government-backed collections for external activities. For places on heavily traveled roads, it must have been an unusual Sunday when they were not encouraged by their minister or in effect required by their churchwardens or constables to contribute to some person or cause. Because poverty had become so severe, the informal and voluntary charity still advocated by the church was not displaced

---

[173] *Elizabethan Underworld*, 84. For below, see ibid., 67.
[174] Ibid., 81–3 for this and below.   [175] Ibid., 105–7. For below, see ibid., 94–8.
[176] Ibid., 98–105.

by the rising importance of payments mandated by the government: the two forms of assistance operated hand in hand. The common historical distinction between religious and secular forms of aid to the poor seems artificial in light of this material. For individuals, giving alms – whether to one's own needy neighbors or to public projects – was both a Christian obligation and a duty imposed by the government. For parishes, charitable activity was only one of the areas in which they had intertwined responsibilities to both church and state.

This discussion illustrates the diversity of responses towards assistance to the poor. At the level of policy, members of Parliament and urban leaders became increasingly concerned about beggars and those who assisted them. Some private people too were beginning to reject the long-established pattern whereby the poor could ask for help at the hands of their neighbors. In 1563, a London haberdasher left 2s. each to twenty poor but honest householders in his parish who lived "in the fear of God," but "to none such as go from door to door"; two decades later, a London scrivener excluded from the recipients of charity in his will "all such poor as go a-begging from door to door."[177] While such responses may perhaps have been influenced by puritan concerns with public order and control, they do not appear to have reflected the later assumption that living in idle poverty indicated an absence of saving grace. But we have also seen that many local people refused to implement the severe statutory measures concerning punishment of vagrants or to demand possession of written permission to beg. When confronted by a poor stranger who provided a convincing explanation of need, some churchwardens were clearly willing to provide assistance. Women deemed worthy of aid were helped alongside men, despite a possible rise in literary anxiety about dishonest female beggars. Private households similarly exercised their own judgment about who should receive alms. Widow Roberts of Boarzell, Sussex gave sums of between 2d. and 6d. each to assorted poor women and poor folks between 1568 and 1574, with no indication that she insisted upon formal documentation of their need.[178] A charitable response to unknown outsiders must have derived largely from individual compassion and/or religious teachings, for such donations did not contribute directly to the bonds said to have held social groups and local communities together.

[177] TNA-PRO PROB 11/47, fol. 60r–v, and PROB 11/65, fol. 8r–v, both as cited by Hickman, "From Catholic to Protestant," 126 and n. 41.
[178] *Accounts of the Roberts Family*, 71–134, passim. For below, see Ben-Amos, *Culture of Giving*, e.g., 376–7.

The central government had learned some important lessons from its experiments with methods of raising money for projects at the county and national level. The parish was the best – perhaps the only possible – unit within which funds could be produced. If local payments were to generate a substantial and predictable yield, they could not rely on voluntary or even semi-obligatory donations. The process of collection must be supervised by some kind of outside but knowledgeable authority, with JPs found to be the most satisfactory. An essential requirement was that written accounts be prepared and submitted to someone external to the project. These lessons were to be applied to the system of parish-based poor relief in the Poor Laws of 1598 and 1601, statutes that brought to an end the era of widespread and sometimes officially sanctioned begging.

7   The changing nature of almshouses and hospitals

The almshouses and hospitals that operated during the second half of the sixteenth century, especially newly founded or re-founded ones, differed from their predecessors in many respects.[1] The number of houses had dropped sharply as a result of the closing of religious institutions and royal confiscation of property between 1536 and 1553. Because institutions founded after 1540 were also generally smaller than their predecessors, the total number of people supported in the 1560s and even in the 1590s was considerably lower than in the 1520s. England's population was rising rapidly, so residential institutions provided accommodation for a much smaller fraction of the population in the late sixteenth century than they had in the fifteenth and early sixteenth centuries. Institutions established after 1540 (the great majority of which were almshouses) were heavily weighted towards elderly poor people, often women, and privacy for residents increased.

Because almshouses could no longer offer prayers for the dead, the reasons for establishing and maintaining such institutions had to be reassessed. Many houses still required prayer and thanksgiving for the generosity of founders and benefactors, but their social role as providers of care within the community became more important and expectations for good behavior increased. Dislike of begging and a belief in labor led many founders of new houses to provide a cash allowance to their residents and sometimes to prohibit idleness. A desire to make the beneficence of the donor visible within the community brought expanded use of distinctive liveries for inmates to wear when they were away from the institution, which in turn reinforced a collective identity.

The form of governance for new foundations changed too. The late medieval movement away from control by a religious house or no external oversight at all in favor of control either by an existing lay-run body such as a town or parish or by a set of formally constituted feoffees intensified.[2] In

---

[1] For definitions used in this chapter, see the opening section of ch. 3 above.
[2] A body of feoffees held property on behalf of a charitable institution, functioning like later trustees.

186

an attempt to provide more effective administration and supervision of their houses, founders often laid down careful rules for accounting and external visitation. Individuals or institutions that governed residential houses gained status through being both charitable and good stewards of resources. Although certain almshouses and hospitals obtained a royal charter of incorporation to gain greater legal and fiscal security, some institutions were plagued by operational problems.[3] It was only with the Poor Laws of 1598 and 1601 that the underlying issues were addressed in a manner that placed almshouses and hospitals on a more solid economic and legal footing, facilitating the establishment of many additional institutions in the following century.

This chapter begins by looking at the number of houses and the growing importance of privacy within them, turning then to the residents and the benefits they received. Later sections examine obligations for prayer and good behavior and the efforts made to improve the governance of institutions. We draw upon textual material from a wide range of local and national sources, the database of information about 1,005 almshouses and hospitals that functioned sometime between 1350 and 1599, and drawings and photographs of buildings that survived into the nineteenth or twentieth centuries.

7.1   The number of institutions and the growth of privacy

After the dramatic closings of the 1530s, 1540s, and 1550s, a smaller number of hospitals and almshouses disappeared later in the century (see Appendix C). The Hospital of Sts. John and Bartholomew in Winchelsea, Sussex, for example, still had at least three residents plus a master and his wife in 1560 and two poor folks in 1571, but in 1586 the mayor, jurats, and commons of the town ordered that the hospital and its lands be sold.[4] Some institutions that survived the Dissolution henceforth played different roles, sometimes operated by urban bodies as part of a wider program of assistance to the poor. Seventy-three houses in my database founded prior to 1540 were reconstituted later in the sixteenth century, with new kinds of residents and/or governance.

Spurred on by the closings, growing need among the poor, Protestant teachings about charity, and a desire to preserve one's name and good deeds into the future, donors founded new houses at an increasing rate. Of

---

[3] See ch. 9.2 below and McIntosh, "Negligence, Greed." For the sentence below, see chs. 9.1.2 and 9.2 below.

[4] ESussRO Winchelsea 51, fol. 70r–v, Winchelsea 53, fol. 13v, and Winchelsea 54, fol. 3r–v. For below, see, e.g., Phillips, "Charitable Institutions," ch. 4.

the institutions I examined, 210 were set up between 1540 and 1599.[5] (See Appendix B.) The kinds of people these houses were intended to serve reflected altered demographic and economic conditions. Only 2 percent of the institutions whose target population we know were meant for lepers or any other kind of sick people (see Appendix A). Three-quarters were described as almshouses for the poor, sometimes said explicitly to be for the elderly; the remainder were hospitals for poor people but with no mention of illness. Most of the latter were actually well-supported almshouses, despite their grander name.

Early modern scholars have drawn attention to the great burst of support for almshouses and hospitals in the Elizabethan period, which increased further between 1600 and 1660. In his analysis of wills and other documents from ten sample counties, W. K. Jordan found that between 1541 and 1600 more than £80,000 (12 percent of all charitable funds, including those for education and municipal projects) went to establishing residential institutions, backed in most cases by a landed endowment.[6] Ian Archer has shown that 32 percent of all citizens in a sample of London wills from the 1570s and 1590s left bequests to the city's hospitals. While those contributions are indeed significant, my database suggests that only in the 1580s did the number of new foundations approach the peak reached in the 1210s.

When we turn to the number of houses in existence per decade, as shown in Appendix D, we see that although the new institutions set up later in the century began to fill the gap, the total number in operation by the 1590s (494) had not quite reached the level seen around 1400; it was far below the values for the rest of the fifteenth and early sixteenth centuries.[7] The regional distribution of new hospitals when compared to late medieval institutions shows an increase in the Midlands/east central area, while almshouses were even more heavily concentrated than before in East Anglia/the southeast.[8] Slightly fewer houses of both types lay in the north/northwest. These shifts in location appear to mirror more general changes in the regional distribution of population and wealth during this period. Both kinds of institutions were more likely to be situated in villages

---

[5] For explanation of the database, see ch. 3.1 above.
[6] Jordan, *Philanthropy in England*, 369. For below, see Archer, "Charity of Early Modern Londoners."
[7] Of those 494, 253 had been founded before 1540, 172 were founded between 1540 and 1599, and 69 earlier institutions had been re-founded since 1540.
[8] See CUP Online App. 3. For definition of regions, see ch. 3, n. 42 above. Three-quarters of the houses of all types established in the north/northwest after 1540 were located in the city of York or elsewhere in Yorkshire.

than had been true previously, with many fewer in the leading cities, but an important cluster in market centers.[9]

The living arrangements offered by houses established after 1540 covered a considerable range. At the simplest end were almshouses in buildings used initially for ordinary domestic purposes, most of them lacking a landed endowment and hence functional only until they needed expensive maintenance. During the 1580s and 1590s on the south coast near Portsmouth, widow Jane Cotton settled two men in a little almshouse during her own lifetime, while widow Honor Wayte placed four poor, honest, and unmarried alms women in another house.[10] When Edward Clere obtained a license in 1576 to found a small almshouse and grammar school in Thetford, Norf., acting to complete the bequests in Richard Fulmerston's will, he said that he intended "to repair a tenement for the inhabitation of four poor." Other institutions were allowed to take over structures that had formerly belonged to a monastery or religious fraternity. The hospital in Warwick founded by Robert Dudley, Lord Leicester, in 1571 was housed in the guildhall, chapel, and secondary buildings of the medieval fraternities of St. George and the Blessed Virgin. Even so, the external appearance of the hospital was similar to the private residences that surrounded it.[11] Newly built institutions, which rarely had their own chapels, were commonly located near the parish church. Christ's Hospital in Abingdon, Berks. erected a set of dwellings known as "Long Alley" in the 1550s, close to St. Helen's church.[12] Rudhall's almshouses in Ross-on-Wye, Heref., founded in 1575, consisted of a row of five two-storey dwellings that opened directly onto the street, with easy access to the church.

A striking feature of Elizabethan institutions was their commitment to privacy for the residents. All newer houses and most of the older ones provided an individual sleeping chamber for every person.[13] In 1584, David Smith, official embroiderer to Queen Elizabeth, built an almshouse at the back of a large mansion in London (Woodmongers' Hall on St. Peter's Hill).[14] The structure contained six comfortable units opening off two sides of a central courtyard. Each consisted of a ground-floor

---

[9] See CUP Online App. 3. For types of communities, see CUP Online App. 1, pt. 6.
[10] Jordan, "Charities of Hampshire," 39–40. For below, see *CPR, Eliz.*, vol. 7, 197–8.
[11] Bailey, *Almshouses*, 84–5 and 90–1.
[12] Ibid., 46. For below, see Prescott, *English Medieval Hospital*, 93–4, and Bailey, *Almshouses*, 91.
[13] E.g., at the Bedford Almshouse in Watford, Herts., where each of the eight poor female residents was to live separately in her own unit (HertsA MS 10056).
[14] *London Surveys of Ralph Treswell*, Survey 34, pp. 108–9 (written description and floorplan).

chamber made of brick, 12.5 feet by 9 or 11 feet in size, with a fireplace and chimney, as well as an upper room with a privy. As pressure on places increased, some institutions allowed two people of the same sex to share a room. In Warwick, this was seen in the houses set up by Thomas Oken in 1571 and in the decisions of Nicholas Eyffeler's executors in the late 1590s.[15] The latter created four two-room apartments in a barn bequeathed by Eyffeler, but they placed two women into each unit, not the single woman specified by the testator. In his 1587 will, Sir Thomas Seckford, a Master of the Court of Requests, stipulated that six of the dwellings in his newly founded almshouse in Woodbridge, Suff. should each house two poor, unmarried men; the man chosen as "Principal of the Poor" was to have his own room.[16]

Some existing buildings were modified to meet the expectation for privacy. When the city of Gloucester took over operation of the old and partially ruined St. Bartholomew's Hospital in 1564, it paid for the cost of repairing the existing buildings and church, but also constructed separate new chambers for twenty-one of the forty poor people who were to be housed there.[17] Whereas the initial residents of Wyggeston's Hospital in Leicester, founded around 1513, were apparently housed in open dormitories, by the time of its 1574 statutes, each of the twelve poor men and twelve poor women had an individual chamber, although they shared kitchens at the end of their lodgings. At God's House in Southampton, the hospital built in 1416–17, where the five to ten residents had lived communally, was replaced around 1588 with a set of almshouses that provided every brother and sister with a separate dwelling.[18] A few institutions furnished locks for the residents' doors. When Ralph Lamb of Winchester left £400 to his executors in 1558 to support an additional group of six people at the Hospital of St. John the Baptist, he specified that each person was to have a private unit, with lock and key.[19] At Trinity Hospital, an almshouse in Bristol, the institution paid for locks for the inmates' chamber doors in 1584.

As part of the same trend, residents now rarely ate together. Some houses contained a fireplace for each resident, intended for cooking as well as warmth. Only a few of the older institutions still listed utensils for

---

[15] WarwsRO CR 2758/1 and CR 1618/WA12/36/13, both references kindly given to me by Angela Nicholls. Eyffeler was a glazier born in Germany who came to Warwick and left funds in his will to found an almshouse for eight female residents ("Nicholas Eyffeler").

[16] *Statutes . . . for Alms-Houses in Woodbridge*, v.

[17] GloucsA GBR K1/3, fol. 1. For below, see ROLeics 10 D 34/1419/1, printed in *Calendar of Charters*, 71–3. All subsequent references will be to the printed version.

[18] *Cartulary of God's House*, lxxxi–lxxxii.

[19] Deverell, *St. John's Hospital*, 9–10. For below, see BristolRO 33041 BMC/1/8.

food in their inventories, and even there, they may no longer have been in regular use. The Hospital of St. Mary Magdalene, Allington, near Bridport, Dorset, which now functioned as an almshouse, contained some cooking and eating equipment in 1587, but an inventory of goods in the personal rooms of two of the residents made in 1593 listed utensils for separate meals.[20] Wyggeston's Hospital was unusual in the ample supplies and comfortable furnishings it provided as late as 1568 for those rooms that were shared by all of the residents, including the kitchen and hall.[21]

An emphasis on individual activity is seen also in the provision of vegetable gardens. Although they are rarely mentioned in the accounts (which list only food that was purchased), many gardens in this period were worked separately, not in common.[22] William Lambarde's almshouse in East Greenwich, Kent, which opened in 1576, included a garden for each of its twenty poor men. As part of their almshouse in Watford, founded in 1581, the Earl and Countess of Bedford granted to their feoffees the barnyard of the parsonage together with eight houses the countess had already built on that land, each with a small croft or garden adjoining it.[23] The ordinances for Seckford's almshouse in Woodbridge stipulated that every room should have its own garden that the residents could "plant, sow, or set with herbs, roots, or any other fruit that shall be most commodious for them."

Institutions founded after 1540 had a weaker religious identity than in the past. Only 14 percent of those in my database had any kind of a religious title, and many of those were generic terms like God's House, Christ's Hospital, or Maison Dieu. More than half of the new almshouses were named after their founders, as were over a third of the hospitals. The title of another 10 percent referred to the location of the house, and the remainder had other kinds of names. A few self-consciously Protestant houses expressly rejected any religious designation. The new statutes prepared for Wyggeston's Hospital in 1574 noted that the institution was to be "for ever hereafter called by the name of William Wygston's Hospital in the town of Leicester . . . and not at any time hereafter [to] bear the name of any fancied saint or other superstitious name."[24]

Some houses used visual means to display their own or their benefactors' identities. Gatehouses might be decorated with the initials or coats of

---

[20] DorsetHC DC/BTB AB49, and see also DorsetHC D/SHA A141.
[21] ROLeics 1 D 50/III/1.
[22] For gardens of unspecified type, see ESussRO Rye 111/1 and *Cartulary of God's House*, lxxxii. For below, see Warnicke, *William Lambarde*, 44.
[23] HertsA MS 10056. For below, see *Statutes . . . for Alms-Houses in Woodbridge*, 1.
[24] *Calendar of Charters*, 55.

arms of founders or present an inscription recording their generosity.[25] When the almshouse founded by Thomas Oken in Warwick was painted in 1573–4, as was one in Binbery Lane in Bath, Som. in 1585, the goal was perhaps purely functional, to preserve exterior surfaces from rain.[26] In 1581–2, however, the governors of Foster's Almshouse in Bristol paid for scaffolding and washing a place on the outside of the house's chapel and gave a man 10s. for painting a picture there. In a quite surprising entry from 1587, Trinity Hospital in Bristol first hired a carpenter for 2 days to make a scaffold and then paid the substantial sum of 25s. 4d. to a painter.[27] His charge was to paint on the house's walls individual portraits of the five poor men and three poor women who lived there, together with three escutcheons of the founders and the city's arms.

7.2   Residents

Nearly all almshouses and hospitals established after 1540 were meant for needy lay people. Among the institutions in the database that described their intended inmates, 98 percent were either almshouses or hospitals for the poor, with no mention of sickness, and every one was for members of the laity.[28] But founders or those who appointed residents often had in mind more specific categories of need, stemming from the multiple meanings of poverty. Here again we see an assumption that friends or family would normally provide help, leaving only atypically detached people dependent upon institutional care. William Wyggeston's Hospital was for people who were "very aged, decrepit, blind, lame, or maimed, or that wanteth [lack] natural wit." But no one was to be accepted "which hath of himself or her self whereon to live, or else friends that be able and willing to keep them."[29] Thomas Cure presented a rank-listed set of criteria for admission into the College of the Poor in the parish of St. Saviour, Southwark, Surrey in 1584. Most of these categories focused on the kinds of people who might also receive licenses to solicit alms.[30]

---

[25] Prescott, *English Medieval Hospital*, 94–6, Tobriner, "Almshouses," and Rawcliffe, "A Word." But at the maison dieu in Hull, E. Yorks. founded in 1414 by John Gregg and his wife, an "ancient" portrait showing them with Jesus was defaced during Elizabeth's reign. A medieval list of the house's regulations, displayed on the wall, was also re-written to omit superstitious practices (Rawcliffe, "A Word").

[26] WarwsRO CR 2758/1, and *Accounts of the Chamberlains of Bath*, 85. For below, see BristolRO 33041 BMC/2/1.

[27] BristolRO 33041 BMC/1/8.   [28] See App. A and CUP Online App. 4.

[29] *Calendar of Charters*, 69. For below, see LondMA P92/SAV/1528, fols. 6v–9v, perhaps an adaptation of the preferences established by Lambarde for his almshouse in East Greenwich (Warnicke, *William Lambarde*, 46).

[30] See ch. 6.2 above.

Cure's priorities were: (1) someone who had previously labored, but is now aged and "past work"; (2) someone who has become lame or maimed by sickness or service in the wars and is thereby unable to labor; (3) someone who was born blind or has become blind; (4) people who have been "despoiled of their goods, and brought from riches to poverty" by a sudden chance event, such as fire, robbery, or shipwreck, so long as it was not through their own fault; (5) someone who had "become continually sick," provided it was not a contagious disease; and (6) people who were "overcharged with a burden of children" whom they could not support through their own work. Cure noted also that people should be favored who had committed no notorious crimes at any time in their lives, who had resided for a longer time in the parish, and who have "utterly no friends or kindred" who could assist them.[31]

While some institutional residents were nearly destitute, the members of houses that offered more generous benefits might be people of at least modest means, as reflected in the common requirement of a cash payment upon entry.[32] At least by the 1590s, new appointees to the almshouse in Stratford-upon-Avon, Warws. were expected to make a contribution at the time of their admission, a payment usually of 6s. 8d. described as the "dues" or "duties belonging to the house." In Rye, Sussex, a "good man or woman" could only be admitted to a place in St. Bartholomew's Hospital in the 1560s without paying the usual entry fee if he or she had previously contributed to the welfare of the town and "be now impoverished and impotent, decayed of their goods and chattels, and little goods have to live with."[33] When Richard Buckmaster was admitted to a room and the accompanying corrody in the Hospital of St. John in Sandwich, Kent in 1583, he was required to pay the standard admission fee of 26s. 8d. Nor were all residents uneducated. The first statutes for Trinity Hospital in Long Melford, Suff. say that each year one of the twelve poor brethren who could read and write was to be chosen by the warden and other residents as sub-warden, to help keep the book of receipts and payments.[34]

The balance of residents continued to shift towards the elderly, especially women. Old age was sometimes a formal requirement for entry, but

---

[31] LondMA P92/SAV/1528, fol. 10v.
[32] For the former, the clothing and utensils of an almsman and alms woman of Wyggeston's Hospital who died in 1541–2 were valued at only 6s. 8d. and 4s. 10d. respectively (ROLeics 1 D 50/II/15). For below, see *Minutes and Accounts*, vol. 5, e.g., 17, 30, 89, 92, and 94.
[33] Holloway, *History . . . of Rye*, 157. For below, see CKentS Ch 10J A1. He paid 20s. at the time, with the remainder to be deducted quarterly from his corrody.
[34] SuffRO-BSE OC 88.

could also be imposed through individual decisions about admission. In Stratford-upon-Avon, borough officials decreed in 1584 that people admitted into the town's almshouse must be at least threescore years old as well as long residents of the community.[35] In 1554–5, John Draper, smith, sent a petition to Hereford's officials, asking for a place as a bede-man in the almshouse of St. Giles. He said that he had been a freeman of the city for about 50 years and warden of the smiths' company for 9 years, but now, aged 80 years and unable to labor for his own support, he had "fallen in to great necessity and poverty" and was "like to perish for want of food and sustenance." In Hadleigh, Suff., thirty-two people (six married couples, sixteen women on their own, and four men) lived in the town's almshouses in 1594.[36] Fifteen were in their 60s, ten in their 70s, and five in their 80s or 90s; the two residents in their 40s or 50s were married to older spouses. In my database, three-quarters of the institutions founded after 1540 accepted women, as compared with 60 percent in the later medieval years and even fewer earlier.[37] We do not know whether the heightened emphasis on widows is because there were more of them in the community for simple demographic reasons, whether they faced particularly severe need, or whether they were thought to be easier to control than men.

Many houses confined their membership to residents of the area. The almshouse called St. Thomas House set up by Thomas Ellys in Doncaster, W. Yorks. in 1557 was to harbor six poor men and women who "have dwelled within the said town or parish, being of good name and fame, and that have fallen in poverty by reason of sickness or other misfortune."[38] When Archbishop Whitgift re-established St. Thomas' Hospital in Canterbury as an almshouse in 1586, he said that all of its brothers and sisters had to be local residents, a stipulation very different from its original and even its early Elizabethan goal of providing accommodation for the itinerant poor. The eight female residents of the almshouse in Watford set up by the Earl and Countess of Bedford were to be "the poorest and most neediest" to be found in that parish or two places in Buckingham.[39]

The marital status of residents was a matter of disagreement. Some houses insisted that inmates not be married. At the hospital in Stoke Poges, Bucks. founded by Lord Hastings of Loughborough at the end of

---

[35] *Minutes and Accounts*, vol. 3, 140. For below, see HerefRO Hereford City documents, Tourn, 1541–58, transcript, 50.
[36] HadlTR 11/A/3.   [37] See CUP Online App. 4.
[38] DoncA DX.War/A/1(a). For below, see Sweetinburgh, "The Poor."
[39] HertsA MS 10056.

Mary's reign, no married people were to be admitted; the poor brothers of the Earl of Leicester's hospital in Warwick were not to take a wife without special consent of the master; and at Wyggeston's Hospital, married people could not enter, and any who wed after being admitted were to be expelled.[40] But the three small almshouses left by Thomas Oken in Warwick in 1571 were intended for married couples or two people of the same sex. Sir William Cordell, founder of Trinity Hospital in Long Melford, expressed some uncertainty about the marital issue in his 1581 will. He wrote that the residents should be at least 55 years old, preferably 60 years, "and sole and unmarried if any such can be found."[41]

The issue of marriage led to problems for the parish of St. Saviour in Southwark. In 1592 the churchwardens approved the proposed marriage of a man named Rodes who was then living in the almshouse run by the parish.[42] The matter came to the attention of the Archbishop of Canterbury, however, who sent an emissary to talk with the churchwardens about why Rodes should not marry. Under pressure, the members of the vestry finally agreed that if Rodes married, he would have to leave the almshouse and his pension. Two years later, however, the orders laid down for the College of the Poor in the parish were more tolerant. If a candidate for admission was married, both members of the couple would be allowed to enter the house, although they would share the quarters and monthly pension of a single person.[43] When a poor person died, a surviving spouse might be offered a separate place if enfeebled, but someone who was "able and valiant of body" would need to leave the institution.

A few houses accommodated specialized types of inmates. At the hospital at Ledbury, Heref., re-founded in 1568, at least some of the twelve brethren were to be former servants of the crown.[44] In a remnant of the earlier pattern of offering overnight shelter to poor travelers, the bailiff of Trinity Hospital in Bristol paid 6d. in 1590 for 2 lbs. of candles "to light the poor wayfaring people to bed, that cometh to lodge in the hospital." Several houses were for ex-sailors or soldiers.[45] In his 1551 will, Henry Tooley of Ipswich said that priority should be given in the almshouse he was founding to people who were "unfainedly lame by occasion of the king's wars"; at the Earl of Leicester's Hospital in Warwick, wounded and

---

[40] CBuckssS CH 7/G.5; *Copy of the Ordinances*, item XXV; *Calendar of Charters*, 69 and 78–9. For below, see WarwsRO CR 2758/1.
[41] SuffRO-BSE FL 509/11/10.   [42] CWA #96, P92/SAV/450, p. 175.
[43] LondMA P92/SAV/1528, fols. 11v–14v.
[44] *CPR, Eliz.*, vol. 4, 215. For below, see BristolRO 33041 BMC/1/8.
[45] E.g., Trinity House in Kingston upon Hull in 1581, for seamen (*CPR, Eliz.*, vol. 9, 19), and an almshouse for sailors in Bristol (*APC*, vol. 25, 10–11). For "alms rooms" for ex-soldiers, see chs. 1.2, 6.2, and 6.4 above.

maimed former soldiers, especially those who had been in troops led by the earl himself or his heirs, received preference.[46] A few urban institutions took in orphaned children until they were old enough to be placed as servants or apprentices or assisted poor parents. At Christ's Hospital in Ipswich, the twenty-three children housed in 1595–6 formed the largest group among its residents.[47] One of York's three city hospitals took in "a girl great with child which named her self Margaret Shawe" for 3 weeks before she gave birth in 1574 or 1575 and for 4 weeks thereafter. Because Margaret Danfold's husband had left her, she and her two children were accepted into St. Anthony's Hospital in York, receiving 8d. weekly.[48] When her husband later returned, however, urban officers ordered that Margaret's payments should cease and that she and the children should leave the institution within the next 3 months.

A requirement for admission mentioned in virtually all statutes from the Elizabethan period was that candidates be known for their godly and moral behavior. The four poor men named to places in the hospital in Stoke Poges were to be "of the age of fifty years and upward, honest and quiet men disposed to serve God in prayer and good conversation"; its two poor women were to be "of good and honest fame."[49] When Cure described criteria for admission into the College of the Poor in Southwark, he said that all candidates should be "honest and godly" men and women.[50] They should be chosen only if they could "say the Lord's Prayer, the articles of the Christian faith or belief, and the Ten Commandments of God in English. No enemy to the Gospel of God or to His religion now established by authority in the realm, no common swearer, adulterer, fornicator, thief, picker, hedge breaker, common drunkard."[51]

A limited number of houses – especially those related in some manner to urban governments – gave at least occasional payments to people living outside their own walls. St. John's Hospital in Winchester awarded money to non-residents for boarding children and tending people when they were sick in 1593–4, and "Fraunces the Blackamore" received 2s. 4d. from Christ's Hospital, Abingdon during an illness in 1596.[52] In Ipswich, the

---

[46] *Poor Relief in Elizabethan Ipswich*, 15–17; *Copy of the Ordinances*, items VII–X. Tooley said that that if ex-soldiers were not available, "aged and decrepit persons" were to be admitted. Later records of the house do not mention maimed soldiers.
[47] *Poor Relief in Elizabethan Ipswich*, 17. For below, see YorkCA E69.
[48] *York Civic Records*, vol. 7, 145.   [49] CBucksS CH 7/G.5.
[50] LondMA P92/SAV/1528, fols. 6v–9v.
[51] Ibid., fol. 11r. A picker was a petty thief; a hedge breaker took wood from common hedges for fuel.
[52] HampsRO W/H1/155 and CHAbing Accounts, vol. 1. For below, see *Poor Relief in Elizabethan Ipswich*, 17–18.

Tooley Foundation used most of its income to support people in its almshouses, but when surplus funds were available, it provided assistance to non-residents. At certain times during the 1590s, as many as seventy townspeople living in their own homes were receiving weekly assistance from the foundation. The statutes of Wyggeston's Hospital say that if the amount of money stored in the common chest reached £100, the master was to use the excess "in relieving of some poor of the town of Leicester" or other charitable deeds.[53]

We can offer a rough estimate of how many people were sheltered in the almshouses and hospitals included in the database during the second half of the sixteenth century. The number of residents that founders of post-1540 institutions hoped would be accommodated continued to drop. New hospitals for the poor still aimed at an average of around thirteen residents, with a median of twelve, but the far more numerous almshouses had an average of only seven inhabitants and a median of five.[54] Information is available about the number of people actually living in 168 residential institutions between 1550 and 1599. Hospitals for the sick, with an average of twenty-five people each (skewed by a few very large municipal institutions) and a median of twelve-and-a-half, were bigger than those for the poor, with an average of twelve and a median of ten. But they were outweighed by the many almshouses, with an average of seven and a median of six. The combined figures for all houses, an average of eleven and a median of six, may be set against the number of estimated houses in existence within a given decade to produce an approximate figure for the total number of people supported in these houses at the time.[55] For the 1560s, which contained the fewest houses of any decade between 1350 and 1600, the total based on the average number per house was 4,560 residents; that based on the median, which is probably more accurate, was 2,530. These figures constitute a reduction of 29 to 49 percent as compared to the number of residents in the 1520s. By the 1590s, when the number of houses had risen to nearly 500, the total number of places based on the average per house was 5,340; that based on the median was 2,960.

We may set the estimates for the 1560s and the 1590s against the total population of England, which was around 3.17 million in the mid-1560s

---

[53] *Calendar of Charters*, 62.
[54] See CUP Online App. 5. Their smaller size derived in part from the fact that founders came from a wider socio-economic range than had been true in the later medieval period, so some could afford to set up only a modest house; donors might also need to invest some of their resources in an endowment for the stipends that would keep their residents from begging. For below, see CUP Online App. 6.
[55] See CUP Online App. 7.

and around 4.06 million in the mid-1590s.[56] The average and median number of places in these institutions would have provided one place in an almshouse or hospital for every 695 to 1,252 people in the 1560s and for every 761 to 1,370 people in the 1590s. There were thus two to three times more people per place at the end of the century than in the 1520s. For the country as a whole, the houses provided between a third and a half of a position per parish.[57] In the 1560s, these institutions contained places for 1.1 to 1.9 percent of all people aged 60 or over; in the 1590s, for 1.0 to 1.8 percent of the elderly.[58] Because the breadth and depth of poverty had increased markedly since the 1520s, residential institutions were now contributing far less to the total volume of need than they had in the past.

Alms people could be named by a variety of patrons and institutions. Few of the newly founded houses followed the common earlier practice of allowing a single person to act independently in choosing new residents.[59] If the master of the institution was involved in appointing residents, he usually had to work with others or accept some degree of supervision. According to the first statutes of the hospital at Stoke Poges, the poor men and women were to be named at a meeting of the master, the vicar of Stoke, and the two churchwardens of the parish.[60] At St. Mary's Hospital in Chichester in 1567, the warden recommended new residents, but they had to be approved by the dean of the cathedral. Although the master of Wyggeston's Hospital was to appoint the poor people, if he granted a place to someone "for any bribe or reward," he was to be deprived of his office.[61] Many houses made provision for a back-up in case the designated appointer did not act. Cordell's instructions for Trinity Hospital in Long Melford stipulated that his heirs were to have the first right to name the master and residents of the hospital.[62] If the heir was not of full age or did not make an appointment within 8 days after a place became vacant, the parson and churchwardens of Melford were to have the nomination; should they not act, the bishop of Norwich was to step in. At Seckford's almshouses in Woodbridge, the lord of the manor was to

---

[56] Wrigley et al., *English Population History*, 613–16. For below, see CUP Online App. 7.

[57] Archer's estimate of the number of almshouse places within given communities as compared to their total aged population, 1589–1600, indicates that two market towns had places for 12–18% of the elderly, two county towns had places for 8–12%, and London had places for 3% ("Hospitals").

[58] For percentages aged 60+, see Wrigley et al., *English Population History*, 614–15, and CUP Online App. 7.

[59] However, the Earl of Derby, who leased the rectory of Prescot, Lancs. in 1592, customarily appointed residents to the almshouse (*Selection from the Prescot Court Leet*, 34).

[60] CBucksS CH 7/G.5. For below, see *Acts of the Dean and Chapter*, 55.

[61] *Calendar of Charters*, 65.

[62] SuffRO-BSE FL 509/11/10, and L&IS, *Cal. Pat. R, 33 Eliz.*, 51.

appoint new residents within two months of a vacancy, but if he did not, the appointment went to the minister and churchwardens or, if necessary, the Chief Justice of the Court of Common Pleas.[63] Many residents were appointed by lay officials. The mayor of Hereford and his fellows granted places in the almshouse of St. Giles in 1554–5; the customal of Rye copied in 1568 said that new residents for St. Bartholomew's Hospital were to be named by the mayor, with the assent of the jurats of the town.[64] In Stratford-upon-Avon, where the almshouse was run by the town after the Reformation, an order of 1577 said that candidates for admission into the institution "shallbe first brought into the chamber of the borough before Mr. Bailiff, aldermen, and burgesses" for questioning.[65] Town officials in Sandwich argued during the 1550s and 1560s about whether the mayor alone or a wider group should select – and receive advance payments from – the twelve brothers and four sisters of St. Bartholomew's Hospital. Parishes too might make appointments to houses under their control. The twenty brothers and sisters of the hospital established in Hemsworth, W. Yorks. by the executors of Robert Holgate, former Archbishop of York, were to be elected by the rector of the parish, the two churchwardens, and four of "the more honest parishioners."[66] At St. Saviour, Southwark, the vestry (a body composed of the leading parishioners) admitted a woman into the almshouse in 1582.

Alternatively, the feoffees who held the institution's property or its governors might have the right of appointment, acting either on their own or with other local people. The residents of Thomas Ellys's almshouse in Doncaster were to be selected by the feoffees to whom he had granted the house's land, joined by the mayor of Doncaster, the vicar, and "four of the most ancient and substantial inhabitants there."[67] At St. Thomas's Hospital in London during the later 1550s, the governors admitted people to the hospital and threatened to expel them. Richard Allman was "elected and chosen into the room of one of the almsmen" at an assembly of the governors of Christ's Hospital in Abingdon in 1583.[68]

Some houses experienced unwelcome outside pressure to appoint particular people to alms places. In 1573, Henry Middlemore, a Groom of the [Royal] Chamber, wrote to the dean and canons of Windsor, Berks.[69]

---

[63] *Statutes . . . for Alms-Houses in Woodbridge*, 2.
[64] HerefRO, Hereford City documents, Tourn, 1541–58, transcript, 50; Holloway, *History . . . of Rye*, 157. See also ShropsA 356/2/1, fols. 7v, 10v, and 13r, for Ludlow.
[65] *Minutes and Accounts*, vol. 2, 112–13. For below, see *Collections for An History of Sandwich*, 8 and 22–3.
[66] *CPR, Ph. & Mary*, vol. 3, 471–2. For below, see CWA #96, P92/SAV/450, p. 174.
[67] DoncA DX.War/A/1(a). For below, see LondMA H.1./ST/A1/1, fols. 3r–7r, passim.
[68] CHAbing Minutes, 1577/8–1694, fol. 20v.   [69] StGeoCh XI.C.7.

His letter, sent from the court, recommended that Silvester Mason, "a poor, honest man," be named to the next vacant almsman's room at St. Anthony's Hospital in London. He ended with a phrase common within a patronage system: if the dean and canons were able to assist Mason, "so you shall find me here assuredly ready to pleasure you any way I can." When Queen Elizabeth herself issued instructions to accept appointees, only powerful houses could resist.[70] In 1579, the queen wrote to St. Thomas's Hospital in London, notifying its officials that she had granted an almsman's place, with all of the wages and other allowances pertaining to it, to Nicholas Harrys due to "his old age, poverty, and impotency."[71] He was to receive the room formerly assigned to Thomas Carye, now deceased. When, however, Harrys presented the queen's letter to officials of the hospital, the governors objected. They not only disliked Elizabeth's interference, they claimed that Carye had received no fees or other financial benefits. When responding to the queen, the governors wrote that out of respect for her they were willing to grant Harrys a place when one opened up in the future, "but they cannot in any wise give him any allowance or pension out of this house."[72]

7.3   Altered benefits

The benefits received by alms people were changing too, for a combination of reasons. The smaller size and more limited resources of some new houses meant that they were able to provide less assistance to their residents. Working in the opposite direction, however, was mounting concern about begging. Because many people admitted into almshouses and hospitals had little if any other income and might be physically unable to do enough labor to support themselves, they would probably be forced to seek alms outside the institution if they did not receive food or cash payments. Although begging by inmates had been accepted in the later medieval period, it was generally regarded as unsuitable by the Elizabethan years.[73] Many almshouses therefore struggled with how to survive on inadequate institutional support without permitting their residents to solicit additional help. While some earlier houses appointed

---

[70] E.g., WarwsRO CR 1600/18.   [71] LondMA H.1./ST/A67/2.

[72] Ibid., A67/3. Thirteen months later, in return for a payment of £3 from the hospital, Harrys agreed to give up his right to a place, promising "never to charge or further to trouble the said hospital or governors in any manner wise" (ibid., A67/4).

[73] In a policy that sounds familiar to modern ears, the city of York reduced the payments given to various men, women, married couples, and children in St. Anthony's Hospital in 1577 and instructed them instead to "labour towards their livings" and not go begging (*York Civic Records*, vol. 7, 145).

collectors to gather assistance for them, founders of new units were strongly encouraged to provide sufficient income for their residents.[74] But our information about the benefits provided is distorted by survival of records. We know most about well-endowed foundations that drew up detailed statutes and kept careful accounts, whereas material about smaller, poorer, and less formal institutions – those less able to provide aid beyond simple shelter – is far more limited.

The most common additional benefit was a weekly cash allowance. The amount varied considerably between institutions and over time, depending upon the financial level of the house and whether it provided any other material assistance in the form of food, bedding, or clothing. The twelve poor folks in the almshouse in Louth, Lincs. each received 6s. 8d. "for their annuity" in the early 1550s, amounting to about 1.5d. per week, not enough to live on.[75] The "salaries" of the seven poor men and seven poor women of St. Thomas's Hospital in York ranged between 2d. and 4d. per week in 1575. The "people of the charity house" at Stratford-upon-Avon probably received 4d. per week each in the later 1580s and 1590s, while the five brothers and sisters of St. Mary's Hospital in Chichester were given 8d. per week in 1570, as they had been in 1549.[76]

Higher stipends were provided to the inmates of several fairly wealthy institutions. In the late 1540s or 1550s, residents of St. Margaret's Hospital in Gloucester and the hospital in Hemsworth received allowances of 12d. per week; Trinity Hospital in Bristol paid 12d. per week in the 1570s and 1580s.[77] Each of the four poor men in the extraordinarily well-endowed hospital at Stoke Poges was to receive £5 annually (23d. per week), and each sister £4 annually (18d. per week), while the residents of God's House, Southampton received 24d. per week in 1584, in place of the former provision of food.[78] Some almshouse and hospital residents were also bequeathed money by charitable testators, and the church courts occasionally freed people found guilty of such offences as sexual misbehavior from other forms of penance if they made a donation to a hospital.

---

[74] See ch. 6.2.2 above.
[75] LincsA Louth Grammar School B/III/1. For below, see YorkCA C104:2.
[76] *Minutes and Accounts*, vol. 3, 160, and vol. 5, 98–9, and Peckham, "St. Mary's Hospital." Stratford's house probably contained twenty-four people at the time, who together received 8s. per week. At Wyggeston's Hospital, the twelve poor men and three women named as keepers were each to receive 8d. weekly; the remaining nine women were to be given 7d. weekly (*Calendar of Charters*, 77).
[77] GloucsA GBR K1/37 and *CPR, Ph. & Mary*, vol. 3, 471; BristolRO 33041 BMC/1/8.
[78] CBucksS CH 7/G.5, and *Cartulary of God's House*, lxxxiv. For below, see, e.g., Archer, *Pursuit of Stability*, 170–4, and NottsAO DDTS 14/26/1, p. 2.

Institutional residents who received a weekly cash allowance that remained fixed across the second half of the century were at the mercy of inflation, which was rising at a rapid clip between 1540 and 1600. Because the purchasing power of money dropped sharply, some alms people must have found it difficult to provide for their needs without begging. We may illustrate the problem by looking at the cost of oats (or oatmeal) and peas, used to make the porridges that were staple items in the diet of many needy folks. While the 6d. per week received by the residents of Magdalen Hospital in Exeter in 1540–1 was probably still sufficient to buy food for one person, by 1564–5 that amount would have purchased only 59 percent as many oats and 69 percent as many peas.[79] By 1594–5, the continued payment of 6d. per week would have purchased only 30 percent as many oats and 37 percent as many peas as in the 1540s.

Some houses therefore increased their stipends in an attempt to compensate at least partially for inflation. Each of the thirty-two poor people in St. Bartholomew's Hospital, Gloucester received around 4.5d. per week in 1545–6, but the amount had risen to 7d. per week by 1570 and to 12d. per week by the end of Elizabeth's reign.[80] The Edwardian charter of Christ's Hospital in Abingdon said that its thirteen "poor alms folk" were each to receive 8d. per week, but by 1575 the stipend had increased to 10d. per week; later it was increased first to 12d. and then to 15d. per week.[81] When the almshouse in Thame, Oxfds. was set up around 1460, its six poor men received 6d. per week, but as Lord Williams of Thame reconstituted the house around 1575, he raised the stipends to 16d. per week.[82] They remained at that level into the 1590s.

Although a few houses still provided some basic foodstuffs for their residents, only those institutions that actually cared for sick people or were exceptionally wealthy offered full meals.[83] St. Thomas's Hospital in London, which stressed the importance of good nutrition for its inmates, described in 1576 the food to be given to "the poor" who were not on a special diet.[84] Each person was to receive daily one loaf of penny bread

---

[79] DevonRO Exeter City Archives G1/N2–4, for this and below. For prices, see *Agrarian History*, Table VIII, 857, based upon average decadal price for oats and peas. Prices for those two items in the 1540s were already 77–91% higher than their average in 1450–99.
[80] GloucsA GBR K1/1 and K1/3, fols. 1–2.
[81] CHAbing Minutes, 1577/8–1694, fols. 1r–6r, and Accounts, vol. 1; Minutes, fols. 17r and 18v.
[82] NewCO MSS 2430 and 3240, for this and below.
[83] E.g., Trinity Hospital in Bristol bought oatmeal, salt, and candles during the 1570s and 1580s (BristolRO 33041 BMC/1/8), and Wyggeston's Hospital provided oatmeal, salt, and – during the winter months – oil for lamps (*Calendar of Charters*, 77).
[84] LondMA H.1./ST/A24/1, fol. 44r.

and three-eighths of a gallon of beer. On Sundays, Mondays, Tuesdays, and Thursdays they were also to eat some beef or mutton, while on Wednesdays, Fridays, and Saturdays their diet was supplemented by butter or cheese. The twelve residents of Trinity Hospital in Long Melford were to share at their midday dinner three batches of meat, fish, butter, or eggs, with simpler fare at supper.[85] In general, however, houses founded after 1540 were more likely to give their inmates a weekly cash sum with which they could purchase their own food. This suggests that many residents were not bedridden, so they could go out to make purchases, and that they cooked and ate individually. At the time of its medieval founding, the hospital in Well, N. Yorks. had provided for each of its residents a loaf of bread, half a gallon of ale, and some meat every day, plus 4s. annually in money; by the mid sixteenth century, however, the few poor folks who lived in the house received only cash – about 6d. per week – "for all their duties and diets."[86] In 1554, the alms people supported in Tewkesbury, Gloucs. were to receive 10d. per week, said expressly to be for food. Heytesbury Hospital in Wiltshire stopped buying food for its seven poor men in the later 1580s, giving them instead a weekly sum "for commons."[87] Each resident received about 8.5d. per week in 1591 and 10d. in 1597.

While most institutions expected their inmates to provide their own clothing, an occasional older house offered assistance. During the 1560s, 1570s, and 1580s, Heytesbury Hospital paid for a shirt made of canvas, shoes of leather and hemp, and stockings of woolen cloth for every resident each year; Trinity Hospital in Bristol made shirts for its five poor men and smocks for its three poor women at Christmas in 1586 and 1590.[88] St. Anthony's Hospital in York paid 8s. 4d. in 1574–5 to a tailor "for raiment for two poor boys called William Davie and John Henryson" who had been "settled" in the institution, and Sherborne Almshouse in Dorset continued to provide a little clothing for its inhabitants in 1589–90. Residents might also receive gifts or bequests of cloth or clothing from outsiders, like the frieze cloth and other apparel given to poor people in the almshouse in Walthamstow, Essex by Elizabeth Alford, widow, in the 1590s.[89]

---

[85] SuffRO-BSE OC 88. See also CBuckss CH 7/G.5 and Wilts&SA 251/4, Booklet #1.

[86] *Certificates of . . . Chantries. . . in County of York*, 110. For below, see *CPR, Ph. & Mary*, vol. 1, 264–5.

[87] Wilts&SA 251/4, Booklet #1, for this and below.

[88] Ibid., 251/1, Bundle 2, Doct. #1, and 251/4, Booklet #1; BristolRO 33041 BMC/1/8. For below, see YorkCA E69 and DorsetHC D/SHA A141.

[89] Bosworth, *History of Walthamstow Charities*, 14.

"Livery gowns" that inmates were to wear when they went out into the community, especially when going to church as a group, became extremely popular among wealthier donors during the Elizabethan years. A few medieval houses continued their former practices, as did Heytesbury Hospital, which once every 3 to 8 years during the mid-Elizabethan period gave robes made of white wool to its six poor men and one woman.[90] But the great majority of houses that spoke of liveries were new or re-founded institutions, and some of their gowns consumed a surprising amount of fabric. Wyggeston's Hospital was already buying 60 yards of frieze cloth in 1541–2 to make robes for its twelve poor men; in 1551–2, the robes required 68 yards of cloth for the same number of people.[91] (Robes requiring 5 to 5.5 yards each were indeed voluminous!) At the almshouse in Thame, the five poor men and one poor woman each received a black frieze gown annually.[92] Christ's Hospital in Abingdon bought 78 yards of frieze wool to make livery gowns for its thirteen poor alms folk in 1575. (Here, we are up to 6 yards per robe).

Distinctive robes filled multiple functions. They marked the residents as members of the institution, thereby strengthening a group identity, but also facilitated supervision of the inmates' behavior. Because the presence of an alms person wearing a flowing gown made of good woolen cloth reminded all viewers of the generosity of the donor, liveries reinforced local memory of founders as praiseworthy people who chose to use their wealth for the good of others. That goal was stated expressly in the statutes for the hospital at Stoke Poges. Each resident was to receive every year "a livery all of one color," made of 3 yards of cloth, so that everyone "beholding the same may understand they be all brethren and sisters, found and maintained by one man," Lord Hastings of Loughborough.[93] Whenever the poor men of Seckford's almshouse in Woodbridge left their institution they were to wear a silver badge attached to the left side of the breast of their livery gowns that displayed the coat of arms "of our name and family, with a sentence written about the same."

---

[90] Wilts&SA 251/1, Bundle 2, Docts. #1–2 and 5.
[91] ROLeics 1 D 50/II/15; ibid., 50/II/23. The revised statutes of the hospital from 1574 confirmed that the twelve poor men were to receive a new gown one year and the twelve women the next, in each case with the letter "W" placed on their breast or sleeve (*Calendar of Charters*, 77).
[92] NewCO MS 2430. For below, see CHAbing Accounts, vol. 1, and also Deverell, *St. John's Hospital*, 10, SuffRO-BSE FL 509/11/10, *Copy of the Ordinances*, items XII and XVIII, *Poor Relief in Elizabethan Ipswich*, 15, and *Accounts of the Chamberlains of Bath*, 105, 111, and 145.
[93] CBucksS CH 7/G.5. For below, see *Statutes . . . of Alms-Houses in Woodbridge*, 4.

Although some institutions bought fuel for their residents, bedding was rarely provided.[94] Many newcomers, even if poor, brought in a few items of their own. Sherborne Almshouse recorded the possessions of twenty-three entrants during the 1590s.[95] Only two widows had no goods at all. Most of the rest, both men and women, brought a sheet and some kind of coverlet or blanket; a smaller number had a bolster, pillow, and/or feather bed. Inmates who lacked bedding could often draw upon institutional supplies acquired through gifts or inheritance from former residents. The Hospital of St. Mary Magdalene in Allington, Bridport and Sherborne Almshouse contained miscellaneous sheets, coverlets, blankets, flock beds, bolsters, pillows, and feather beds in inventories taken in 1587 and 1590.[96] Sir William Cordell said that part of any excess profits from the lands he bequeathed to his hospital in Long Melford should be used to renew the bedding and linens of the residents.

Well-funded institutions commonly hired a woman to look after the routine needs of the residents. At St. Thomas's Hospital in York, the "housewife," usually a widow, provided domestic care for the seven poor men and seven poor women.[97] Sherborne Almshouse likewise had a resident housewife, who received wages, clothing, and board and room; she was assisted by another woman "in lifting the poor," presumably when bedridden people were washed or their bedding changed. At Trinity Hospital in Long Melford, two women were to be hired to attend to the poor.[98] Ideally these would be "honest widows of the age of fifty years at the least," but if such could not be found, the employees could be "poor men's wives of good conversation." At Wyggeston's Hospital in Leicester, three of the female residents, those who had sufficient strength and skill, were appointed by the master as keepers of the others: two to look after the men and their kitchen, the third to tend to the women.[99] Sherborne Almshouse and Heytesbury Hospital paid barbers to cut the hair of their male residents.

---

[94] For fuel, see, e.g., Deverell, *St. John's Hospital*, 10–11, YorkCA E69, and *Calendar of Charters*, 77.
[95] DorsetHC D/SHA D24.
[96] DorsetHC DC/BTB AB49 and D/SHA A141. For below, see SuffRO-BSE FL 509/11/10.
[97] YorkCA E66, p. 21, and C104:2. The hospital occasionally paid an outsider for attempting to heal residents, such as two boys with scaly growths on their heads and a man suffering from syphilis (ibid., E69, from 1574–5). For below, see DorsetHC D/SHA A93 and A157.
[98] SuffRO-BSE FL 509/11/10.
[99] *Calendar of Charters*, 72–3 and 78. For below, see DorsetHC D/SHA A157 and Wilts&SA 251/4, Booklet #1, for 1583.

Almost none of the new institutions, even those that called themselves hospitals, provided trained medical attention for their inmates. Any care for sick people was provided on an ad hoc basis. At the hospital in Stoke Poges, the master and each resident were to contribute a small amount of money every quarter into a fund, kept in the common box, that would be "employed upon them in sickness if need be."[100] Trinity Hospital in Bristol made special payments for care of several sick inmates in the 1580s, including 4d. given "for lancing Maurice Hall's sore under his arm which he hath had this three weeks and for salve." Seckford's alms-house in Woodbridge paid poor widows of the town to look after the male residents when sick, weak, or infirm.[101] John Chapman, one of the poor men living in Sherborne Almshouse, received extra food when he lay sick in 1598 or 1599. If a resident died but did not have sufficient personal possessions to pay for burial, most houses would cover the costs.[102]

A few exceptional institutions did provide a medical staff. St. Thomas's Hospital in London hired doctors and surgeons for its 200 poor inmates. An order made in 1566/7 said that no one should be admitted from its sister institution, London's Bridewell, unless first seen by "a surgeon of this house" who could verify that the person was "so diseased that of need they ought to be received."[103] When Queen Elizabeth granted St. Bartholomew's Hospital in Gloucester to the mayor and burgesses of the city in 1564, the latter agreed to pay for one physician, one surgeon, and a minister for its forty poor people.[104] But some houses expressly prohibited the admission of people suffering from what were believed to be contagious ailments. The revised statutes for Wyggeston's Hospital say that no one was to be appointed to a place who had leprosy, "the French pox" (syphilis), the falling sickness (epilepsy), "or any such other foul and loathsome disease"; should people already living in the house become infected with those illnesses, they were to be removed at once, sent either to a leper hospital or to some place where their friends could provide for them.[105] Even at St. Thomas's in London, much of the money expended upon staff went to the matrons and sisters who provided simple bedside care for the inmates and were assigned wool, flax, and hemp "to set the poor on work."

---

[100] CBuckss CH 7/G.5. For below, see BristolRO 33041 BMC/1/8, esp. for 1584.
[101] *Statutes ... for Alms-Houses in Woodbridge*, 6–7. For below, see DorsetHC D/SHA A158.
[102] E.g., *Canterbury Chantries*, 6, HMC, *Eighth Report*, Appendix, "MSS of Ewelme Almshouse," 630, and *Calendar of Charters*, 70.
[103] LondMA H.1./ST/A1/1, fol. 5r.   [104] GloucsA GBR K1/3, fol. 1.
[105] *Calendar of Charters*, 70–1. They were, however, to continue receiving their weekly stipends. For below, see LondMA H.1./ST/D5/1 and ST/A24/1, fol. 35v.

7.4   Obligations for prayer and good behavior

Many houses established between 1540 and the end of the century imposed explicitly defined religious and social obligations on their residents. These requirements created new identities for the inmates, positive in tone so long as they conformed to the rules. Although the contents and setting of their prayers changed with the ending of Catholicism and the move towards smaller and less wealthy institutions, inmates were still expected to pray, often several times each day.[106] After 1559, they were no longer to pray for the souls of the dead, but they were commonly instructed to remember (and remind God of) the generosity of the founder and other benefactors of the institution. At the hospital at Stoke Poges, erected chiefly for "th'advancement of God's glory by divine service and good and devout prayer," residents were required to pray three times daily at church for "the good estate of me their founder" (the religiously conservative Lord Hastings) and many of his named relatives, as well as for Queen Elizabeth and the late Queen Mary.[107] The master of the house was also to say a grace at each meal that included a prayer for the founder. The residents of Cordell's hospital in Long Melford were to assemble twice daily in the institution's hall to say a considerable round of prayers and give "thanks unto God for their several good benefactors."[108] In 1586, the sexton of Trinity Hospital in Bristol was paid to ring the bell that called its poor inhabitants to assemble at 7 o'clock in the morning and 7 in the evening "to give God thanks for his great benefits and mercies showed unto them."

Only a few of the older houses still had their own chapels and clergymen. New statutes for the Charterhouse or God's House in Hull, from 1572, said that the residents were to come to the chapel twice each day to pray or hear the word of God read by their master, a cleric.[109] When the staunchly Protestant Robert Dudley, Earl of Leicester, founded his hospital in Warwick, he insisted that its master be a preacher of God's word, and Leicester himself wrote lengthy prayers to be said by the residents when they assembled in the common hall (formerly the medieval guild

---

[106] For the liturgy in post-Dissolution hospitals and almshouses, see Phillips, "Charitable Institutions," 53–70.

[107] CBuckksS CH 7/G.2.

[108] SuffRO-BSE OC 88. The poor men were to say the ordinary Confession, the Creed, the Ten Commandments, the Lord's Prayer, the Collect for the Queen, and the ordinary Collects for morning and evening as "set forth in the Book of Common Prayer in the Church of England." For below, see BristolRO 33041 BMC/1/8.

[109] HullCA BRB/2, fols. 100v and 98r–v. For below, see *Copy of the Ordinances*, items I and XXX.

chapel). Both of the chaplains at Wyggeston's Hospital in Leicester, one of whom served as its master, had to be men "learned and admitted into one of th'ecclesiastical orders now established within the Church of England."[110]

Some houses required collective prayer in a public area of the institution. Residents of Whittington's Almshouse or College in London gathered in the dining hall three times weekly at 8 o'clock in the morning to recite a designated list of prayers.[111] Those who were literate were to read a chapter of the Old or New Testament in English to their fellows, but should not offer their own exposition of the text. The orders made by Cure in 1584 for the College of the Poor in St. Saviour, Southwark said that the residents were to assemble in some common place when a hand bell was rung each evening after the gates had been shut and again in the mornings before the gates were opened.[112] On their knees, with loud and audible voices, they should say several prayers in English (presumably to remove any hint of Catholicism) written especially for them by the bishop of Winchester. These included the Lord's Prayer followed by prayers for the sovereign, nobility, and councilors of the realm, the clergy, the wardens and governors of St. Saviour's, and "the whole commonalty of this land" (the Protestant equivalent of the "all Christian souls" with which earlier prayers had ended). Sherborne Almshouse, following a more traditional schedule, noted in 1591 the times at which its residents were to pray together.[113] Between February 2 and November 2, their first prayer was to be at 6 o'clock in the morning, followed by ones before, during, and after their midday dinner at 1 o'clock in the afternoon and before and after their supper in the evening; during the darker winter months, the requirements were reduced somewhat.

Many of the newer almshouses expected their residents to pray at their parish church, either instead of or in addition to activities within the institution. When Thomas Ellys set up St. Thomas House in Doncaster in 1557, he said simply that its residents should come daily to the parish church "to hear the divine service … and to attend their prayer."[114] Cordell indicated that the poor men of his hospital in Long Melford were to attend services at the parish church as well as to say morning and evening prayer and conduct "other godly exercises" within the house.

---

[110] *Calendar of Charters*, 56.   [111] Imray, *Charity of Richard Whittington*, 51–2.
[112] LondMA P92/SAV/1528, fols. 18r–21r. The poor were also to attend services at the parish church four days each week and on holy days.
[113] DorsetHC D/SHA A141, back cover.
[114] DoncA DX.War/A/1(a). For below, see SuffRO-BSE FL 509/11/10. Cordell assigned to four bishops and deans the job of preparing detailed statutes for the hospital (ibid., OC 88).

Alms people often sat together in a designated section of the church, presumably to make their collective presence more visible. Residents of Christ's Hospital in Abingdon were instructed in 1558 to go every day to their seats in a special area at the back of St. Katherine's aisle in the church.[115] When the twenty-four poor men and women of Wyggeston's Hospital went to their parish church, they were "to sit together in those two seats which are appointed now for them, the men on the north side and the women on the south side of the west door." The executors of Nicholas Eyffeler, who left funds to found an almshouse in Warwick for eight female residents, spent 5s. 4d. in 1598 "for making of the poor women['s] seats in the church & for mats for the same seats."[116] The role of the founder/patron was more overt at Roger Manwood's almshouse in Canterbury, founded in the 1590s, where the residents collected their daily loaves of bread from a board set up beside his tomb in the church. Seeing alms people worshipping as a group not only reminded the congregation of the beneficence of the founder of the house, it emphasized the deference owed by its residents and the social service performed by the institution, perhaps encouraging parishioners to contribute to its support.

A few houses provided religious instruction for their residents.[117] The second chaplain of Wyggeston's Hospital in Leicester, known as "the Brother," was to be "a man learned, of sound judgment in the Christian religion ... and a preacher of the word of God."[118] When new inmates entered the hospital, he was to examine "their faith and religion, to th'end that if they be well instructed, they may be not only confirmed therein but trained to farther increase of knowledge, or that, their ignorance being known, they may be the rather charged to be diligent to learn." The Brother was to teach the latter to recite in English and understand the Ten Commandments, the Lord's Prayer, and the articles of the Christian faith as expressed in the Apostles' Creed.[119] In addition, he was to see that they gained "such understanding as is necessary for good Christians touching the nature and use of the sacraments of Christ, and to live holily, as good Christians ought to do." A few wealthier houses paid a minister to

[115] CHAbing Minutes, 1577/8–1694, fol. 10r. For below, see *Calendar of Charters*, 76.
[116] "Nicholas Eyffeler," esp. 71. For below, see Sweetinburgh, "The Poor."
[117] Edward VI's injunctions of 1547 said that every master of a hospital who was a priest should preach to its residents at least twice each year, but this requirement was not repeated in Elizabeth's injunctions of 1559 (*VAI*, vol. 2, 125, and ibid., vol. 3, 16, the gap between old injunctions 25 and 27).
[118] *Calendar of Charters*, 65–6. For below, see ibid., 76.
[119] Ibid., 66–7, for this and below. The Brother was also responsible for saying prayers in the hospital's chapel every evening and for seeing that the poor went to their parish church of St. Martin's for morning and evening prayer, to hear sermons, and to receive communion.

give occasional sermons to their own residents and perhaps to others in the parish church.[120]

In contrast to the later medieval period, when many institutions assumed that their residents would gain at least part of their support by seeking alms, begging was now expressly prohibited by some houses, replaced by an obligation to labor. The statutes for the Earl of Leicester's hospital in Warwick said that if any brother were "found begging, either at or about the hospital itself, or elsewhere abroad," he would be fined 18d. for the first offence and 6s. for the second; if caught begging a third time, he was to be expelled.[121] Sir Thomas Seckford ordered that none of the poor men in his almshouse in Woodbridge "shall wander or go abroad to demand or to ask any alms or charity"; those who did were to suffer a reduction in their weekly stipends. Instead, "in avoiding of idleness, each of them according to their ability and strength of body [shall] labor and be occupied, either in digging, planting, or setting the gardens and grounds allotted unto them ... or else to be occupied in some other commendable exercise." Residents of Wyggeston's Hospital in Leicester were not to beg, but were to carry out "some such labor as they be able to do."[122] If an inmate became so sick and weak that he or she could not "go abroad to labor, nor to get for his or her necessary sustentation, nor have any friends by whose benevolence they may be relieved," the master was allowed to augment the weekly allowance at least temporarily. The feoffees of Jankyn Smith's almshouses in Bury St. Edmunds required in 1583 that new residents take an oath to "eschew all idleness & keep them selves in some profitable & commendable occupation or exercise to the best of their power and knowledge."[123]

Some houses expected residents to do a little work on behalf of the institution itself. The statutes of the hospital at Stoke Poges said that every brother and sister was to work in the common garden or orchard or carry out other tasks appointed by the master.[124] When William Lambarde established his almshouse in East Greenwich, he attached to the institution a plot for growing hemp; the lessee of the woodland associated with the foundation was to plough, dung, and sow the plot, but the residents were to harvest the hemp and work it into cloth for the good of the house, not for their own profit. Labor might be associated with a concern for sanitation. Statutes for the hospital at Long Melford instructed the poor

---

[120] CBucksS CH 7/G.5, CHAbing Accounts, vol. 1, for 1556–97, passim, and SuffRO-BSE FL 509/11/10.
[121] *Copy of the Ordinances*, item XXVII. For below, see *Statutes ... of the Alms-Houses in Woodbridge*, 5–6.
[122] *Calendar of Charters*, 77–8, for this and below.   [123] SuffRO-BSE H 2/1/1(a).
[124] CBucksS CH 7/G.5. For below, see Warnicke, *William Lambarde*, 44–7.

men to sweep the hall twice daily and to clean their own chambers; keeping their rooms "sweet" was likewise a responsibility of the residents of the Earl of Leicester's hospital in Warwick.[125] At Wyggeston's Hospital in Leicester, three of the women were to keep all public areas "swept and clean from all filth, and from every thing which may breed any evil or unwholesome air."[126] Twice each year, in March and October, they were to "refresh all the beds of the poor men and women with fresh straw." Unlike workhouses, however, such labor was seen not as a punishment, but rather as a way to keep the residents busy and help maintain the institution.

In a few cases residents were asked to tend sick people, either other inmates of their house or members of the wider community. The burghmote of Maidstone, Kent ordered in 1564 that the mayor or his deputy could appoint anyone dwelling in the almshouses belonging to the town to take care of sick people in "the time of plague or pestilence."[127] Should the designated people refuse to provide this "comfort, help, and succour," they would be turned out of the almshouse. Residents of the guildhall almshouses in Bury St. Edmunds were told in 1583 that they should be "ready at all times to keep such persons as shallbe sick within this town of Bury and attend diligently upon them" when required.[128] But other authorities worried that alms people who tended the sick might bring contagion into the house. Sir George Monoux's ordinances for his almshouse in Walthamstow specified that "none of the almsfolks shall keep any person being sick of the pestilence or plague."[129] The manor court of Croydon, Surrey ordered in 1582 that if any woman living in the local almshouse left the town or parish "to keep any sick person" without consent of the vicar, bailiff of the manor, constables, or churchwardens of Croydon, she was to lose her dwelling until an officer said she could return.

Although conduct had been regulated in a few earlier foundations, more vigorous and widespread control in this period may have been influenced by reformed Protestant or puritan concern with enforcing godly behavior. Alms people were generally told to remain within the institution, presumably so they could attend to their prayers and would not increase the number of wandering and begging poor. Christ's Hospital in Abingdon ordered in 1558 that if any of the residents was

---

[125] SuffRO-BSE OC 88; *Copy of the Ordinances*, item XXIII.
[126] *Calendar of Charters*, 73. For below, see ibid., 78.   [127] *Records of Maidstone*, 20.
[128] SuffRO-BSE H 2/1/1(a).
[129] Gibson, *Walthamstow Charities*, 8. For below, see LambPL T.H. 41.

absent from the required church services (unless sick) or roamed abroad into the countryside without special license, he or she was to be fined 4d. for each offence, a sum that would be distributed among the other poor folk.[130] The brothers and sisters of the house in Stoke Poges were instructed in 1564 not to "go out of the circuit of the parish of Stoke" or to "lie out of the hospital" without permission of the master. When Queen Elizabeth appointed Nicholas Harrys as an almsman of St. Thomas's Hospital in London in 1579, the grant specified that he "shall always be resident upon the same room after his placing and shallbe present at divine service for the same hospital appointed" unless he had been excused due to sickness or some other legitimate reason.[131]

Social wrongdoing was often proscribed and could lead to expulsion. New residents of the almshouses in Bury St. Edmunds had to vow that they would "live in peace and quietness without brawling, drunkenness, idleness, or any other disorder."[132] Inmates of the hospital at Stoke Poges were to be "of good behaviour, no drunkers, no whisperers, quarrelers, ill sayers, no contentious people." The ordinances of Christ's Hospital in Abingdon said that "if any of the said poor persons do use to brawl, fight, or chide with any of his companions or be given to drunkenness or any other viciousness of life," he or she was to be warned three times by the head of the institution, but could then be expelled; "some other sober and quiet person" would be placed into that room.[133] The poor men in the hospital in Long Melford were not to play any card or dice games (usually accompanied by betting), nor were they to operate or even go to any alehouse or "any suspected place of misdemeanor or crime."[134] Presumably to help them avoid such temptations, they were required to go to bed at 9 o'clock in the evening between March and September (unless excused due to illness); during the winter, they were to go to bed at 8 o'clock. They could be removed from their places "for notable and common drunkenness, for common swearing, lying, and slandering, or for any other notable crime."

Despite the efforts of founders and administrators of institutions, their members did sometimes misbehave. A petition sent to Hereford's city officials in 1567 complained that the bedemen living in the almshouse of St. Giles were going out of the house to beg; they haunted alehouses and

---

[130] CHAbing Minutes, 1577/8–1694, fol. 10r. For below, see CBuckesS CH 7/G.5.
[131] LondMA H.1./ST/A67/2.
[132] SuffRO-BSE H 2/1/1(a). For below, see CBuckesS CH 7/G.5.
[133] CHAbing Minutes, 1577/8–1694, fol. 10r, and see HertsA MS 10056.
[134] SuffRO-BSE OC 88, for this and below. For even more detailed listings of prohibited behavior, see *Copy of the Ordinances*, items XIII–XXIX, and *Calendar of Charters*, 77.

were daily drunk.[135] At Heytesbury Hospital, almsman William Browne was accused in 1576 of "slanderous words" against Margaret Scamell, the woman who attended to the hospital; he also worked illicitly on Ascension Day, and every Saturday he traveled to Warminster, neglecting his duty to go to church and say prayers with the other almsmen. In 1583, after the mayor of the Devizes, Wilts. and his brethren received a written complaint charging two widows in the almshouse with various misdeeds, the women were dismissed from the institution "for their abuses and disorderly behavior."[136] Widow Butt was removed from the almshouse in Ludlow, Shrops. by town officials in 1594 "for that she hath lived incontinently." When Katheryn Symonds, a resident of Sherborne Almshouse, committed a "misdemeanor" against the master and brethren in 1597, she was punished by exclusion from group meals in the common hall and restricted to one meal per day for 3 days.[137] She was warned that if she erred again, she would miss normal meals for 6 days; and on a third offense, she would be expelled from the house. People put out of institutions might need to rely on alms to sustain themselves. Ellen Davy, "great with child," was arrested and punished as a vagrant by the constable of Kelvedon, Essex in 1566.[138] She said she had previously lived in a poor house, perhaps in Ipswich, but was now obliged to beg.

In an atypical case, "Mother Margery" was expelled in the early 1560s not only from the almshouse at Rye, but also from the entire town.[139] Her removal was initially said to be for certain notorious offences "such as any Christian heart would abhor to hear spoken of, much less to be used." A fuller report explained that because she was suspected of witchcraft, the mayor had ordered that the almshouse be searched. There they found "a good quantity of raw beef" that was said to have been used by Margery: "as the beef decayed, so the bodies of diverse persons against whom she bore malice should also decay." Ten years later the mayor and jurats commented that the charges against her had been proven true. A man whom she had "cruelly tormented in his body at last hanged himself," demonstrating her evil power; and the town had not been troubled with similar problems since her banishment.

---

[135] HerefRO Hereford City Documents, bound vol. 6, transcript, 154–5. For below, see Wilts&SA D5/28/4, #34. The visitation record notes that Browne promised to depart from the hospital within the following week, but he was still there 7–9 years later (ibid., D/5/28/5, #49).

[136] Wilts&SA G20/1/15, fol. 23r. For below, see ShropsA 356/2/1, fol. 16v.

[137] DorsetHC D/SHA D1, fol. 4v.   [138] EssexRO-Ch Q/SR 19A, #25.

[139] ESussRO Rye/47/2/10, used through A2A, a certificate from 1571–2 reporting on earlier events, for this paragraph.

7.5   Efforts to improve governance

Many founders of almshouses or hospitals gave thought to the mechanisms through which their institutions would operate and be supervised. They needed to decide how responsibilities would be divided between the master (or warden or keeper) who commonly ran the house on a day-to-day basis and the feoffees, governors, or civic body that held the house's landed property, made policy decisions, and provided general oversight. Someone needed to ensure that the buildings belonging to the house were well maintained, that its endowment was protected, that income due to the institution was collected and used properly, and that suitable residents were chosen and their conduct monitored. To achieve better control, external visitors might be named to conduct occasional inspections and order correction of any faults. (Women were never chosen either as routine administrators of institutions or as their governors or visitors.)

People who established houses between 1540 and 1599 continued to move in the directions that were beginning to appear in the later medieval years with regard to the governance they prescribed for their institutions (see Appendix E). Monasteries were no longer an option, and self-governing institutions were apparently regarded as too vulnerable to dishonesty or neglect: only 3 percent of the new almshouses and a fifth of the hospitals had no outside regulation. Supervision of just over a third of all almshouses and hospitals was assigned to existing lay institutions, especially to urban bodies, while the greatest increase came in houses that were to be governed by a formal body of lay feoffees, accounting for 58 percent of new almshouses and 44 percent of new hospitals.

Towns that ran or helped to run almshouses and hospitals maintained buildings, hired masters, admitted residents, audited accounts, and/or kept the institution's records under lock and key.[140] The borough of Bridgwater, Som., which had repaired the local almshouse in the fifteenth century, organized a major rebuilding in 1558, to which twenty-nine people contributed money, their labor, or food and drink for the workers. Between 1569 and the mid 1590s, the Chamberlains of Bath paid for work on the almshouses and in some years gave money or cloth to the alms folks.[141] Stratford-upon-Avon's borough officers, who had replaced the former Guild of the Holy Cross, operated the local almshouse throughout

---

[140] E.g., ESussRO Winchelsea 51, fol. 70r–v, HullCA BRB 2, fols. 230v–31r, and *Ordinances of Bristol*, 81. For below, see SomstRO D/B/bw 1768.

[141] *Accounts of the Chamberlains of Bath*, 18–145, passim. See also W&FM Wisbech Corp. Records, 1566–99, fol. 105r.

Elizabeth's reign.[142] Other towns found the money with which to purchase back the buildings and property that had sustained residential institutions run by religious bodies before royal confiscation.

Parishes too might support almshouses.[143] During the second half of the century, the churchwardens of Mildenhall, Suff. paid for repairs and improvements to their local institution.[144] The directors of a new house in Stoneleigh, Warws., sheltering five poor men and five poor women, were to be the churchwardens of the parish. St. Mary's parish in Nottingham received rental income on behalf of the bedehouse on Malin Hill during the 1580s and 1590s, and the churchwardens bought loads of coal and made occasional small gifts to the poor there.[145] Even when a house was run by others, the parish in which it lay might feel some sense of ownership. At Archbishop Whitgift's metropolitan visitation of the diocese of Salisbury in 1584, the parish of Heytesbury reported that "our almshouse of St. Katherine's" (Heytesbury Hospital) was not being run in accordance with its foundation statutes, supporting only eight people instead of the stipulated thirteen.[146] In a pattern that was to expand in the seventeenth century, some parishes maintained houses bequeathed to them as free housing for the poor.

In urban centers, other lay groups might be in charge of residential institutions. In 1582, seventy-one members of York's "fellowship of Merchants and Mercers" (the Company of Merchant Adventurers) contributed money to support "the poor in the Hospital of Trinity in Fossgate"; other members gave goods.[147] The feoffees of Jankyn Smith's charity in Bury St. Edmunds, which became known as the Guildhall Feoffment, operated almshouses and other projects, with considerable overlap between its members and town officers. The governors of Christ's Hospital in Abingdon were chosen from among the leaders of the borough: in 1598, nine of the governors had been or were to become mayors.[148] A few older institutions were backed by a "confraternity" of wealthy local people, resembling the boards of charitable institutions today. Sherborne Almshouse received £4 in 1589 from Peter Game,

---

[142] E.g., *Minutes and Accounts*, vol. 1, 120–2, and vol. 5, 98–9. For below, see, e.g., HMC, *Report on MSS of the Corp. of Beverley*, 178.
[143] See also ch. 8.2.2 below.
[144] CWA #92, 110/5/3 and 5. For below, see *CPR, Eliz.*, vol. 7, p. 213.
[145] NottsA CA 4611–15B.
[146] Wilts&SA D1/43/5, fol. 29v, from "Hatchburye." For below, see Broad, "Housing the Rural Poor."
[147] BIA Company of Merchant Adventurers, Trinity Hospital Benevolences for the Poor, #1. For below, see SuffRO-BSE, section H, e.g., H 2/3/4.1–4.5 and H 2/6/2.1.
[148] Carter and Smith, *Give and Take*, 85.

"one of the confraters of this house," to sustain one poor man and his successors in the house in perpetuity.[149]

Almshouses were sometimes run in conjunction with other charitable projects. Among the institutions associated with schools were the bede-houses in Louth, operated by the wardens or governors of Louth Grammar School. During the 1550s and 1560s, they paid the annual stipends of the alms people and repaired the building.[150] A set of alms-houses founded in Worcester in 1561, comprising twenty-four cottages for the residence of forty-eight poor people of the town, was controlled by "the Six Masters," a group that also governed the local grammar school. The "bridgemen" of Henley, Oxfds., whose primary function was to maintain the important bridge across the Thames, paid for work on the almshouse in 1578 and provided coats for six poor men who lived in it during the 1550s, 1560s, and 1570s.[151] The almshouse attached to the College of St. Mary Magdalen at Kingston on Thames, Surrey was supervised by the parish's bridgewardens, while Christ's Hospital in Abingdon was responsible for repairing four local bridges.

The master of a charitable house played a vital role in its operation, but these positions were often awarded as a form of patronage, with little regard for the qualifications of the men appointed. Founders or patrons commonly named the initial master and sometimes specified that their heirs were to have the right of appointment thereafter. The monarch was an important patron, and some people acquired that role through pur-chase of land confiscated by the crown that had formerly supported an almshouse or hospital. Robert Dudley, first Earl of Leicester, used his position of authority within several hospitals to appoint radical religious reformers to what he probably hoped would be safe positions as mas-ters.[152] Larger institutions generally paid a salary to their head, together with a residence that could be leased out if the master chose not to live there in person, and the position offered opportunities for sub-patronage through naming people to other offices or alms places within the house. In the medieval period, heads had not always been required to submit formal accounts or justify why they had selected particular residents or servants

---

[149] DorsetHC D/SHA A140.

[150] LincsA Louth Grammar School B/III/1. For below, see WorcsRO 261.1, BA 3617/7, and also LancsRO PR 3332.

[151] OxfdsRO D.D. Henley C.I. 4, 8, and 10. For below, see Groom, "Piety and Locality," 89–90, and Carter and Smith, *Give and Take*, 2–3. Two of the bridges had formerly been supported by the Fraternity of the Holy Cross based in St. Helen's church, Abingdon.

[152] Thomas Lever at Sherburn Hospital in Durham and Thomas Cartwright, first master of Leicester's hospital in Warwick.

for the house. Holding a mastership had thus invited lax or dishonest administration.

In response to these problems, some later founders attempted to exert long-term control over the master and financial probity of their houses by preparing detailed instructions or ordinances. These statutes commonly emphasize the quality of the person appointed as head and specify his duties, including the accounts to be submitted to the institution's governors. The rules for the hospital at Stoke Poges say that the master was to be a cleric "of good conversation, discreet, and of good fame."[153] In return for the sizeable salary of £10 annually, he was to be in actual residence, away from the house no more than 40 days annually. On the last day of December each year he was to submit to the founder or his heirs and the institution's visitors a detailed account of all income received and expended. The money belonging to the house was to be stored in a chest, for which there were to be three keys, one to be kept by the visitors. Should the master permit the house to suffer any economic loss, through negligence or wrongdoing, or if he were found guilty of heresy, incontinency, murder, drunkenness, or any other "notable crime," the residents were to inform the founder or visitors and the man would be expelled. The statutes of Trinity Hospital in Long Melford specify that its warden was to be at least 56 years in age, "a man of gravity and wisdom, of good experience and able to govern the others with discretion and to be of honest life and conversation and an example to others of all virtue"; he was also to be able to read and write and "cast accounts."[154] At the Charterhouse or God's house in Hull, where it was found that the current master had personally received a large amount of customary but illegal income, new ordinances prepared in 1572 described in detail the duties of subsequent heads of the house and the accounts to be submitted annually to town officials.[155] "A sure and strong chest" called "the Treasury Chest or Ark" was to be provided, with two of its three keys kept by urban officials. The master of Wyggeston's Hospital in Leicester was required to deliver a formal book of accounts to representatives of the Chancellor of the Duchy of Lancaster each year. After the audit, the book was to be placed with the institution's other records into a locked chest.

Statutes might try also to force masters to issue proper leases and protect the possessions of their houses. Excessively long leases, granted

---

[153] CBuckss CH 7/G.5, for this and the following sentences.
[154] SuffRO-BSE OC 88. Documents belonging to the house were to be stored in a strong chest, bound with iron, with its three keys kept by the warden, Melford's parson, and the most senior churchwarden of the parish. For below, see *Calendar of Charters*, 60.
[155] HullCA BRB/2, fols. 88v–102r, esp. 98r–v.

for many decades, were generally accompanied by a generous cash payment to the current head, but made it impossible to raise rents during the term of the award; it might also be difficult to re-claim institutional ownership of the property at the end of the lease. At Long Melford, the master could only lease or demise lands belonging to the hospital with the approval of the majority of the poor residents and the parish's parson.[156] Grants would normally run for no more than 5 years, and only with the written consent of the hospital's visitor could land be leased for as much as 10 years. The head was never to award "reversions" (an agreement to award a lease in the future, in return for a present payment) or grants of woodland. Rules for the Earl of Leicester's hospital in Warwick insisted that no lease or demise be issued for a term longer than 21 years or the lives of three consecutive tenants and that no reversions be granted.[157] Wyggeston's Hospital's statutes limited the length of leases and ordered that an inventory of all the possessions of the institution be prepared immediately and renewed upon the appointment of each new master. If a master left office without accounting for all of those goods, he was to be sued in the court of the Duchy of Cornwall.

Some founders specified who would serve as their feoffees and what they were expected to do. Sir George Monoux's will conveyed the property for the almshouse he had recently founded in Walthamstow to six men: two fellow members of the Drapers' Company of London, a gentleman of Walthamstow, two of Monoux's kinsmen, and his attorney.[158] They were to keep the premises in repair, supervise the operation of the almshouse and a school associated with it, pay salaries to the officers and stipends to the alms people, and meet annually as a group on the day of his death to inspect the governance of the institution. Cordell took several steps designed to provide good administration for his hospital in Long Melford. In his will, he ordered that within three years after his death, the feoffees to whom he had already granted land should obtain from the queen "a corporation of one warden and twelve brethren of the Hospital of the Holy Blessed Trinity of the foundation of Sir William Cordell, knight. And to make the said warden and brethren one body politic and to have capacity to take lands to them and their successors . . . to the clearly yearly value of two hundred marks," with all other privileges normally granted to an incorporated institution.[159] Cordell obviously thought that high-status trustees would be more successful in establishing his foundation: the

[156] SuffRO-BSE OC 88, for this and below.
[157] *Copy of the Ordinances*, item XXXIV. For below, see *Calendar of Charters*, 57–9.
[158] Gibson, *Walthamstow Charities*, 8–9.
[159] SuffRO-BSE FL 509/11/10, and see ibid., OC 88.

fifteen feoffees all held top offices at court or in the church, and at least one of them – William Cecil, Lord Burghley – took an active interest in the project.[160] The first governors of the almshouse in Woodbridge founded by Thomas Seckford were to be the Chief Justice of the Court of King's/ Queen's Bench and either an heir of the founder or the Master of the Rolls of the Court of Chancery.

Governors occasionally scrutinized and corrected their own activities. At Christ's Hospital in Abingdon, the governors were very conscious of their position (although they often had violent and protracted disagreements among themselves).[161] Their meetings were held in a special room of the house under a cupola, featuring a bay window and seats with mats and carved decorations.[162] But in 1596, an assembly of the governors noted that in recent years "a great charge of expenses hath grown unto this hospital by the charge of the dinner made unto the master and governors and auditor of this house" on the day when the annual accounts were submitted, "more than was necessary to be spent."[163] The assembly therefore ordered that no more than 33s. 4d. should henceforth be spent on food for the audit dinner, an amount "thought good to be allowed in consideration of the great business and pains always taken that day yearly by the said master, governors, auditor, and other officers about the account aforesaid."

Many founders, especially those whose houses were to have their own feoffees, named external visitors to inspect the house. Lord Hastings of Loughborough appointed the dean of Windsor and the provost of Eton College as visitors of his hospital in Stoke Poges.[164] When the first governors of Cordell's hospital in Long Melford prepared institutional statutes after his death, they instructed the bishop of Norwich to visit the house, either in person or through a special commissary, at least once every 3 years; should he find that the statutes were not being properly observed or discover anything else amiss, he was authorized to implement necessary reforms. The Earl of Leicester appointed the bishop, dean, and archdeacon of Worcester as the visitors of his hospital in Warwick, to hold inspections at their pleasure but at least once every 3 years.[165] Heytesbury Hospital was visited every 3 years in the 1570s by the dean of Sarum, accompanied by four lay officials of the parish.

---

[160] BritL Lansdowne MS 66, nos. 49–51. For below, see *Statutes . . . of the Alms-Houses in Woodbridge*, vii.
[161] For their disputes, see McIntosh, "Negligence, Greed."
[162] Godfrey, *English Almshouse*, plate 34 (b), and CHAbing Accounts, vol. 1, for 1586.
[163] CHAbing Minutes, 1577/8–1694, fol. 31v, for this and below.
[164] CBuckss CH 7/G.5. For below, see SuffRO-BSE OC 88.
[165] *Copy of the Ordinances*, item XXXII. For below, see Wilts&SA 251/1, Bundle 2, Doct. #2.

It is interesting that high ecclesiastical figures were so often appointed as visitors, suggesting that as individuals they were held in high regard for their administrative acumen and moral probity even if the English church seemed too insecure an institution to be given full control over an almshouse or hospital. Some religious leaders used their authority in other ways too. During the 1560s, Archbishop Parker brought about the refounding of the hospitals of St. Bartholomew's in Sandwich and St. John the Baptist in Canterbury; in 1571 Archbishop Grindal's intervention led to the survival of the Charterhouse (or God's House) in Hull.[166] After St. Katherine's Hospital in Ledbury was robbed of its lands by its master – Bishop John Story – the dean and chapter of Hereford Cathedral moved decisively and successfully in 1580 to recover its estates.

Parliament took steps to secure ongoing income and good governance for charitable institutions. The Poor Laws of 1555 and 1563 stipulated that some of the money gathered by parish officials in London should be paid to and distributed by the governors of Christ's Hospital.[167] The latter measure had a similar provision for the civic hospital in Coventry, and a statute of 1572 added St. Bartholomew's Hospital in Gloucester and St. Thomas's Hospital in Southwark. Better external supervision was the goal of sections of the 1572 act that ordered Justices of the Peace to join with bishops in visiting hospitals and almshouses and compelling their governors to render account of how they had used their revenues.[168] Other statutes attempted to secure property given to charitable institutions and to address the problem of overly long leases. A measure of 1571 declared void any leases of property belonging to hospitals, among other institutions, if granted for more than 21 years or three lives.[169] A follow-up measure in 1572 provided clarification of what kinds of institutions were covered, saying that the term "hospitals" as used in 1571 was to include "all hospitals, maisondieus, bedehouses, and other houses ordained for the sustentation or relief of the poor."[170] The statute of 1572 also declared valid all former grants of property to hospitals, especially ones founded by previous monarchs, that had received gifts or bequests in which the name of the institution was inaccurately stated in the written document. These measures did not, however, make it easier to set up a new institution, nor did an act of 1576, which exempted from normal requirements for a

[166] Archer, "Hospitals," for this and below.
[167] 2 & 3 Philip & Mary, c. 5, sec. 12, and 5 Elizabeth, c. 3, sec. 14, *SR*, vol. 4, 281 and 414.
For below, see 5 Elizabeth, c. 3, sec. 15, and 14 Elizabeth, c. 5, secs. 31 and 41, *SR*, vol. 4, 414, 596, and 598.
[168] 14 Elizabeth, c. 5, secs. 32 and 37, *SR*, vol. 4, 596–7.
[169] 13 Elizabeth, c. 10, sec. 2, *SR*, vol. 4, 544–5.
[170] 14 Elizabeth, c. 14, *SR*, vol. 4, 605, for this and below.

founding license only the "abiding houses" and Houses of Correction created at the district or county level.[171] The church likewise tried to promote the economic and administrative stability of almshouses and hospitals, using two familiar techniques. It encouraged bequests on the part of people writing their wills, as seen in Bishop Bonner's Injunctions for the Diocese of London, from 1555, which said that all curates were to visit the sick, exhorting them in their last wills "to remember the poor, and especially to solicit for the maintenance of the hospitals of the city of London."[172] The church also used episcopal visitations to supervise houses. During Cardinal Pole's visitation of Canterbury Diocese in 1557, churchwardens and clergy were asked "whether there be any hospitals within your parishes, and whether the foundations of them be duly and truly observed and kept, and whether the charitable contributions of the same be done accordingly?"[173] In similar terms despite the official shift to Protestantism, Archbishop Parker of Canterbury inquired in 1560 "whether your hospitals and almshouses be justly used, according to the foundation and ancient ordinances of the same" and whether any institutions had been pulled down or closed. Bishop Parkhurst of Norwich was particularly concerned with the religious condition of these houses. He asked in 1561 "whether the master and governors of the hospital within Norwich, and other hospitals within the diocese of Norwich, do look diligently to the well ordering and godly instructing of the sick and sore people within the same hospitals."[174] Visitation articles asked further about the kinds of people who had been named to these institutions, trying to limit the temptation to appoint more prosperous residents in return for a payment. Archbishop Parker's articles of 1560 inquired "whether there be any other placed in them than poor, impotent, and needy persons that hath not otherwise wherewith or whereby to live."[175] All of these concerns were echoed in later Elizabethan visitations.

Several wider themes are addressed by this material. After 1540 founders of institutions described more specifically what kinds of people they intended to assist, in most cases respectable old people, often women, and they laid down more detailed requirements for religious and social behavior. Any distinction between public and private administration was

---

[171] 18 Elizabeth, c. 3, sec. 9, *SR*, vol. 4, 612–13. See also ch. 6.3 above.
[172] *VAI*, vol. 2, 368.   [173] Ibid., 426. For below, see ibid., vol. 3, 84 and 82.
[174] Ibid., vol. 3, 103.
[175] Ibid., 84. For below, see, e.g., ibid., 213 and 268, and *Documentary Annals*, vol. 1, 411–12, and vol. 2, 26–7.

blurred. Some houses established and at least partially funded by individual donors were operated by towns or parishes, while many feoffees or governors of privately run charitable institutions also held public office. Participating in the successful operation of an almshouse or hospital reinforced a man's or a community's reputation as socially humane but fiscally provident stewards, a pairing of concerns commonly associated with but not limited to puritanism. Apart from some parish involvement, the church was replaced almost entirely by secular institutions and lay individuals in the operation of almshouses and hospitals. Only through visitations did religious leaders remain active. The marked determination of founders to ensure better governance for their institutions accords with the movement towards closer supervision and more stringent accounting practices seen in both charitable gathering and the operation of parish-based poor relief.[176] Many of these features continued to characterize the numerous almshouses founded in the seventeenth century.

Yet residential institutions often faced serious operational problems. Some were specific to particular houses, stemming from negligence or an illegitimate desire for personal profit on the part of their administrators or those who held property from them.[177] But several features of English law caused more systemic difficulties. Although assigning the property and management of residential institutions to feoffees became far more common in the second half of the sixteenth century, the legal situation of these bodies was ill-defined. The law with regard to what were emerging as de facto charitable trusts developed gradually as part of the broader late medieval concept of "uses."[178] In a use, the legal owner of property was differentiated from the beneficiary of the income that derived from it. Because many pre-Reformation charitable activities were run by religious organizations, they were affected also by growth of procedures whereby land could be granted to individuals for the benefit of an ecclesiastical entity. But because the common law did not recognize or enforce uses, disputes involving them had to be resolved through equity jurisdiction. By the fifteenth century, the Court of Chancery was accepting petitions concerning religious or charitable uses, joined later by the Court of Requests. The Statute of Uses of 1536 was intended to eliminate the distinction between legal and beneficial ownership of secular property, but it did not entirely succeed.

---

[176] See chs. 6.3 above and 8.3.2 below.
[177] For such challenges, see ch. 9.2 below and McIntosh, "Negligence, Greed."
[178] Jones, *History of the Law of Charity*, 3–22, and Jordan, *Philanthropy in England*, 109–12, for this paragraph and the next.

After the Reformation, although the crown joined Chancery in trying to protect property given to charitable activities, the standing of many alms- houses and hospitals remained unclear. If an institution did not have independent legal status, it could not sue or be sued collectively in a common law court, the normal venue, but instead had to petition for an equity hearing. Chancery had for some time treated parish officers as if they were a corporation, entitled in the law to receive and hold property, but feoffees serving in effect as trustees for private charitable activities were not similarly acknowledged. Who then was allowed to act on behalf of an almshouse or hospital if the master and residents lacked a shared legal identity? If people who had been granted land to hold for the benefit of the institution appropriated its property or income for their own use, or if tenants failed to pay their rents, could the house sue them? How were future feoffees or governors to be appointed in order to ensure an ongoing succession?

Prior to 1598, the only way to gain legally recognized status was to go through the process of incorporating the institution, which would hence- forth function as a legal body distinct from its individual members or feoffees and have the right of continuous succession. Some founders were able and willing to obtain a royal license, usually through letters patent, which granted corporate status and the use of an institutional seal to their new institutions.[179] The license for a hospital in Hemsworth in 1557 said that its master and twenty brothers and sisters were to be "a body corpo- rate with a perpetual succession, able in law to plead and be impleaded in any courts or places, to purchase and hold lands, liberties and goods, and to grant and lease the same as amply as the master and brothers of any other hospital within the realm; and they shall have a common seal for the business of the hospital."[180] Even the founders of small, local houses sometimes sought incorporation, as did the executors of Richard Twedy, who established an almshouse for four poor people in Stock, Essex in 1591. If an existing house was found to be legally invalid, it too could be re-established as a corporate body.[181] Paul Slack has identified seventy-five new or reorganized almshouses and hospitals that obtained letters patent for incorporation between 1540 and 1570.[182] Because,

---

[179] As an extreme way of obtaining a license for the hospital he was founding in Warwick, the Earl of Leicester put through a private act of Parliament in 1571 (13 Elizabeth, c. 17, *SR*, vol. 4, 552).

[180] *CPR, Ph. & Mary*, vol. 3, 471. For below, see L&IS, *Cal. Pat. R., 33 Eliz.*, 62.

[181] E.g., L&IS, *Cal. Pat. R., 39 Eliz.*, 130–1, where the governors – not the master and residents – were incorporated.

[182] Slack, *From Reformation to Improvement*, 26. He places these institutions into the same general category as incorporated urban bodies, all of which he describes as "little

however, obtaining a license required knowledge of legal practice as well as time, money, and access to the crown, some founders did not bother. That left in doubt the legal situation of their houses – and of the many medieval ones that had not been incorporated – until the Poor Laws of 1598 and 1601 defined and protected charitable trusts.

common weals" (ibid.). During the Tudor period, many boroughs did indeed obtain incorporation, motivated by similar problems and a desire for visible civic recognition (Tittler, *Reformation and the Towns*, 345–7).

8   Support for the parish poor

During the reigns of Mary and Elizabeth, poor relief within the parishes developed more fully. Of 119 parishes whose churchwardens' accounts were used between 1554 and 1598, seventy-one (60 percent) reported some activity on behalf of the poor. Although statutes of 1555 and 1563 modified the foundational Edwardian legislation of 1552 in limited ways, and although acts of 1572 and 1576 created new institutions at the county level, the expansion in parish involvement with the poor derived not from new laws but rather from the concerns of local people. Churchwardens experimented with techniques for generating and awarding funds to their poorer neighbors, especially children, and they served as legal spokespersons for the parish, representing it at ecclesiastical visitations and in court cases involving assistance to the poor. We can rarely determine the full level of parish involvement, however, for in some churches the wardens worked alongside Collectors for the Poor, who submitted separate but highly perishable accounts.

Collectors for the Poor have received no more than passing mention in previous studies. The sources used here show that Collectors were at work in 208 parishes by 1598, a number that is probably a small fraction of the total number. Their duties were complex, time consuming, and capable of creating ill-will. Perhaps in consultation with the churchwardens and minister, they had to decide which parishioners would contribute to the poor on a regular schedule, and in some parishes they imposed fixed assessments that might be resented or resisted. The Collectors were to report anyone who refused to pay to the churchwardens, who would in turn ask for the help of the bishop or Justices of the Peace (JPs) in forcing them to contribute. The Collectors also determined which parishioners should receive assistance and how much they should get, probably requiring visits to their homes to assess the level of need. Their decisions involved subjective value judgments about an individual's or family's sources of income, ability to work, and the reasons for poverty: whether the result of circumstances outside their control or due to their own idleness or wastefulness. In many parishes early in Elizabeth's reign and in smaller parishes even later, the assistance given by Collectors might be limited to short-term help for people with particular problems, similar to the aid given by churchwardens. Increasingly, however, Collectors moved towards ongoing weekly payments for a subset of the poor deemed unable to support themselves. In addition to distributing the money, Collectors had to submit written accounts every quarter and sometimes carry out tasks normally assigned to the churchwardens, including pursuing legal action on behalf of the poor. It is no wonder that men tried to avoid an office that brought no pay and little prestige in return.

While the increase in parish responsibility for the poor could perhaps be regarded as an "organic" growth of approaches first employed in the late medieval period, the range and volume of activity present by the 1590s, including the work of Collectors, was substantively different from the occasional assistance that had been provided by some parishes prior to 1547. For the poor, the existence of predictable support within their own community presumably provided some sense of security. Those who received weekly assistance were especially comfortable, but even in parishes that granted only temporary help, it would have been reassuring to know that if exceptional hardship struck, they could ask for aid. It is not clear, however, to what extent the rise of parish-based relief constituted a net increase in help provided to the poor, for such aid replaced some of the assistance given in the past by religious houses, chantries, fraternities, and/or manorial institutions and possibly some of the informal help provided by relatives, friends, and other members of the community. The wide array of often unpredictable forms of medieval aid was thus narrowing in favor of fewer but more reliable sources of support. In this chapter we look first at orders from the central government and church concerning the developing system of poor relief and at some changes in the functions of parishes. The role of churchwardens in raising and distributing money for the poor is considered next, while a final section examines Collectors for the Poor and their duties.

8.1   The changing legislative and parochial environment

During the first half of this period, through 1576, the job of raising and distributing money for the poor became more complicated due to several Parliamentary laws that described parish duties in more detail and established some new institutions at a higher level. Church officials used injunctions and visitation articles to enforce compliance with those rules and ensure that all sums due to the poor were rendered. Motivated in part by a desire to reduce public begging, both lay and ecclesiastical leaders were presumably influenced also by humanist or commonwealth thinking and Protestant beliefs, now embedded in the curricula and religious programs of the grammar schools and universities that most of them had attended.

The first Parliamentary measure, passed in 1555, adjusted only slightly the statute of 1552. Despite the restoration of Catholicism, Mary's government made no effort to abolish the fledgling approach beginning to emerge within parishes. The act stated that Collectors should be appointed at Christmas time by the minister and churchwardens in parishes and by the mayor and two of the chief inhabitants of cities and towns; anyone refusing to accept the office was to be fined 40s.[1] The Marian church does not seem to have gone much beyond those guidelines. Thus, Bishop Brooks's injunctions for Gloucester Diocese in 1556 say only that "the poor people of every parish shall be charitably provided for" according to the statute of 1555 and the decree of a recent synod that instructed the clergy to spend on the poor and educating scholars whatever they might save out of their ecclesiastical income.[2]

Shortly after her accession to the throne, Elizabeth issued a proclamation that repeated verbatim Edward's injunctions about religion, including those dealing with poor relief, and added a few new orders on other subjects.[3] An act of 1563 re-stated the relevant section of the statute of 1552. After the minister and churchwardens (or urban officials) had prepared the required listing of inhabitants and householders and of the poor who warranted assistance, the Collectors were to ask each parishioner in public at a church service how much he or she was willing to pay every week to assist the needy and write those amounts into the book. Whether intentionally or not, the imprecise wording of these statutes permitted considerable latitude in how individual parishes applied it. Some communities let parishioners decide for themselves what they were willing to give on a regular basis, hence allowing semi-voluntary contributions, whereas in other settings the Collectors defined fixed assessments or rates, due each week, month, or quarter.[4] Regardless of how the individual amounts were determined, the Collectors were then to gather and distribute the money to the poor each week. The measure suggests some reluctance on the part of local people to assume the office of Collector, for the fine for refusing to serve when elected was raised to £10. Any churchwarden who failed to report and prosecute such a person was to forfeit £20, and Collectors who did not submit quarterly accounts could be jailed.

---

[1] 2 & 3 Philip & Mary, c. 5, *SR*, vol. 4, 280–1. [2] *VAI*, vol. 2, 407.
[3] *TRP*, vol. 2, 117–32, esp. 120–1 and 123–4. For below, see 5 Elizabeth, c. 3, and 5 & 6 Edward VI, c. 2, *SR*, vol. 4, 411–14 and 131–2.
[4] A rate was a local tax.

The 1563 act added teeth to enforcement of the sums demanded by the Collectors. A person who was unwilling to pay was first to be sent to the bishop for exhortation, but if he remained recalcitrant, he was to give a money bond that he would appear at the next General Sessions held by JPs.[5] Should he refuse to post bond, the bishop could send him to jail. When he appeared before the JPs, they were to assess him for his contributions to the parish poor, and if he once more refused, imprison him until he agreed to pay. The measure emphasized that none of its provisions was to be prejudicial to any voluntary gifts or legacies given to relief of the poor, which were to be employed and accounted for as in the past.[6]

The new Protestant church was working in parallel with the state to promote charitable giving. A homily about almsgiving published in 1563 was joined by episcopal exhortation.[7] In a letter to the parishes of the diocese of Ely in July 1569, Bishop Cox required lay people to "deal liberally and charitably" with their poor neighbors, for three rather pragmatic reasons: (1) they no longer had to give to former religious practices like ungodly beggars and friars or to the costs of pilgrimages and "decking of images," so they had more with which to comfort the poor; (2) the queen and Privy Council were laboring every day to deliver people from the demands of healthy vagabonds and idle beggars; and (3) the queen and Council "have given express commandment that the effect and matter of the statute for the provision for the poor shallbe put in use."[8]

Two later statutes erected additional institutions above the level of parish support, each with its own set of collectors. The act of 1572 that authorized district-wide "abiding places" for those poor who could not be supported by their own communities implies that the assistance provided by parishes was proving insufficient.[9] The act of 1576 not only ordered that a House of Correction be established in every county, it instructed counties and towns to set up a stock of materials on which the unemployed poor could (and must) work, and it required that bastard children be supported by their parents.[10]

The multiplicity of "collectors" in these statutes has caused some scholarly confusion. Neither of the later two acts referred to the parish system for assisting the poor or to the Collectors for the Poor who implemented it. The collectors named in 1572 were those who gathered rates within districts to support the abiding places, operating under the

[5] 5 Elizabeth, c. 3, secs. 7–8, *SR*, vol. 4, 412–13.   [6] Ibid., sec. 17, *SR*, vol. 4, 414.
[7] See ch. 1.3 above.
[8] CorpCCC MS 168. I am grateful to Scott Wenig for this reference.
[9] 14 Elizabeth, c. 5, sec. 16, *SR*, vol. 4, 593–4. The acts of 1572 and 1576 are discussed more fully in ch. 6.3 above.
[10] 18 Elizabeth, c. 3, secs. 4 and 1, *SR*, vol. 4, 611–12 and 610.

supervision of JPs. The two sets of collectors and assessments described in 1576, for Houses of Correction and work projects, were likewise to be overseen by county JPs. William Lambarde's account of the lesser officers of the peace, from 1584, discusses the three new kinds of collectors created by the laws of 1572 and 1576.[11] Lying outside Lambarde's purview were the Collectors for the Poor who continued to function at the parish level, responsible to their own ministers and churchwardens.

Several additional misreadings apply to the statute of 1572. The measure has sometimes been described by historians as having introduced for the first time a compulsory poor rate.[12] That rate, however, applied only to support for the abiding houses, not to parish assistance. When the law discusses people who obstinately refuse to "further this charitable work" and defines the penalties imposed upon them, it is referring to those who are unwilling to pay their assessments for the new residential institutions. Further, the punishments described in 1572 were more direct, but no more severe than those prescribed in 1563 for non-payers to the parish poor.[13] The variation in wording between the opening paragraph of the 1572 act and the heading in the margin beside it is misleading too. The text itself says that it nullifies several earlier measures, including that of 1563 concerning relief of the poor, but the marginal summary is more specific, repealing only the section of the 1563 act dealing with beggars and vagabonds. In practice, the chapters of the 1563 statute that discuss parish assistance remained in effect until the 1598 Poor Laws.

The most striking feature of the second half of this period, 1577 to 1598, is that although activity by parishes and churchwardens on behalf of the poor increased, their efforts were not mandated by any new Parliamentary statutes or ecclesiastical injunctions. Greater involvement in poor relief as documented in many parishes cannot therefore be explained merely as conformity to orders coming down from above. It resulted instead from a conjunction of other factors. The number of poor people continued to mount and their need deepened, especially after the bad harvests of the later 1580s and 1590s, evoking human compassion.[14] The ongoing spread of the Protestant social message together with humanist thinking, as communicated to less educated people through laws and the pulpit, probably persuaded some churchwardens that as

---

[11] Lambarde, *Duties of Constables*, 66–7, 70–1, and 74–5. I was incorrect in saying that the 1572 act "authorized the Justices of the Peace to supervise parish and town relief" ("Local Responses to the Poor," 233).

[12] E.g., Slack, *Poverty and Policy*, 124.

[13] In the 1572 statute, people who refused to pay the county rate were to be brought before two JPs and if necessary jailed (14 Elizabeth, c. 5, sec. 21, *SR*, vol. 4, 412 and 594).

[14] See ch. 1.3 above.

local representatives of both church and state, they had an obligation to help the poor. Spread of information and competition played a part as well, as seen in the cluster of towns and villages in southeast Suffolk that seem to have been keenly aware of what their neighbors were doing and eager to demonstrate their own charitable nature. In areas marked by manufacturing or mining, employers may have put pressure on the parish to help their workers get through hard economic times so as to have a trained labor force ready at hand when conditions improved. A powerful consideration must have been fear that if the poor became desperate, they might rise out of their usual obedience and deference to those above them and resort to physical violence to obtain food or other resources. To pay for expanded assistance, communities had to have some level of economic surplus in the form of people who enjoyed more ample resources and were prepared to contribute to the poor. In implementing a system of organized aid, parishes may have drawn upon experience gained from their secular governments. Administering poor relief in a socially concerned but fiscally responsible manner could be a positive identity component for churchwardens and Collectors individually and for communities as a whole.

Activity on behalf of the needy took place amidst some changes in the operation of parishes. Like their predecessors, post-Reformation churchwardens continued to raise funds for such purposes as maintaining the church's physical structure, paying for communion bread and wine, and sometimes providing the salary for a parish clerk. Some churches still held ales, although official disapproval contributed to a decline in their use; others had special collections for targeted purposes.[15] But parishes were now more likely to employ formal assessments to generate money, at least for special projects.[16] When the church in Northill, Beds. needed income for work on its bells and bell tower in 1573, the wardens imposed a "leyer" or "levye." Some parishes acknowledged that obligatory assessments were needed even for routine church expenses. The wardens of Aston Abbots, Bucks. collected payments from the parishioners at communion services in 1563 to pay for bread and wine, demanding 3d. per household (but with the poor exempted).[17] Kirton Lindsey, Lincs. normally based its "sess" or rate on the amount of land held by parishioners, but in 1593 it experimented with a levy based on the number of animals they owned.

---

[15] For the former, see CWA #110b, from 1554–5 and 1570–71, CWA #16a, fol. 81r, and CWA #4, pp. 1–2 and 45.
[16] Ware, *Elizabethan Parish*, 88–9. For below, see CWA #2, 15–19. The churchwardens noted that the tax had been "agreed on by the body of the parish."
[17] CWA #13, fol. 3r. For below, see LincsA Kirton Lindsey par. 7/1, fols. 51r–55r.

In the mid sixteenth century, parishes acquired some new duties, ones that we would consider secular. They were probably chosen to carry out these tasks because they were the only geographical and administrative units that spanned the entire country and remained active. The Highways Act of 1555 assigned to them the job of keeping in good repair all roads leading to market towns.[18] The churchwardens and constables (the latter normally chosen for hundreds and responsible primarily to JPs) were to call together some of the parishioners annually to elect two men as surveyors of the highways. On four days each year, all parishioners were required to assemble for work on the roads, bringing at least their picks and shovels and if possible their draft animals and carts. An act of 1566 "for preservation of grain" placed responsibility on the parish for destroying "vermin."[19] (Vermin included crows and hedgehogs that ate seed and young crops or damaged thatched roofs, as well as foxes and badgers that attacked poultry and lambs.) The churchwardens and six other parishioners were to meet each year to determine how much money should be collected from wealthier people in the community in order to pay rewards to those who killed vermin. The parish of St. Thomas in Launceston, the site of Cornwall's county jail, had additional though atypical secular functions. Elizabethan churchwardens rented out their high ladder for use in hangings, after the assize justices had given judgment, and they received money from sale of the clothing of executed prisoners; in return they had to pay for washing the bodies and clothes of dead prisoners as well as digging their graves and carrying them to the churchyard for burial.[20]

The wardens of some parishes were instrumental in attempts to hide or recover property affected by royal confiscation of land that had formerly supported "superstitious" religious purposes. At Cratfield, Suff., the parish concealed earlier uses of church property and kept possession of the land by redirecting its income to support an almshouse and school; the parish of Long Melford, Suff. petitioned royal visitors to spare at least part of their endowment for the sake of poor people as well as for highways and the needs of the church.[21] Some Elizabethan parishes gained royal leases of former monastic, fraternity, or chantry property. Such grants were for a

---

[18] 2 & 3 Philip & Mary, c. 8, *SR*, vol. 4, 284–5, amended slightly in 1562 and 1575–6. Hundreds were sub-divisions of counties; for the parish's role in other kinds of public collections, see ch. 6.3 above.
[19] 8 Elizabeth, c. 15, *SR*, vol. 4, 498–9, expanding a measure of 1532–3 (24 Henry VIII, c. 10, *SR*, vol. 3, 425–6).
[20] CornwRO P 221/5/5–8.
[21] Kümin, "Secular Legacy," 107. For below, see, e.g., L&IS, *Cal. Pat. R.*, *32 Eliz.*, pt. 1, 56–7, 117–18, and 185.

limited number of years, however, and they could be revoked if the crown decided to sell the property permanently to someone else.

Across the sixteenth century, large and wealthy parishes commonly developed a hierarchy of local officers. A designated group of high status men might set policy and watch over the activities of lesser officers, or "the vestry" (a meeting of the principal parishioners) could fill that role.[22] Increased intra-parish supervision was necessary because of the wider array of tasks to be carried out, the greater sums of money handled, and the need to watch over not only the churchwardens and sometimes a clerk, but now also the Collectors for the Poor. A movement towards elite control was often reinforced by the increasing social and cultural distance between leading members of the community and the men of middling rank who filled parish offices.

8.2   Churchwardens and the poor

In analyzing the role of churchwardens in gathering and distributing funds for the poor, I have divided the second half of the sixteenth century into two shorter segments: 1554 to 1576, and 1577 to 1598 (see Appendix F). They allow us to distinguish between the period that contained some new orders from the government and church concerning poor relief and the later expansion of assistance by parishes based entirely upon their own concerns. Between 1554 and 1576, even though Collectors for the Poor were being introduced, some churchwardens remained actively involved in poor relief. Of the ninety-four parishes whose wardens' accounts were examined for those years, 37 percent reported that they generated, protected, or distributed funds for the poor, as did thirty-one additional parishes documented in other sources. Although the percentage was lower than in Edward's reign (down from 52 percent, despite a longer span), the diversity of activities was slightly greater. Between 1577 and 1598, the proportion of churchwardens in 110 parishes who gathered or gave out assistance rose to 48 percent, plus references from ninety-six other places.

If we look at the location of parishes that were implementing poor relief, we find that between 1554 and 1576 they lay in types of communities similar to those seen in the Edwardian years, though with fewer in villages and more in towns and market centers.[23] They were also found in similar

---

[22] E.g., "the Masters" of St. Mary at Hill, London in 1522–3, "the Four Men and Receivers" of Chagford, Devon in 1570, and "the Eight Men" of Prescot, Lancs. in the 1590s; for vestries, e.g., St. Saviour parish, Southwark, Surrey, Addlethorpe, Lincs., and St. Dunstan, Stepney, Middx. (see References, pt. 1).

[23] See CUP Online App. 9 for this paragraph.

regions of the country, in eighteen counties plus the city of York. But different patterns are visible among thirty-seven parishes that reported activity between 1577 and 1598 for the first time. None of the new parishes, distributed among twenty-one counties, was located in a city, and the fractions in market centers and villages rose. Further, the regional distribution had shifted. Although the north/northwest and East Anglia/ the southeast changed only slightly, the Midlands/east central became far more active, with a relative decline in the southwest/west.

8.2.1 Generating and protecting income

Churchwardens' efforts to raise or preserve income for the poor are summarized in Part A of Appendix F. In the first half of the period, through 1576, 15 percent of the accounts examined reported such roles, as did 14 percent in the second half; by the later decades, they were joined by ninety-three other parishes. Wardens were increasingly likely to receive gifts from living people and legacies for the poor. As parishes developed techniques for identifying and assisting genuinely needy people, some donors and testators clearly felt that churchwardens (working sometimes with the minister and/or Collectors) would be more knowledgeable and reliable vehicles for distributing alms than executors or heirs. In his 1556 will, George Clarke the elder of Bennington, Herts. left the tithes of grain he had bought from Henry VIII to his son William and his heirs, under condition that every year at Christmas – in perpetuity – they make specified distributions of money and cloth to the poor of three nearby communities.[24] Each of the grants was to be handled by the vicar, churchwardens, and two or three of "the honest men" of the relevant parishes. In 1571 the wardens of Lambeth, Surrey accounted for 20s. given by James Fonyard to the poor, while in 1575 the wardens of Spelsbury, Oxfds. listed sixteen people to whom they had awarded 12d. each from the money given by several gentlemen "to the poor of this parish."[25] Even when testators asked their executors to deal with their bequests, they might work with or through parish officers.

By the 1580s and 1590s, gifts and bequests for the poor awarded to churches and their wardens had become common.[26] Although large donations, especially landed endowments, are better documented, most

---

[24] *Hellard Almshouses*, 62–3.
[25] CWA #94, Pt. 1, 111, and CWA #81, 63. For below, see, e.g., Bosworth, *History of Walthamstow Charities*, 13, and Archer, "Charity of Early Modern Londoners."
[26] Both Archer and Schen found that by the later sixteenth century, London testators were likely to specify that bequests to the poor should go directly to churchwardens rather than being distributed by executors ("Charity of Early Modern Londoners" and *Charity*, 172).

bequests by local people were modest. In 1588, the churchwardens of Steeple Aston, Wilts. listed five legacies given to the church for the poor that year: one at 12d., one at 18d., and three at 13s. 4d.; seven years later the wardens recorded bequests of 10s., 40s., and £3.[27] In Ludgershall, Bucks. in 1593, a local gentleman left 40s. in money to the minister and churchwardens "to be bestowed and given to the poorest people there at their discretion and to their most commodity, which money was distributed according to the consciences of the distributors and according to his bequest." Some bequests were in kind. Margaret, the wife of Pascow Tresillyan of Nuland, gent., bequeathed 40s. to the poor of St. Columb parish, Corn. in 1586. Her gift took the form of 24 yards of grey frieze cloth "to be bestowed in clothes for the poor" plus 20s. in cash to be used for linen for them.[28]

Whereas gifts and bequests were a welcome but unpredictable source of income, some churchwardens themselves raised money for the poor, generally using techniques seen prior to 1554. Whether or not their church had implemented a system of regular payments gathered by Collectors, wardens might solicit "benevolences" or other contributions at church services, especially when communion was offered.[29] Some churches took special collections for the poor during outbreaks of plague or crop failure or in conjunction with royally decreed fasting days. Aid for local people would have supplemented any contributions made to individual outside alms seekers and proctors for charitable institutions as well as the collections mandated by the central government or county JPs for public causes.[30] Other kinds of fundraising by groups within the parish gradually disappeared, but the men, women, and maidens of the parish of St. Mary's, Reading, Berks. continued to gather money at Hocktide until the mid-1570s, perhaps giving some of their income to the poor.[31] An occasional parish in the 1560s and early 1570s used church ales to raise money at least in part for needy people.

Poor men's boxes in churches were still used to promote charitable giving, although apparently with less success than under Edward. A royal proclamation of 1559 repeated the Edwardian rules about the box and its functions; Elizabeth's injunctions of the same year modified them only by saying that the chest used for alms should be placed in "a most convenient place" in the church, not necessarily near the high altar.[32] Bishops too

---

[27] CWA #109. For below, see CWA #15.   [28] CWA #32, 24.

[29] See, e.g., CWA #26, 322/1, fol. 102, and 322/2, fol. 107, and CWA #83, fol. 11r. For below, see Hindle, "Dearth, Fasting and Alms" and GoucsA P 154/6/OV/2/1.

[30] See chs. 6.2 and 6.3 above.

[31] CWA #9, introduction. For below, see CWA #33, 160 and 168.

[32] TRP, vol. 2, 120–1 and 123–4; VAI, vol. 3, 16–17.

promoted use of the poor box. The interrogatories prepared for an unidentified visitation in 1560 and those used by Bishop Parkhurst in Norwich in 1561 asked "whether the churchwardens have provided a strong chest for the poor man's box, and hath fastened it in a fit place?"; they inquired whether income from church stocks that had formerly been used for now banned religious practices was being "employed to the poor man's box?"[33] In his visitation of the diocese of Canterbury in 1569 Archbishop Parker focused on how money from the box was distributed: he asked "whether the store of the poor men's box be openly and indifferently given where need is, without partial affection."[34]

Although fewer testators made the contributions so common in Edwardian wills, gifts to the box continued to supplement other sources of income.[35] In a sample of Sussex wills between 1554 and 1560, testators who left bequests to the poor men's box of their own and occasionally other churches gave an average of 2s. 1d., slightly less than during the Edwardian period; the median remained 12d. Living people contributed too. Between 1569 and 1575, the Roberts family of Boarzell, Sussex, gave 6d. to "the poor folk's box" several times each year, and the household of Henry Percy, ninth Earl of Northumberland, gave 20s. in alms to "the poorman's box of St. Clement's" in London in the mid-1580s.[36] During the late 1550s and 1560s more parishes in the north and northwest began to install this receptacle.[37] In several places the box had some kind of writing above it, perhaps a reminder of the importance of charity to the poor or a list of major donors. Churchwardens in Ludlow, Shrops. paid 4d. to William Stockton in 1559 "for writing over the poor men's box," while St. Michael's in Chester laid out 4d. in 1562 for making "the table over the poor men's box" and another 10s. 6d. to Pycke "for painting the table."[38] Parishes that had not installed a box could be reported to the church courts. Between 1578 and 1597 these included places in the dioceses of York, Gloucester, and Norwich and in Cheshire and

---

[33] *VAI*, vol. 3, 91 and 104. For Archbishop Grindal's articles for the Province of York, 1571, see ibid., 260.

[34] *Documentary Annals*, vol. 1, 361.

[35] Sweetinburgh, "The Poor," and Litzenberger, "Local Responses." For below, see CUP Online App. 8.

[36] *Accounts of the Roberts Family*, 74–146, passim, and *Household Papers*, 48.

[37] E.g., CWA #116, p. 2, and CWA #23, fol. 16r. The Pevsner volumes report two boxes in parish churches in the north of England as well as two in the south that date definitely or possibly from the late sixteenth century (Pevsner, *The Buildings of England*, as described in ch. 4, n. 72 above). The latter were in St. Helen Auckland, Durham, Knaresborough, W. Yorks., Winchcombe, Gloucs., and Dovercourt, Essex.

[38] CWA #85, 94, and CWA #23, fol. 16r.

Wiltshire.[39] We cannot be sure whether such parishes had no organized system of poor relief at all or whether they named Collectors who were gathering and storing funds in other ways. Even when contributions to the box declined, it remained in use for storing funds for the poor generated in other ways.[40]

A growing number of parishes had a landed endowment or stock of cash or animals, derived usually from previous bequests, the rental income from which was directed specifically at the poor. The churchwardens of Ely St. Mary's received 37s. 6d. from "rents for the poor" in 1572, and Henry Giles, a London ironmonger, gave 5 acres of land in Stondon Massey, Essex to the churchwardens and a group of other men as feoffees in 1575, with the income to be "charitably expended yearly among the poor inhabitants."[41] The bishop of Winchester reported in 1584 that two large gifts, of £120 and £80, had been converted into cash stocks by their respective parishes, to be loaned out at 10 percent interest; the income would go to the use of the poor. In Elm in the Isle of Ely, John Allen left £13 8s. 4d. in 1579 to relief of the poor, instructing the churchwardens and constables to loan it out and use the income to help needy people.[42] The parish's officers decided to buy animals and land with the money, but once they had rented out the stock, they had trouble collecting the rents due from it. Parishes might also be able to use church land to assist the poor less directly. Churchwardens in St. Giles, Reading noted in 1598 that they had issued a lease to William Nethercliffe "upon condition that he shall pay weekly towards the relief of his mother Agnes Nethercliffe, widow, 12d. during her life."[43] We note that William was not expected or required to support his own mother voluntarily: he had to be given a financial incentive.

Another potential source of income stemmed from the requirement that non-resident beneficed clergy were to give one-fortieth of their income to the poor and/or perform other traditional acts of charity.[44] Churchwardens in Nottinghamshire, Cheshire, Yorkshire, Gloucestershire, and Wiltshire reported to the church courts absentee clerics who failed to distribute the required fraction of their livings. Such

[39] *Tudor Parish Documents*, 193, GloucsA GDR 20, pp. 1–6, passim, *Diocese of Norwich*, 12, BIA V.1578–9/CB.3, fol. 29v, and Wilts&SA D1/43/5, fol. 28r.

[40] E.g., CWA #92, 110/5/5, fol. 4, CWA #83, fols. 11r and 12v–21v, passim, and CWA #18, P22/5/2, fol. 61v.

[41] CWA #19, p. 3, and Reeve, *Stondon Massey*, 110. Feoffees held property for the use of another person or purpose. For below, see TNA-PRO SP 12/173/62.

[42] TNA-PRO PRO C 2/Eliz/C.6/10.   [43] CWA #7.

[44] *VAI*, vol. 3, 12 and 378–9. For below, see NottsA DDTS 14/26/2, p. 35, and DDTS 14/26/6, pp. 28 and 39, BIA V.1578–9/CB.3, fols. 5r, 8v, and 17r, GloucsA GDR 20, pp. 1–6, passim, 10, and 27, and Wilts&SA D1/43/5, fols. 35r and 40v.

complaints were often joined by other allegations. The rector of Brinkley, Cambs. was presented in 1569 because "he doth not distribute the 40th part of his benefice to the poor" and had not even been to the parish for 7 years; Master Calvert, vicar of Haslingfield, did not give the fortieth part and did not read the homilies according to the queen's injunctions.[45] In an extreme case, the parish of Gargrave, W. Yorks. complained in 1575 against Anthony Forrest, their non-resident vicar, who not only failed to relieve the poor, but had only been to his benefice once in the past 20 years; "neither is it known where he is." Occasionally, however, payments of the one-fortieth were made and acknowledged.[46]

The "hospitality" required of resident clergymen was sometimes an issue in the later Elizabethan period.[47] For lesser clerics, that term probably included providing excess food to the poor and/or awarding simple overnight accommodations to legitimate travelers. Among the faults ascribed by the churchwardens of Southwell, Notts. to vicar Thomas Barkar in 1595 or 1596 were that he "keepeth no hospitality, relieveth not the poor, and he denieth to visit the sick."[48] Concern at the parish level must have been heightened by the church's own attempt to promote hospitality and by the central government's campaigns in 1587 and 1596–7 to encourage regular fasting, with unused food distributed as alms to the poor.[49] When a book of articles was presented to Parliament in the early 1580s recommending changes in church financing, including limiting the number of livings a clergyman might hold, the bishops responded that such measures would impoverish the clergy and make them unable to give hospitality: due to inflation, everything costs more "yet as great or greater hospitality [is] looked for."

Fines for wrongdoing by lay people, imposed by governments or the church, constituted a welcome new source of income for the parish poor. While churchwardens' accounts do not mention implementation of an order of 1547, repeated in an Elizabethan proclamation of 1559, that fines for failure to keep a register of baptisms, marriages, and burials were to go into the poor men's box of their church, other types of misbehavior were later added to the list of offences the fines for which should assist the

---

[45] CambUL D/2/8, fol. 52v; ibid., fol. 60r. For below, see BIA V.1575/CB.1, fol. 49v.
[46] CWA #58, 80, and ESussRO Par 465/10/3/1, fol. 33r.
[47] E.g., *VAI*, vol. 2, 332 and 423, and vol. 3, 3, 212, and 340, and see Heal, *Hospitality*, ch. 7.
[48] BIA V.1595–6/CB.3, fol. 83r, and see UNottL PB 292/1587, fol. 10r, and BIA V.1578–9/ CB.3, fol. 8v.
[49] Heal, "Archbishops of Canterbury," her *Hospitality*, ch. 7, and Hindle, "Dearth, Fasting and Alms." For below, see *Documentary Annals*, vol. 2, 17.

poor.[50] A royal proclamation of 1560 enforcing abstinence from meat during Lent and other fasting days ordered offending butchers, victualers, and innkeepers to pay £20; half was to go to the queen, with the other half "disposed by their churchwardens to their poor people inhabiting the parish where the offense shall be found." Penalties for misdeeds like selling goods wrongly were to be divided between the borough government of Hull, E. Yorks. and the poor in 1566, while the Saddlers' Company of Lichfield, Staffs. assigned part of the fines for violating its ordinances to the poor men's box.[51] In 1562, urban officials in Newark-upon-Trent, Notts. prohibited expensive feasting after the "churching" of women who had given birth, ordering that the offerings traditionally given to the church on such occasions should instead be paid to the use of the town's poor.

Ecclesiastical authorities added fines for not attending church to the revenues. Interrogatories for a visitation in 1560 asked:

whether the churchwardens of every parish do duly levy and gather of the goods and lands of every such person that cometh not to his own parish church upon the Sundays and holy days, and there hear the divine service, and God's word read and preached, twelve pence for every such offence; and whether they have distributed the same money to the poor?[52]

When the crown appointed a large commission to enforce religious conformity in the province of York in 1577, its tasks included seeing that churchwardens were duly levying the fines for absence from services and applying them to the poor.[53] Enforcement of these orders varied between parishes, based presumably on local attitudes towards people who were unwilling to attend Protestant services as well as the rigor of diocesan officials. Churchwardens in Bishop's Stortford, Herts. received 11s. in 1587 from fines for absence, but the parish of Wilmslow, Ches. was reported to an ecclesiastical court in 1578 or 1579 because "they levy no money for the poor of such as absent them selves from the church," a complaint echoed in the presentments for several other nearby places.[54] Social pressure was a factor too. During a Parliamentary discussion in 1571 concerning attendance at services, a member from Suffolk said that presentment of defaults should not rely on churchwardens, who were

---

[50] *VAI*, vol. 2, 121, and *TRP*, vol. 2, 120. For below, see *TRP*, vol. 2, 139–40.
[51] HullCA BRB 2, fol. 64v, and LichfRO D77/4/5/3, from 1594. For below, see N-u-TrMus D6.75/HT 8, fol. 14r.
[52] *VAI*, vol. 3, 91, and see ibid., 104, 266–7, and 311, and *Documentary Annals*, vol. 1, 359. Some injunctions instructed the churchwardens to collect such fines but then give them to the Collectors for the Poor for distribution (ibid., 289).
[53] *CPR, Eliz.*, vol. 7, 382–3, and see *Documentary Annals*, vol. 2, 24, and HullCA BRL 109.
[54] CWA #49b, 64, and BIA V.1578–9/CB.3, fols. 5v, 22r, and 30r.

simple men and might fear to offend: they would be willing to pay the fine for non-reporting rather than displease some of their neighbors.[55] During the earlier part of Elizabeth's reign, religious authorities sometimes authorized payments to the poor as commutations of penance. In 1564, the York High Commission ordered a man who had been walking and talking in church during divine service to give 12d. to the poor men's box as part of his punishment.[56] Some men found guilty of sexual misbehavior, working on Sundays or holidays, or disrupting services in the archdeaconry of Nottingham during the 1560s and 1570s were to pay their fines to the poor. A Stapleford layman had to give the singularly large fine of £5 to the poor men's box because he was not performing "the conjugal duties due to his wife," although they kept house together.[57] Hugh Pullen, the vicar of Marnham, was ordered to give 6s. 8d. to the poor box because he was not delivering quarterly sermons, while the vicar of Edwinstowe had to contribute 2s. 6d. for failure to read the homilies. But when Archbishop Whitgift issued a public letter with instructions concerning church matters in 1583, he ordered that penance not be commuted to a money fine (even if employed for relief of the poor or other godly uses) except under rare circumstances, and then only by the bishop.[58]

Churchwardens were becoming more careful to acquire appropriate written documentation concerning charitable gifts and bequests and more aggressive in ensuring that all sums due to the poor were paid. Wardens in Ashburton, Devon paid John Caunter the considerable sum of 13s. 4d. in 1575–6 "for making of the writings between Leonard Bound and Mr. Hayman, and between Mr. Heyman and the parish, for the lands that he gave to the poor."[59] Lambeth laid out 5s. 3d. in 1588 "for the search of the last will and testament of Mr. William Marshall for certain legacies given to the poor of the parish and for sermons." When John Tacye of Ordsall, Lancs. detained an annual sum due to the poor of Elkesley, Notts. in 1566, the churchwardens presented him to the archdeacon's court; a few years later, the wardens of Rolleston, Notts. complained against Richard Bull "for detaining the rent of an house given to the poor men's box."[60] Wootton Basset, Wilts. reported in 1586 that for the

[55] *Proceedings in the Parls. of Eliz.*, vol. 1, 202.
[56] BIA HC.AB.1, fol. 97v. For below, see NottsA DDTS 14/26/1, pp. 2 and 20–31, *passim*, and 14/26/2, pp. 4–5.
[57] NottsA DDTS 14/26/2, p. 95. For below, see ibid., 14/26/1, pp. 46 and 56.
[58] *Documentary Annals*, vol. 1, 470.
[59] CWA #33, 178. For below, see CWA #94, pt. 2, 172.
[60] NottsA DDTS 14/26/1, p. 32; ibid., p. 75. The court ordered Bull to pay rent of 6s. annually to the use of the poor, to account every year for having rendered that sum, and to cooperate with the wardens.

past 3 years, James Leet had not paid his rent for a cow leased from the parish, income that ought to go to the poor.[61]

By the 1580s and 1590s, some parishes had decided that it was worth the cost in time and money to bring more formal legal action in hopes of gaining or re-gaining property that provided ongoing support for the poor. The equity Courts of Chancery and Requests and the Court of the Arches (the top ecclesiastical authority) all received complaints from churchwardens throughout the country who were attempting to preserve income to assist the poor.[62] Some time in the 1580s, the churchwardens of Chislet, Kent petitioned the Court of Requests against a group of men and their wives concerning an unfulfilled bequest to the poor. They alleged that John Taylor in his 1581 will had left 44 acres of land to his son William and his heirs for a term of 4 years. After that, the land was to go to the wardens, who were to lease out the premises "and the issues and profits thereof for ever to distribute to maintain the poor people of the said parish." But after William's death, a group of other relatives had entered the property and refused to convey the lands to the churchwardens. In 1595, the leading parishioners of Sherborne, Dorset, ordered their wardens to continue demanding the legacy given by Andrew Tynewe to the church and the poor and, if necessary, to bring suit against his executors in the Court of the Arches.[63]

8.2.2   Distributing assistance to the needy

Churchwardens also awarded aid (see Part B of Appendix F). Even if their parish now appointed Collectors for the Poor, the wardens often continued to provide ancillary help. Of the churchwardens' accounts used between 1554 and 1576, 31 percent recorded some role in handing out aid to the poor, the same proportion as during Edward's reign, but between 1577 and 1598 the fraction rose to 45 percent.[64] Testators increasingly asked churchwardens to distribute legacies to the poor or to advise their executors in doing so. Some wills left the decision about how to use their bequest entirely in the hands of the wardens, while others laid

---

[61] Wilts&SA D3/7, fol. 6v.
[62] See McIntosh, "Negligence, Greed," and for cases brought by Collectors for the Poor, ch. 8.3.2 below. For below, see TNA-PRO REQ 2/152/22.
[63] CWA #36b, fol. 4r.
[64] For the very start of this period, 1553–58, Kümin's analysis of churchwardens' expenditures shows that only four of ten sample parishes paid anything for the poor, down from eight under Edward, and the proportion of total expenditures was in each case smaller than in the previous period (*Shaping of a Community*, 276–315, passim; explanations on 270–4).

out instructions of their own.[65] Awards that spanned multiple years meant that good records were needed to ensure that successive officers remained aware of their obligations. Early in Elizabeth's reign, executors were usually responsible for handing out small sums of money, food, or clothing at funerals or the few residual commemorative services.[66] Later, as some testators of Protestant or even puritan beliefs continued to encourage the attendance of poor people at their funerals, such gifts were more likely to be awarded by the wardens.[67] The popularity of occasional doles declined sharply from the previous period, although some parishes still gave a little money or bread to the poor on holy days.

Parishioners who were not being assisted by Collectors or who encountered special problems sometimes received short-term help from churchwardens. At Trinity Church, Cambridge, the wardens contributed 4s. 1d. in 1576–7 to "Warde's wife, Watson's wife, Mother Joan, and to Dawson at several times in their great need."[68] The parish of Shillington, Beds. gave the unusually large sum of 5s. in 1581 to "Robert Hill, the lame fellow." Long Melford made many one-time payments to local poor people between 1585 and 1595, in amounts between 2d. and 12d., although the parish also had an active system of regular relief.[69] In many parishes, strangers who came to the church asking for alms, either for themselves or for a charitable organization, were given a few pennies by the wardens.

Although Collectors were supposed to handle regular distributions to the poor, the churchwardens of a few parishes awarded multiple payments to selected people, at least in the later 1550s and early 1560s. These may have been parishes that had not yet appointed the new officers. In Ashburton, one married couple, one woman, and six men received sums ranging from 12d. to 8s. 2d. each in 1560–1; the following year the same woman (now described as a widow) plus two other women, a married couple, and two men received between 16d. and 27s. 4.5d.

---

[65] E.g., CWA #114, 99–139, passim, CWA #18, fols. 76r and 77v, and ESussRO Par 414/24/1. For below, see, e.g., CWA #60, 1556–71, CWA #102, 17–82, passim, and CWA #21, fols. 10v–15r, passim.

[66] E.g., CWA #116, p. 6, and MacKinnon, "Charitable Bodies." Many testators in Sussex between 1554 and 1560 instructed that food, drink, or – more commonly – money should be given to the poor at their funerals, although it is not clear who distributed these rewards (see CUP Online App. 8).

[67] Archer, *Pursuit of Stability*, 175–7. Archer found that among London testators in the 1590s who made some kind of bequest to the poor, 32% expected that poor people would be present at their funerals ("Charity of Early Modern Londoners"). For below, see, e.g., CWA #57, 10, CWA #104, from 1560 and 1573, and CWA #114, 30–2, 42, and 51–3.

[68] CWA #18, P22/5/2, fol. 193r. For below, see CWA #3, 75.

[69] CWA #91, FL 509/5/1(b). For below, see ch. 6.2 above.

each.[70] Churchwardens in Romford, Essex, spent nearly 50s. in assisting thirteen women and seventeen men in 1564–5. Half of the people received aid only once during the year, but the others received several payments.

Churchwardens might also help to operate almshouses or subsidize housing for the poor.[71] Charges for repairs of almshouses were recorded in both rural and urban parishes, and some provided cloth, fuel, and/or money to the poor people living in them, at least during sickness. Among the fullest accounts are those of the churchwardens of Thatcham, Berks. between 1562 and 1576. They bought loads of wood and straw and had them carried to the almshouse for the use of the occupants, and they purchased canvas and had it made into sheets.[72] They bought additional bedding, clothing, and shoes for some of the residents and paid for the burials of those who had no resources (and in one case "for the people's drinking at the same time"). They invested in a pound of flax with which Mother Beyckefylde could work and gave small money payments to some of the other alms people, especially when ill or at Easter. All of this activity was supported by rent from landed property assigned to the almshouse and from a special stock for the poor. Some parishes managed dwellings that had been left to them to house needy people, although if the houses lacked an endowment to finance repairs, they may have lasted for only a generation or two.[73] A few parishes paid rent for a poor person living in his or her own home. The expectation that the poor would be helped with housing is illustrated by a complaint submitted to the JPs meeting in Hatfield, Herts. in 1591.[74] Faith Rancey, a widow with a precocious awareness of her rights, said that she and her children had not been provided with "sufficient house room and dwelling in Clothall, contrary to the statute for the relief of the poor."

A few parishes in the earlier part of Elizabeth's reign hired poor women or men to do occasional jobs other than boarding or caring for their needy neighbors. Some of these tasks could be handled by people with limited

---

[70] CWA #33, 144 and 146 and, for later, 149, 151, and 153. One of the 1560–61 payments was said to be "by order of the parishioners." For below, see EssexRO-Ch T/R 147/1, after baptisms, and McIntosh, *A Community Transformed*, 283–4. Most of the recipients were old, and three lived in Roger Reede's almshouse.

[71] E.g., CWA #74, CA 4611, 4613, and 4615B, CWA #92, 110/5/5, from 1578, CWA #94, pt. 2, 160, and DevonRO 482 A/Tavistock PW30 B from 1588–9. See also ch. 7.5 above. For below, see CWA #46a, pp. 198–207, CWA #40a, P/AS/ChW/3, and CWA #94, pt. 1, 91 and 114–15. For detailed accounts, see, e.g., BristolRO P/St.J./Ch/33, fols. 1r–2v, and CWA #10, fols. 5v–73r, passim.

[72] CWA #10, fols. 2r–27v, passim, for this and below.

[73] E.g., CWA #21, fol. 6v. For below, see, e.g., CWA #114, 136.

[74] HertsA HAT/SR 3/148. For later entitlement, see, e.g., Hindle, *On the Parish?*, 398–405.

physical strength. Wardens in St. Mary's, Chester paid "the poor woman" for cleaning the church's pathway in 1561, and in the early 1560s Stratford-upon-Avon, Warws. gave a small sum each quarter to Mother Margaret for sweeping "before the chapel."[75] Other work was more demanding. Melton Mowbray, Leics. laid out 14d. in 1567–8 "in expenses to the poor folk for the carriage of the gravel of the church, 2 days," while a poor woman in Northill received 1d. in 1574 for carrying a load of sand into the church.[76] By the later Elizabethan years, churches were generally kept clean by more regular parish employees, some of whom may have been poor, although they were not identified as such.

A limited number of parishes had loan funds from which poor people could borrow small sums of money, paying little if any interest. (These were distinct from stocks of cash that were loaned out to others, with the interest going to the use of the poor.) The vestry book of Addlethorpe for 1584 notes that one-year loans from "the poor man's money" were made in units of 5s. (four loans), 10s. (seven loans), 20s. (two loans), and 40s. (one loan).[77] Churchwardens of Witham on the Hill, Lincs. made twenty-three loans of between 2s. 6d. and 8s. each in 1590; similar grants in 1594 were described as "money lent to the poor." A bequest of £4 made to the parish of Childrey, Berks. in 1530 was still being loaned out by the churchwardens to poor men and widows in the 1580s and 1590s, usually in individual amounts of 6s. 8d. or slightly larger.[78]

Occasional purchases of clothing, shoes, food, and coal or wood for fuel, which had previously been rare, became far more common after the mid-1570s.[79] In 1585–6, churchwardens in Long Melford paid 20d. for a smock for Innocent Burdon and 8d. for making a petticoat for Mother Reffen, both described as poor, while Exning, Suff. laid out 3s. 9d. "for as much cloth as made Mother Woodes a petticoat, coat, and a waistcoat." Camborne parish in Cornwall was among the most active in providing clothing. In 1577 and 1578, churchwardens reported expenses for making four shirts for poor men, one pair of men's britches, and seven pairs of men's shoes or clouts, plus three smocks for women and girls, one petticoat and bodice, and five pairs of women's shoes.[80] Similar payments

[75] CWA #22 and *Minutes and Accounts*, vol. 1, 120–1. See also CWA #18, P22/5/2, fol. 20r.
[76] CWA #59, DG 36/140/13, and CWA #2, 19.
[77] CWA #60. For below, see CWA #68, fols. 5r–v and 9v, and also CWA #18, P22/5/2, fol. 190v.
[78] CWA #4, pages at end of the book.
[79] E.g., CWA #26, 322/1, fols. 80, 87–8, and 91–2, CWA #52a, fol. 5r, and CWA #33, 171–9, passim. For below, see CWA #91, FL 509/5/1(b), and CWA #90, p. 24.
[80] CWA #26, 322/1, fols. 97 and 102. For below, see ibid., 322/2, fols. 129–30.

in 1592–3 were heavily weighted towards clothes for children. Like many of the larger towns and cities, a few parishes bought bread or grain that was made available to the poor at reduced cost. Long Melford collected more than £30 in 1586–7 to be used "for the provision of barley for the poor."[81]

Helping sick, injured, or old people or a woman having a difficult pregnancy – by giving them money or food, paying another parishioner to board or care for them, or even hiring a medical person to attend to them – was a growing concern across the Elizabethan period.[82] By 1577 to 1598, 12 percent of the churchwardens' accounts used here recorded such assistance. Because many of those who provided care were themselves poor, parish payments performed several functions. St. Aldate parish in Gloucester gave 7s. 5d. in 1587 "to Thomas Wood's wife lying sick," and the parish of St. John, Winchester, paid Widow Cicell in 1590 "for tending to Mathew Wotten in his sickness."[83] In Trinity parish, Ely, the wardens gave 7s. in 1566 to "Robert Clement the surgeon for helping John Keye's arm, being bitten with a dog," and they paid for "a surgeon for Fennell" in 1584–5.[84] A few adults were boarded longer term with other people. Camborne paid the very large sum of 28s. 6d. to George Sander in 1577 "for the board of the Old Joan," and in St. Peter's parish in St. Albans, Herts., Kinge received 5s. 10d. in 1590–91 "for keeping the Lunatick woman."

Activity increased during plague outbreaks, presumably in part because churchwardens wanted to limit the spread of infection by keeping sick people within their own homes. Wardens in Sherborne parish paid a total of 22s. 3d. in the late 1570s "for the charges of Joan Masters, being sick of the plague," while those in Camborne submitted a detailed account in 1592 of what they had expended "in relieving the sick people that were infected with the plague."[85] Melyor Gere was given 6s. in cash plus bread, a gallon of drink (probably ale), honey, and candles; the churchwardens later laid out 3s. 4d. for her shroud and 2d. for her grave. The wardens paid 25s. 3d. for tending Thomas Buswainnes and later burying him, but Reynold Vyans must have died more quickly, as he needed only 3s. 11d. for his nursing and burial. And there were others. Many of the payments went directly to sick people, but Whitford's wife received money for looking after others, and John William received regular weekly wages. This was a major financial and human undertaking, one that must have

[81] CWA #91, FL 509/5/1/49.
[82] See also Willen, "Women in the Public Sphere," Wear, "Caring for the Sick Poor," and Schen, *Charity*, 188–90.
[83] CWA #44, CW/1/21, and CWA #45.
[84] CWA #20. For below, see CWA #26, 322/1, fol. 97, and CWA #52a, fol. 33v.
[85] CWA #36a, CW 1/51, and CWA #26, 322/2, fol. 124r, for this and the examples below.

taxed the churchwardens' resources whether or not they were assisted by Collectors. In some cases, parishes had more ready cash with which to assist people smitten by plague than did urban bodies. In 1595, Sherborne parish loaned £5 9s. 6d. from the church stock to the town to cover "part of the charge in relief of the sick of the plague."[86]

More parishes were now paying for shrouds, winding sheets, and/or burials, a sad indicator of destitution. Churchwardens in St. Mary's, Ely gave 11d. in 1587 to Father Hall for burying his wife, and the wardens of Poughill, Corn. paid 2s. 7d. for Hugh Bear's shroud in 1596.[87] Mildenhall, Suff. laid out 20d. for a sheet for Lucy Druwrye to bring her to the ground and 10d. for one yard of cloth to bury Firmyne's child in 1596, as well as giving 18d. to "Edmund Docking for eight graves making for poor folks." It is even more painful to encounter so many references to the burials of completely unknown strangers, especially in urban parishes. (Towns probably attracted sick and destitute immigrants, and mortality was higher there.) In 1570, the churchwardens of St. Mary's, Chester spent 4d. "for covering of a stranger's grave which died in Robert Crossys," and wardens in Trinity parish, Ely gave 3s. in 1588 "for the burying of a poor boy which was found frozen to death."[88] The wardens of St. Thomas's church, Salisbury noted as an extraordinary charge in 1587–8 the 3s. spent for "a shroud and the burial of a soldier," while Lambeth paid "for a sheet and for bearers to carry a poor Irish woman to church which died in Faukes Hall" and for making her grave.

In a particularly interesting development, care for poor children became far more common. Orphaned, abandoned, or illegitimate infants or children were usually boarded initially with another household. If they survived to the age of around 6 to 12 years, they might be sent by the parish into (unpaid) service until they reached adulthood. Between 1554 and 1598, forty parishes encountered in this study recorded some assistance to infants or youngsters (31 among the 119 parishes in the main analysis, or 26 percent, plus nine others). The active parishes were located in all four regions of the country, although the largest number lay in East Anglia/the southeast.[89] None of the communities in which the parishes were situated

---

[86] CWA #36b, fol. 3v.
[87] CWA #19, 32, and CWA #30, fol. 58. See also CWA #33, 153, 162, and 165, and CWA #26, 322/1, fols. 87–8, 91–2, 97–9, and 102. For below, see CWA #92, 110/5/5, fols. 20r–v, and see also 5r.
[88] CWA #22 and CWA #20, and also the latter, under 1585 and 1586. For below, see CWA #108, 297, and CWA #94, pt. 2, 149. Lambeth's wardens also laid out 14d. for food for the woman's children and later 6d. for burying one of them.
[89] For definition of regions, see ch. 3, n. 42 above; for types of communities, see CUP Online App. 1, pt. 6.

was a city and only three were towns, as compared to thirteen market centers and twenty-four villages. That distribution suggests that larger places dealt with orphans primarily through urban institutions. Increased parish activity evidently stemmed from a rising number of young children who lacked families to look after them, for no statutes assigned additional responsibilities to parishes for their care. The poor laws of 1552 and 1563 did not mention children specifically, nor did they impose residency requirements for the people to be assisted by parishes.[90] Several acts dealing with begging and vagrancy, however, stipulated that legitimately needy folks qualified for help in the parish where they were born or where they had lived for at least 3 years.

Many of the children who were boarded or "kept" by a person other than their parents at the parish's expense were orphans of local people, while a few were evidently the offspring of poor families that could not provide for them.[91] Trinity parish in Ely paid 10s. in 1576 to John Harvie, who had "a poor boy of Turpyns," and gave 20s. the following year to Tyllingham, who had "a poor wench of Turpins."[92] Churchwardens in Heckington, Lincs. delivered to Paramore's wife a total of 50s. in 1584 and 1585 for keeping Ellen Cowper's child for 18 months and gave more than 43s. to William Jeffrey for keeping Pope's boy for two years. St. Peter's parish in St. Albans paid Goodwife (later Widow) Grave around 50s. annually for nursing one of Richard Carter's children between 1591–2 and 1596–7.[93] Because boarding costs were so high, it is unsurprising that parishes hoped to avoid responsibility for any additional children. In 1579–80, parishioners in Debden, Essex asked the Quarter Sessions whether they were required by law to provide for children whose parents "are of a manual occupation but will neither use the same nor any other kind of labour."[94] We do not know what the JPs replied. In a different pattern, churchwardens in the rural community of Eaton Socon, Beds. hired a woman in 1596 to train poor children "to work bone lace," a skill they must have hoped would allow the youngsters to earn their own living subsequently.[95]

---

[90] 5 & 6 Edward VI, c. 2, and 5 Elizabeth, c. 3, *SR*, vol. 4, 131–2 and 411–14. For below, see chs. 2.1, 5.1, and 6.1 above.

[91] E.g., CWA #89, 68–9 and 74, CWA #85, 106 and 111, CWA #34, 218, CWA #4, from 1573, and McIntosh, "Networks of Care." See also CWA #88, fols. 2r and 8r, CWA #122, pp. 128–9, CWA #121 for 1595, CWA #57, 16, 34, and 38, CWA #32, 12, and CWA #52a, fol. 20v.

[92] CWA #20. For below, see CWA #62, fols. 30v–31r.

[93] CWA #52a, fols. 36v–47v, passim.

[94] Essex RO-Ch Cal. QS Records, vol. 9, 74/51, used through HarvUA 17729, Box 2, QS Records, MSS, Essex, 146.

[95] Beds&LA P 5/12/1, p. 78.

Wardens were legally obliged to provide for illegitimate children born in the parish whose parents were unable to pay for their keep. Increasing activity at the parish level mirrors the rise in a national illegitimacy ratio, which went from 2.2 in the 1560s to 4.0 in the 1590s.[96] The heavy financial burden shouldered by parishes for care of such children was cited in a statute of 1576, which referred to "bastards begotten and born out of lawful matrimony" who were "left to be kept at the charges of the parish where they be born."[97] The measure ordered that the mother and/or reputed father of such children pay a weekly sum, as determined by the JPs, to the parish where the child was being raised. Although justices attempted to enforce the statute, their efforts were often unsuccessful.[98] Some communities took aggressive action to prevent the birth of illegitimate children whom the parish would thereafter be required to support. The manor of Shrawley, Worcs. fined widow Alice Cooke a shilling in 1565 for keeping a pregnant prostitute in her house, ordering that the woman be removed and no other pregnant women be taken in under penalty of 10s.; in 1591 Robert Bruar had to pay 40s., an exceptionally high penalty, because he received into his house a pregnant woman who gave birth there.[99]

Parishes were also responsible for children who had been abandoned within their bounds. The minute book of the parish vestry in St. Dunstan, Stepney, Middx. contains a poignant entry for September 2, 1581:

> Whereas a child was left in the church porch on Sunday the 25th of August last, with a note left written in the breast of it, that it was a Christian soul named Jane, we call her Jane. It is agreed that for the same child there shall be a nurse provided (for as small a charge as may), and the money for it, as also for necessary charges, shallbe disbursed by the church wardens, who shall keep account of the same charge.[100]

The kind of situation every parish presumably feared was described to the Wiltshire Quarter Sessions in 1589. A "wandering woman" had come to the house of John Hiscockes at Preshute, bringing with her a baby girl about 6 weeks old. During the middle of the night, the mother departed,

---

[96] The ratio compares illegitimate births to total baptisms: Adair, *Courtship, Illegitimacy*, 48–50.

[97] 18 Elizabeth, c. 3, sec. 1, *SR*, vol. 4, 610. In 1593 Parliament discussed whether the 1576 measure "for relieving of bastards" may "cherish the vice" and hence should be discontinued, but no action seems to have been taken (*Proceedings in the Parls. of Eliz.*, vol. 3, 131).

[98] E.g., *Wiltshire Co. Recs.: Mins. of Procs. in Sessions*, 129.

[99] WorcsRO 705:7:BA 7335/50/22, Views held 7 Eliz. and 33 Eliz. For an earlier private arrangement by a man accused of adultery and fornication who agreed to support his bastard children, see TNA-PRO STAC 2/34/91.

[100] CWA #72, fol. 9v. For below, see *Wiltshire Co. Recs: Mins. of Procs. in Sessions*, 132.

leaving the infant behind. The JPs therefore ordered that the parishioners of Preshute be rated, "every man according to his living," to produce the 54s. that Hiscockes had already spent in caring for the girl as well as the cost of maintaining her until she reached the age of 12 years. Anyone who refused to pay the assessment was to be called before the next Quarter Sessions.

Churchwardens struggled with ways to pay for such children. They were occasionally able to extract support from relatives or friends. Wardens in Ashburton recorded an agreement made on May 17, 1562 "before the whole parish" concerning the care of Hugh Fursse, son of Richard Fursse, tanner, deceased, who was then in the keeping of Thomasine Conott.[101] Eight people agreed to pay between 2d. and 8d. quarterly, yielding a total of 14s. per year: four men surnamed Fursse, a widow Fursse, and three other men. But in the absence of individual payments like those, a special assessment on the whole parish might be necessary. An entry from Great Paxton, Hunts. from the 1590s records "the names of all such the inhabitants of Much Paxton which contribute towards the bringing up of Michael Hallam and Joane Hallam . . . children of John Hallam deceased, left to the said town to be brought up. The said inhabitants being levied towards the said 2 children finding after 2d. the half yardland according as need require."[102] Some churchwardens were prepared to expend a great deal of effort, time, and money to get outside assistance (or perhaps to be relieved of responsibility entirely) for a child abandoned in the parish.

Elizabethan wardens experimented with two further methods of dealing with unwanted children, neither of which provided for any future parish inspection of the quality of care received by the youngsters. In one arrangement, they granted a child permanently into the care of an often unrelated adult. That person received an immediate cash payment from the parish and would be able to utilize the child's labor as he or she grew older, while the parish was legally freed from subsequent financial liability. In 1574, Harry Man's wife received the sizeable sum of £3 7s. from churchwardens in Ashwell, Herts. "for the bastard," and in Northill, William Ball was paid 40s. by the wardens as "agreed upon in presence of Mr. Hardynge, Mr. Barnard[iston] and the rest of the parish, for the keeping of a poor child."[103] The parish of Great Berkhamstead, Herts.

---

[101] CWA #33, 147. Hugh Fursse was still being boarded in 1565 (ibid., 153).
[102] CWA #53, after burials. Twenty-three people were listed, paying between 1d. and 2s. 2d. each, for a total of 13s. 5d. A yardland usually contained around 30 acres. For below, see, e.g., CWA #33, 181.
[103] CWA #46a, p. 207, and CWA #2, 18. See also CWA #94, pt. 1, 93, and CWA #57, 30. For below, see CWA #50, VI-1.

was unusually explicit about its motivation with regard to the baby daughter of Alice Sheppard in 1585. Thomas Sheppard, a merchant tailor of London, and Hugh Brassington of Berkhamstead, glover, gave bond for £40 to the churchwardens that they would keep and bring up the child, discharging the parish of all responsibility for her. The condition of the bond explained that Alice Sheppard had recently given birth in Hugh Brassington's house in Berkhamstead. Due to that event, the parish, "by force of certain statutes, is charged with the bringing up of the child unless some other proviso be sought and done." The two bonded men agreed to "save harmless the parish and parishioners from all loss, troubles, or pains of money by reason of the keeping or bringing up of the said child, so that she is maintained by them for ever." If they filled that agreement, their obligation to render the £40 would be void. Nothing was said about how they should raise or train the girl.

Transferring illegitimate, abandoned, or vagrant children into the hands of another person became even more common in the 1590s. St. Aldate, Oxford, took a bond from a local carpenter in 1590 concerning "one maiden child late found in the parish of St. Aldate named Joan."[104] He agreed to raise her at his own costs for 16 years, excusing the parish from all expenses. The churchwardens of Warfield, Berks. delivered 11s. 2d. to Foster in 1595 "for the discharge of the child base born," while John Warde of Linton, Cambs. received £5 in 1594 "to bring up Richard Humphrey, a poor child, and to discharge the town."[105] Some parishes offered inducements other than a cash payment. In Lacock, Wilts., the churchwardens noted in 1598 that they had assigned two female children to local men, to be kept at their own costs.[106] In return, the parish agreed to give beneficial leases to the men and to provide clothing for the girls once each year.

An alternative strategy was to bind slightly older children as servants for a period of years until they reached full adulthood.[107] Their masters would subsequently cover all their expenses, but there was no mention of the cash wages normally paid to servants. Most of a cluster of bonds from the parish of Walsham le Willows, Suff. between 1576 and 1593 pertain to children who were being granted out as servants, even when

---

[104] CWA #77, c. 23, file D.
[105] CWA #11 and CWA #21, fol. 13v. See also CWA #52a, fol. 50r, and CWA #75, fol. 64a.
[106] Wilts&SA 173/1, after churchwardens' accounts.
[107] A statute of 1572 modified the Edwardian order about beggars' children, saying they could be placed as servants by General Sessions of the Peace (14 Elizabeth, c. 5, sec. 24, *SR*, vol. 4, 595). Vagrant children under the age of 14 if defined as rogues were to be whipped or punished in the stocks (ibid., sec. 14, *SR*, vol. 4, 593).

their masters were craftspeople. Robert Purdye, aged 5, the base child of Robert Wadroke, was assigned as a servant to Toby Wood, a shoemaker of Ditchingham, Norf., and Richard Carter, the base child of Mary Carter, aged probably around 7, went as a servant to Richard Clarke, an Ipswich weaver.[108] The transition from boarding an orphaned child to sending him into service is visible in Exning. In 1596, the churchwardens paid 2s. 6d. to Widow Bettes for doing laundry for Climes' boy "ever since his father died" and 11s. to Thomas Blanne "towards the keeping of Climes' child."[109] The following year, Widow Bettes and Blanne received more for the lad, but in 1598 the wardens paid the schoolmaster 6d. "for making a pair of indentures to bind Clymes boy with John Horn."

Churchwardens rarely paid to place poor children as true apprentices, where they would gain craft skills that would enable them to support themselves as adults. Nearly all of the nominal apprenticeship contracts signed by parishes in this period committed needy youngsters to what was in fact an exceptionally long period of service, receiving no wages and with no indication that they would receive any specialized training.[110] In 1598, churchwardens in Lacock placed a young girl as an apprentice for 12 years; the parish was to pay her master 2s. 8d./month during the first two years of the term, but nothing was said about teaching her skills. This pattern in parishes, probably due largely to lack of funds, contrasted with the burst of interest in real apprenticeships among wealthy donors in the 1590s.[111] Their endowed schemes allowed poor boys to get training as actual apprentices, part of an approach designed to help people rise out of poverty.

Urban or suburban parishes overburdened with the poor sometimes paid to have children or enfeebled adults removed from their area lest they acquire the right to relief through 3 years of residence.[112] Churchwardens in Lambeth paid 12d. in 1588–9 "for conveying away a child that was brought to the parish," and in 1594–5 they spent 22d. "for two warrants for the remove of certain poor folks that new came into the parish."[113] In St. Saviour, Southwark, one of the churchwardens, with the consent of the vestry, paid 20s. in 1582 to James Bartlett, a shoemaker of Fenny

---

[108] SuffRO-BSE EL 159/7/29/5 and 2.
[109] CWA #90, pp. 22–3, 25–7, and 29, for this and below.
[110] Ibid., pp. 20 and 23, and see McIntosh, *Working Women*, 135–8. Most of the documents described by modern archivists as "pauper apprenticeship indentures" were actually contracts for service (e.g., Emmison, "Care of the Poor," esp. 13). For below, see Wilts&SA 173/1, after churchwardens' accounts, and also SuffRO-BSE EL 159/7/29/3 and DerbRO D/1955/E292.
[111] Jordan, *Philanthropy*, 370–1 and 263–74.   [112] E.g., CWA #27, fol. 22.
[113] CWA #94, pt. 2, 175 and 195. For below, see CWA #96, P92/SAV/450, p. 173, and also CWA #114, 136.

Stratford, Bucks., "for the carrying away out of this parish an old widow woman, his mother, named Elizabeth Johnsonne, into Buckinghamshire aforesaid; which James hath entered into bond to save this parish harmless for ever hereafter from the keeping or finding of his said mother." Again we see an adult child being paid to provide for an elderly parent. Some parishes turned to JPs for help in trying to expel poor people. The inhabitants of Hertingfordbury, Herts. petitioned the Sessions held in Hatfield in 1596 concerning widow Margaret Watkyns, who was originally from Woollaston, Gloucs. but had moved to their area.[114] Because Margaret could no longer maintain herself "and has become a charge upon the parish," the JPs ordered that she be sent back to Woollaston, conveyed by the constables of each parish through which she traveled.

The amount of money that late Elizabethan churchwardens devoted to the poor, and the fraction of their total expenses used in that way, varied widely. The differences are illustrated by a small sample of ten parishes the wardens' accounts of which survive from around 1590 (a period of only moderate hardship) and 1596 (a time of acute hardship). Three parishes in villages and one in a market center reported no payments at all to either local poor or outside alms seekers in those years, although several made the required contributions to the county jail and/or injured soldiers.[115] We do not know whether those parishes actually did nothing for the poor or had Collectors who were submitting separate accounts. Churchwardens in two other parishes reported small contributions to the poor in 1590–1 (2s. 6d., or 8 percent of the total expenses in the village of Ashwell, and 2s. 6d., or 1 percent of the total expenses in the suburban community of Lambeth), but nothing in 1596–7.[116] Given the severe problems with poverty in the latter year, Collectors were probably dealing with the poor. The remaining parishes listed larger contributions in at least one year. In the village of Clifton, Beds., the 14s. 7d. spent on the poor in 1589–90 (income from "the town land") formed 31 percent of the churchwardens' total expenses.[117] Wardens in the rural parish of Shillington spent just 1s. 8d. for the poor in 1590–1 (1 percent of the total), but 11s. 7d. in 1595–6 (16 percent of the total), due to repairs to the almshouse and donations to needy strangers, even though Collectors were by then operating a separate system of collection for the local poor. The two parishes in larger towns had the highest percentages. In Worcester, St. Michael's in Bedwardine

---

[114] HertsA HAT/SR 8/41.
[115] Strood, Kent, Pyrton, Oxfds., Northill, Beds. and Prescot, Lancs.: CWA #57, 67–70 and 74–5; CWA #79, 85 and 88; CWA #2, 37–9; and CWA #58, 116–18 and 124–6.
[116] CWA #46b, 28–9 and 36–8; CWA #94, pt. 2, 182–4 and 199–202.
[117] CWA #1, 1–2. For below, see CWA #3, 88–90 and 94–8.

devoted £2 10s. 8d. to the poor in 1590–1 (57 percent of the church-wardens' total expenses), with some of the money coming from a bequest; the amount dropped to 18s. (15 percent of the total) in 1596–7.[118] Churchwardens in St. Peter's parish in the market center of St. Albans gave only 8s. to needy people in 1590–1 (3 percent of the total), but the following year it was agreed "by the parish" that 55s. 3d. should be devoted to poor relief; in 1596–7 the parish spent the startling sum of £11 2s. 10d. (59 percent of the total), much of it going to provision for children.

8.3   Collectors for the Poor

According to the statute of 1552, modified slightly in 1563, all parishes should henceforth have appointed Collectors for the Poor to assess and collect regular payments from wealthier parishioners and distribute the money each week to those in need. Historians have generally assumed, however, that the system was rarely implemented, at least not on a regular basis, prior to the Poor Laws of 1598 and 1601. W. K. Jordan thought that the poor rates he identified before that time were imposed only during "periods of acute local distress."[119] Paul Slack, when discussing the development of parish poor relief, concluded that although most of the larger towns had poor rates by 1600, "only a small minority of rural parishes, most of them probably in the south-east," did so. Not until after 1601, he suggested, was the law implemented more widely, and he estimates that even by 1660, just one-third of all parishes were accustomed to using poor rates. Steve Hindle commented that in a handful of counties, especially in market towns and large villages, "the closing years of the sixteenth century witnessed the growing sophistication and bureaucratization of poor relief under the authority of collectors for the poor."[120] He nevertheless proposed that most parishes did not adopt the new system before 1598, in some cases not beginning to appoint poor relief officials until the 1620s or 1630s.

This project presents a more positive picture. The fragility of Collectors' accounts and their rare preservation among parish documents mean that the absence of records cannot be taken as evidence that Collectors were not at work. The information presented here about the number of parishes

[118] CWA #114, 102–4 and 130–4. For below, see CWA #52b, 141–3; ibid., 160–2.

[119] Jordan, *Philanthropy in England*, 129–30. For below, see Slack, *English Poor Law*, 26 (which says that "in some places rating was tried only for a year or two; in others it was said to be unnecessary; many parishes did nothing") and his *Poverty and Policy*, 170. Neither of these works discusses Collectors.

[120] Hindle, *On the Parish?*, 233. For below, see ibid., 233–53.

that did have Collectors and/or fixed assessments (which would have been imposed by these officers) suggests that in southern and central England, many parishes were indeed making use of the new system before 1598. Other historians and archivists will probably be able to add further examples from their own research. We can also observe for the first time how Collectors functioned during the Elizabethan period.

8.3.1   Collectors' accounts and the extent of implementation

Some of the material about when parishes began appointing Collectors and collecting fixed assessments comes from the quarterly accounts prepared by those officials. By the 1560s they were commonly written on loose sheets of paper set up as a lined grid in which each payer was listed down the left-hand side, together with the amount that he or she was supposed to contribute each week or month. The sheet had thirteen vertical columns (one per week) in which the Collectors could check off whether the person had rendered the stipulated amount. A similar sheet was prepared for distributions, with the names of recipients and their allocation down the left-hand side and checks showing whether they received that sum each week. The total amount collected and disbursed could then be calculated on a weekly and quarterly basis. But once the account had been submitted to the minister and churchwardens, the paper sheets were no longer needed. Sadly from our perspective, they were rarely stored with other parish records, and even if they were preserved initially, the paper was generally too fragile to survive. Lack of Collectors' accounts from a given parish does not mean that those officers were not in place and carrying out their designated functions.

Fortunately, one also finds occasional references to Collectors in other records. Their summary income and expenditures were sometimes noted in churchwardens' accounts or parish registers, where they have not always been identified as related to the poor.[121] Additional material comes from reports about their activity or complaints submitted to the church courts, Quarter Sessions, and central equity counts. The parishes for which Collectors or regular assessments are documented in this discussion derive from their own accounts plus the additional references I encountered while working on the project. The number would have been much higher had I gone beyond those sources to include references to Collectors and assessments in wills and secondary studies of particular communities. To avoid any artificial inflation of the figures, I have

---

[121]   A suggestion previously made by Emmison, "Care of the Poor."

counted city parishes that had their own Collectors, but excluded Collectors named for urban wards.

Despite the patchiness of the records, it is clear that a significant number of parishes appointed Collectors and/or imposed obligatory assessments for the poor between 1552 and 1598.[122] Even between 1552 and 1559, Collectors are documented in twenty-two parishes, while formal assessments for the poor were noted in three additional places. During the 1560s, the number of parishes with some type of reference rose to thirty-eight, while in the 1570s it jumped to 104. That increase stemmed in part from an aggressive campaign by the bishops in 1569–71 to enforce the appointment of Collectors and payment of the sums assessed by them. In the 1580s I encountered references from just seventy-nine parishes, but in the 1590s, the number rose to ninety-eight. The total number of different parishes for which Collectors or assessments are recorded some time between 1552 and 1598 was 208. These figures constitute an unknown but probably very small fraction of all parishes that complied with central government orders.

In geographical terms, the 208 parishes were located within twenty-seven counties plus the cities of London and York. They were not, however, distributed evenly throughout England. Of the four geographical regions used in this analysis, East Anglia/the southeast provided nearly two-thirds of all sites.[123] Its 135 parishes with references to Collectors or assessments were distributed among all eleven counties plus London. The southwest/west was next, with active parishes in seven of its ten counties, coming to a total of forty-three parishes; the Midlands/east central region included twenty-seven parishes spread between eight of eleven counties. The north/northwest, however, was almost entirely absent, represented only by two parishes in the city of York and one from the East Riding. Although the regional distribution is certainly affected by the better survival of records in the southern and central parts of the country, it is likely that the north of England was slower to begin implementation of the poor relief system. Parishes with Collectors or fixed payments were located in all four types of communities, but just over half were in villages. That cluster in rural settings parallels the increasing frequency of villages as the site for almshouses founded between 1540 and 1599, attesting to a rise in rural poverty.

---

[122] CUP Online App. 10 distinguishes between two types of entries: surviving accounts or specific mentions of Collectors; and references to fixed individual payments, rates for the poor, or people who refused to pay them.

[123] See CUP Online App. 9, pt. 2.

Some parishes – and in certain regions probably many parishes – did not want to spend the time required to implement the new system or to force their wealthier members to support the poor.[124] If the churchwardens who were summoned to visitations and sometimes the local lay representatives who came before the Quarter Sessions agreed to hide the absence of Collectors and assessments (which meant they had to violate their oath to reply honestly to the questions posed to them), outside authorities might not become aware of the problem. Occasional reports indicate, however, that some parishes had not appointed Collectors and/or did not have regular collections. The parish of Little Thurrock, Essex was named at the Essex Quarter Sessions in 1566 for having no collection for the poor, and a complaint was made at a visitation in 1578–9 that the parish of Holt, Ches. had no Collectors and no collection.[125] At a visitation in Nottinghamshire in 1587, the parish of Burton in Fabis admitted that they had no Collectors, nor did the parish of Granby cum Sutton, although the latter said that their churchwardens gathered a collection for the poor before the communion. The fact that Archbishop Grindal of York thought it necessary to send out detailed instructions in 1571 about how the new system was supposed to function suggests that it had not yet been widely implemented. Nearly twenty years later, a survey of ecclesiastical conditions in the county of Lancashire reported that "the provision for the poor by a common and certain collection according to statute in all churches is utterly neglected."[126]

8.3.2   Collectors and their duties

The responsibilities of Collectors for the Poor were described in unusual detail in Archbishop Grindal's injunctions of 1571.

Yearly at midsummer, the parson, vicar, or curate and churchwardens shall choose two collectors or more for the relief of the poor of every parish, according to a statute made in that behalf in the fifth year of the Queen's Majesty's reign, entitled an act for the relief of the poor, and renewed in the last parliament, which collectors shall weekly gather the charitable alms of the parishioners, and distribute the same to the poor where most need shall be, without fraud or partiality; and shall quarterly make unto the parson, vicar, or curate, and churchwardens, a just account thereof in writing: and if any person of ability shall obstinately and

---

[124] Some townspeople actively opposed taxation for the poor (Slack, *Poverty and Policy*, 125–6).
[125] EssexRO-Ch Cal. QS Records, vol. 2, 18/46, used through HarvUA 17729, Box 2, QS Records, MSS, Essex, 145, and BIA V.1578–9/CB.3, fol. 22r. For below, see UNottL PB 292/1587, fols. 6v and 4v.
[126] "The State, Civil and Ecclesiastical," esp. 12.

frowardly refuse to give reasonably towards the relief of the poor, or shall willfully discourage others from so charitable a deed, the churchwardens and sworn men shall present to the Ordinary [the convener of a church court] every such person so refusing to give, discouraging others, or withdrawing his accustomed alms, that reformation may be had therein.[127]

Appropriately for his conservative archdiocese, Grindal did not mention required payments or fixed assessments as determined by the Collectors, nor did he refer to enforcement by JPs.

Because the method for determining how much people should pay for the parish poor was imprecisely described in the statutes, parishes could choose between several procedures. In some settings, individual parishioners were allowed to state how much they were willing to give each week or month. Since that declaration was made in public at a church service, they might face some pressure to offer a fair amount. The "wardens of the poor" in Camborne used an ambiguous wording in the mid-1570s that suggests regular but voluntary payments: they accounted for money "received upon the book of the benevolence of the parish to the poor."[128] In other parishes, Collectors imposed fixed assessments on those considered able to pay. In the early 1570s, the Kentish parish of St. Nicholas, Strood referred to its payments explicitly as "the rate of the poor."[129] But an older conception of voluntary almsgiving sometimes held sway even when parish officials specified the amount to be rendered. In May 1555, Sir William Petre of Ingatestone Hall, Essex, then Secretary of State, paid 46s. 8d. to the Collectors for the Poor of Ingatestone for the previous 28 weeks, at the imposed rate of 20d. per week.[130] Yet his steward's account book described those sums as "my master's charity to the poor of Ingatestone."

Assistance to the poor was normally rendered in cash. Money could easily be distributed to recipients, with any excess placed into the poor men's box or loaned out at interest until needed. Occasionally, however, perhaps especially during food shortages, the obligation might be met in kind. The parish of Aston Clinton, Bucks. listed the people who had paid either money or bushels of beans towards support of the poor in 1596–7.[131] In some settings it was possible to pay off one's total lifetime contribution in advance, allowing the Collectors to use the money as they wished. In Wisbech in the Isle of Ely, William Skortred sold a gelding in

---

[127] *VAI*, vol. 3, 290.   [128] CWA #26, 322/1, fol. 97.
[129] CWA #57, 29. The term "rate" was used for a compulsory local tax.
[130] Emmison, "Care of the Poor." He also paid 26s. to the Collectors of each of two adjacent parishes where he held land, at the rate of 12d. per week.
[131] LincsA Lincoln Diocesan Records, Charities and Briefs, #3.

1591 to cover "the weekly payment for the collection for the poor of Wisbech" for the rest of his life.[132] We are rarely told how parish officers decided which people should pay and at what level. Some communities may have relied on a subjective appraisal of each individual's overall economic status, but others used more quantified measures. In Alvingham, Lincs. in 1592, the poor rate was based on the number of acres of meadow held by parishioners.[133] The parish of Ludgershall decided in 1592 that every yardland of arable should pay 1d. per month. A certain amount of individual negotiation is suggested by a comment from St. Saviour's parish in Southwark in 1583: one parishioner agreed to give 6d. weekly to the poor if another paid 8d.[134] At times of special need, the normal impositions might be revised upwards. The suburban London parish of St. James Clerkenwell ordered in 1597 that every person previously "sessed to pay towards the poor" must now double the amount, due to "the hardness of the times" and to satisfy the Privy Council.[135]

Collectors may have found it difficult to demand payment from more prominent households. These officers were generally of somewhat lower socio-economic and educational level than churchwardens and had far less standing than the local elite.[136] They were also appointed by and responsible to parish leaders. The statutes of 1552, 1555, and 1563 said that Collectors were to be named by the minister and churchwardens in the presence of all the parishioners after a church service, although a more democratic process is suggested by a note in the records of Betrysden, Kent from 1560–1: money left from the previous accounting was handed over to the two "collectors for the poor men's box chosen by the whole parish."[137] Guidelines for the laity of the northern archdiocese issued in 1571 say that churchwardens were to assist the minister in the choice of two Collectors for the Poor.[138]

We gain further information about the size of payments for poor relief and the sex of payers from selected parishes for which detailed Collectors' accounts have survived.[139] In market centers, the amounts given covered a wide range, but women formed a small minority because they were far

---

[132] *VCH Cambridgeshire*, vol. 4, 260.   [133] CWA #61. For below, see CWA #15.
[134] CWA #96, P92/SAV/450, p. 190.   [135] LondMA P76/JS1/80.
[136] E.g., in Hadleigh, Suff., 1579–98 (HadlTR 21/7–29), and Archer, *Pursuit of Stability*, 65–6.
[137] 5 & 6 Edward VI, c. 2, sec. 2, 2 & 3 Philip & Mary, c. 5, sec. 2, and 5 Elizabeth, c. 3, sec. 2, *SR*, vol. 4, 131, 280, and 411, and CWA #54, 132.
[138] *Tudor Parish Documents*, 184.
[139] McIntosh, *Charity, Family*, will discuss these accounts more fully, setting the numbers of payers and recipients against estimates of total population (done thus far only for Hadleigh).

less likely to own property than men. In Hadleigh, Suff., which had an exceptionally ambitious system of poor relief, around 150 people (25 to 30 percent of all household heads) were assessed each year between 1579 and 1596.[140] Individual payments, rated by the week or quarter, ranged from 4d. to £1 6s. annually, but no more than a handful of widows paid in most years. About a quarter of the payers in Bishop's Stortford between 1563 and 1569 owed less than a half-penny per week (below 2s. 2d. annually), but individual amounts went as high as £1 6s. per year.[141] Only 5 percent of the payers were women, and they gave in fewer years. Assessments were generally lower in Melton Mowbray between 1564 and 1595.[142] Nearly one-third of the payers (6 to 7 percent of whom were women) owed no more than 1d. per quarter (4d. annually) and another two-fifths paid between 4d. and 2s. 2d. But men described as "mister" paid four times as much as their fellows of lower status, and twelve payments were between 13s. and £1 15s.

In agricultural villages, the size of payments was smaller and the range narrower, but women were still relatively unimportant. More than four-fifths of the payments in the little Oxfordshire village of Whitchurch between 1569 and 1591 were 4d. or less annually, and only three people ever gave 2s. 2d. or more.[143] Twelve percent of the payers were women, described in most cases as widows. In the larger village of Eaton Socon between 1591 and 1598, where women constituted 5 percent of all payers, three-fifths of the payments were no larger than 4d. per month or quarter, with only five people assessed at 2s. 2d. or more.[144] For Broadclyst, Devon during the mid-1580s and 1590s, we do not have lists of payers, but in bad years the Collectors excused some people who had been assessed for the rates because they had themselves fallen into poverty.[145]

To enforce the system of Collectors and regular payments, outside supervision was needed. Especially during the 1560s and 1570s, bishops played a key role. Bishop Parkhurst's injunctions for Norwich Diocese in 1569 asked representatives of the parishes whether they had "the collection and distribution for the poor, made according to a statute in that behalf provided."[146] Archbishop Parker's articles for the diocese of Canterbury in the same year make clear that even in parishes that had appointed Collectors, some still used self-defined contributions – not imposed rates – to raise funds. In a new article he asked "whether the

[140] McIntosh, "Networks of Care," and her "Poverty, Charity." Another 60–65% neither paid nor received relief. Hadleigh's Collectors were appointed by the principal inhabitants who controlled most aspects of the parish's and community's public life.
[141] HertsA D/P 21 12A/1, #1a-6.   [142] ROLeics DG 36/159/1–13.
[143] OxfdsRO Par 207/5/F1/1.   [144] Beds&LA P5/12/1.   [145] DevonRO 1310 F/A3, B.
[146] VAI, vol. 3, 210, and see ibid., 228. For below, see ibid., 216.

parishioners of every parish duly pay unto the collectors of the same for the poor, according to the statute in that behalf provided, all such sums of money as they be cessed at, or by benevolence have granted, for the relief of the poor, or no; and whether they have or do refuse to pay the same or no." Bishop Cox of Ely seems to have been especially assiduous. In a letter of 1569 sent to Downham, Cambs. and perhaps to other parishes, he required the minister of the church, churchwardens, and Collectors for the Poor to certify to him or his chancellor within a month the names of those who give weekly to the poor and how much, as well as the names of any who are able to contribute but "yet will depart with nothing."[147] His articles for the diocese in 1571 instructed parish representatives "to certify and present whether you have collectors for the poor of your parish, whether they do their duty in gathering weekly, and distributing the alms of the poor."

At least in the southern two-thirds of the country, the church courts backed local efforts to obtain payment of the sums imposed by Collectors. They did so usually through the normal mechanism of having the church-wardens, as the official spokesmen for the parish, report problems to visitations or sessions of the court convened by a bishop or lesser official.[148] But such complaints were based upon information provided by the Collectors. Several people from Romford were reported to the archdea-con's court in 1569 for failure to contribute to the poor; Robert Smith was told specifically that "he must pay quarterly as he is sessed."[149] The consistory court of the archdeaconry of Norwich heard cases in 1563 and 1568, and ecclesiastical courts in Nottinghamshire and Warwickshire received many reports of people who refused to pay for the poor or were behind on their payments (often described as "assess-ments") from 1570 through the late 1590s.[150] Presumably to seek help from diocesan officials, churchwardens in Ashburton reported 4s. in expenses in 1565–6 for "riding to Exeter against those who did not pay to the poor."[151] When wardens in Danbury, Essex reported in 1574 that Anthony Cadell "hath paid but half so much as he is appointed to pay for the poor," he replied that he was a very poor man with only an acre of ground, but was willing to pay a penny per week.

---

[147] As printed in Nichols, *Progresses and Public Processions*, 257, n. 1. For below, see *VAI*, vol. 3, 300.
[148] *VAI*, vol. 3, 90 and 104.   [149] EssexRO-Ch D/AEA 5, fol. 5r.
[150] Houlbrooke, *Church Courts*, 155, and NottsA DDTS 14/26/1, p. 99, DDTS 14/26/2, pp. 36 and 51, 14/26/6, pp. 13, 27, 29, and 35, UNottL PB 292/1587, fol. 13r (bis), and LichfRO B/V/1/22, p. 15.
[151] CWA #33, 155. For below, see Hopkirk, "Administration of Poor Relief."

Ecclesiastical authorities could exert considerable spiritual pressure. The consistory court of Ely backed up Bishop Cox's letters of 1569. Five men from Hinton, Cambs., cited for not paying to the poor, to the evil example of others, initially failed to appear, but eventually came in after one of them was excommunicated; they were told to bring certificates from the Collectors indicating that they had delivered what they owed.[152] A man from Waterbeach who refused to give anything to the poor was warned to pay "the sum taxed against him" and to certify that he had done so. Parishes may have been especially likely to ask for outside backing when dealing with local residents of higher status. One of the people reported for refusing to pay in Clarbourgh, Notts. in 1587 was described as "Mr. Smith of Bollam in our parish," and the churchwardens of "Eastcombe" (probably Castle Combe), Wilts. reported George Scrope, esquire, a powerful local figure, plus two other men in 1590 for not paying "to the book made for the poor."[153]

Trying to force payment of poor rates led to serious legal problems for the Collectors and churchwardens of Lewisham, Kent around 1590. They had failed to persuade John Greeneway, a gentleman who had recently acquired a house and extensive lands in the parish, to render the sum of 10s. 6d. assessed against him towards relief of the poor and repair of the church.[154] When the churchwardens took the problem before the commissary court of the diocese of Rochester, Greeneway complained against them to the Court of Star Chamber, causing them "extreme charges, trouble, and hindrance." Because other people followed Greeneway's bad example, the poor were left "altogether unprovided for" and the church was likely to fall into utter ruin and decay. The parishioners therefore appealed to the Privy Council, which wrote to the archbishop of Canterbury in 1592, instructing him to call parish officials and the obstinate Greeneway before him and issue a final order to end the matter.

By the 1580s and 1590s, JPs were becoming more active in prosecuting defaulters, as authorized in 1563. In Wiltshire, Thomas Turner was first reported to a Petty Sessions (a meeting of three JPs from a given district) in 1580 for not "paying to the poor" and later taken before the Quarter Sessions.[155] Between 1581 and 1590, several husbandmen and laborers, a mercer, and a woman were summoned and fined 2s. to 3s. 4d. by Wiltshire's JPs.[156] In 1588, they ordered that anyone unwilling to contribute to relief of poor and impotent people (among other kinds of

---

[152] CambUL MS D/2/8, fols. 46r–v, 50r, 62v, and 65r–v. For below, see ibid., fol. 63r.
[153] UNottL PB 292/1587, fol. 13r, and Wilts&SA D3/7, fol. 43v.
[154] *APC*, vol. 22, 482–3.   [155] *Wiltshire Co. Recs., Mins. of Procs. in Sessions*, 58.
[156] Ibid., 64, 67, 121, 135, and 123. For below, see ibid., 121–2.

refusals) could be sent to prison by a JP. In Essex, people from multiple communities were reported to the Sessions for not paying their contributions, rates, or taxes for the poor between 1581 and 1593, including the minister of Leadon Roding and a gentleman of Walthamstow.[157] In Hertfordshire, Thomas Hearn, a yeoman of Weston, came before the Quarter Sessions in 1593–4 for tearing up "the bill of sessment" for the poor of that parish and erasing his name out of the bill for the collection.[158] The Quarter Sessions of Kent received notice in 1594 of twenty-four "defaulters of the poor rate" in Dartford, whereupon they sent a warrant to the constable of Dartford instructing him to warn those people to render their assessments.

Collectors occasionally dealt with other kinds of income too, filling roles normally played by churchwardens. A few people gave or bequeathed money for the poor to Collectors. In 1580, Margaret Clerke, a widow of Wortwell, Norf., assigned an annual rent of 6s. 8d. to the Collectors for relief of poor inhabitants there; yeoman William Aneston bequeathed a legacy of 20s. annually for 5 years to the Collectors of Hooe and Catsfield, Sussex in 1596.[159] In his 1584–5 will, John Elsam of Sutterton, Lincs. left land to his wife for her life, but if she died childless, the property was to go to "the use of the poor people of Sutterton for ever." Elsam specified that "the Collectors of the said town from year to year do let the said houses and lands and the benefit thereof to redound to the use of the said poor people quarterly by equal distribution by the said Collectors," acting with the advice and consent of the churchwardens and others. Current donations to churchwardens or the poor men's box might likewise be turned over to Collectors for distribution.[160]

To obtain delivery of bequests for the poor, Collectors sometimes resorted to the equity courts. Robert Thorowgood and Edward Robynson, described as "Collectors for the poor, aged, and impotent persons" of Meldreth, Cambs., petitioned the Court of Requests in the early 1560s.[161] They alleged that when Warren Ashe died in 1554, he left lands to his daughter and her husband, Edward Thomysin, under condition that they distribute £6 to the poor of the town over a 6-year period. Although Thomysin was now in possession of Ashe's lands, he had not handed out the money. The Collectors claimed that this legacy was needed to prevent begging: the poor of their community were "so many

---

[157] EssexRO-Ch Cal. of QS Records, used through HarvUA 17729, Box 2, QS Records, MSS, 146–8.
[158] Ibid., 471. For below, see CKentS QM/SB 50/1 and SB 45.
[159] NorfRO PD 295/150; ESussRO ASH/4501/369, both used through A2A. For below, see TNA-PRO REQ 2/270/71.
[160] E.g., CWA #92, 110/5/5, fol. 4.   [161] TNA-PRO REQ 2/279/22.

in number that they do daily go abroad into the country to be relieved by the charitable alms and liberality of others." The Collectors for the Poor of Steyning, Sussex plus four other inhabitants appealed to the Court of Requests in 1578 concerning a bequest left by Jane Walle, a widow of Wadesmill, Herts. who had died probably in the 1560s.[162] Walle ordered that the income from a meadow containing 19 acres that she had recently purchased in Steyning "should be and remain forever towards the relief, sustentation, and maintenance of the poor people within the said parish of Steyning in weekly payment towards their maintenance every Sunday after service in the forenoon." She left the meadow to her cousin, instructing him to devise it to such persons as he thought most expedient for accomplishing her intent, but he had kept the land for himself. Collectors for the Poor in Hitchin, Herts. wrote to the Court of Requests some time in Elizabeth's reign about another unfilled bequest.[163] They alleged that Edward Catliner had left £10 "to buy gowns for certain poor to be distributed by the Collectors for the time being for the poor of the town of Hitchin," as well as an unknown amount of money that was to provide a yearly annuity of 50s. "for the better relief of the poor of the same town, to be employed by the Collectors." Those bequests had not been rendered. Collectors might be joined by people of higher status in their parish when taking action on behalf of the poor. Two esquires, the two churchwardens, and the two Collectors of the parish of Burnham (on Crouch), Essex complained to the Court of Chancery in 1595–6 that £150 left to the poor of the parish three years before had still not been handed over by the executors.[164]

In considering how to award the money they had brought in, Collectors (and those who may have advised them) had to make several policy decisions. Because providing full support for all poor parishioners would have been prohibitively expensive, Collectors needed to consider how much – if any – of their income would be used to provide regular weekly assistance to a subset of their needy neighbors, and at what level, and how much would be reserved for people who experienced particular need at certain times. Occasional grants to tide a person or family over for a few weeks or months were the only option for parishes with very limited funds, but even wealthier places that provided some weekly support often awarded secondary assistance to people who faced temporary hardship. Additional issues must likewise have been perplexing. How should the Collectors evaluate the relative needs of women and men, and to what

---

[162] TNA-PRO C 2/Eliz/S.26/48.   [163] TNA-PRO REQ 2/178/124.
[164] TNA-PRO C 2/Eliz/B.1/16. The petition said that the parish contained nearly sixty poor households.

extent and in what ways should poor children be helped? What about needy people who had more prosperous relatives living in the same community? Should they be regarded more favorably, because they were deeply imbedded locally, or should extended families be required to look after their own kin? Collectors needed also to decide whether they would impose religious and behavioral requirements.

More specific information about recipients is again provided by Collectors' accounts.[165] In Hadleigh, forty-seven to seventy-five poor or disabled people (who together constituted 10 to 11 percent of the total population) received regular weekly payments each year between 1579 and 1594, with an average award of 4.5d. per week. Collectors also gave occasional cash, clothing, or fuel to people who were normally self-sufficient, covered the cost of boarding orphans, poor children, and adults who were injured or ill, and operated two almshouses (for thirty-two elderly people) and a workhouse. In the other market centers and large villages, however, regular payments averaged around 1d. to 2d. per week.[166] The amounts awarded by Collectors in the village of Whitchurch between 1569 and 1591 were initially very small, averaging less than a half-penny per week through the 1570s, but they rose in the early 1580s to around 1d. Broadclyst's payments were a little larger, averaging somewhat over 2d. in most years between 1582 and 1597.

In most of these settings, women did not greatly outnumber men as beneficiaries of relief, unlike the pattern noted in other places during the first half of the seventeenth century.[167] But women – most of them widows – generally received more money per year than men and might be helped over a longer period of years. Of 583 people who received some kind of help in Hadleigh in the full span between 1579 and 1596, 46 percent were women. They were less likely than men to be assisted in only a single year and were more likely to receive aid over a span of 10 years or more. Among the people given regular weekly payments in the mid-1590s, however, 64 percent were women and they received slightly larger payments than men, perhaps indicating a movement towards the early seventeenth-century pattern. In Bishop's Stortford, 48 percent of the recipients of ongoing aid were women. Both sexes were given the same average amount per week, but women were assisted for

---

[165] For references to the accounts below, see nn. 140–5 above.
[166] Payments at that level were seen in Bishop's Stortford between 1563 and 1569 (where a few other people were assisted with clothing, wood, or by being boarded), in Melton Mowbray between 1564 and 1574, and in Eaton Socon between 1589 and 1598.
[167] E.g., Wales, "Poverty, Poor Relief," W. N. Brown, "Receipt of Poor Relief," and Botelho, *Old Age*, 116, where a shift to more even sexual distribution of pensions is visible in the second half of the seventeenth century.

longer periods than men. Melton Mowbray was atypical, for women formed 61 percent of its recipients even in the 1560s and 1570s, and they were given 28 percent more than men. In the villages, women (nearly all widows) received considerably larger payments than men. Female recipients in Whitchurch – who formed one-third of the total – were given an average of 24d. per year, as opposed to 13d. for men. In Eaton Socon, only 26 percent were women, an imbalance due largely to the many men who received assistance in just a single year, but women were awarded nearly twice as much as men on an annual basis. In Broadclyst, 56 percent of those relieved were women, and they gained 50 percent more than men.

We have a little evidence about other possible criteria for relief. Collectors in these places were willing to help needy people regardless of whether they had relatives nearby. In Hadleigh, more than a third of those who received relief between 1579 and 1596 had the same surname as other residents of the town. In Whitchurch, two men and two women named Sparrock were assisted between 1570 and 1591, even though two other people with that name paid poor rates, sometimes in the very same years. In Broadclyst, 64 percent of the male recipients had apparent relatives who paid to the parish, as did 39 percent of the women. It is hard to determine how much assistance went to children, as aid was normally given through their parents. Occasionally, however, Collectors listed some children in their own names. In both Whitchurch and Broadclyst, 7 to 8 percent of recipients were said to be children; in Hadleigh, 5 percent of those given direct aid in 1579 were children or adolescents. But Collectors' accounts for Hadleigh can be used in conjunction with parish registers to construct mini family trees for the poor. They show that a quarter of the recipients of regular, weekly payments in 1594 were parents of children younger than around 15 years, although only a single child was listed in his own name. The social criteria used by seventeenth-century Overseers of the Poor when deciding upon recipients of relief (for example, respectable behavior, churchgoing, and deference) seem to have been imposed less vigorously in the Elizabethan period.[168] Hadleigh was prepared to give support to illegitimate children living with their mothers, but conditions were laid down for a lame boy with a Welsh name living in the parish of St. Chad's, Shrewsbury, who was assisted if he "apply his book at school."[169] A poor woman of St. Chad's received aid provided that she come to church when capable of doing so. Occasionally we are told that money or goods were distributed after church services, implying attendance by recipients.[170]

---

[168] E.g., Hindle, *On The Parish?*, 379–98.
[169] McIntosh, "Networks of Care," and ShropsA MS 3365/723, for this and below.
[170] E.g., TNA-PRO C 2/Eliz/S.26/48 and Andrews and Springall, *Hadleigh*, 97.

Also unclear is the extent to which getting help from the parish was seen as a reflection that the person suffered from poverty for legitimate reasons and was a part of the community, making this a respectable status, as opposed to the possibility that recipients were shamed or lost credit because they were not economically independent.[171] The rarity with which witnesses before the church courts mentioned that they or their spouse received alms suggests that people who relied upon relief were thought to lack sufficient standing to be neutral observers: they might be susceptible to improper pressure from people to whom they were indebted or loyal.

In assisting the poor, some Collectors were assigned duties usually handled by churchwardens, such as boarding incapacitated adults. In Broadclyst, the Collectors paid Joan Marten each year between 1585–6 and 1591–2 for keeping her former servant Alice Warren in her house, "being both aged and impotent."[172] They gave Ralph Beare 20d. to 24d. monthly between 1586 and 1590 for housing Thomasin Holwill, described as his servant and "a decrepit woman"; in 1591–2 they paid for a shroud for her. Eaton Socon's Collectors gave Valentine Smythe 8s. in 1596 "for keeping of a cripple."[173]

Much of their activity focused on orphaned, abandoned, or illegitimate children. In Great Bentley, Essex, the Collectors reported in 1575 that they had laid out the sizeable sum of 22s. 3d. for boarding a child.[174] The vestry of St. Saviour, Southwark agreed in late November 1586 that "Widow Pryce shall have 4d. a week more of the Collectors besides that which already she hath towards the keeping of a poor child til Easter next because the weather is so hard and everything so dear." Martin Davie of Broadclyst had been getting relief from the Collectors before his death in 1589, after which his widow Joan received larger weekly payments; when she died in 1592–3, the Collectors sold her few household goods to help pay for boarding her son Michael with Grace Warren, an arrangement that continued until 1597.[175] A painful case came before the JPs of Kent in 1594. What the justices described as "a foul abuse offered by the township of Newenden unto the parish of Sandhurst" began when Joan Bott, formerly of Newenden, was arrested elsewhere as a vagrant and sent back to her original home.[176] Because she was about to give birth, some Newenden people deliberately lodged her in a barn across the border with

---

[171] E.g., Hindle, "Dependency" and his *On the Parish?*, esp. 353–60, Snell, *Parish and Belonging*, esp. chs. 1 and 3, vs. Shepard, "Poverty, Labour" and personal communication.
[172] DevonRO 1310 F/A3, B, for this and below.   [173] Beds&LA P5/12/1, p. 93.
[174] EssexRO-Ch D/P 171/8/1, used through HarvUA 17729, Box 2, Essex, A-L, Batch 9a, 1. For below, see CWA #96, P92/SAV/450, p. 217.
[175] DevonRO 1310 F/A3, B.   [176] CKentS QM/SB 36.

Sandhurst, so that her bastard child would become the responsibility of the latter. In response, the JPs, deeming that action shameful and not to be tolerated, ordered that the inhabitants of Newenden were henceforth to pay 16d. weekly to the Collectors for the Poor of Sandhurst for support of the child.

After the statute of 1576 that required the parents of illegitimate children to pay for their support, Quarter Sessions sometimes ordered that their assistance be delivered to Collectors of the parish. In 1577, JPs in Hampshire ordered the putative father of a child to pay 4d. weekly to the Collectors of Overton, while in Framfield, Sussex in 1594, the supposed father of an illegitimate child was required to pay to the Collectors 10d. per week at first and then 8d. per week for an additional 5 years.[177] Two JPs in Essex ruled in 1595 that after Alice Francke of Steeple Bumpstead and the alleged father of her bastard child had been tied to the back of a cart, stripped to the waist, and given ten lashes with a whip, they were each to pay 4d. weekly to the Collectors until the child was 10 years old.

Because Collectors were now dealing with sizeable amounts of cash, sometimes more than the churchwardens controlled, careful accounting procedures became essential. In the absence of strict requirements for written records and frequent audits, a careless Collector could easily lose track of some of the money that came through his hands, while a dishonest one might be able to line his own pockets quite nicely. The statute of 1552 said that Collectors were to submit their accounts quarterly to the minister and churchwardens of the parish, or – in towns – to the mayor and other head officers.[178] Should they fail to do so or leave office at the end of their term without turning over any remaining funds, the bishop of the diocese could compel them to comply. No changes were made in 1555, but the act of 1563 imposed harsher penalties. A Collector who failed to submit his accounts or hand in excess funds could be reported and sent to jail by the bishop, acting with a JP and one churchwarden from the parish.[179] By the late Elizabethan period, some counties and cities were organizing audits of the Collectors' accounts within larger geographical areas. Parishes in the area around Guildford and Shere, Surrey were summoned together in 1591 to submit the accounts of their Collectors, probably before the JPs of that district.[180] In London, the accounts of all Collectors for the city's parishes were audited by Christ's Hospital's officials.

---

[177] HampsRO Q3/1, fol. 147r, and ESussRO QR/E 2, #79. For below, see EssexRO-Ch Q/ SR 132/50, and also CKentS QM/SB 194.
[178] 5 & 6 Edward VI, c. 2, sec. 4, *SR*, vol. 4, 131.
[179] 5 Elizabeth I, c. 3, sec. 6, *SR*, vol. 4, 412.
[180] SurreyHC LM/COR/3/459, used through A2A. For below, see Archer, *Pursuit of Stability*, 160.

The actions of Collectors were subject to scrutiny by religious and secular authorities at several levels. In 1562, one of the Collectors of the parish of St. Saviour, Southwark was reported to the vestry because he did not "do his duty with his fellows" and failed to come to meetings. Despite his apology, the vestry ordered him to give 5s. to the poor box.[181] The parish of Babraham, Cambs. reported its Collectors to the bishop's court in 1569 for keeping the sums they had collected in their own hands rather than distributing and accounting for them. A Babraham man called before the court that year for not paying "his enjoined portion to the poor" likewise countered that the Collectors there had brought in 49s. but distributed only 12s. to the poor; the court ordered the Collectors to appear.[182] A husbandman of Berwick St. John was fined 2s. by the Wiltshire sessions in 1581 for refusing to serve as Collector for the Poor, while the Collectors of Goldhanger were reported to the Essex sessions in July 1585 for not gathering money for the poor since the previous Michaelmas.

Edward Wilson, a Collector in Water Lambeth, Surrey, responded aggressively when he was accused of wrongdoing. Robert Ridgway and other named men and women, described as "poor parishioners and inhabitants" of Water Lambeth, complained against Wilson to the Court of Requests sometime in Elizabeth's reign.[183] They claimed that he had gathered "diverse and sundry sums of money" for the use of the poor but had refused to distribute it, instead detaining most of it in his own hands. When Ridgway approached Wilson on behalf of the poor, asking him to give out the money as previous Collectors had done, Wilson first gave him "hard and bad speeches" and then sued Ridgway in the Court of King's Bench (a common law court) for defaming him, resulting in Ridgway's arrest. Because Wilson was "very familiar and well acquainted" with the people who might testify in the case, Ridgway and his fellows asked the Court of Requests to intervene.

Within cities and towns, poor relief was handled in various ways. Some communities appointed their own Collectors for the Poor to assess, gather, and distribute payments by wards. These Collectors might either replace ones normally appointed by parishes or work in parallel with them.

---

[181] CWA #96, P92/SAV/449, p. 27. For below, see CambUL MS D/2/8, fol. 41v.
[182] CambUL MS D/2/8, fols. 35r and 41v. For below, see *Wiltshire Co. Recs.: Mins. of Procs. in Sessions*, 69, and Essex RO-Ch Cal. of QS Records, used through HarvUA 17729, Box 2, QS Records, MSS, 146. But in 1573, the half-hundred of Becontree told the Essex sessions that all of the Collectors in their region "have made a just account of their collection and distribution for impotent poor and are to keep office for another year for they are just and honest men" (ibid., 145).
[183] TNA-PRO REQ 2/260/33.

In the borough of Ludlow, the Collectors who accounted for weekly poor rates and distributions in 1565–6 were named by wards; in Queenborough, Kent, the borough court chose Collectors for the Poor around 1587.[184] In another arrangement, parishes named and used their own Collectors, but city authorities supervised their work. In Exeter in the 1580s, the mayor was to call all the parish Collectors to account once each year; in Chester, a laborer appealed to the mayor in 1585, asking him to order the Collectors of St. Oswald's parish to give some relief to him and his family.[185] The subcollectors for the poor in the parish of St. Trinity, York were reported to the City sessions in 1591 for failing to collect the sums that had been taxed by the chief collector. Even when the town exercised no official control over parish Collectors, the latter's accounts are occasionally preserved with urban records.

By the later Elizabethan years – but before passage of the Poor Laws of 1598 and 1601 – many parishes were helping their needy members, acting through churchwardens and/or Collectors for the Poor. Although the latter were supposed to collect regular payments from 1552 onwards, and in some parishes they did so, other churches, especially in the north and conservative rural areas, continued to rely primarily upon optional contributions, including current gifts, bequests, and benevolences collected at services. The shift in balance between voluntary and required payments was thus both chronologically and geographically uneven. The transition to compulsory rates for the local poor was probably assisted by the growing number of obligatory payments imposed upon parishes from outside, to support activities at a county or national level.[186] The ongoing importance of individual donations and endowments distributed by parish officers obscures any distinction between private and public assistance, and the aid given was selective. Churchwardens and Collectors knew the history and situation of people who needed help, and they made value judgments about who would receive assistance. Their goal was not to eliminate poverty, but rather to sustain those people most severely in want, so long as their problems did not derive from their own idleness or wrongdoing. The government assumed greater control over poor relief through orders from Parliament and the crown, through the actions of JPs, and through the parish itself insofar as it functioned in a secular capacity while administering aid. But the emerging forms of assistance

---

[184] ShropsA LB/15/2/143 A and CKentS Qb/JMs 3, fol. 59r.
[185] Hooker, *Pamphlet of the Offices*, no page numbers, under Mayor; ChChRO QSF/35, no. 67, used through A2A. For below, see YorkCA F6, fol. 7r.
[186] See ch. 6.3 above.

were successful in both ideological and practical terms only because the Protestant church backed them through teachings from the pulpit and the power of its ecclesiastical courts. Parishes themselves and churchwardens might gain new respect as charitable but careful managers of resources, although Collectors were probably more often resented than admired by those who had to pay.

While the general plan introduced in 1552 and 1563 was operational in many parts of the country by 1598, some weaknesses in the details had become apparent. Church courts and JPs were willing to receive and act upon complaints about the absence of Collectors or collections, but they learned about such problems only when local representatives chose to mention them. Supervision of the people who gathered and distributed money for the poor was weak. Collectors were named by the minister and churchwardens, and they submitted their quarterly accounts to the same people. That was an overly cozy relationship. While this project encountered few examples of local officials who were said to have pocketed money intended for the poor, if the churchwardens and Collectors in a given parish chose to act dishonestly, it would have been hard for others to document and punish their actions. Nor was the relationship between churchwardens and Collectors for the Poor clearly defined, leading in some cases to inefficient duplication of functions. The modest socioeconomic status of the Collectors made it difficult for them to assert their authority with people of higher standing. The parish could be too small a unit to cover the needs of its poor members, lacking sufficient resources to provide necessary assistance. If an entire parish was suffering from economic hard times, there might not be enough people with money to relieve others, and the district-wide abiding houses authorized in 1572, intended to deal with that problem, had not been widely established.[187] The statutes of 1552 and 1563 did not specify whether people who held land in the parish but were not resident there had to pay for the poor. Since many people owned or rented property in more than one parish, Collectors' income might be greatly reduced if only actual dwellers could be assessed. Existing laws had also not addressed the question of whether family members had to support their own needy relatives rather than leaving them to the care of the parish. Methods of dealing with orphaned or illegitimate children offered little protection to the youngsters. All of these problems were to be addressed in the Poor Laws of 1598 and 1601.

---

[187] The statute of 1563 had permitted civic officials to assess wealthier parishes to assist needier ones (5 Elizabeth, c. 3, sec. 12, *SR*, vol. 4, 413), but the provision did not extend to smaller communities.

Part IV

Responding to the problems

9   The Poor Laws of 1598 and 1601

The late Elizabethan Poor Laws contained a series of measures that addressed how assistance should be given to the kinds of poor people we have considered in previous chapters. Statutes of 1598 dealt with alms seekers and ex-soldiers, hospitals and almshouses, and parish relief, while also defining "charitable uses" or trusts and creating a new form of ready access to equity justice.[1] That legislation grew out of a mixture of ideological and practical pressures. The teachings of the Church of England about Christian charity and the impact of humanist or commonwealth thinking played a part. But more pressing was the rise in poverty, due in a longer perspective to demographic growth that outstripped economic development, but in immediate terms to a series of disastrous harvests in the later 1580s and 1590s that depressed the economy and brought issues of population rise and unemployment to a head. The ad hoc solutions already tried (clerical calls from the pulpit for more generous almsgiving, days of fasting imposed each week, and importation of subsidized grain for the poor by some counties as well as urban bodies) were insufficient. Particularly worrying was the large number of able-bodied men who were willing to labor but could not find work. As the hunger and desperation of many poor people intensified, leading to occasional food riots and threatened uprisings, leaders at both national and local levels became willing to accept a more active role for the state in defining appropriate aid and addressing the obstacles that hampered current forms of relief.

---

[1] 39 Elizabeth, c. 4 ("for punishment of rogues, vagabonds, and study beggars," which also refers to Houses of Correction, *SR*, vol. 4, 899–902), c. 17 ("against lewd and wandering persons pretending themselves to be soldiers or mariners," ibid., 915–16) and c. 21 ("for the necessary relief of soldiers and mariners," ibid., 923–4), c. 5 ("for erecting of hospitals or abiding and working houses for the poor," ibid., 902–3), c. 3 ("for the relief of the poor," also county rates for prisons and hospitals, ibid., 896–9), and c. 6 ("to reform deceits and breaches of trust, touching lands given to charitable uses," ibid., 903–4). For whether destitute people were henceforth "entitled" to relief, see, e.g., Charlesworth, *Welfare's Forgotten Past*, ch. 1, vs. Hindle, *On the Parish?*, esp. 398–405.

When Parliament convened in October 1597, its debates ranged over multiple causes and symptoms of the current crisis, including agrarian problems and the rise in vagabondage as well as the plight of the needy. Seventeen bills dealing with such issues were introduced, some by private members, which were then pared down by a committee to the measures approved early in 1598.[2] Several of the statutes (concerning soldiers, parish aid, and trusts) were modified slightly when the next Parliament sat in 1601.[3] All of these measures counted on the willingness and ability of the Privy Council, Justices of the Peace (JPs), and parish officials to enforce their provisions.

In his undergraduate lectures at Harvard University in the early 1960s, W. K. Jordan described the Poor Laws of 1598 and 1601 in glowing terms. Calling these omnibus acts "one of the finest achievements of the human spirit," he praised their Parliamentary framers for accepting that the state had a moral obligation to ensure that all members of the community were helped to meet their basic needs if they were unable to provide for their own support. He lauded the courageous decision to require wealthier people to furnish aid to their less fortunate neighbors, and he noted Parliament's acknowledgement that many vagrants and beggars had been pushed into poverty by broader economic and social changes. Although Jordan's comments resonate powerfully with debates over poor relief in the early twenty-first century, the Elizabethan Poor Laws did not fully achieve their goal of providing minimal assistance to all impoverished people. Nonetheless, after clarification of where the poor were entitled to receive support in the "settlement acts" of the 1660s and some further adjustments in the 1790s, the basic system of parish relief remained in effect until 1834.

The present study examines the Poor Laws of 1598 and 1601 from a different vantage point. It argues that they were an attempt to address the specific problems that were then hindering the various forms of assistance to the poor. The late Elizabethan statutes abolished the older system of licensed begging and gathering entirely, eased procedures for founding, incorporating, and financing almshouses and hospitals, and made a series of relatively minor changes to the system of parish relief. Parliament also addressed two underlying weaknesses that had contributed to the legal

---

[2] Slack, *Poverty and Policy*, 126, and Jordan, *Philanthropy in England*, 93–4. Francis Bacon commented during a debate in 1601 that in the Parliament of 1598 there had been "so many other bills for the relief of the poor that he called it a feast of charity" (*Proceedings in the Parls. of Eliz.*, vol. 3, 441).

[3] 43 Elizabeth, c. 3 ("for the necessary relief of soldiers and mariners," *SR*, vol. 4, 966–8), c. 2 ("for the relief of the poor," ibid., 962–5), and c. 4 ("to redress the misemployment of lands, goods, and stocks of money heretofore given to charitable uses," ibid., 968–70).

difficulties faced by many projects for the poor when attempting to deal with the challenges they confronted. It provided a secure legal status for charitable trusts, and it created a new equity process to investigate complaints about the malfunctioning of charitable activities. In this chapter we consider how the Poor Laws dealt with the three major forms of assistance and the systemic legal issues. Because the Commissions for Charitable Uses authorized in 1598 went into immediate action, we can also examine a sample of cases heard during the next five years, seeing what kinds of wrongdoing were alleged, what procedures were used, and what judgments were given.

9.1   The three main types of relief

9.1.1   Alms seeking and charitable gathering

By the late sixteenth century, serious problems surrounded begging and gathering.[4] Too many people were moving through the countryside and towns while requesting alms for themselves or charitable institutions. The system of licensing or giving protection to certain beggars and gatherers was riddled with flaws: it was too easy to obtain a fraudulent document or to travel under the name of the person to whom permission had been issued, and there was little assurance that money gathered for a charitable institution would ever reach the intended recipient. For large-scale public projects, the amount brought in by collectors from voluntary contributions was unpredictable and often insufficient to meet the need. Compulsory levies imposed upon parishes for county-wide or infrastructural projects were proving more effective.

In response, a statute of 1598 banned virtually all begging by or for individuals. By defining those who sought alms while on the road as "rogues, vagabonds, and sturdy beggars," subject to whipping and perhaps forcible removal to a House of Correction, the act made it illegal for most people who had previously requested aid to continue doing so.[5] Anyone who repeatedly refused to abandon a wandering and begging life could be committed to jail, banished out of the realm of England, or forced to work in the galleys by Quarter Sessions or members of the Privy Council; should a person expelled from the country return, he or she would be declared a felon, punishable by death. Public assistance to the

---

[4] See ch. 6 above for the earlier history.
[5] 39 Elizabeth, c. 4, secs. 2–3, *SR*, vol. 4, 899, for this and below. Other groups of travelers, including minstrels, acting companies, and petty traders, were likewise prohibited from begging.

poor was henceforth to be provided only within their home parishes. The focus of strategies on the part of the poor themselves about how to gain help subsequently shifted to negotiation with those who controlled parish relief or operated private charities.

A few exceptions were allowed, at least initially. A measure situated obscurely within a different statute of 1598 authorized churchwardens and the new Overseers of the Poor to permit certain poor people to solicit relief, but only for food and only within their own parish.[6] No mention was made of licensing such people. Provision for local begging was dropped in 1601, however, which should have meant that henceforth no one was allowed to request alms even locally. In practice, the fuller legislative prohibition of begging went unnoticed or was ignored by some local officials, who continued to issue permissions and occasionally written licenses to request aid throughout the seventeenth century.[7] The other exemption concerned soldiers discharged from their service and shipwrecked mariners, who were allowed to ask for relief on their way home, but only if they carried a letter from a JP stating where and when they had arrived in England, the destination to which they were traveling, and how many days were allowed for their passage.[8] Soldiers and sailors who traveled with falsified testimonials were declared felons.

Parliament also abolished traditional gathering for charitable causes, whether or not the collector had a valid license. "All persons that be or utter themselves to be Proctors, Procurors, Patent Gatherers or Collectors for Gaols, Prisons or Hospitals" were to be punished as rogues.[9] To provide an alternative – and more regular – form of assistance for prisoners, almshouses, and hospitals, another statute drew upon the experiments with obligatory payments made since 1572 to support county jails and since 1593 for maimed soldiers. The new measure ordered the JPs of every county to assess a rate upon all parishes in their area, ranging from 0.5d. to 6d. per week each.[10] The way in which those sums were to be distributed within the parish could be determined either by an "agreement of the parishioners within themselves" or by the churchwardens and

---

[6] 39 Elizabeth, c. 3, sec. 10, *SR*, vol. 4, 897.
[7] Hindle, "Technologies of Identification," and his *On the Parish?*, esp. 69–76. Alms seeking as approved by the parish was most common in poor regions of the country and during times of economic hardship. Begging remained a concern in the eighteenth century too, whether done in traditional ways or through creative use of media like newspapers (Ben-Amos, "Gifts and Favors").
[8] 39 Elizabeth, c. 3, sec. 16, and c. 4, sec. 14, *SR*, vol. 4, 898–9 and 901. For below, see ibid., c. 17, sec. 2, *SR*, vol. 4, 915–16. For alms given to seventeenth-century sailors, soldiers, and other itinerant people, see Hobbes, "Payments."
[9] 39 Elizabeth, c. 4, sec. 2, *SR*, vol. 4, 899.
[10] 39 Elizabeth, c. 3, secs. 12–14, *SR*, vol. 4, 898, for this and below.

constables. At least 20s. annually generated by each county's rate was to be sent to the Marshalsea and King's Bench prisons for relief of their inmates, with the rest given to hospitals and almshouses in that county. Should any extra money be left after those distributions (which seems unlikely), the JPs were authorized to award it to "those that shall sustain losses by fire, water, the sea, or other casualties" or to other types of poor relief.

Apart from that last clause, the 1598 measure did not mention the needs of people struck by sudden calamities, nor did it explain how support was to be obtained for large-scale projects formerly financed by means of gatherers authorized by the crown (such as towns struck by fire and damaged churches and harbors). It is not clear whether Parliament intended those needs to be met in the manner that subsequently became common practice: royal briefs that authorized collection on behalf of specific individuals or causes.[11] As was true with earlier licenses and letters of protection, these warrants explained why assistance was needed and urged people to contribute, but now they had also to include a dispensation from the 1598 act. Because briefs were printed on paper, with identifying royal insignia or other illustrations, they could not be copied so readily as earlier licenses handwritten onto parchment strips, and it was much more difficult to scratch out the name of the original bearer and replace it with another. In the seventeenth century, most briefs were awarded for the kinds of issues familiar from the Elizabethan period, but puritan-leaning towns and parishes responded with particular generosity to those supporting foreign Protestant churches or refugees in England.[12] Over time, however, the system of briefs became encumbered by many of the same problems that had previously accompanied licensed collection.

The statutes expanded the use of rates imposed on parishes by county JPs. Although county jails were not explicitly named, they continued to be supported in that way. Because the act of 1593 had failed to generate sufficient funds for maimed servicemen, a measure in 1598 authorized JPs sitting in Quarter Sessions to increase parish rates for their support.[13] However, the problem continued to intensify. In 1601, noting that "it is

[11] Briefs are not mentioned in any of the 1598 and 1601 statutes. For later briefs, see Harris, "Inky Blots," and Ben-Amos, *Culture of Giving*, 337–40.

[12] See, e.g., Underdown, *Fire from Heaven*, 126–7, and Schen, "Constructing the Poor." The issuance of briefs reached its peak between 1660 and 1665, but their use continued into the eighteenth century (Ben-Amos, *Culture of Giving*, 338–40).

[13] 39 Elizabeth, c. 21, *SR*, vol. 4, 923–4. Churchwardens and constables were ordered to assist in the collection of those rates, and no parish was to pay less than 2d. per week or more than 8d.

now found more needful . . . to provide relief and maintenance to soldiers and mariners that have lost their limbs and disabled their bodies in the defense and service of her majesty and the state," Parliament raised still further the amount imposed upon parishes to help former soldiers and tightened the mechanisms for collecting and distributing funds.[14] The "abiding places" introduced in 1572 were described more accurately in 1598 as "working houses for the poor" in a measure that encouraged individuals to found and endow such institutions voluntarily, supplementing the assistance generated by the rates assessed by JPs upon their districts.[15] County and city Bridewells came into widespread use thereafter. The 1576 statute concerning Houses of Correction was repealed; in its place, the Justices in Quarter Sessions were authorized to erect one or more Houses of Correction in their counties and to take all necessary orders for their operation and the punishment of those sent to them.[16] How these houses were to be supported financially is not stated, but an act of 1609 said that they should receive money from the county rate charged against parishes for support of prisoners and hospitals.

9.1.2   Almshouses, hospitals, and future endowed charities

Several measures simplified the creation and improved the functioning of almshouses and hospitals.[17] These provisions established the basis for the operation not only of current institutions, but also of other kinds of endowed charities in the future. A statute of 1598 made it easier to found new houses. For the next 20 years – and by extension thereafter – people with a valid title to property were permitted to use their land to set up and endow a hospital (a term that covered all residential institutions) for "maimed, poor, needy, or impotent people" without needing to obtain a royal license in the form of letters patent under the Great Seal.[18] Further, provided that the yearly income from those possessions did not exceed £200, such institutions would automatically be incorporated when the founder obtained a deed in Chancery, gaining the right to receive and

---

[14] 43 Elizabeth, c. 3, secs. 2–4, *SR*, vol. 4, 966–7. In 1601, Sir Robert Cecil commented in a Parliamentary discussion that whereas previous poor laws had provided relief for "our ordinary begging poor," the streets were still "full of soldiers, some maimed, some poor, but all distressed" (*Proceedings in the Parls. of Eliz.*, vol. 3, 428–9, and see ibid., 460).

[15] 39 Elizabeth, c. 5, *SR*, vol. 4, 902–3. The orders laid down for hospitals regarding incorporation, visitation, and term of leases applied also to these working houses. For below, see Innes, "Prisons for the Poor."

[16] 39 Elizabeth, c. 4, sec. 1, *SR*, vol. 4, 899. For below, see 7 James I, c. 4, *SR*, vol. 4, 1159–61.

[17] For these institutions, see ch. 7 above.

[18] 39 Elizabeth, c. 5, *SR*, vol. 4, 902–3, for this and below.

hold all landed property and goods and to enjoy continuous succession forever. Corporate houses could sue or be sued in any courts of the realm, both ecclesiastical and secular, they might have a common seal, and they were to be supervised by a designated visitor. Any leases they granted were limited to terms of no more than 21 years.

The new legislation was less helpful with regard to support for existing almshouses and hospitals that had insufficient landed endowments or none at all. The abolition of charitable gathering by proctors was probably offset only in part by the money raised within counties to support prisoners and residential institutions for the poor. We do not know how county officials decided which houses should receive assistance or how much the new approach yielded for them. In the seventeenth century, briefs were not normally used to gather aid for the routine operation of almshouses and hospitals. Many houses were run by charitable trusts, while urban governments, merchant companies, and parishes administered others. Those institutions solicited gifts and bequests, with donors often providing "meticulous and elaborate instructions regarding the manner in which the gift was to be appropriated and handed out, attesting to a sense of piety and social obligation but also to a determined intention ... to establish lasting control over the gift and the manner in which it would be distributed."[19] Whereas managing the property of charitable institutions, distributing income, and receiving additional donations placed heavy responsibilities upon their governing bodies, the projects might accumulate considerable material wealth. Their officers also became patrons, gaining discretionary power in naming beneficiaries and supervising the lives of the residents.[20]

9.1.3 A parish-based system of poor relief

Although the statutes of 1598 and 1601 continued the basic system of parish assistance as laid down in 1552 and 1563, they included some new provisions that addressed the practical problems that had emerged in recent decades.[21] Some of the corrections drew upon the experience of the central government in raising money for county- and national-level

---

[19] Ben-Amos, *Culture of Giving*, 185.
[20] Ibid., 186–9. By around 1700, however, problems associated with the administration of charitable activities by trusts or corporate bodies were attracting considerable criticism. Institutions therefore began to utilize annual or life subscriptions to gain funds. Published lists of benefactors echo earlier "bede rolls" and the records of donors to charitable causes within the parishes as submitted to bishops or JPs during the later sixteenth century (ibid., 191–2).
[21] See ch. 8.1 above. For below, see ch. 6.3 above.

projects. Those experiments had confirmed that the parish was the most viable unit within which to generate funds for public activities, but they demonstrated that voluntary or even semi-obligatory donations could not produce a sufficient and predictable amount of money. Collection and distribution of funds had to be supervised by some kind of outside authority, with JPs proving the most effective, and written accounts needed to be submitted to and audited by someone external to the parish. All of these lessons were applied to the revision of earlier poor laws.

The new legislation replaced parish Collectors for the Poor with Overseers of the Poor, men whom the authors of the acts clearly hoped would be of higher local status than their predecessors. Overseers were to be "substantial householders" of the parish, if possible sufficiently wealthy that they were assessed for national subsidies.[22] A handbook published in 1601 said when discussing "what persons be fit to be made Overseers of the Poor," that only men of substance who had "competency of wealth and wisdom and care of a good conscience" would be able to carry out the office in a way that avoided current problems with "corruption, negligence, and abuse."[23] But the 1601 statute removed the statement about subsidy payers, and Steve Hindle found that in practice, most Overseers during the first half of the seventeenth century were of lower economic and social standing than the churchwardens, thus resembling the former Collectors.[24] The change in title from Collector to Overseer is interesting. It may have occurred in part to distinguish these parish officers from the people collecting rates for county projects, but the new name also implies governance of the poor, not merely gathering and distributing money. Thus it parallels growing efforts to supervise almshouses and regulate the people living in them.[25]

The late Elizabethan measures clarified and in some areas expanded the duties of Overseers and churchwardens. These officers were instructed in 1598 to raise money for the poor through "taxation of every inhabitant & every occupier of lands in the said parish in such competent sum and sums of money as they shall think fit."[26] (Self-assessment for voluntary contributions was now gone.) The 1601 statute specified that the people subject to poor rates included not only non-resident owners and renters of land,

---

[22] 39 Elizabeth, c. 3, sec. 1, *SR*, vol. 4, 896. Four Overseers per parish were required in 1598, but two to four in 1601 (43 Elizabeth, c. 2, sec. 1, *SR*, vol. 4, 962).

[23] *An Ease for Overseers of the Poore*, 9–11.

[24] Personal communication, and see his *On the Parish?*, 256–62. Hindle thinks that Overseers of higher standing were often chosen after the settlement laws of the 1660s, as the amount of money they handled and their discretionary powers rose.

[25] See ch. 7 above.

[26] 39 Elizabeth, c. 3, sec. 1, *SR*, vol. 4, 896. For below, see 43 Elizabeth, c. 2, sec. 1, 962.

but also vicars of parishes and the owners of tithes, mines, and any under-
wood that could be sold. Should parishioners "refuse to contribute
according as they shall be assessed," churchwardens and Overseers,
with warrant from two JPs, were authorized to seize the offenders'
money or animals and/or sell their goods.[27] If that was not successful,
non-payers could be sent to prison by the JPs, as had been true in the past.
People who thought they had been unfairly treated by parish officials or
local JPs were allowed to appeal to the full Quarter Sessions.[28] In response
to another problem, the 1598 act stated that if a given parish could not
bring in enough money to provide assistance for all of its own poor, JPs
could authorize a rate on other parishes within that same hundred – or
even more widely – to make up the difference.[29] That statute also
extended the parish-based system uniformly throughout the country,
whereas cities and towns had previously been allowed to choose their
own Collectors for wards or other units.[30]

From their income, Overseers and wardens were to provide "necessary
relief of the lame, impotent, old, blind and such other among them being
poor and not able to work."[31] Building upon the requirement for labor
within the "abiding places" initiated in 1572 and the system of supplies
imposed in urban areas and counties in 1576, parishes were also
instructed to assemble "a convenient stock of flax, hemp, wool, thread,
iron & other necessary ware & stuff to set the poor on work." A person who
refused to labor, having been offered such supplies, could be sent to the
county's House of Correction or jail by a JP.[32] If housing for the poor
within a parish was inadequate, its officers were allowed to build dwellings
on waste land in the community (with the approval of the lord of the
manor) and place needy people into them.

Several measures concerned children and family relations. In an extension of a practice used in some places before 1598, poor children whose
parents could not provide for them were to be required to work or sent out

---

[27] 39 Elizabeth, c. 3, sec. 3, *SR*, vol. 4, 897.   [28] Ibid., sec. 6, 897.
[29] 39 Elizabeth, c. 3, sec. 2, *SR*, vol. 4, 896–7. This replaced the act of 1563, which said that
if the poor of one parish were too numerous to be relieved, they could be licensed by JPs to
beg; in cities, parishes were to contribute to each other's needs (5 Elizabeth, c. 3, secs. 10
and 12, *SR*, vol. 4, 413).
[30] 39 Elizabeth, c. 3, sec. 3, *SR*, vol. 4, 896. The JPs of urban areas were, however, given the
same power as those operating in counties to supervise the system (ibid., sec. 8, 897).
[31] Ibid., c. 3, sec. 1, *SR*, vol. 4, 896, for this and below.
[32] Ibid., c. 3, sec. 3, *SR*, vol. 4, 897. For below, see ibid., sec. 5, 897. The latter measure
followed the unrealistically rigorous act of 1589 that prohibited the building of new cottages
unless they were accompanied by at least 4 acres of land and barred more than a single
family or household from living in one cottage (31 Elizabeth, c. 7, *SR*, vol. 4, 804–5).

as "apprentices," probably in fact as servants.[33] But to provide greater protection for the children and their families, churchwardens and Overseers were now obliged to obtain approval from two JPs before doing so. The act of 1598 also said that the children or parents of poor people, so long as they had sufficient means, must relieve and maintain their relatives at their own expense.[34] Should they be unwilling to do so, JPs sitting in Quarter Sessions were authorized to assess them at an appropriate level, with a penalty of 20s. for each month in which they refused to pay.

The Poor Laws included a new emphasis on supervision, record-keeping, and accounting. Local JPs were given greater authority over the process, lessening the independence of parish officials. Each year in Easter week, two or more JPs – no longer the minister and churchwardens – were to appoint Overseers of the Poor for the parishes in their district. Overseers were instructed to work together with churchwardens in handling relief, eliminating inefficient duplication.[35] To permit oversight by fellow parishioners, the wardens and Overseers were required to meet publicly at least once each month – in the parish church on Sunday afternoon after the service – to make decisions about assessing and distributing money for the poor. Churchwardens and outgoing Overseers had to submit to JPs an annual account, in writing, of all sums received and awarded, any payments assessed but not rendered, and the condition of the parish's stock of supplies for setting the poor to work; the cash balance was to be delivered to the next Overseers. If a parish official was negligent in his duties on behalf of the poor or failed to submit the required accounts, he could be fined 20s. or sent to prison by two JPs.

Because payments for the poor were now categorically required, at levels determined by the Overseers, and because they had to be made by everyone with an economic interest in the area, the sums raised in many parishes increased considerably. We can observe the financial impact in several parishes that had previously conformed only to the extent of appointing Collectors to gather semi-voluntary contributions, an approach that yielded unpredictable and often limited amounts for the poor. In Market Deeping, Lincs. during the decade after 1588, the Collectors

---

[33] 39 Elizabeth, c. 3, secs. 1 and 4, *SR*, vol. 4, 896–7, for this and below. Boys could be required to stay in service until they reached the age of 24, girls to the age of 21 or, according to the act of 1601, until they married (43 Elizabeth, c. 2, sec. 3, *SR*, vol. 4, 963).

[34] 39 Elizabeth, c. 3, sec. 7, *SR*, vol. 4, 897, for this and below.

[35] Wardens continued to provide occasional assistance beyond that offered by the Overseers and to handle many charitable gifts and bequests. Of ninety-one trusts to benefit the poor set up in Somerset parishes before 1660, only two were vested solely in the Overseers; the remainder were assigned to churchwardens, clergymen, and/or other lay inhabitants (Hindle, "Good, Godly and Charitable Uses").

received between £2 6s. 8d. and £3 12s. annually.[36] In 1598–9, however, after the imposition of fixed and obligatory payments, their income rose to £11 12s. 6d. Detailed Collectors' accounts from Pitminster, Som. show that between 1589 and 1598, anywhere from two to nine people were listed as contributing each year, with the bulk of the money usually coming from William Person, a large landholder in the parish.[37] The total annual income varied widely, between £3 2s. and £10 2s. The sums given by named people were sometimes supplemented by a small amount "gathered of the parish" (probably at church services) or by income from bequests. Only in 1598 did the collectors begin to "rate" the parish for the poor. That change led to an increase in the amount received and in the reliability of the income from one year to the next. In 1601, a total of £13 12s. was received through regular payments from eleven people living in the main village of Pitminster itself, at individual levels of between 1s. and 12s. per year; another fifty-three people from smaller hamlets and twenty-six non-residents who held property in the parish were also assessed. (Those "outdwellers" included one knight and two men termed "misters," people who had not contributed before.) After a revised set of rates was imposed in 1602–3, the yield rose to £17 10s. Parishes could henceforth offer more support to the poor and make better financial plans because they knew how much would be coming in.

9.2   Generic operational problems

The effective operation of activities intended to help the poor was sometimes hampered by the negligence or greed of those who administered or held property from them. Whereas the kinds of fraud described in the chapter on licensed begging and gathering were generally committed by people seeking aid or their associates, here we see wrongdoing by those who ran or owed financial support to charitable projects. Especially for activities that had no external supervision or were governed by outside bodies that paid little attention to them, opportunities for illegitimate personal profit were rife. Careful administration and oversight were thus of prime importance to the successful functioning of a wide range of charitable projects, as we have noted with regard to the operation of almshouses and hospitals and parish-based assistance to the poor. Both church and state provided mechanisms through which allegations of malfeasance could be made public and corrected. We have information about such problems from 187 complaints submitted to various legal,

---

[36] CWA #66.   [37] SomstRO SAS C795/CH 20, for this paragraph.

religious, and urban bodies between 1350 and 1603 by people who spoke for the poor or for projects that should have assisted them.[38] The activities at issue included small and informal ones, like a meadow left by a testator to his heirs with the rent to be given to needy people in the future, as well as parish and town projects and privately run residential institutions. The obstacles mentioned in those complaints may be summarized within four main groupings.

A first set of challenges concerned the establishment of a charitable activity for the poor, particularly the difficulty of extracting bequests. Because executors and heirs commonly had use of a deceased person's property – land, cash, and personal possessions – until it was handed over to the designated beneficiaries, they had a strong incentive to avoid distribution as long as possible or to try to escape their obligation entirely. Especially in cases involving large bequests, lengthy legal action might be required to force payment.[39] One-sixth of the references encountered in this study stemmed from unfulfilled bequests to the poor.

A second cluster, constituting somewhat under half of the cases, described financial problems with charities once they were up and running. The most common complaint was that income intended for the poor was not being rendered, such as the money rent or in-kind payments due from a tenant of land. Property that had initially supported a charitable activity might later be claimed by other individuals as their own. Disputes increased after the mid sixteenth century, as land that had previously supported projects for the poor was appropriated by the crown and then conveyed into private hands. It might be genuinely unclear whether the new owners were obligated to continue the charitable payments, and such confusion provided a good excuse for ceasing to deliver former dues. Leases of property often caused trouble. Masters or feoffees sometimes put money into their own pockets by demanding a fee at the time they awarded a new lease, or they might grant land to their own friends and relatives for an inappropriately low rent or long period. Conflict could stem also from uncertainty concerning the legal validity of an endowment and from jurisdictional issues.

Another type of difficulty, mentioned in just over a fifth of the references, stemmed from bad administrative or operating practices. Many complaints focused on the masters (or wardens or keepers) of residential institutions, alleging that they had not performed their duties, had granted leases for their own personal gain, or had allowed damage through

---

[38] For fuller discussion, see McIntosh, "Negligence, Greed."
[39] For efforts by churchwardens and Collectors for the Poor to obtain delivery of bequests, see chs. 8.2.1 and 8.3.2 above.

neglect. Some of these careless or dishonest masters had been named by patrons of their houses, who regarded such appointments as a valued right but felt no obligation to provide actual supervision. The governors of a foundation might contribute to its malfunctioning, getting into disputes among themselves that hampered their ability to act collectively for the good of the project. Other conflicts involved multiple parties who had interests in a charitable activity. Successful administration of a project required good record keeping, adequate protection of key documents, and a willingness to defend its rights. By the later sixteenth century, groups that managed activities for the poor sometimes took deliberate steps to obtain and preserve relevant manuscripts. An important negative consequence of lost or incomplete records was that organizations could not plead successfully in the common law, as those courts required written evidence. Going to court might be a necessity if the people in charge of a charity wanted to protect its possessions and income. Administrators of a project who were thinking about bringing suit had to weigh the immediate costs of legal action against the chances of longer-term gain; if sued themselves, they had no choice but to respond.

A final category of problems, amounting to nearly a fifth of the instances, involved the appointment of people to residential institutions and their support or misconduct once there.[40] Places might be contested by several potential recipients, or residents might be wrongly threatened with expulsion. Positions in wealthier houses were highly desirable, leading some inmates who needed cash to rent or even sell their place to someone else. Further problems stemmed from the requirement in some settings that new residents had to offer a payment. Entry fees could undermine the role of residential institutions in caring for the genuinely needy, with corrodies open to particular abuse.[41] Other complaints referred to the level of payment or non-payment of stipends to the residents of almshouses and hospitals. A specialized set of problems concerned the maimed soldiers named to alms rooms in cathedrals and certain other institutions.

Prior to 1598, the ability of people concerned about the malfunctioning of charitable activities to seek legal remedies was limited by two underlying problems: the often shaky standing of their projects in the eyes of the law, and the difficulty of obtaining a hearing in a secular court. The legal status of people acting on behalf of projects for the poor, including the feoffees who held property for the use of a charitable activity, was ill defined during the Elizabethan years, for trusts were not yet recognized in English common law.[42] To prosecute suits via a normal common law

[40] For severe misbehavior by residents, see pp. 88 and 212–13 above.
[41] For corrodies, see ch. 3.2 above.   [42] See pp. 222–4 above.

court, a charitable activity had to have a collective legal identity, gained either through its own incorporation or by being run by an external body that was allowed to plead in the courts, like a chartered borough. Moreover, even if a project possessed the required corporate standing, the common law courts would only hear cases that fell within certain defined forms, and it demanded written documentation as evidence. Another challenge was that the common law respected current practice and possession, so if income originally owed to the poor had been not been rendered recently or if property had fallen into private hands, it might be unrecoverable.

Many charitable activities therefore had to seek equity help. The equity courts accepted oral evidence, were less bound by immediate precedents, and were thought to be particularly receptive to pleas from the poor and powerless. Yet before the creation of special Commissions for Charitable Uses in 1598, relatively few local people possessed the knowledge, time, money, and sometimes ability to travel needed to submit a petition and prosecute a case. Although the number of complaints to existing equity courts about charities for the poor rose across the Elizabethan years, the enormous popularity of Commissions for Charitable Uses beginning immediately upon their creation indicates that only a fraction of the need had previously been met.

While the Poor Laws of 1598 and 1601 could not address all of the specific problems that hampered the effective operation of charitable activities, they tackled both of the underlying legal issues. Acts of 1598 and 1601 created a secure status for those projects operated by a group of individuals for the benefit of the poor, defining them as charitable trusts (a subset of all "uses").[43] Trustees recognized by the law were henceforth allowed to run such projects in place of legally uncertain feoffees. The statutes began by laying out the range of activities that came under their provision. While the 1598 measure spoke particularly of hospitals, almshouses, and colleges, the 1601 act was much broader.[44] Reflecting the multiple definitions of poverty that had been developing over time, the statute specified the forms of aid:

[43] 39 Elizabeth, c. 6, and 43 Elizabeth, c. 4, *SR*, vol. 4, 903–4 and 968–70, and Jones, *History of the Law of Charity*, 22–56. For the earlier history of "uses," see pp. 222–4 above. One provision of an act of 1593 had sanctioned gifts and bequests of land to the use of the poor (35 Elizabeth, c. 7, sec. 9, as in 18 Elizabeth, c. 3, sec. 9, *SR*, vol. 4, 856 and 612), but there was no statute of charitable uses in 1593 (cf. Hindle, *On the Parish?*, 135).

[44] 39 Elizabeth, c. 6, sec. 1, and 43 Elizabeth, c. 4, sec. 1, *SR*, vol. 4, 903–4 and 968–9, for this and below. The 1601 list included also assistance to schools, free schools, and scholars at the universities; repair of bridges, ports, havens, causeways, churches, sea banks, and highways; the education and preferment of orphans; and stocks or maintenance for Houses of Correction.

some for relief of aged, impotent, and poor people, some for maintenance of sick and maimed soldiers and mariners . . . some for marriages of poor maids, some for supportation, aid, and help of young tradesmen, handicraftsmen, and persons decayed, and others for relief or redemption of prisoners or captives, and for aid or ease of any poor inhabitants concerning payment of fifteenths [= subsidies], setting out of soldiers, and other taxes.

The 1601 listing, a secular conception of charity – though resembling rather closely the forms of assistance described by William Langland in *Piers Plowman* more than two centuries before – remained the official formulation of what kinds of projects would be entitled to legal protection as charitable activities into the second half of the twentieth century.[45] The statutes also established a new and more forceful legal mechanism whereby projects could be enabled or forced to carry out their intended functions, thereby making it far easier for local people to seek correction for wrongdoing on the part of those who operated or held property from charitable activities. The 1598 act noted that many funds for relief of the poor, among other worthy causes, "have been and are still like to be most unlawfully and uncharitably converted to the lucre and gain of some few greedy and covetous persons, contrary to the true intent and meaning of the givers and disposers thereof."[46] To remedy the problem, the measure permitted the Lord Chancellor to appoint commissions within individual counties to inquire whether charitable endowments were being employed in accordance with the wishes of the donors. The commissions, which had to include the bishop of the diocese or his representative and "other persons of good and sound behavior," were charged with correcting or preventing the misapplication of charitable funds as they derived from landed property.[47] In a modification that greatly benefited smaller activities, the 1601 measure widened its protection to include all stocks of money and any movable goods given for charitable purposes, not just land. The assignment given to these commissions reflects the types of operational problems described above: they were to investigate "any abuses, breaches of trusts, negligences, misemployments, not employing,

---

[45] Jordan, *Philanthropy in England*, 112–13. Repair of churches, the only religious item on the list, appears amidst other infrastructural causes that serve public needs. The increased legal security of charitable trusts no doubt contributed to their increasing popularity with donors. The capital endowments of those organizations in Jordan's ten sample counties rose from £808,000 in 1600 to £2,525,000 by 1660 (ibid., 118–19).

[46] 39 Elizabeth, c. 6, sec. 1, *SR*, vol. 4, 903.

[47] Ibid. The act of 1601, a fuller and more carefully worded version of the earlier measure, specified that commissions had to include at least four people in addition to their episcopal member (43 Elizabeth, c. 4, sec. 1, *SR*, vol. 4, 969). We see the same assumption that bishops were honest and competent overseers of aid to the poor that we noted with regard to visitors of residential institutions. For below, see ibid.

concealing, defrauding, misconverting, or misgovernment" concerning all property donated to charitable activities.[48] The acts exempted certain institutions that already had a clear legal identity and external supervision, among them any hospitals with "special visitors, governors, or overseers appointed them by their founders."

9.3   Commissions for Charitable Uses

The Commissions for Charitable Uses that began to act in 1598 opened up a new era of legal pleading for charities of many kinds. People concerned about the malfunctioning of projects for the poor henceforth had access to tailor-made inquiries that offered a sympathetic hearing and appropriate procedures within their own county. The process began with submission of a petition to the Chancellor requesting a hearing by a special county commission. Cases were heard locally, eliminating travel to Westminster, and once there the commissioners could initiate additional inquiries of their own. Information about each complaint was provided by a sworn jury of twelve people from the parish or town at issue who were familiar with the details of the matter. The commissions followed equity procedures, and they were powerful, for if the allegation of wrongdoing was supported by the jury, they could issue a formal order for correction of the problem. That ruling had the force of the central government behind it, although it could be appealed to the Chancellor.

People unhappy with the operation of charities immediately began to send in petitions. The sample of forty-nine inquisitions and orders between 1598 and 1603 used for this project, some of which include complaints about multiple problems within a given county at a particular time, constitute just a small fraction of the initial total. In the reign of James I, more than 1,000 decrees were issued on the basis of Commissions for Charitable Uses, with another 2,800 by 1688.[49] Most of the projects in my sample lay in smaller towns and villages, and they were distributed throughout England.[50] The records of these inquiries are

---

[48] Ibid., c. 4, sec. 1, *SR*, vol. 4, 969, and Jones, *History of the Law of Charity*, ch. 3. For below, see 39 Elizabeth, c. 6, secs. 2–3, *SR*, vol. 4, 904. Also exempted were universities and cathedrals, activities operated by cities and corporate towns, those in urban areas with their own governors, and colleges and free schools with their own visitors.

[49] Jones, *History of the Law of Charity*, 52, 25–26, and 251–6, and *List of Proceedings of Commissioners for Charitable Uses*. Although the process was less frequently employed after 1688, commissions continued to hear complaints through the first half of the eighteenth century.

[50] They came from three counties in the north/northwest region, seven in the southwest/ west, six in the Midlands/east central area, and seven in East Anglia/the southeast. See ch. 3, n. 42 above for definition of regions.

unusually rich, for they typically include the initial petition, a report of what the parties and local jury said, and a final ruling.[51]

The procedures of the commissions were based on standard equity practices, but included some extra features that benefited charities. As was common, they accepted oral evidence, rather than requiring written documentation, and they tried whenever possible to bring parties in a dispute into agreement and to persuade people who owed rents or other money to the poor to render those sums voluntarily.[52] But they were also prepared to enforce charitable practices that had operated far in the past but had been discontinued in more recent times, ruling with interesting frequency in favor of earlier projects as against the interests of people who had now discovered ways to gain personal profit from them. The commissions' orders sometimes raised the amount of rental income that had previously been assigned to the poor, presumably to account for inflation in the intervening years.[53] They were aggressive in gathering information that might benefit the charitable activity. If they felt that the picture obtained from a jury was insufficient, they employed other means of obtaining a fuller account, such as making an announcement in a parish church after the service asking interested people to appear before them.[54] They went head-to-head with attorneys hired by defendants. One commission interviewed the legal counsel of two men who claimed title to land given to the parish of St. Stephen in St. Albans, Herts. for support of the poor, "but they could not deliver any good matter to satisfy us touching any right they pretended to have to the premises."[55] Another order issued in favor of the petitioners noted that the defendants "have this day appeared before us with their learned counsel and have not alleged nor showed unto us any matter or cause at all to stay our proceedings upon the said inquisition."

Many cases concerned bequests to the poor that should have been delivered to parish officials for distribution. An inquisition summoned by a commission in Essex reported that John Turner, late of Crepping Hall in the parish of Wakes Colne, esquire, had left sums ranging from 6s. 8d. to 40s. to the poor men's boxes of eight nearby parishes.[56] Although

---

[51] TNA-PRO C 93 for inquisitions and decrees, with supplemental material in C 90, 91, and 92. Individual dates within the period 1598–1603 will not be provided for the examples cited here.

[52] E.g., TNA-PRO C 93/1/9, #1 and 13, and C 93/1/12, #2. Richard Hoyle pointed out that disputes over copyhold land sometimes referred to events in the distant past recorded only in people's memory (personal communication).

[53] Tim Wales likewise found in seventeenth-century Norfolk that decrees by Commissions for Charitable Uses adjusted the value of land upwards to reflect current prices and rents (personal communication).

[54] TNA-PRO C 93/1/19, #10.   [55] Ibid., C 93/1/18. For below, see C 93/1/19, #10.

[56] TNA-PRO C 93/1/19, #3 and 6.

Turner had died in 1578, his wife as executrix had not yet paid those legacies. When the commissioners ordered her to do so, she complied. Some of the amounts involved were very small, suggesting that parish officers thought that even the most limited support for the poor was worth pursuing now that a mechanism for doing so had become readily available. Churchwardens of Adderbury, Oxfds. were ordered by a commission to distribute bread worth 3s. to the poor each year, in accordance with a previous bequest.[57] "The poor people of the parish" of Easthorpe, Essex reported John Binder and others for detaining from the parish a yearly rent of 7s. 2d.

Most of these complaints concerned land or animals. When John Cooke of Belchamp Otton, Essex died in 1555–6, he bequeathed land to the churchwardens, who were supposed to distribute its income of 13s. 10d. annually to the poor.[58] The wardens took possession of the property and gave out its rents to appropriate recipients for about 25 years, but then Cooke's nephew entered the land and began taking its profits for his own use. The commission ordered the current and future tenants to pay a larger amount – 22s. annually – to the churchwardens and Overseers. In Woodchurch, Ches., a local man had given 20 marks (£13 6s. 8d.) to the poor of the parish around 1520, in the form of twenty pairs of oxen for twenty ploughs that the poor could use in return for small payments.[59] Because the rental income had been used to buy additional animals, the stock had grown to thirty-four pairs by 1600, but a local esquire now claimed control of the cattle. The commission ruled that several overseers acting on behalf of the poor should henceforth supervise the animals and their hire.

Stocks of money might also be an issue. A commission for Cheshire dealt with an allegation that many years before, a parson of the church of Alderley had left £47 8s. 6d. to the parish, under condition that the money be granted out as small loans to poor people.[60] A local jury stated that the money had been duly loaned for some time, but because of the negligence of previous wardens, "sufficient sureties have not been taken for the repayment thereof, so there is not now in good debt any more to be had but £36 7s. 7d. The rest is lent out to such as are not able to pay but is very doubtful never to be had, nor we do not know upon whom to lay the fault, for that such as did lend it are alleged to be dead." The commission ordered that four "substantial men" of the parish be named overseers of the money and that adequate sureties for repayment henceforth be required.

---

[57] Ibid., C 93/1/24, #3. For below, see C 93/1/19, #11.   [58] Ibid., C 93/1/12, #4 and 5.
[59] Ibid., C 93/1/17, #4.   [60] Ibid., C 93/1/17, #5.

In cases concerning property held by feoffees or other private individuals for the use of the poor, commissions commonly brought parish officials into the process of distributing the income. An inquisition at Bicester, Oxfds. dealt with land in a group of nearby towns and villages that had been assigned to feoffees. The petitioners alleged that the profits – amounting to £8 7s. 8d. annually – were to go to relief of the poor of Bicester as well as to other charitable causes.[61] Now, however, several people were wrongly claiming a private estate in those lands, on the grounds that the requirement to support the poor had been filled and was ended. The commission ordered that income from the land in question should continue to support the poor but be awarded with the consent of the vicar, churchwardens, Overseers of the Poor, and the four wealthiest inhabitants of the community. Sometime before 1587, William Wodley, a salter of London, bequeathed land in Berrow, Worcs. to his uncle, Thomas Hall, for 12 years.[62] After that time, its income was to be distributed by the churchwardens to the poor of the parish of Berrow. A commission was told, however, that the property had gone to Thomas Hall and then been passed on to Hall's son, rather than being used for the poor. The commissioners decreed that the land should be conveyed to a group of ten men as trustees, who would lease the land back to its current tenant for 31 years; the rent was to be given to the poor by the churchwardens.

Land and rents might become detached from their original charitable purposes when the property changed hands. At an inquiry about eight cottages and a room plus 2 acres of land in Holme, in the parish of Glatton, Hunts., jurors reported that the property, worth £4 annually, had since the early sixteenth century been copyhold land belonging to the Duchy of Lancaster, paying an annual rent of 10s. 5.5d.[63] In 1575, John Somersham, its tenant at the time, surrendered the property into the hands of the queen's steward with the stipulation that it be re-granted to him and two others and their heirs, with its income used for relief of the poor of Holme and other charitable purposes. That was done, but after Somersham's death in 1585, a different man obtained a 21-year lease of the same property from the queen, paying a slightly higher rent, but with no charitable provisions. The commissioners allowed the later lease to stand, but they ordered the tenant to pay 50s. annually to the poor, an increase of almost five-fold over the initial distribution.

Commissions heard cases involving the loss of records that documented charitable acts. Jurors from Canewdon, Essex said that in 1519,

[61] Ibid., C 93/1/36.   [62] Ibid., C 93/1/35.   [63] Ibid., C 93/1/33.

two men had conveyed land to a group of feoffees, with the intent that the income be used to relieve poor local inhabitants "of honest name and fame."[64] In 1560, the remaining survivor of those men conveyed the land to another set of feoffees, for the same purpose. The written records concerning the property and its conveyances were kept in a chest with five locks located in the steeple of the parish church. But recently several of the feoffees had broken into the chest, removed the records, and converted the land to their own use.

Other petitions concerned financial support for almshouses or hospitals, especially control over property.[65] One inquiry looked into land in Lincolnshire that had been bequeathed by John Fuller, late of Stepney, Middx. to a group of feoffees. They were to build two almshouses in Stepney, one for twelve poor single men aged 50 or more, the other for twelve poor, elderly widows; the houses were to be governed and visited by the Mercers' Company of London. When the jury reported that the institutions had not yet been erected, the commission ordered Fuller's widow and his male executor to build the houses and get them incorporated at their own costs. A commission in Newcastle upon Tyne, Northumb. heard evidence that in 1579 a local man and his son had granted during their lifetimes four tenements and one little garden in the town to the churchwardens of All Saints' parish.[66] Those dwellings, occupied at the time by four widows, were to be kept for the use of the poor of the parish. The churchwardens had employed the property as intended until recently, when doubt was raised about the validity of the original gift. The commission backed the continued use of the property for the poor.

Some inquiries focused on the right to control and appoint people into free housing. Jurors in Wye, Kent reported that in his 1568 will Robert Searles, clerk, had left a tenement and some land as an almshouse for three poor people, who were to be appointed at first by his brother-in-law and sister and subsequently by the churchwardens.[67] Suitable residents had been named, but now one of Searles' cousins, a gentleman, claimed that property and had moved a different person into the house without consulting the wardens. The commissioners ordered that the people originally placed in the tenement were to return, keeping their places for life, with subsequent vacancies filled by parish officers. Witnesses from Castle Morton, Worcs. deposed that a house near Morton Green had for at least 80 years been used as "a common and free almshouse to and for the sustentation, maintenance, and relief of poor people of the parish."[68]

---

[64] Ibid., C 93/1/12, #9.
[65] E.g., ibid., C 93/1/13 and C 93/1/12, #3. For below, see C 93/1/25, #2 and 3.
[66] Ibid., C 93/1/21, and also C 93/1/19, #8.   [67] Ibid., C 93/1/27.   [68] Ibid., C 93/1/8.

John Hill, a gentleman living in London, now said that he had title to that house and was taking its profits for his own use. When summoned to appear before the bishop and another member of the commission, Hill failed to do so. He was given one more chance, but if he defaulted again, the Overseers and the churchwardens, with the approval of four other substantial members of the parish, were henceforth to appoint poor people to live in the house.

Commissions were even prepared to investigate institutions that had ceased operation entirely after serious neglect. An inquisition in Buckinghamshire was told that the little Hospital of St. John the Baptist in Newport Pagnell, founded many years before and supported by lands worth £7 annually, had initially housed poor people.[69] More recently, however, the master had leased the site of the hospital and its lands to a gentleman, who pulled down the chapel and carried away its stones. When the commissioners were shown evidence that the hospital had indeed accommodated poor residents previously but now supported only the master, they ordered that the ruins be repaired and needy people again be appointed. The current tenant of the hospital's lands was to prepare a full listing of its property and deliver it to the master within the next three months; the latter was to recover at his own expense any land that had been lost. In addition, the tenant and master were ordered to pay £4 6s. 8d. annually to the Overseers of the parish, to be used in rebuilding the hospital as well as providing stipends for the residents.

These cases illustrate the value of Commissions for Charitable Uses in providing legal access and a favorable hearing for projects that assisted the poor. Like the other elements of the Poor Laws of 1598 and 1601, they can best be understood as attempts to remedy the problems that had emerged over the past half-century in the emerging forms of poor relief, not as one feature within the creation of a new system of support.

---

[69] Ibid., C 93/1/10.

10 Conclusion

This study has shown how religious and social thought joined with changes in the demographic and economic environment and with emerging political practices to shape attitudes, policies, and behavior concerning the poor between 1350 and 1600. The nature and extent of poverty shifted over time in accordance with the size and mobility of the population and particular economic conditions. During the later medieval years, when the proportion of needy people was comparatively small, alms gathering was facilitated by Catholic views about charity and a belief in indulgences. Hospitals and almshouses provided shelter for several thousand others, and some parishes distributed occasional aid. These forms of assistance supplemented the mutual help provided by the poor themselves, among friends, relatives, and neighbors.

Beginning around 1530, a rise in the number and visibility of poor people, especially in urban areas, created new concern. A combination of humanist and early Protestant idealism during the 1530s, 1540s, and early 1550s led to critiques of existing provisions for the poor, helped to justify the dismantling of earlier forms of church-run assistance, and led to the initiation of a system of parish-based poor relief. That early experimentation was made possible by cooperation between the crown, Privy Council, and leaders of the national church and by the interest and energy of Parliament, which was becoming more actively involved in many areas of legislation.

After 1563, no new laws addressed the operation of aid within the parishes, although poverty continued to worsen. Begging was widespread, with permission to seek alms now granted to some of the chronically poor and elderly as well as to those hit by some particular misfortune. Almshouses and hospitals, the numbers of which had been significantly reduced by the closings of the 1530s to 1550s, struggled to provide privacy and sufficient financial resources for their inmates, most of whom gained welcome security because their places were granted for life. Churchwardens and Collectors for the Poor in the parishes displayed considerable ingenuity as they worked to generate and protect income for the poor and to devise appropriate ways to offer aid. Justices of the

Peace (JPs) gained increasing responsibility for supervising not only poor relief, but also other forms of collection. Discomfort with begging became stronger in the late sixteenth century, as did an emphasis upon labor and good behavior among almshouse dwellers. Calls for good governance, strict oversight, and careful financial stewardship with regard to all charitable projects intensified. These changes may have been influenced by puritan thinking as well as a more general desire to maintain control over the poor and the activities that assisted them so as to preserve social and political stability.

The Poor Laws of 1598 and 1601, rather than creating a new system of parish-based relief, made relatively minor modifications to existing practices. It also ended the entire system of licensed begging and eased the process for founding and incorporating residential institutions. The statutes created a more solid legal status for charitable activities and set up a new process whereby allegations of malfeasance could be heard and remedies ordered. They thus reinforced the movement away from a wide array of unconnected forms of largely occasional assistance, as found prior to 1530, towards a network that was still loosely joined but contained fewer and more predictable kinds of relief.

This research has found little evidence to support either of two common historical assumptions: (1) that the inflated rhetoric of some clerical or literary writers with regard to the able-bodied but idle poor expressed attitudes shared by ordinary people, and that sometimes drastic Parliamentary legislation was actually enforced on the ground; and (2) that charitable aid moved away from casual assistance to all comers in favor of greater discrimination in some period (after the plague, in response to Protestant beliefs, or among puritans). Parish officers and private households were willing to help unknown strangers who offered a persuasive explanation of their need even if they did not carry the written permission required by Parliament; constables punished only a few of the itinerant people who requested alms, often ignoring the laws about vagrants. Although Catholic theology taught that almsgiving was meritorious for the donor regardless of the condition of the recipient, and although some monasteries and medieval hospitals provided food or temporary shelter to those who requested it, nearly all of the private individuals, institutions, and parish officers who assisted the poor throughout these centuries made deliberate and selective decisions about which people warranted help, based upon the reason for and depth of their need. Their choices were shaped not only by ideological constructions of poverty and charity, but also by personal sympathy for suffering people and concern about order and authority. The exceptions to this general pattern of careful awarding of assistance by lay people occurred only under certain specific circumstances: when testators instructed that alms be distributed to all of the poor who came to their funerals or commemorative services. In those contexts, the primary goal was to generate as many prayers for the souls of the deceased or statements of thanksgiving for their generosity as possible.

A more useful question is what specific kinds of people were selected to receive aid at different times and in various settings. Whereas late medieval licenses to solicit individual alms were largely confined to those struck by misfortune, chronically poor or old people were sometimes permitted to beg as poverty intensified during the later sixteenth century. Founders of residential institutions displayed a mounting preference for the laity and the elderly, especially women. Churchwardens and Collectors for the Poor made value judgments about which outside alms seekers would receive a few pennies; they used their own knowledge in determining which of their neighbors would be given occasional help or – if fixed assessments had been introduced – more regular aid. We have observed their assistance to old, sick, and disabled adults, not only widows, and their particular attention to poor children.

Several standard approaches to poor relief have used dichotomous concepts that do not promote effective analysis. The church and state should not be seen as separate and competing mechanisms through which aid might be delivered. From 1547 onwards they worked in tandem to implement many kinds of help. In that partnership, based upon shared social and religious goals, the government may have been the dominant member, but it could not have succeeded without the church's backing from the pulpits and in its courts. Nor were voluntary and compulsory contributions to the poor in opposition: Catholicism imposed considerable pressure to contribute, long before the introduction of fully obligatory payments, and both kinds of assistance expanded during the second half of the sixteenth century in an effort to meet mounting demand. Likewise, the categories of private and public support were so often blurred in practice that they do not constitute a meaningful distinction.

From the perspective of poor people themselves, the most important development was the emergence after 1552 of an ongoing source of assistance within the parish. Occasional alms of unpredictable value as given previously by charitable people, executors, or churchwardens had provided welcome help, but offered no security. When, however, Collectors for the Poor had a regular source of income thanks to the payments made by wealthier parishioners, people could ask for help at times of special need. If they met local criteria, funds would probably be available. In parishes that imposed fixed poor rates, selected people might be granted an ongoing weekly allowance, placing them in a highly privileged situation. We cannot be sure, however, whether those people – who were to evolve into the "parish poor" or "dependent poor" of the seventeenth and eighteenth centuries – regarded their selection as evidence that others recognized that they needed aid through no fault of their own, that they were respectable and "belonged" to the community, or whether they feared that receiving alms was demeaning and might weaken their personal credit.

Other themes have extended our horizon. Dishonesty was a recurring problem, whether as fraud in begging and gathering or as greed in the operation of charitable activities. Concern about effective administration led to changes in the governance of residential institutions beginning in the later medieval period that became far more pronounced after 1540. Methods used to collect funds for larger projects in the later sixteenth century and the emerging system of parish relief likewise focused attention on control, supervision, and accountability. Identity formation is another interwoven thread. Unlike the sympathetic terms used to refer to people licensed to request alms, proclamations and statutes of the 1530s and 1540s expressed a more negative conception of beggars. Generally positive if constraining identities for those poor who lived in almshouses during the second half of the sixteenth century were created by detailed rules for prayer and good behavior. The individuals and institutions (like towns, guilds, and parishes) that served as administrators or governors of charitable projects could gain favorable reputations as generous and socially concerned but at the same time effective and hard-headed managers of resources and distributors of aid. Because benefactors of almshouses and other institutions were increasingly concerned to have their names and contributions known not only to their contemporaries, but also to future members of the community, they insisted upon institutional titles and policies – including distinctive liveries for the residents – that contributed to the visible identity of their houses. For parishes, handling poor relief created a new arena for self-definition, helping to compensate for the loss of traditional religious functions during the early Reformation period.

This evidence has shed a little light on gender issues. While some medieval women begged within their own communities, most – but not all – licensed alms seekers were men. By the later sixteenth century, women appear more frequently as authorized and unauthorized beggars, and literary representations suggest that poor female wanderers may have evoked disproportionate concern. Women founded some residential institutions or assisted their husbands in setting them up, and they were increasingly the intended residents of almshouses, although they never ran them. The relatively few female landholders were assessed alongside men to pay for the poor within parishes, but widows did not yet constitute the great majority of recipients of relief as they would become in the early seventeenth century.

Cooperative relations between local, county, and national levels of government were key elements of this history. The central government sometimes took the lead, as in the initiatives for the poor at parish and county levels introduced under Edward VI and Elizabeth, but church-wardens and Collectors for the Poor developed their own practices. Their interactions were often mediated by JPs, who also gained new duties in supervising collections for larger projects. When problems developed that could not be resolved by individual parishes, charitable bodies, or the JPs of a district, Parliament came to their aid, as seen in the Poor Laws of 1598 and 1601. While demographic, economic, and ideological factors were essential to the gradual development of English poor relief across the fifteenth and sixteenth centuries, those pressures alone would not have produced the system of parish-based assistance that was henceforth to provide the central ingredient within the fabric of assistance to the poor. The emergence of parish relief depended upon the constructive interaction of several components: thoughtful measures introduced by the crown, Privy Council, and Parliament; moral support for that legislation by the church; effective enforcement of new policies by both secular and religious authorities; the ability of JPs to work with people above and below them; and the willingness of parish officers to take on additional roles within their communities.

Appendices included in the printed volume

Appendix A: Type of institution and intended residents of houses operative 1350–1599, by date of founding

	Founded pre-1350	Founded 1350–1539	Founded 1540–1599	Total
Hospitals				
For lepers, lepers+sick, or lepers+poor	149[1] = 41% of houses of specified type	20 = 9% of houses of specified type	2 = 1% of houses of specified type	171
For other sick/sick+poor	110 = 31%	16 = 7%	2 = 1%	128
For the poor (sickness not mentioned)	101 = 28%	55 = 24%	39 = 22%	195
Total, hospitals	360 = 100%	91 = 40%	43 = 24%	494
Almshouses	0	138 = 60%	138 = 76%	276
Total, all hospitals and almshouses of specified type	360 = 78% of all houses	229 = 69% of all houses	181 = 86% of all houses	770
Hospitals with unspecified type of residents/unspecified type of house	102[2] = 22%	104[3] = 31%	29[4] = 14%	235
Total, all hospitals and almshouses	462	333	210	1,005

Notes :
[1] Includes two hospitals founded sometime in the fourteenth century that may have been founded after 1350.
[2] Includes two hospitals founded sometime in the fourteenth century that may have been founded after 1350.
[3] Includes two institutions founded sometime in the sixteenth century to be operated by a monastic house that were assigned to the pre-Reformation period.
[4] Includes twenty-two institutions founded sometime in the sixteenth century that were assigned to the post-Reformation period.

Appendix B: Date of founding or first reference, hospitals and almshouses in the database

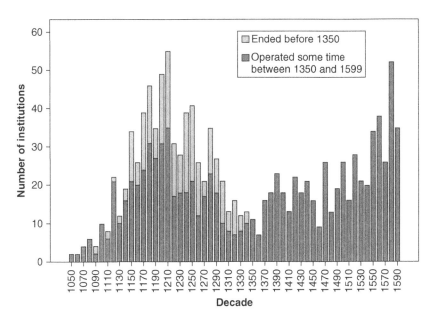

For the numbers displayed here and the methods used to produce them, see CUP Online Apps. 1 and 2.

Appendix C: Date of closing or last reference, hospitals and almshouses in the database

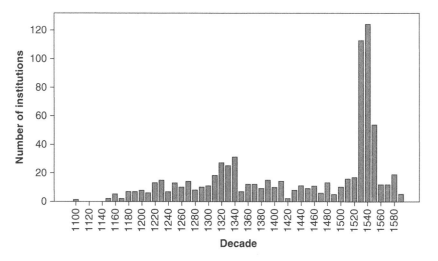

For the numbers displayed here and the methods used to produce them, see CUP Online Apps. 1 and 2.

Appendix D: Number of houses in existence, 1350–1599, hospitals and almshouses in the database

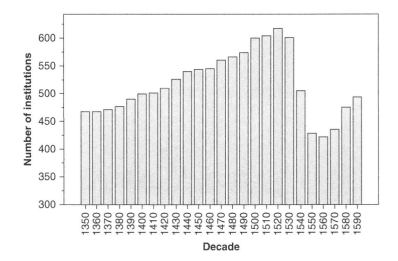

Note that the base shown here is 300. For the numbers displayed and the methods used to produce them, see CUP Online Apps. 1 and 2.

Appendix E: Operators or governors of hospitals and almshouses

Type of operator or governance	Founded pre-1350	Founded 1350–1539			Founded 1540–1599		
	Hospitals of all types plus institutions of unspecified types	Hospitals of all types	Almshouses	Institutions of unspecified type	Hospitals of all types	Almshouses	Institutions of unspecified type
Type of operator or governance							
Monastic house	201 = 56%	10 = 16%	7 = 8%	13 = 26%	0	0	0
Self-governing (no outside supervision)	122 = 34%	26 = 43%	3 = 3%	9 = 18%	7 = 21%	3 = 3%	1 = 6%
Existing lay-run institution							
Town/city	14 = 4%	5 = 8%	9 = 10%	2 = 4%	7 = 21%	16 = 15%	1 = 6%
Parish	0	2 = 3%	12 = 13%	4 = 8%	4 = 12%	12 = 12%	2 = 13%
Religious fraternity or urban guild/company	3 = 1%	7 = 11%	16 = 18%	7 = 14%	0	9 = 9%	2 = 13%
School or college	4 = 1%	1 = 2%	6 = 7%	9 = 18%	1 = 3%	3 = 3%	0
Total, lay-run bodies	21 = 6%	15 = 25%	43 = 47%	22 = 44%	12 = 35%	40 = 38%	5 = 31%
Private lay feoffees or governors	11 = 3%	8 = 13%	37 = 41%	4 = 8%	15 = 44%	60 = 58%	9 = 56%
Other	4 = 1% (1 chantry, 2 the crown, 1 lay operator but no other info.)	2 = 3% (1 chantry, 1 lay operator)	1 = 1% (1 chantry)	2 = 4% (2 chantries)	0	1 = 1% (1 lord of the manor)	1 = 6% (1 lay operator)
Number and % of total houses for which information	359 = 78%	61 = 67%	91 = 66%	50 = 53%	34 = 76%	104 = 75%	16 = 59%

Appendix F: Churchwardens' assistance to the poor in the fifteenth and sixteenth centuries, by type of activity and period

	1404–1546		1547–1553		1554–1576		1577–1598	
	Chwdns' accounts	Other primary sources	Chwdns' accounts	Other primary sources	Chwdns' accounts	Other primary sources	Chwdns' accounts	Other primary sources
Number of parishes whose churchwardens' accounts or church books were used for at least some years within this period[1]	58		62		94		110	
Number and % of those parishes that reported some activity by churchwardens on behalf of the poor (other than through bequests, funerals, or obits)	16 = 28%		32 = 52%		35 = 37%		53 = 48%	
Number of additional parishes mentioned in other primary sources where churchwardens engaged in some kind of activity on behalf of the poor		3		11		31		96
Part A: Activities that acquired or protected income used to assist the poor								
1. Indirect: receiving gifts/bequests to the poor (when not done by executors/-trices)	probably rarely		occasionally		sometimes		commonly	
2. Collecting alms/gathering for the poor (apart from activities of Collectors for the Poor)	2 = 3%	Stat, EccVA/I		Stat, RoyPr/I	1 = 1%	Stat, RoyPr/I		
3. Soliciting/receiving money for a box in the church for alms for the poor, or (after 1547) failing to do so	2 = 3%	Stat and 1 parish	18 = 29%	RoyPr/I, Stat, EccVA/I, and 5 parishes	11 = 12%	RoyPr/I, EccVA/I, and 3 parishes	7 = 6%	47 parishes

stocks (or animals, cash, land, or houses), with income designated specifically for the poor; handling parish endowments for the poor							
5. Organizing church ales for the poor	1 = 2%			1 = 1%	RoyPr/I, EccVA/I, and 5 parishes	1 = 1%	EccVA/I and 7 parishes
6. Receiving fines for wrongdoing, for use of poor			RoyPr/I			1 = 1%	
7. Reporting vicars who were not paying 1/40th of their beneficed income to the poor/giving hospitality/rendering other dues	RoyPr/I		RoyPr/I, EccVA/I, and 7 parishes		RoyPr/I, EccVA/I, and 8 parishes		13 parishes
8. Enforcing: (a) payment of assessments on parishioners for relief of the poor; or (b) appointment/action by parish Collectors for the Poor			Stat and 1 parish	3 = 3%	Stat, EccVA/I, and 11 parishes	3 = 3%	19 parishes
9. Taking action to preserve sources of income for the poor (other than in 7 and 8 above)	3 = 5%		1 parish	1 = 1%	2 parishes	3 = 3%	7 parishes
Number of parishes engaged in one or more activities in Part A	19 = 31%		10 parishes	14 = 15%	27 parishes	15 = 14%	93 parishes

Part B: Activities that assisted the poor

1. Indirect: distributing gifts and bequests to the poor (when not done by executors/-trices)	probably rarely	occasionally		sometimes		commonly	
2. Indirect: distributing alms (money, bread, clothing) at funerals and obits/anniversaries (when not done by executors/-trices)	rare at funerals, perhaps more common at obits	rare at funerals, obits prohibited		occasionally at funerals		occasionally at funerals	
3. Distributing small doles (money, bread, clothing) to local people on special religious days/feasts	3 = 5%	10 = 16%	1 parish	6 = 6%		4 = 4%	
4. Giving money occasionally to individual local poor people or outsiders	3 = 5%	5 = 8%	1 parish	5 = 5%	2 parishes	14 = 13%	2 parishes

	1404–1546		1547–1553		1554–1576		1577–1598	
	Chwdns' accounts	Other primary sources	Chwdns' accounts	Other primary sources	Chwdns' accounts	Other primary sources	Chwdns' accounts	Other primary sources
5. Giving small sums to poor people who came to the parish with licenses/briefs/testimonials			1 = 2%		6 = 6%	1 parish	11 = 10%	2 parishes
6. Making multiple/regular payments to individual local poor people, not linked to religious occasions	1 = 2%		7 = 11%		4 = 4%	1 parish		
7. Maintaining almshouses or subsidizing housing for the poor	5 = 9%		2 = 3%		6 = 6%		9 = 8%	2 parishes
8. Paying poor people to do work for the church (other than caring for children or adults)	5 = 9%				4 = 4%			1 parish
9. Loaning stock to the poor	1 = 2%			RoyPr/I	1 = 1%		1 = 1%	
10. Giving clothing/bedding/food/fuel to the poor	2 = 3%		3 = 5%		3 = 3%	1 parish	6 = 5%	3 parishes
11. Giving money to/paying for care of/ boarding sick, injured, or old people					4 = 4%	1 parish	13 = 12%	4 parishes
12. Paying for shrouds/burials for local or outside poor	1 = 2%		2 = 3%		4 = 4%	1 parish	10 = 9%	3 parishes
13. Children: paying for the temporary boarding/raising of orphaned, abandoned, or illegit. children			5 = 8%		9 = 10%	1 parish	14 = 13%	5 parishes
14. Children: granting poor children permanently into another person's care					3 = 3%	1 parish	4 = 4%	7 parishes
15. Children: placing poor children as servants/apprentices or helping them to travel elsewhere					2 = 2%		3 = 3%	3 parishes

16. Paying to get undesirable poor people out of the parish							5 = 5%	
Number of parishes engaged in one or more activities in Part B	14 = 24%	2 parishes	19 = 31%	1 parish	29 = 31%	4 parishes	50 = 45%	16 parishes

Key to symbols

Stat = mentioned in one or more statutes

RoyPr/I = mentioned in one or more royal proclamations and/or royal injunctions

EccVA/I = mentioned in one or more ecclesiastical visitation articles and/or injunctions

Sources

Chwdns' accounts: churchwardens' accounts or church/vestry books from 125 parishes in 32 counties (counting Yorkshire's Ridings as separate counties) plus London and York, as listed in References, pt. 1.

Other primary sources: churchwardens' comperta/presentments, other visitation records, ecclesiastical court Act Books, notes in parish registers, and other parish documents, including contracts concerning children; records of the Justices of the Peace. Many of these sources are cited in the text. Material from wills was not used for this table.

Stat entries: *Statutes of the Realm*, vols. 3–4.

RoyPr/I entries: *Tudor Royal Proclamations*, vols. 1–3, plus royal injunctions in the collections below.

EccVA/I entries: R. M. Haines, "Bishop Carpenter's Injunctions"; *Visitation Articles and Injunctions of the Period of the Reformation*, vols. 2 and 3; *Documentary Annals of the Reformed Church of England*, vols. 1 and 2; and *Diocese of Norwich: Bishop Redman's Visitation, 1597*.

Note

[1] In some cases, the churchwardens' accounts were not continuous, and for a few sets of accounts I sampled certain periods, focusing on the 1530s, 1547–53, the 1560s, and the 1590s. Under either of those circumstances, I made entries on this chart only for the periods in which I actually used the records.

References

1 MANUSCRIPT AND PRINTED CHURCHWARDENS' ACCOUNTS OR CHURCH/VESTRY BOOKS

These materials are cited in all notes as CWA followed by the number shown below.

BEDFORDSHIRE

#1. Clifton, CWA, 1589–1608. *Elizabethan Churchwardens' Accounts.* Ed. J. E. Farmiloe and R. Nixseaman. Bedfordshire Historical Record Society, vol. 33, 1953, 1–5.

#2. Northill, CWA, 1561–1612. *Elizabethan Churchwardens' Accounts.* Ed. J. E. Farmiloe and R. Nixseaman. Bedfordshire Historical Record Society, vol. 33, 1953, 6–59.

#3. Shillington, CWA, 1571?–1603. *Elizabethan Churchwardens' Accounts.* Ed. J. E. Farmiloe and R. Nixseaman. Bedfordshire Historical Record Society, vol. 33, 1953, 60–109.

BERKSHIRE

#4. Childrey, CWA, 1568–88, with a few entries from 1526 and 1530. BerksRO D/P 35/5/1.

#5. Hungerford, vestry minute book, 1581–1823. BerksRO D/P 71/8/1.

#6. Kintbury, CWA, 1583–c. 1844. BerksRO D/P 78/5/1.

#7. Reading St. Giles, CWA, 1518–1808. BerksRO D/P 96/5/1.

#8. Reading St. Laurence, CWA, 1498–1626. BerksRO 97/5/2.

#9. Reading St. Mary, CWA, 1550–1662. *The Churchwardens' Accounts of the Parish of St. Mary's, Reading, Berks, 1550–1662.* Ed. Francis N. A. Garry, and A. G. Garry. Reading, 1893.

#10. Thatcham, CWA, 1561–1633. BerksRO D/P 130/5/1A.

#11. Warfield, CWA, 1586–1728. BerksRO D/P 144 5/1.

#12. Winkfield, CWA, 1521–1606. BerksRO D/P 151 5/1A.

BUCKINGHAMSHIRE

#13. Aston Abbots, CWA, 1562–1669. CBuckss PR 7/5/1.

#14. Great Marlow, CWA, 1593–1675. CBucksS PR 140/5/1.
#15. Ludgershall, CWA, 1565–1631. CBucksS PR 138/5/1.
#16. Wing, CWA, 1527–1723. (a) CBucksS PR 234/5/1; and (b) "The Accounts of the Churchwardens of Wing." Ed. A. Vere Woodman. Records of Buckinghamshire, vol. 16, pt. 5, 1960, 307–29.

CAMBRIDGESHIRE

#17. Bassingbourn, CWA, 1497–1538. CambsA P 11/5/1 and 2.
#18. Cambridge Holy Trinity, CWA, 1504–1638. CambsA P 22/5/1 and 2.
#19. Ely St. Mary, CWA, 1570–1656. CambsA parish records, typed catalogue.
#20. Ely Trinity, CWA, 1565–1738. CambsA parish records, uncatalogued.
#21. Linton, parish officers' account book, 1577–1692. CambsA L 95/14.

CHESHIRE

#22. Chester St. Mary, CWA, 1536–1690. ChChRO P 20/13/1.
#23. Chester St. Michael, CWA, 1558–1678. ChChRO P 65/8/1.
#24. Wilmslow, CWA, 1585–1632. ChChRO P 23/3466/9/1.

CORNWALL

#25. Anthony, CWA, 1538–84. CornwRO P7/5/1.
#26. Camborne, CWA, vol. 1, 1535–79, and vol. 2, 1581–1628. CornwRO PD 322/1 and 2.
#27. Kilkhampton, near Bude, CWA, 1563–1603. CornwRO P102/5/1.
#28. Launceston St. Thomas, CWA, 1559–96, scattered years. CornwRO P221/ 5/5–9.
#29. North Petherwin, parish accounts, 1493–1591, scattered. CornwRO P167/5/1.
#30. Poughill, parish accounts, 1525–98. CornwRO P192/5/1.
#31. St. Breock, CWA, 1529–98, passim. CornwRO P19/5/1.
#32. St. Columb, church book, 1585–1604. "The St. Columb' Green Book." Ed. Thurstan Peter. Supplement to Journal of Royal Institution of Cornwall, vol. 19, Truro, 1912.

DEVONSHIRE

#33. Ashburton, CWA, 1479–1580. Churchwardens' Accounts of Ashburton, 1479–1580. Ed. Alison Hanham. Devon and Cornwall Record Society, new ser., vol. 15, 1970.
#34. Chagford, CWA, 1480–1600. The Church Wardens' Accounts of St. Michael's Church, Chagford, 1480–1600. Ed. Francis M. Osborn. Trowbridge, 1979.
#35. Morebath, CWA, 1520–73. The Accounts of the Wardens of the Parish of Morebath, Devon, 1520–1573. Ed. J. Erskine Binney. Exeter, 1904.

DORSET

#36. Sherborne: (a) CWA, 1512–97, passim. DorsetHC PE/SH CW 1/1–68, passim; (b) vestry book, 1592/3–1833. DorsetHC PE/SH VE 1.
#37. Wimborne Minster, account books, 1475–1636. DorsetHC PE/WM CW 1/ 40–41.

ESSEX

#38. Saffron Walden, CWA, 1439–90. EssexRO-Ch D/DBy Q 18.
#39. Wivenhoe, CWA, 1562–1649. EssexRO-Colch D/P 277/5/1.

GLOUCESTERSHIRE

#40. Bristol All Saints: church book, 1407–81, and CWA, 1446–1662. (a) BristolRO P/AS/ChW/1 and 3; (b) The Pre-Reformation Records of All Saints', Bristol: Part I. Ed. Clive Burgess. Bristol Record Society, 1995.
#41. Bristol St. Ewen, church book, 1454–1584. *The Church Book of St. Ewen's Bristol, 1454–1584.* Ed. Betty R. Masters and E. Ralph. Bristol and Gloucestershire Archaeological Society, Records Section, vol. 6, 1967.
#42. Bristol St. James, CWA, 1566–1623. BristolRO P/St.J/ChW/1(a).
#43. Bristol St. Werburgh, CWA, 1548–1615. BristolRO P/St.W/ChW/3(a).
#44. Gloucester St. Aldate, CWA, 1563–1619. GloucA P 154/6/CW/1/1–44.

HAMPSHIRE

#45. Winchester St. John, CWA, 1549–1605. HampsRO 88M81W/PW1.

HERTFORDSHIRE

#46. Ashwell, CWA, 1563–1603. (a) HertsA D/P 7 5/1; and (b) *Tudor Churchwardens' Accounts.* Ed. Anthony Palmer. Hertfordshire Record Society, 1985, 1–52.
#47. Baldock, CWA, 1500–53. (a) HertsA D/P 12 5/1 and 18/1; and (b) partially in *Tudor Churchwardens' Accounts.* Ed. Anthony Palmer. Hertfordshire Record Society, 1985, 53–70.
#48. Barkway, CWA, 1558–1640. HertsA D/P 13 5/1.
#49. Bishop's Stortford, CWA, 1440–1785. (a) HertsA D/P 21 5/1–2; and (b) *The Records of St. Michael's Parish Church, Bishop's Stortford.* Ed. J. L. Glasscock. London, 1882.
#50. Great Berkhamstead, parish records, 1584–97. HertsA D/P 19 1, classes V, VI, XI, and Miscell. Charity Papers.
#51. Munden, Little, CWA, 1589–1615. HertsA D/P 71/1 5/1.
#52. St. Albans, St. Peters, CWA, 1573–1639. (a) HertsA RO D/P 93 5/1; and (b) *Tudor Churchwardens' Accounts.* Ed. Anthony Palmer. Hertfordshire Record Society, 1985, 89–183.

HUNTINGDONSHIRE

#53. Great Paxton, parish record book, 1588 ff. HuntsA 2119/2.

KENT

#54. Betrysden, CWA, 1515–73. *Churchwardens' Accounts at Betrysden, 1515–1573.* Ed. Francis R. Mercer. Kent Archaeological Society, Records Branch, vol. 5, 1928.
#55. Cranbrook, CWA, 1509–1694. CKentS P 100/5/1.
#56. Harrietsham, CWA, 1565–99. CKentS P 173/5/1.
#57. Strood St. Nicholas, CWA, 1555–1600. *The Churchwardens' Accounts of St. Nicholas, Strood.* Ed. Henry R. Plomer. Kent Archaeological Society, Records Branch, vol. 5, 1927.

LANCASHIRE

#58. Prescot, CWA, 1523–1607. *The Churchwardens' Accounts of Prescot, Lancashire, 1523–1607.* Ed. F. A. Bailey. Record Society of Lancashire and Cheshire, vol. 104, 1953.

LEICESTERSHIRE

#59. Melton Mowbray, CWA, 1547–98. ROLeics DG 36/140/1–27.

LINCOLNSHIRE

#60. Addlethorpe (with Ingoldmells), vestry book, 1542–1825. LincsA Addlethorpe par. 7/10.
#61. Alvingham, CWA, 1573–1644. LincsA Alvingham par. 7/1–2.
#62. Heckington, CWA, 1560–1729. LincsA Heckington par. 7/1.
#63. Horbling, "town book" with CWA, 1533–1702. LincsA Horbling par. 7/10.
#64. Kirton Lindsey, CWA, 1484–1766, passim. LincsA Kirton Lindsey par. 7/1–3.
#65. Louth St. James, CWA, 1500–1623. LincsA Louth (St. James) pars. 7/1–3.
#66. Market Deeping, parish accounts, 1570–1647. LincsA Market Deeping par. 7/10.
#67. Scothorne, CWA, 1588–1769. LincsA Scothorne par. 7/1.
#68. Witham on the Hill, CWA, 1548–1833. LincsA Witham on the Hill par. 7/1.

LONDON

#69. Allhallows, London Wall, CWA, 1455–1536. *The Churchwardens' Accounts of the Parish of Allhallows, London Wall ... 1455–1536.* Ed. Charles Welch. London, 1912.
#70. St. Andrew Hubbard, Eastcheap, CWA, c. 1450–c. 1570. *The Church Records of St Andrew Hubbard Eastcheap.* Ed. Clive Burgess. London Record Society, 1999.

#71. St. Mary at Hill, CWA, 1420–1559. *The Medieval Records of a London City Church, St. Mary at Hill, 1420–1559.* Ed. Henry Littlehales. Pt. I, Early English Text Society, vol. 125, 1904; Pt. II, Early English Text Society, vol. 128, 1905.

MIDDLESEX

#72. Stepney St. Dunstan, vestry book, 1579–1662. LondMA P93/DUN/327.

NOTTINGHAMSHIRE

#73. Holme Pierrepont, CWA, 1560–1722. NottsA PR 547.
#74. Nottingham St. Mary, CWA, 1582–93. NottsA CA 4611–4615B.
#75. Worksop Priory, CWA, 1544–1750. NottsA PR 22,765.

OXFORDSHIRE

#76. Marston, CWA, 1529–71. *Churchwardens' Accounts of Marston, Spelsbury, Pyrton.* Ed. F. W. Weaver and G. N. Clark. Oxfordshire Record Society, vol. 6, 1925.
#77. Oxford St. Aldate, CWA, 1410–1609, and Miscell. papers, 1590–1660. OxfdsRO D.D. Par. Oxford, St. Aldate c. 15–16 and 23.
#78. Oxford St. Michael, CWA, 1404–1600. (a) OxfdsRO D.D. Par. Oxford, St. Michael a.1–2; and (b) accounts to 1562 published in *The Churchwardens' Accounts of St. Michael's Church, Oxford.* Ed. H. E. Salter. Transactions of the Oxfordshire Archaeological Society, 1933.
#79. Pyrton, CWA, 1548–1613. *Churchwardens' Accounts of Marston, Spelsbury, Pyrton.* Ed. F. W. Weaver and G. N. Clark. Oxfordshire Record Society, vol. 6, 1925.
#80. South Newington, CWA, 1553–1684. *South Newington Churchwardens' Accounts, 1553–1684.* Ed. E. R. C. Brinkworth. Banbury Historical Society, vol. 6, 1964.
#81. Spelsbury, CWA, 1524–75. *Churchwardens' Accounts of Marston, Spelsbury, Pyrton.* Ed. F. W. Weaver and G. N. Clark. Oxfordshire Record Society, vol. 6, 1925.
#82. Thame, CWA, 1442–1617. OxfdsRO D.D. Par. Thame c.5 and b.2.
#83. Witney, CWA, 1569–1643. OxfdsRO D.D. Par. Witney c.9.

SHROPSHIRE

#84. Cheswardine, CWA, 1544–1628. *Shropshire Parish Documents.* Ed. E. C. Peele and R. S. Clease. Shrewsbury, n.d. (extracts only).
#85. Ludlow, CWA, 1506 and 1540–1605. *Ludlow Churchwardens' Accounts, 1540–1603.* Ed. Thomas Wright. Camden Society, 1869 (full accounts through 1574, extracts thereafter).

SOMERSET

#86. Bridgwater, CWA, 1548–9. SomstRO D/B/bw 1447.
#87. Yatton, CWA, 1445–1560. *Church-Wardens' Accounts of Croscombe, Pilton, Yatton, Tintinhull, Morebath, and St. Michael's, Bath, ranging from A.D. 1349 to 1560*. Ed. Edmund Hobhouse. Somerset Record Society, vol. 4, 1890.

STAFFORDSHIRE

#88. Pattingham, CWA, 1583–1646. StaffsRO D3451/2/2.

SUFFOLK

#89. Boxford, CWA, 1530–61. *Boxford Churchwardens' Accounts, 1530–1561*. Ed. Peter Northeast. Suffolk Records Society, vol. 23, 1982.
#90. Exning, CWA, 1590–1624. SuffRO-BSE FL 567/5.
#91. Long Melford, CWA, 1549–1641. SuffRO-BSE FL 509/1/15 and 509/5/1 (a) and (b).
#92. Mildenhall, CWA, 1446–54 and 1504–1602. SuffRO-BSE EL 110/5/1 and 3–5.

SURREY

#93. Kingston on Thames, CWA, 1503–38 and 1561–1650. SurreyHC KG 2/2/1–3.
#94. Lambeth, CWA, 1504–1645. *Lambeth Churchwardens' Accounts, 1504–1645, and Vestry Book*, 1610, Pt. 1. Ed. Charles Drew and Hilary Jenkinson. Surrey Record Society, vol. 40, 1940; and Pt. 2. Ed. Charles Drew. Surrey Record Society, vol. 43, 1941.
#95. Mortlake, vestry minute book, 1578–1652. SurreyHC 2414/4/1.
#96. Southwark St. Saviour, vestry minute book, 1557–1628. LondMA P92/SAV/449–450.
#97. Wandsworth, CWA, 1545–58. "Early Churchwardens' Accounts of Wandsworth, 1545 to 1558." Ed. Cecil T. Davis. *Surrey Archaeological Collections*, vol. 15, 1900.

SUSSEX

#98. Hellingly, vestry minutes, 1591–1780. ESussRO Par 375/12/1.
#99. Lewes St. Andrew and St. Michael, CWA, 1522–1601. ESussRO Par 414/9/1/1a–b.
#100. Rye, CWA, 1513–95. ESussRO Rye 147/1–11.

WARWICKSHIRE

#101. Coventry Holy Trinity, CWA, 1462–1662, passim. WarwsRO DR 801/12.
#102. Rowington, CWA, 1550–1600. *Records of Rowington*, vol. 2. Ed. John W. Ryland. Oxford, 1922.

WESTMORELAND

#103. Salkeld, Great, CWA, 1583–98. CumbAS-C PR116/107.

WILTSHIRE

#104. Devizes St. Mary, CWA, 1499–1633. Wilts&SA 189/1.
#105. Marlborough St. Peter, CWA, 1555–1700. Wilts&SA 1197/21.
#106. Salisbury St. Edmund, CWA, 1443–1603. *Churchwardens' Accounts of S. Edmund and S. Thomas, Sarum, 1443–1702.* Ed. H. J. F. Swayne. Wiltshire Record Society, 1896.
#107. Salisbury St. Martin, CWA, 1567–1653. Wilts&SA 1899/65.
#108. Salisbury St. Thomas, CWA, 1545–1690. *Churchwardens' Accounts of S. Edmund and S. Thomas, Sarum, 1443–1702.* Ed. H. J. F. Swayne. Wiltshire Record Society, 1896.
#109. Steeple Aston, CWA, 1542–1668. Wilts&SA 730/97.

WORCESTERSHIRE

#110. Badsey, CWA, 1525–1821. (a) WorcsRO 850: Badsey/BA 5013/2; partly published in (b) *Churchwardens' Accounts of the Parish of Badsey with Aldington in Worcestershire from 1525 to 1571.* Ed. W. H. Price and E. A. B. Barnard. Hampstead, 1913.
#111. Halesowen, CWA, 1487–1582. *Halesowen Churchwardens' Accounts, 1487–1582.* Ed. Frank Somers and M. O'Brien. Worcestershire Historical Society, 1957.
#112. South Littleton, CWA, 1548–1707. WorcsRO 850: South Littleton/BA 1284/1.
#113. Stone, CWA, 1591–1770. WorcsRO 850: Stone/BA 5660/2–3.
#114. Worcester St. Michael's in Bedwardine, CWA, 1539–1603. *The Churchwardens' Accounts of St. Michael's in Bedwardine, Worcester, 1539–1603.* Ed. John Amphlett and A. S. Porter. Worcestershire Historical Society, 1896.

YORK, CITY OF

#115. All Saints Pavement, CWA, 1568–98. BIA PR Y/ASP F14/2.
#116. Holy Trinity Goodramgate, CWA, 1559–1712. BIA PR Y/HTG 12.
#117. St. Martin Coney Street, CWA, 1552–1638. BIA PR Y/MCS 16–17.
#118. St. Michael Spurriergate, CWA, 1518–47. BIA PR Y/MS 4.

YORKSHIRE EAST RIDING

#119. Beverley St. Mary, CWA, 1592–3. ERYoAS-B PE 1/51.
#120. Howden, CWA, 1593–1666. ERYoAS-B PE 121/37.

YORKSHIRE NORTH RIDING

#121. Bedale, CWA, 1583–1734. NYksRO PR/BED 2/1.
#122. Masham, CWA, 1542–1677. NYksRO PR/MAS 3/1/1.
#123. Sheriff Hutton, CWA, 1524–68. BIA PR S.H. 13.
#124. Thornton Watlass, CWA, 1574–1722. NYksRO PR/TW 3/1.

YORKSHIRE WEST RIDING

#125. Kirkby Malzeard, CWA, 1576–1655. NYksRO PR/KMZ 2/1.

2 OTHER PRINTED PRIMARY SOURCES

The Accounts of the Chamberlains of the City of Bath, 1568–1602. Ed. F. D. Wardle.
   Somerset Record Society, vol. 38, 1923.
Accounts of the Roberts Family of Boarzell, Sussex, c. 1568–1582. Ed. Robert Tittler.
   Sussex Record Society, vol. 71, 1977–9.
The Acts of the Dean and Chapter of the Cathedral Church of Chichester, 1545–1642.
   Ed. W. D. Peckham. Sussex Record Society, vol. 58, 1959.
Acts of the Privy Council of England, 1542–1604. Ed. J. R. Dasent. 32 vols. London,
   1890–1907.
"Ancient Statutes of Heytesbury Almshouse." Ed. Canon Jackson. *Wiltshire
   Archaeological and Natural History Magazine* **11** (1869): 289–308.
Aubrey, John. *Wiltshire: The Topographical Collections.* Ed. John E. Jackson.
   London, 1862.
Awdeley, John. *The Fraternity of Vagabonds.* Orig. publ. 1561; reprinted in *The
   Elizabethan Underworld,* 51–60. Ed. A. V. Judges. London, 1930.
Becon, Thomas. "The Pathway unto Prayer" and "A Pleasant New Nosegay."
   In *The Early Works of Thomas Becon ... Published by Him in the Reign of
   King Henry VIII,* 123–87 and 188–229. Ed. John Ayre. Parker Society,
   1843.
Beverley Town Documents. Ed. Arthur F. Leach. Selden Soc., vol. 14, 1900.
The Boke for a Justyce of Peace neverso wel and dylygently set forth. London,
   c. 1538.
The Boke of Justices of Peas, the charge with all the processe of the cessions. London,
   1506.
The Book of John Fisher, Town Clerk and Deputy Recorder of Warwick (1580–1588).
   Ed. Thomas Kemp. Warwick, [1900].
Books of Examinations and Depositions [of Southampton], 1570–1594. Ed. Gertrude
   H. Hamilton and E. R. Aubrey. Southampton Record Society Publications,
   vol. 16, 1914.
Boyle, J. R. "Orders for the Town and Borough of Morpeth, 1523." (App. to his
   "The Insignia and Plate of the Corporation of Morpeth.") *Archaeologia
   Aeliana* new ser. **13** (1889): 209–15.
Bridgwater Borough Archives, 1445–1468. Ed. Thomas B. Dilks. Somerset Record
   Society, vol. 60, 1948.

Brinklow, Henry. "Complaynt of Roderyck Mors." Orig. publ. 1542. Ed. J. Meadows Cowper. Early English Text Society, Extra Ser., vol. 22, 1–76, 1874.

"The Lamentacyon of a Christen Agaynst the Cytye of London, made by Roderigo Mors." Orig. publ. 1542. Ed. J. Meadows Cowper. Early English Text Society, Extra Ser., vol. 22, 77–140, 1874.

Calendar of Charters and Other Documents belonging to the Hospital of William Wyggeston at Leicester. Ed. A. Hamilton Thompson. Leicester, 1933.

Calendar of Letters and Papers, Foreign and Domestic, of the Reign of Henry VIII. 22 vols. in 37 parts. London, 1864–1932.

Calendar of State Papers, Domestic Series, Edward VI, Mary, Elizabeth, James I. 12 vols. London, 1856–72.

Calendar of State Papers, Domestic Series, of the Reign of Edward VI, 1547–1553. Revd. edn. Ed. C. S. Knighton. London, 1992.

Calendar of the Patent Rolls (1452–1582). 25 vols. London, 1911–86.

A Calendar to the Records of the Borough of Doncaster, vol. 4. Doncaster, 1902.

The Cartulary of God's House, Southampton, vol. 2. Ed. J. M. Kaye. Southamptonshire Record Society, vol. 20, 1976.

Cartulary of St. Mark's Hospital, Bristol. Ed. C. D. Ross. Bristol Record Society, vol. 21, 1959.

A Catalogue of the Manuscripts in the Cottonian Library deposited in the British Museum. London, 1802.

Certaine Sermons or Homilies. Ed. Mary Ellen Rickey and T. B. Stroup. Gainesville, Flo., 1968.

The Certificates of the Commissioners appointed to Survey the Chantries, Guilds, Hospitals, etc. in the County of York. 2 vols. Ed. W. Page. Surtees Society, 1894.

Chapter Acts of the Cathedral Church of St. Mary of Lincoln, A.D. 1520–1536. Ed. R. E. G. Cole. Publications of the Lincoln Record Society, vol. 12, 1915.

Chaucer, Geoffrey. *The Canterbury Tales.* London, 2005.

Collections for An History of Sandwich in Kent. Ed. William Boys. Canterbury, 1792.

Copland, Robert. *The Hye Way to the Spyttell Hous,* published sometime after 1531; reprinted in *The Elizabethan Underworld,* 1–25. Ed. A. V. Judges. London, 1930.

A Copy of the Ordinances, Statutes and Rules for the Order and Government of the Hospital in the Town of Warwick called "The Hospital of Robert Earl of Leicester in Warwick." Warwick, 1840.

Court Leet Records [of Southampton]. Vol. 1, pt. 1. Ed. F. J. C. Hearnshaw and D. M. Hearnshaw. Southampton Record Society Publications, vol. 1, 1905.

The Courts of the Archdeaconry of Buckingham, 1483–1523. Ed. E. M. Elvey. Buckinghamshire Record Society, vol. 19, 1975.

The Coventry Leet Book or Mayor's Register. Part 3. Ed. Mary D. Harris. Early English Text Society, vol. 138, 1909.

Cratfield: A Transcript of the Accounts of the Parish. Ed. William Holland. London, [1895].

Diocese of Norwich: Bishop Redman's Visitation, 1597. Ed. J. F. Williams. Norfolk Record Society, vol. 18, 1946.

Documentary Annals of the Reformed Church of England. 2 vols. Ed. Edward Cardwell. Oxford, 1844.

"The Earliest Book of the Drapers' Company, Shrewsbury." Pt. 1. *Transactions of the Shropshire Archaeological Society* **36** (1913): 135–262.

An Ease for Overseers of the Poore. [London], 1601.

The Elizabethan Underworld. Ed. A. V. Judges. London, 1930.

The Fifteenth Century Cartulary of St. Nicholas' Hospital, Salisbury. Ed. Christopher Wordsworth. Wiltshire Record Society, 1902.

The First Ledger Book of High Wycombe. Ed. R. W. Greaves. Buckinghamshire Record Society, vol. 2, 1956.

Fish, Simon. *A Supplicacyon for the Beggers.* Ed. Frederick J. Furnivall. Early English Text Society, Extra Ser., vol. 13, 1–15, 1871.

FitzRalph, Richard. "Defensio Curatorum." In *Trevisa's Dialogus* [and other translations]. Ed. Aaron J. Perry. Early English Text Society. London, 1925.

The Gild of St. Mary, Lichfield. Ed. F. J. Furnivall. Early English Text Society. London, 1920.

Grafton, Richard. *A Chronicle at Large and Mere History of the Affayres of England.* London, 1569.

Harman, Thomas. *A Caveat or Warning for Common Cursitors, Vulgarly Called Vagabonds.* Orig. publ. 1566; reprinted in *The Elizabethan Underworld,* 61–118. Ed. A. V. Judges. London, 1930.

Harrison, William. *The Description of England.* Ed. Georges Edelen. Ithaca, New York, 1968.

The Hellard Almshouses and Other Stevenage Charities, 1482–2005. Ed. Margaret Ashby. Hertfordshire Record Publications, vol. 21, 2005.

Henley Borough Records: Assembly Books i–iv, 1395–1543. Ed. P. M. Briers. Oxfordshire Record Society, 1960.

Historical Manuscripts Commission. *Calendar of the Manuscripts of the Dean and Chapter of Wells.* Vol. 1. London, 1907.

    Calendar of the Manuscripts of the . . . Marquis of Salisbury: vol. 6, London, 1895; vol. 7, London, 1899; vol. 14, London, 1923.

    Eighth Report, Appendix: "Manuscripts Belonging to the Ewelme Almshouse in the County of Oxford" and "Manuscripts Belonging to Bishop Bubwith's Almshouses, Wells, Somerset." London, 1881.

    Fifth Report, "Manuscripts of the Corporation of Fordwich." London, 1876.

    Fourth Report, "MSS of Magdalene College, Oxford." London, 1874.

    Report on the Manuscripts of the Corporation of Beverley. London, 1900.

    Report on the Manuscripts of Lord de L'Isle and Dudley. Vol. I. London, 1925.

    Report on the Manuscripts of Lord Middleton, Preserved at Wollaton Hall, Nottinghamshire. London, 1911.

    Seventh Report, "Manuscripts of G. A. Lowndes, Esq., Barrington Hall, Co. Essex." London, 1879.

    Twelfth Report, App. 4, "Manuscripts of the Duke of Rutland, Belvoir Castle." London, 1888.

History of Chesterfield. Vol. 5. Ed. Philip Riden, and John Blair. Chesterfield, 1980.

Hooker, John. *A Pamphlet of the Offices, and Duties of Every Particular Sworne Officer, of the City of Excester*. London, 1584.

Household Accounts from Medieval England. Pt. 2. Ed. C. M. Woolgar. Oxford, 1993.

The Household Papers of Henry Percy, Ninth Earl of Northumberland (1564–1632). Ed. G. R. Batho. Camden Society, third ser., vol. 93, 1962.

Ilchester Almshouse Deeds . . . 1200–1625. Ed. W. Buckler. Yeovil, 1866.

The Injunctions and Other Ecclesiastical Proceedings of Richard Barnes, Bishop of Durham, from 1575 to 1587. Surtees Society, vol. 22, 1850.

John Howes' MS., 1582. Ed. William Lempriere. London, 1904.

Kent Chantries. Ed. A. Hussey. Kent Archaeological Society, Records Branch, vol. 12, 1936.

Kentish Visitations of Archbishop William Warham and His Deputies, 1511–1512. Ed. K. L. Wood-Legh. Kent Archaeological Society, Kent Records, vol. 24, 1984.

Lambarde, William. *The Duties of Constables, Borsholders, Tithingmen, and such other low Ministers of the Peace*. London, 1584.

Langland, William. *The Vision of Piers Plowman [B-Text]*. Ed. A. V. C. Schmidt. London, 1978.

Lever, Thomas. *"A Sermon Preached . . . before the Kinges Maiestie."* Ed. Edward Arber. Orig. publ. 1550; London, 1870.

Life, Love and Death in North-East Lancashire, 1510 to 1537: A Translation of the Act Book of the Ecclesiastical Court of Whalley. Ed. Margaret Lynch. Remains Historical and Literary . . . of Lancaster and Chester, Chetham Society, third ser., vol. 46, 2006.

List and Index Society. *Calendar of Patent Rolls, 32 Elizabeth I. Pt. 1*. London, 2004.

Calendar of Patent Rolls, 33 Elizabeth I. London, 2005.

Calendar of Patent Rolls, 39 Elizabeth. Pt. 1. London, 2008.

List of Proceedings of Commissioners for Charitable Uses . . . Preserved in the Public Record Office. PRO Lists and Indexes, vol. 10, 1899.

Liverpool Town Books: Proceedings of Assemblies, Common Councils, Portmoot Courts, etc., 1550–1862. Vol. 2. Ed. Jesse A. Twemlow. Liverpool, 1935.

London and Middlesex Chantry Certificates, 1548. Ed. C. J. Kitching. London Record Society, vol. 16, 1980.

The London Surveys of Ralph Treswell. Ed. John Schofield. London Topographical Society, vol. 135, 1987.

Memorials of St. Giles's, Durham. Ed. J. Barmby. Surtees Society, Durham, 1896.

Minutes and Accounts of the Corporation of Stratford-upon-Avon and Other Records. Vol. 1. Ed. Richard Savage. Dugdale Society Publications, vol. 1, 1921; vol. 2. Ed. Richard Savage and E. I. Fripp. Dugdale Society Publications, vol. 3, 1924; vol. 3. Ed. Richard Savage and E. I. Fripp. Dugdale Society Publications, vol. 5, 1926; vol. 5. Ed. Levi Fox. Dugdale Society Publications, vol. 35, 1990.

More, Thomas. *Utopia*. Ed. George M. Logan and R. M. Adams. Revd. edn., Cambridge, 2002.

"Nicholas Eyffeler of Warwick, Glazier: Executors' Accounts and Other Documents." Ed. M. W. Farr. In *Miscellany I*, 29–110. Dugdale Society Publications, vol. 31, 1977.

The Norwich Census of the Poor, 1570. Ed. John F. Pound. Norfolk Record Society, 1971.

The Ordinances of Bristol, 1506–1598. Ed. Maureen Stanford. Bristol Record Society, vol. 41, 1990.

Oxford Council Acts, 1583–1626. Ed. H. E. Salter. Oxford Historical Society, vol. 87. Oxford, 1928

Oxford English Dictionary. Compact edn., 2 vols. Oxford, 1971.

The Papers of Nathaniel Bacon of Stiffkey. Vol. 3. Ed. A. Hassell Smith and G. M. Baker. Norfolk Record Society, 1990.

Poor Relief in Elizabethan Ipswich. Ed. John Webb. Suffolk Records Society, vol. 9, 1966.

Poverty in Early-Stuart Salisbury. Ed. Paul Slack. Wiltshire Record Society, vol. 31, 1975.

The Pre-Reformation Records of All Saints' Church, Bristol: Wills, The Halleway Chantry Records and Deeds. Ed. Clive Burgess. Bristol Record Society, 2004.

Proceedings in the Parliaments of Elizabeth I. 3 vols. Ed. T. E. Hartley. Leicester, 1981–95.

Records of the Borough of Crossgate, Durham, 1312–1531. Ed. Richard Britnell. Surtees Society, vol. 212, 2008.

Records of the Borough of Leicester. Vol. 3. Ed. Mary Bateson. Cambridge, 1905.

Records of the Borough of Nottingham. Vol. 3. London, 1885; vol. 4. London, 1889.

The Records of the City of Norwich. Vol. 2. Ed. William Hudson and J. C. Tingey. Norwich, 1910.

Records of Maidstone, being selections from documents in the possession of the Corporation. Ed. K. S. Martin. Maidstone, 1926.

The Register of the Guild of Corpus Christi in the City of York. Surtees Society, vol. 57, 1872.

Reports of the Charity Commissioners for England and Wales. 44 vols. Parliamentary Papers, London, 1819–42.

Rites of Durham, being a Description … of all the Ancient Monuments, Rites, and Customs [of] the Monastical Church of Durham before the Suppression. Ed. J. T. Fowler. Surtees Society, vol. 107, 1903.

Sandys, Edwin. *The Sermons of Edwin Sandys.* Ed. John Ayre. Parker Society, vol. 41, 1842.

Selected Rentals and Accounts of Medieval Hull, 1293–1528. Ed. Rosemary Horrux. Yorkshire Archaeological Society Record Series, vol. 141, 1983.

A Selection from the Prescot Court Leet and Other Records, 1447–1600. Ed. F. A. Bailey. The Record Society of Lancashire and Cheshire, vol. 89, 1937.

Selections from English Wycliffite Writings. Ed. Anne Hudson. Cambridge, 1978.

Staffordshire Quarter Session Rolls. Vol. 1. Ed. S. A. H. Burne. William Salt Archaeological Society. Kendal, 1931.

"The State, Civil and Ecclesiastical, of the County of Lancaster, about the year 1590." In *Chetham Miscellanies*, vol. 5, 1–13. Chetham Society, vol. 96, 1875.

Statutes of the Realm. 12 vols. London, 1810–28.

The Statutes, and Ordinances, for the Government of the Alms-Houses, in Woodbridge … Founded by Thomas Seckford. Ed. Robert Loder. Woodbridge, 1792.

Steer, Francis W. "The Statutes of Saffron Walden Almshouses." *Transactions of the Essex Archaeological Society*, new. ser. **25** (1958): 160–221.

A Supplication of the Poore Commons. Ed. J. Meadows Cowper. Early English Text Society, Extra Ser., vol. 13, 60–93, 1871.

"Terumber's Chantry at Trowbridge." Ed. W. H. Jones. *Wiltshire Archaeological and Natural History Magazine* **10** (1867): 240–52.

The Third Book of Remembrance of Southampton. Vol. 1. Ed. A. L. Merson. Southampton Records Series, vol. 2, 1952.

Transcripts of Sussex Wills . . . to the year 1560. 4 vols. Ed. R. G. Rice. Sussex Record Society: vol. 41, 1935; vol. 42, 1936–7; vol. 43, 1938; and vol. 45, 1940–41.

Tudor Economic Documents. Vol. 2. Ed. R. H. Tawney and Eileen Power. London, 1924.

Tudor Parish Documents of the Diocese of York. Ed. J. S. Purvis. Cambridge, 1948.

Tudor Royal Proclamations. Ed. Paul L. Hughes and James F. Larkin. Vol. 1. New Haven, Conn., 1964; vols. 2 and 3. New Haven, Conn., 1969.

Tyndale, William. *The Obedyence of a Christian Man*. [Antwerp], 1528.

Visitation Articles and Injunctions of the Period of the Reformation. Vol. 2. Ed. W. H. Frere and W. M. Kennedy. London, 1910; vol. 3. Ed. W. H. Frere. London, 1910.

Visitations in the Diocese of Lincoln, 1517–1531. Ed. A. Hamilton Thompson. Vol. 1. Lincoln Record Society, vol. 33, 1940; vol. 3. Lincoln Record Society, vol. 37, 1947.

West Riding Sessions Rolls, 1597/8–1602. Ed. John Lister. Yorkshire Archaeological and Topographical Association, Record Series, vol. 3, 1888.

Wiltshire County Records: Minutes of Proceedings in Sessions, 1563 and 1574 to 1592. Ed. H. C. Johnson. Wiltshire Archaeological and Natural History Society, Records Branch, vol. 4. Devizes, 1949.

York Civic Records. Ed. Angelo Raine.
Vol. 2. Yorkshire Archaeological Society Record Series, vol. 103, 1941;
vol. 3. Yorkshire Archaeological Society Record Series, vol. 106, 1942;
vol. 4. Yorkshire Archaeological Society Record Series, vol. 108, 1945;
vol. 5. Yorkshire Archaeological Society Record Series, vol. 110, 1946;
vol. 7. Yorkshire Archaeological Society Record Series, vol. 115, 1950;
vol. 8. Yorkshire Archaeological Society Record Series, vol. 119, 1953.

York Memorandum Book. Vol. 2. Ed. Maud Sellers. Surtees Society, vol. 125, 1915.

3 SECONDARY STUDIES

Adair, Richard. *Courtship, Illegitimacy and Marriage in Early Modern England*. Manchester, 1996.

Aers, David. "*Piers Plowman* and Problems in the Perception of Poverty: A Culture in Transition." *Leeds Studies in English*, new ser. **14** (1983): 5–25.

Andrews, Sue and Tony Springall. *Hadleigh and the Alabaster Family*. Self-published, Bildeston, Suffolk, 2005.

Archer, Ian W. "The Arts and Acts of Memorialization in Early Modern London." In *Imagining Early Modern London*, ed. J. F. Merritt, 89–113. Cambridge, 2001.

"The Charity of Early Modern Londoners." *Transactions of the Royal Historical Society* 12 (2002): 223–44.

"The Charity of London Widows in the Later Sixteenth and Early Seventeenth Centuries." In *Local Identities in Late Medieval and Early Modern England*, ed. Norman L. Jones and Daniel Woolf, 178–206. Basingstoke, 2007.

"Hospitals in Sixteenth- and Seventeenth-Century England." In *Europäisches Spitalwesen. Institutionelle Fürsorge in Mittelalter und Früher Neuzeit*, ed. Martin Scheutz, Andrea Sommerlechner, Herwig Weigl, and Alfred Stefan Weiss, 53–74. Munich, 2008.

The Pursuit of Stability: Social Relations in Elizabethan London. Cambridge, 1991.

Atherton, Ian, Eileen McGrath, and Alannah Tomkins. "'Pressed Down by Want and Afflicted with Poverty, Wounded and Maimed in War or Worn Down with Age?' Cathedral Almsmen in England 1538–1914." In *Medicine, Charity and Mutual Aid: The Consumption of Health and Welfare in Britain, c. 1550–1950*, ed. Anne Borsay and Peter Shapely, 11–34. Aldershot, 2007.

Ault, Warren O. "By-Laws of Gleaning and the Problems of Harvest." *Economic History Review* 2nd ser. 14 (1961): 210–17.

"Manor Court and Parish Church in Fifteenth-Century England: A Study of Village By-Laws." *Speculum* 42 (1967): 53–67.

"The Village Church and the Village Community in Mediaeval England." *Speculum* 45 (1970): 197–215.

Aydelotte, Frank. *Elizabethan Rogues and Vagabonds. Orig. publ.* 1913; London, 1967.

Bailey, Brian. *Almshouses*. London, 1988.

Bainbridge, Virginia R. *Gilds in the Medieval Countryside*. Woodbridge, 1996.

Barron, Caroline M. *London in the Later Middle Ages*. Oxford, 2004.

"The Parish Fraternities of Medieval London." In *The Church in Pre-Reformation Society*, ed. Caroline M. Barron and C. Harper-Bill, 13–37. Woodbridge, 1985.

Beier, A. L. *Masterless Men: The Vagrancy Problem in England, 1560–1640*. London, 1985.

"On the Boundaries of New and Old Historicisms: Thomas Harman and the Literature of Roguery." *English Literary Renaissance* 33 (2003): 181–200.

The Problem of the Poor in Tudor and Early Stuart England. London, 1983.

"The Social Problems of an Elizabethan Country Town." In *Country Towns in Pre-Industrial England*, ed. Peter Clark, 46–85. Leicester, 1981.

"Vagrants and the Social Order in Elizabethan England." *Past and Present*, 64 (1974): 3–29.

Belfield, Gervase. "Cardinal Beaufort's Almshouse of Noble Poverty at St Cross, Winchester." *Proceedings of the Hampshire Field Club and Archaeological Society* 38 (1982): 103–111.

Ben-Amos, Ilana Krausman. *The Culture of Giving: Informal Support and Gift-Exchange in Early Modern England*. Cambridge, 2008.

"Gifts and Favors: Informal Support in Early Modern England." *Journal of Modern History* 72 (2000): 295–338.

Bennett, Judith M. "Conviviality and Charity in Medieval and Early Modern England." *Past and Present* **134** (1992): 19–41.

Bewes, Wyndham Anstis. *Church Briefs*. London, 1896.

Bittle, William G. and R. T. Lane. "Inflation and Philanthropy in England: A Re-Assessment of W. K. Jordan's Data." *Economic History Review* 2nd ser. **29** (1976): 203–10.

Blanchard, Ian. "Population Change, Enclosure, and the Early Tudor Economy." *Economic History Review* 2nd ser. **23** (1970): 427–45.

Bosworth, G. F. *History of Walthamstow Charities, 1487–1920*. Walthamstow Antiquarian Society Publications, vol. 8, 1920.

Botelho, Lynn A. *Old Age and the English Poor Law, 1500–1700*. Woodbridge, 2004.

Brigden, Susan. "Religion and Social Obligation in Early Sixteenth-Century London." *Past and Present* **103** (1984): 67–112.

Britnell, Richard. "English Agricultural Output and Prices, 1350–1450: National Trends and Regional Divergences." In *Agriculture and Rural Society after the Black Death*, ed. Ben Dodds and Richard Britnell, 20–39. Hatfield, 2008.

Broad, John. "Housing the Rural Poor in Southern England, 1650–1850." *Agricultural History Review* **48** (2000): 151–70.

Broadberry, Stephen, Bruce M. S. Campbell, and Bas van Leeuwen. "English Medieval Population: Reconciling Time Series and Cross Sectional Evidence," working paper, University of Warwick, July 27, 2010. Online at: www2.warwick.ac.uk/fac/soc/economics/staff/academic/broadberry/wp/medievalpopulation7.pdf

Brown, Andrew D. *Popular Piety in Late Medieval England*. Oxford, 1995.

Brown, W. Newman. "The Receipt of Poor Relief and Family Situation." In *Land, Kinship and Life-Cycle*, ed. Richard M. Smith, 405–22. Cambridge, 1984.

Burgess, Clive. "The Benefactions of Mortality: The Lay Response in the Late Medieval Urban Parish." In *Studies in Clergy and Ministry in Medieval England*, ed. David M. Smith, 65–86. Borthwick Studies in History, vol. 1. York, 1991.

"The Broader Church? A Rejoinder to 'Looking Beyond'." *English Historical Review* **119** (2004): 100–16.

"London Parishioners in Times of Change: St Andrew Hubbard, Eastcheap, c. 1450–1570." *Journal of Ecclesiastical History* **53** (2002): 38–63.

"Pre-Reformation Churchwardens' Accounts and Parish Government: Lessons from London and Bristol." *English Historical Review* **117** (2002): 306–32.

"A Service for the Dead: The Form and Function of the Anniversary in Late Medieval Bristol." *Transactions of the Bristol and Gloucestershire Archaeological Society* **105** (1987): 183–211.

"Time and Place: The Late Medieval English Parish in Perspective." In *The Parish in Late Medieval England*, ed. Clive Burgess and Eamon Duffy, 1–28. Donington, 2006.

Burgess, Clive and Beat Kümin. "Penitential Bequests and Parish Regimes in Late Medieval England." *Journal of Ecclesiastical History* **44** (1993): 610–30.

Campbell, Bruce M. S. "Four Famines and a Pestilence: Harvest, Price, and Wage Variations in England, 13th to 19th Centuries." In *Agrarhistoria på Många Sätt; 28 studier om manniskan och jorden. Festskrift till Janken Myrdal [Agrarian History Many Ways]*, ed. Britt Liljewall, I. A. Flygare, U. Lange, L. Ljunggren, and J. Söderberg, 23–56. Stockholm, 2009.

"Grain Yields on English Demesnes after the Black Death." In *Town and Countryside in the Age of the Black Death: Essays in Honour of John Hatcher*, ed. Mark Bailey and S. H. Rigby. Turnhout, forthcoming.

"Physical Shocks, Biological Hazards, and Human Impacts: The Crisis of the Fourteenth Century Revisited." In *Le interazioni fra economia e ambiente biologico nell'Europe preindustriale. Secc. XIII-XVIII [Economic and Biological Interactions in Pre-Industrial Europe from the 13th to the 18th Centuries]*, ed. Simonetta Cavaciocchi, 13–32. Prato, 2010.

Cannan, Edwin. *The History of Local Rates in England*. London, 1912.

Carlin, Martha. "Medieval English Hospitals." In *The Hospital in History*, ed. Lindsay Granshaw and Roy Porter, 21–39. London, 1989.

Carter, John and Jacqueline Smith. *Give and Take: Scenes from the History of Christ's Hospital, Abingdon, 1553–1900*. Privately published, Abingdon, 1981.

Cavallo, Sandra. "The Motivations of Benefactors: An Overview of Approaches to the Study of Charity." In *Medicine and Charity before the Welfare State*, ed. Jonathan Barry and C. Jones, 46–62. London, 1991.

Cavill, P. R. "The Problem of Labour and the Parliament of 1495." In *The Fifteenth Century V: Of Mice and Men*, ed. Linda Clark, 143–55. Woodbridge, 2005.

Charlesworth, Lorie. *Welfare's Forgotten Past: A Socio-Legal History of the Poor Law*. Abingdon, 2010.

Clark, Elaine. "Charitable Bequests, Deathbed Land Sales, and the Manor Court in Later Medieval England." In *Medieval Society and the Manor Court*, ed. Zvi Razi and Richard Smith, 143–61. Oxford, 1996.

"City Orphans and Custody Laws in Medieval England." *American Journal of Legal History* **34** (1990): 168–87.

"The Custody of Children in English Manor Courts." *Law and History Review* **3** (1985): 333–48.

"Institutional and Legal Responses to Begging in Medieval England." *Social Science History* **26** (2002): 447–73.

"Mothers at Risk of Poverty in the Medieval English Countryside." In *Poor Women and Children in the European Past*, ed. John Henderson and Richard Wall, 139–59. London, 1994.

"Social Welfare and Mutual Aid in the Medieval Countryside." *Journal of British Studies* **33** (1994): 381–406.

"Some Aspects of Social Security in Medieval England." *Journal of Family History* **7** (1982): 307–20.

Clarke, Basil. "Norfolk Licenses to Beg." *Norfolk Archaeology* **35** (1972): 327–34.

Clay, Rotha M. *The Mediaeval Hospitals of England*. London, [1909].

Collinson, Patrick. "Puritanism and the Poor." In *Pragmatic Utopias*, ed. Rosemary Horrox and Sarah Rees Jones, 242–58. Cambridge, 2001.

Cooper, C. M. *Annals of Cambridge*. Vol. 1. Cambridge, 1842.

Cox, J. Charles and Alfred Harvey. *English Church Furniture*. New York, 1907.

Craig, John S. "Co-operation and Initiatives: Elizabethan Churchwardens and the Parish Accounts of Mildenhall." *Social History* **18** (1993): 357–80

"Reformers, Conflict, and Revisionism: The Reformation in Sixteenth-Century Hadleigh." *The Historical Journal* **42** (1999): 1–23.

Crassons, Kate. *The Claims of Poverty: Literature, Culture, and Ideology in Late Medieval England*. Notre Dame, Indiana, 2010.

Crowe, Ken. "Charity and the Economy of the Poor in an Essex Parish: Canewdon in the Early Modern Period." *Essex Archaeology and History* **33** (2002): 310–22.

Cruickshank, C. G. *Elizabeth's Army*. 2nd edn. Oxford, 1966

Cullum, Patricia H. "'And Hir Name Was Charite': Charitable Giving by and for Women in Late Medieval Yorkshire." In *Women in Medieval English Society*, ed. P. J. P. Goldberg, 182–211. Stroud, 1997.

"Cremetts and Corrodies: Care of the Poor and Sick at St Leonard's Hospital, York, in the Middle Ages." Borthwick Paper no. 79. York, 1991.

"'For Pore People Harberles': What was the Function of the Maisonsdieu?" In *Trade, Devotion and Governance*, ed. Dorothy J. Clayton, R. G. Davies, and Peter McNiven, 36–54. Stroud, 1994.

Hospitals and Charitable Provision in Medieval England. In preparation.

"Leperhouses and Borough Status in the Thirteenth Century." In *Thirteenth Century England III*, ed. P. R. Coss and S. D. Lloyd, 37–46. Woodbridge, 1991.

"Medieval Colleges and Charity." In *The Late Medieval English College and Its Context*, ed. Clive Burgess and Martin Heale, 140–53. York, 2008.

"Poverty and Charity in Early Fourteenth-Century England." In *England in the Fourteenth Century*, ed. Nicholas Rogers, 140–51. Stamford, 1993.

Cullum, Patricia H. and P. J. P. Goldberg. "Charitable Provision in Late Medieval York: 'To the Praise of God and the Use of the Poor.'" *Northern History* **29** (1993): 24–39.

Davies, C. S. L. "Slavery and Protector Somerset; the Vagrancy Act of 1547." *Economic History Review* 2nd ser. **19** (1966): 533–49.

Davies, Matthew. "The Tailors of London: Corporate Charity in the Late Medieval Town." In *Crown, Government and People in the Fifteenth Century*, ed. Rowena E. Archer, 161–90. Stroud, 1995.

Deverell, John. *St. John's Hospital and Other Charities in Winchester*. London, 1879.

Dyer, Christopher. *An Age of Transition? Economy and Society in England in the Later Middle Ages*. Oxford, 2005.

"Deserted Medieval Villages in the West Midlands." *Economic History Review* 2nd ser. **35** (1982): 19–34.

"Did the Peasants Really Starve in Medieval England?" In *Food and Eating in Medieval Europe*, ed. Martha Carlin and J. T. Rosenthal, 53–71. London, 1998.

"The English Medieval Village Community and Its Decline." *Journal of British Studies* **33** (1994): 407–29.

"The Political Life of the Fifteenth-Century English Village." In *Political Culture in Late Medieval Britain*, ed. Linda Clark and Christine Carpenter, 135–57. Woodbridge, 2004.

Standards of Living in the Later Middle Ages. Cambridge, 1989.

"Taxation and Communities in Late Medieval England." In *Progress and Problems in Medieval England*, ed. Richard Britnell and John Hatcher, 168–90. Cambridge, 1996.

Elton, Geoffrey R. "An Early Tudor Poor Law." *Economic History Review* 2nd ser. **6** (1953): 55–67.

Emmison, F. G. "The Care of the Poor in Elizabethan Essex." *Essex Review* **62** (1953): 7–28.

Evans, Vivienne. *Dunstable with the Priory, 1100–1550*. Dunstable, 1994.

Fideler, Paul A. "Introduction: Impressions of a Century of Historiography." In "Symposium on the Study of the Early Modern Poor and Poverty Relief," *Albion* **32** (2000): 381–407.

"Poverty, Policy and Providence: The Tudors and the Poor." In *Political Thought and the Tudor Commonwealth*, ed. Paul A. Fideler and T. F. Mayer, 194–222. London, 1992.

Social Welfare in Pre-Industrial England: The Old Poor Law Tradition. Basingstoke, 2006.

Fleming, P. W. "Charity, Faith, and the Gentry of Kent, 1422–1529." In *Property and Politics*, ed. Anthony J. Pollard, 36–53. Gloucester, 1984.

French, Katherine L. *The Good Women of the Parish*. Philadelphia, 2008.

"Parochial Fund-Raising in Late Medieval Somerset." In *The Parish in English Life, 1400–1600*, ed. Katherine L. French, G. G. Gibbs, and B. A. Kümin, 115–32. Manchester, 1997.

The People of the Parish. Philadelphia, 2001.

"Women Churchwardens in Late Medieval England." In *The Parish in Late Medieval England*, ed. Clive Burgess and Eamon Duffy, 302–21. Donington, 2006.

Frohnsdorff, Mike. "The Maison Dieu and Medieval Faversham." Lecture published by the Faversham Society, 1997.

Fumerton, Patricia. "Making Vagrancy (In)Visible: The Economics of Disguise in Early Modern Rogue Pamphlets." *English Literary Renaissance* **33** (2003): 211–27.

Unsettled: The Culture of Mobility and the Working Poor in Early Modern England. Chicago, 2006.

Gibson, James M. *The Walthamstow Charities*. Chichester, 2000.

Gilchrist, Roberta. *Gender and Material Culture: The Archaeology of Religious Women*. London, 1994.

Given-Wilson, Chris. "Service, Serfdom and English Labour Legislation, 1350–1500." In *Concepts and Patterns of Service in the Later Middle Ages*, ed. Anne Curry and Elizabeth Matthew, 21–37. Woodbridge, 2000.

Godfrey, Walter H. *The English Almshouse*. London, [1955].

Good, Michael. *A Compendium of Pevsner's Buildings of England on Compact Disc*. Oxford, 1995.

Goodall, John A. A. *God's House at Ewelme*. Aldershot, 2001.

Goose, Nigel. "The English Almshouse and the Mixed Economy of Welfare: Medieval to Modern." *The Local Historian* **40** (2010): 3–19.

"The Rise and Decline of Philanthropy in Early Modern Colchester." *Social History* **31** (2006): 469–87.

Gould, J. D. "Bittle and Lane on Charity: An Uncharitable Comment." *Economic History Review* 2nd ser. **31** (1978): 121–3.

Gransden, Antonia. "Letter of Recommendation from John Whethamstede for a Poor Pilgrim, 1453/4." *English Historical Review* **106** (1991): 932–8.

Groom, Matthew. "*Piety and Locality: Studies in Urban and Rural Religion in Surrey, c. 1450–c. 1550.*" University of London Ph.D. thesis, 2001.

Hadwin, J. F. "Deflating Philanthropy." *Economic History Review* 2nd ser. **31** (1978): 105–17.

Haines, R. M. "Bishop Carpenter's Injunctions to the Diocese of Worcester in 1451." *Bulletin of the Institute of Historical Research* **40** (1967): 203–7.

Hampson, E. M. *The Treatment of Poverty in Cambridgeshire, 1597–1834.* Cambridge, 1934.

Hanawalt, Barbara A. "Keepers of the Lights: Late Medieval Parish Gilds." *Journal of Medieval and Renaissance Studies* **14** (1984): 21–37.

"Reading the Lives of the Illiterate: London's Poor." *Speculum* **80** (2005): 1067–86.

Hanawalt, Barbara A. and Ben R. McRee. "The Guilds of *Homo Prudens* in Late Medieval England." *Continuity and Change* **7** (1992): 163–79.

Harris, Barbara J. "The Fabric of Piety: Aristocratic Women and Care of the Dead, 1450–1550." *Journal of British Studies* **48** (2009): 308–35.

Harris, Mark. "'Inky Blots and Rotten Parchment Bonds': London, Charity Briefs and the Guildhall Library." *Bulletin of the Institute of Historical Research* **66** (1993): 98–110.

Harrison, Christopher. "The Great Fire of Nantwich." Unpublished paper.

Harvey, Barbara. *Living and Dying in England, 1100–1540.* Oxford, 1993.

Hatcher, John. "The Great Slump of the Mid-Fifteenth Century." In *Progress and Problems in Medieval England*, ed. Richard Britnell and John Hatcher, 237–72. Cambridge, 1996.

"Mortality in the Fifteenth Century: Some New Evidence." *Economic History Review* 2nd ser. **39** (1986): 19–38.

"Understanding the Population History of England, 1450–1750." *Past and Present* **180** (2003): 83–130.

Hatcher, John, A. J. Piper, and David Stone. "Monastic Mortality: Durham Priory, 1395–1529." *Economic History Review* **59** (2006): 667–87.

Heal, Felicity. "The Archbishops of Canterbury and the Practice of Hospitality." *Journal of Ecclesiastical History* **33** (1982): 544–63.

"Concepts of Generosity in Early Modern England." In *Luxury and Austerity*, ed. Jacqueline Hill and Colm Lennon, 30–45. Dublin, 1999.

Hospitality in Early Modern England. Oxford, 1990.

Heale, Martin R. V. "Monastic-Parochial Churches in Late Medieval England." In *The Parish in Late Medieval England*, ed. Clive Burgess and Eamon Duffy, 54–77. Donington, 2006.

Heath, Peter. "Urban Piety in the Later Middle Ages: The Evidence of Hull Wills." In *The Church, Politics and Patronage in the Fifteenth Century*, ed. Barrie Dobson, 209–29. Gloucester, 1984.

Hewitt, H. J. *The Organization of War under Edward III*. Manchester, 1966.

Hickman, David. "From Catholic to Protestant: The Changing Meaning of Testamentary Religious Provisions in Elizabethan London." In *England's Long Reformation, 1500–1800*, ed. Nicholas Tyacke, 117–38. London, 2003.

Hicks, Michael. "St Katherine's Hospital, Heytesbury." *Wiltshire Archaeological and Natural History Magazine* 78 (1984): 62–9.

Hill, Christopher. "Puritans and the Poor." *Past and Present* 2 (1952): 32–50. *Society and Puritanism*. London, 1964.

Hindle, Steve. "Dearth, Fasting and Alms: The Campaign for General Hospitality in Late Elizabethan England." *Past and Present* 172 (2001): 44–86.

"Dependency, Shame, and Belonging: Badging the Deserving Poor, *c.* 1550–1750." *Cultural and Social History* 1 (2004): 6–35.

"'Good, Godly and Charitable Uses': Endowed Charity and the Relief of Poverty in Rural England, *c.* 1550–1750." In *Institutional Culture in Early Modern Society*, ed. Anne Goldgar and R. I. Frost, 164–88. Leiden, 2004.

On the Parish? The Micro-Politics of Poor Relief in Rural England, c. 1550–1750. Oxford, 2004.

"Technologies of Identification under the Old Poor Law." *The Local Historian* 36 (2006): 220–36.

Hitchcock, Tim. *Down and Out in Eighteenth-Century London*. London, 2004.

Hitchcock, Tim, Peter King, and Pamela Sharpe, eds. *Chronicling Poverty: The Voices and Strategies of the English Poor, 1640–1840*. Basingstoke, 1997.

Hobbes, Stephen. "Payments to Itinerant Travellers Seeking Alms in Hartland, 1612–1706." *The Devon Historian* 78 (2009): 21–46.

Holloway, William. *The History and Antiquities of the Ancient Town and Port of Rye*. London, 1848.

Hopewell, Peter. *Saint Cross: England's Oldest Almshouse*. Chichester, 1995.

Hopkirk, Mary. "The Administration of Poor Relief, 1604–1834." *Essex Review* 58 (1949): 113–21.

Horden, Peregrine. "A Discipline of Relevance: The Historiography of the Later Medieval Hospital." *Social History of Medicine* 1 (1988): 359–74.

"Small Beer? The Parish and the Poor and Sick in Later Medieval England." In *The Parish in Late Medieval England*, ed. Clive Burgess and Eamon Duffy, 339–64. Donington, 2006.

Houlbrooke, Ralph. *Church Courts and the People during the English Reformation, 1520–1570*. Oxford, 1979.

Howson, Brian. *Houses of Noble Poverty*. Sunbury-on-Thames, 1993.

Hudson, Geoffrey L. "Disabled Veterans and the State in Early Modern England." In *Disabled Veterans in History*, ed. David A. Gerber, 117–44. Ann Arbor, Mich., 2000.

Hunt, William. *The Puritan Moment*. Cambridge, Mass., 1983.

Imray, Jean. *The Charity of Richard Whittington*. London, 1968.

Innes, Joanna. "The 'Mixed Economy of Welfare' in Early Modern England: Assessments of the Options from Hale to Malthus (*c.* 1683–1803)." In

Charity, Self-Interest and Welfare in the English Past, ed. Martin Daunton, 139–80. London, 1996.

"Prisons for the Poor: English Bridewells, 1555–1800." In *Labour, Law, and Crime: An Historical Perspective*, ed. Francis Snyder and Douglas Hay, 42–122. London, 1987.

Jones, Gareth. *History of the Law of Charity, 1532–1827*. Cambridge, 1969.

Jordan, W. K. "The Charities of Hampshire, 1480–1660." Unpublished essay in Harvard University Archives HUG (FB)-7.60, Box 1.

The Charities of London, 1480–1660. London, 1960.

The Charities of Rural England, 1480–1660. London, 1961.

"The Charities of Worcestershire, 1480–1660." Unpublished essay in Harvard University Archives HUG (FB)-7.60, Box 1.

Edward VI: The Young King. Cambridge, Mass., 1968.

The Forming of the Charitable Institutions of the West of England. Philadelphia, 1960.

Philanthropy in England, 1480–1660. London, 1959.

Social Institutions in Kent, 1480–1660. Archaeologia Cantiana, vol. 75, 1961.

The Social Institutions of Lancashire. Chetham Society, 3rd ser., vol. 11, 1962.

Kitching, C. J. "Fire Disasters and Fire Relief in Sixteenth-Century England: The Nantwich Fire of 1583." *Bulletin of the Institute of Historical Research* **54** (1981): 171–87.

Knowles, David. *The Religious Orders in England*. 3 vols. Cambridge, 1948–59.

Knowles, David and R. N. Hadcock. *Medieval Religious Houses, England and Wales*. London, 1971.

Kreider, Alan. *English Chantries: The Road to Dissolution*. Cambridge, Mass., 1979.

Kümin, Beat. "Late Medieval Churchwardens' Accounts and Parish Government: Looking beyond London and Bristol." *English Historical Review* **119** (2004): 87–99.

"Parish Finance and the Early Tudor Clergy." In *The Reformation of the Parishes*, ed. Andrew Pettegree, 43–62. Manchester, 1993.

"The Secular Legacy of the Late Medieval English Parish." In *The Parish in Late Medieval England*, ed. Clive Burgess and Eamon Duffy, 95–111. Donington, 2006.

The Shaping of a Community: The Rise and Reformation of the English Parish, c. 1400–1560. Aldershot, 1996.

Lehmberg, Stanford E. *The Reformation of Cathedrals*. Princeton, New Jersey, 1988.

Leonard, E. M. *The Early History of English Poor Relief*. Cambridge, 1900.

Lepine, David. "'And Alle Oure Paresshens': Secular Cathedrals and Parish Churches in Late Medieval England." In *The Parish in Late Medieval England*, ed. Clive Burgess and Eamon Duffy, 29–53. Donington, 2006.

Litzenberger, Caroline. "Local Responses to Changes in Religious Policy Based on Evidence from Gloucestershire Wills (1540–1580)." *Continuity and Change* **8** (1993): 417–39.

Macfarlane, Alan. *Witchcraft in Tudor and Stuart England*. London, 1970.

MacKinnon, Dolly. "Charitable Bodies: Clothing as Charity in Early-Modern Rural England." In *Practices of Gender in Late Medieval and Early Modern*

Europe, ed. Megan Cassidy-Welch and Peter Sherlock, 235–59. Turnhout, 2008.

McIntosh, Marjorie Keniston. *Autonomy and Community: The Royal Manor of Havering, 1200–1500*. Cambridge, 1986.

Charity, Family, and Community in Elizabethan Hadleigh, Suffolk. In preparation.

A Community Transformed. Cambridge, 1991.

Controlling Misbehavior in England, 1370–1600. Cambridge, 1998.

"The Diversity of Social Capital in English Communities, 1300–1640 (with a Glance at Modern Nigeria)." *Journal of Interdisciplinary History* **29** (1999): 459–90. Reprinted in *Patterns of Social Capital*, ed. Robert I. Rotberg, 121–52. Cambridge, 2001.

"Local Change and Community Control in England, 1465–1500." *Huntington Library Quarterly* **49** (1986): 219–42.

"Local Responses to the Poor in Late Medieval and Tudor England." *Continuity and Change* **3** (1988): 209–45.

"Negligence, Greed, and the Operation of English Charities, 1350–1603." *Continuity and Change*, forthcoming in 2012.

"Networks of Care in Elizabethan English Towns." In *The Locus of Care*, ed. Peregrine Horden and Richard Smith, 71–89. London, 1998.

"Poverty, Charity, and Coercion in Elizabethan England." *Journal of Interdisciplinary History* **35** (2005): 457–79.

Working Women in English Society, 1300–1620. Cambridge, 2005.

McRee, Ben R. "Charity and Gild Solidarity in Late Medieval England." *Journal of British Studies* **32** (1993): 195–225.

Meade, Dorothy M. "The Hospital of Saint Giles at Kepier, near Durham, 1112–1545." *Transactions of the Architectural and Archaeological Society of Durham and Northumberland* new ser. **1** (1968): 45–57.

Mollat, Michel. *Les Pauvres au Moyen Age*. Paris, 1978.

New, Elizabeth. "Signs of Community or Marks of the Exclusive? Parish and Guild Seals in Later Medieval England." In *The Parish in Late Medieval England*, ed. Clive Burgess and Eamon Duffy, 112–28. Donington, 2006.

Nichols, John. *The Progresses and Public Processions of Queen Elizabeth*. 3 vols. London, 1823.

O'Donoghue, Edward G. *The Story of Bethlehem Hospital*. London, 1914.

Orme, Nicholas. "Indulgences in the Diocese of Exeter, 1100–1536." *Reports and Transactions of the Devonshire Association for the Advancement of Science* **120** (1988): 15–32.

"A Medieval Almshouse for the Clergy: Clyst Gabriel Hospital near Exeter." *Journal of Ecclesiastical History* **39** (1988): 1–15.

"The Other Parish Churches: Chapels in Late-Medieval England." In *The Parish in Late Medieval England*, ed. Clive Burgess and Eamon Duffy, 78–94. Donington, 2006.

Orme, Nicholas and Margaret Webster. *The English Hospital, 1070–1570*. New Haven, Conn., 1995.

Ottaway, Susannah R. *The Decline of Life: Old Age in Eighteenth-Century England*. Cambridge, 2004.

Owst, G. R. *Preaching in Medieval England*. Cambridge, 1926.

Page, Frances M. "The Customary Poor-Law of Three Cambridgeshire Manors." *Cambridge Historical Journal* **3** (1930): 125–33.

Patriquin, Larry. "Agrarian Capitalism and Poor Relief in England, *c.* 1500–1790." In *The Capitalist State and Its Economy*, ed. Paul Zarembka, 3–50. Research in Political Economy, vol. 22, 2005.

Peckham, W. D. "St. Mary's Hospital, Chichester." *Sussex Notes and Queries* **8** (1941): 207–13.

Pelling, Margaret. "Healing the Sick Poor: Social Policy and Disability in Norwich, 1550–1640." In her *The Common Lot: Sickness, Medical Occupations and the Urban Poor in Early Modern England*, 79–102. London, 1998.

"Old Age, Poverty, and Disability in Early Modern Norwich." In her *The Common Lot, 134–54.* London, 1998.

Peters, Christine. *Patterns of Piety*. Cambridge, 2003.

Pevsner, Nikolaus. *The Buildings of England*, orig. publ. London, 1951; second and sometimes third editions were written with or by other authors and published variously.

Phillips, Elaine M. "Charitable Institutions in Norfolk and Suffolk, *c.* 1350–1600." University of East Anglia Ph.D. thesis, 2001.

Ping, Lilian G. "Raising Funds for 'Good Causes' during the Reformation." *Hibbert Journal* **35** (1936–7): 53–66.

Post, J. B. "Manorial Amercements and Peasant Poverty." *Economic History Review* 2nd ser. **28** (1975): 304–11.

Pound, John. *Poverty and Vagrancy in Tudor England*. London, 1971.

Prescott, Elizabeth. *The English Medieval Hospital, 1050–1640*. Broughton Gifford, 1992.

Rawcliffe, Carole. "Dives Redeemed? The Guild Almshouses of Later Medieval England." In *The Fifteenth Century VII*, ed. Linda Clark, 1–27. Woodbridge, 2008.

"The Earthly and Spiritual Topography of Suburban Hospitals." In *Town and Country in the Middle Ages*, ed. Kate Giles and Christopher Dyer, 251–74. Leeds, 2005.

The Hospitals of Medieval Norwich. Norwich, 1995.

Leprosy in Medieval England. Woodbridge, 2006.

"Medicine for the Soul: The Medieval English Hospital and the Quest for Spiritual Health." In *Religion, Health and Suffering*, ed. John R. Hinnells and Roy Porter, 316–38. London, 1999.

"A Word from Our Sponsor: Advertising the Patron in the Medieval Hospital." In *The Impact of Hospitals, 300–2000*, ed. John Henderson, Peregrine Horden, and Alessandro Pastore, 167–93. Oxford, 2007.

Reeve, Edward H. L. *Stondon Massey*. Colchester, 1900.

Resl, Brigitte. "Hospitals in Medieval England." In *Europäisches Spitalwesen. Institutionelle Fürsorge in Mittelalter und Früher Neuzeit*, ed. Martin Scheutz, Andrea Sommerlechner, Herwig Weigl, and Alfred Stefan Weiss, 41–52. Munich, 2008.

Rexroth, Frank. *Deviance and Power in Late Medieval London*. Orig. publ. in German, 1999; Engl. transl., Cambridge, 2007.

Richmond, Colin. "Victorian Values in Fifteenth-Century England: The Ewelme Almshouse Statutes." In *Pragmatic Utopias*, ed. Rosemary Horrox and Sarah Rees Jones, 224–41. Cambridge, 2001.

Rigby, Stephen H. "Urban Population in Late Medieval England: The Evidence of the Lay Subsidies." *Economic History Review* 63 (2010): 393–417.

Robison, William B. "The Bawdy Master of St. Thomas's Hospital." *Historical Research* 83 (2010): 565–74.

Rowe, Joy. "The Medieval Hospitals of Bury St. Edmunds." *Medical History* 2 (1958): 253–63.

Rubin, Miri. *Charity and Community in Medieval Cambridge.* Cambridge, 1987.

"Development and Change in English Hospitals, 1100–1500." In *The Hospital in History*, ed. Lindsay Grandshaw and Roy Porter, 41–59. London, 1989.

"Imagining Medieval Hospitals: Considerations on the Cultural Meaning of Institutional Change." In *Medicine and Charity before the Welfare State*, ed. Jonathan Barry and Colin Jones, 14–25. London, 1991.

Rushton, Neil S. "Monastic Charitable Provision in Tudor England." *Continuity and Change* 16 (2001): 9–44.

Savine, Alexander. *English Monasteries on the Eve of the Dissolution.* Oxford, 1909.

Schen, Claire S. *Charity and Lay Piety in Reformation London, 1500–1620.* Aldershot, 2002.

"Constructing the Poor in Early Seventeenth-Century London." *Albion* 32 (2000): 450–63.

Shepard, Alexandra. "Poverty, Labour and the Language of Social Description in Early Modern England." *Past and Present* 201 (2008): 51–95.

Shepherd, Geoffrey. "Poverty in Piers Plowman." In *Social Relations and Ideas: Essays in Honour of R. H. Hilton*, ed. T. H. Aston, P. R. Coss, Christopher Dyer, and Joan Thirsk, 169–89. Cambridge, 1983.

Slack, Paul. *The English Poor Law, 1531–1782.* Basingstoke, 1990.

From Reformation to Improvement: Public Welfare in Early Modern England. Oxford, 1999.

"Hospitals, Workhouses and the Relief of the Poor in Early Modern London." In *Health Care and Poor Relief in Protestant Europe, 1500–1700*, ed. Ole Peter Grell and Andrew Cunningham, 234–51. London, 1997.

Poverty and Policy in Tudor and Stuart England. London, 1988.

"Social Policy and the Constraints of Government, 1547–58." In *The Mid-Tudor Polity, c. 1540–1560*, ed. Robert Tittler and J. Loach, 94–115. London, 1980.

"Vagrants and Vagrancy in England, 1598–1664." *Economic History Review* 2nd ser. 27 (1974): 360–79.

Smith, Richard M. "Charity, Self-Interest and Welfare: Reflections from Demographic and Family History." In *Charity, Self-Interest, and Welfare in the English Past*, ed. Martin Daunton, 23–49. London, 1996.

"The Manorial Court and the Elderly Tenant in Late Medieval England." In *Life, Death, and the Elderly*, ed. Margaret Pelling and R. M. Smith, 39–61. London, 1991.

"Putting Benedictine Monks in Context: Mortality in England, 1350–1540." In *Town and Countryside in the Age of the Black Death: Essays in Honour of John Hatcher*, ed. Mark Bailey and S. H. Rigby. Turnhout, forthcoming.

Snape, Robert H. *English Monastic Finances in the Later Middle Ages.* Cambridge, 1926.

Snell, Keith D. M. *Parish and Belonging: Community, Identity and Welfare in England and Wales, 1700–1950.* Cambridge, 2006.

'*So Long as the World Shall Endure': The Five Hundred Year History of Bond's and Ford's Hospitals.* Coventry, 1991.

Somerscales, M. I. "Lazar Houses in Cornwall." *Journal of the Royal Institution of Cornwall* new ser. 5 (1965–8): 61–99.

Stone, Lawrence. *The Family, Sex and Marriage in England, 1500–1800.* London, 1977.

Sutton, Anne F. "The Hospital of St Thomas of Acre of London." In *The Late Medieval English College and Its Context,* ed. Clive Burgess and Martin Heale, 199–229. York, 2008.

Swanson, R. N. *Indulgences in Late Medieval England.* Cambridge, 2007.

"Tales to Tug at Purse-Strings: Publicizing Indulgences in Pre-Reformation England." In *Freedom of Movement in the Middle Ages,* ed. Peregrine Horden, 123–36. Donington, 2007.

Sweetinburgh, Sheila. "Clothing the Naked in Late Medieval East Kent." In *Clothing Culture, 1350–1650.* Ed. Catherine Richardson, 109–21. Aldershot, 2004.

"The Poor, Hospitals and Charity in Sixteenth-Century Canterbury." In *Pieties in Transition: Religious Practices and Experiences, c. 1400–1640,* ed. Robert Lutton and Elisabeth Salter, 59–73. Aldershot, 2007.

The Role of the Hospital in Medieval England. Dublin, 2004.

Tanner, Norman P. *The Church in Late Medieval Norwich, 1370–1532.* Toronto, 1984.

Thirsk, Joan (ed.). *The Agrarian History of England and Wales.* Vol. 4, *1500–1640.* Cambridge, 1967.

Thomas, Keith. *Religion and the Decline of Magic.* New York, 1971.

Thomson, J. A. F. "Piety and Charity in Late Medieval London." *Journal of Ecclesiastical History* 16 (1965): 178–95.

Tierney, Brian. *Medieval Poor Law.* Berkeley, Calif., 1959.

Tittler, Robert. *The Reformation and the Towns in England.* Oxford, 1998.

Tobriner, Alice. "Almshouses in Sixteenth-Century England: Housing for the Poor Elderly." *Journal of Religion and Aging* 1 (1985): 13–41.

Todd, Margo. *Christian Humanism and the Puritan Social Order.* Cambridge, 1987.

Underdown, David. *Fire from Heaven.* New Haven, Conn., 1992.

Van der Slice, Austin. "Elizabethan Houses of Correction." *Journal of Criminal Law and Criminology* 27 (1936): 45–67.

Vickers, Michael. "An Elizabethan Contact with Greece." *Journal of Ecclesiastical History* 24 (1973): 51–8.

The Victoria History of the County of Cambridge. Vol. 4. London, 1953.

The Victoria History of the County of Northampton. Vol. 2. London, 1906.

Wales, Tim. "Poverty, Poor Relief and the Life Cycle." In *Land, Kinship and Life-Cycle.* Ed. Richard M. Smith, 351–404. Cambridge, 1984.

Ward, Jennifer C. "The Reformation in Colchester, 1528–1558." *Essex Archaeology and History* 15 (1983): 84–95.

Ware, Sedley L. *The Elizabethan Parish in Its Ecclesiastical and Financial Aspects.* Baltimore, 1908.

Warnicke, Retha M. *William Lambarde, Elizabethan Antiquary.* Chichester, 1973.

Watson, Sethina. "City as Charter: Charity and the Lordship of English Towns, 1170–1250." In *Cities, Texts and Social Networks, 400–1500,* ed. Caroline Goodson, Anne E. Lester, and Carol Symes, 235–62. Farnham, 2010.

"The Origins of the English Hospital." *Transactions of the Royal Historical Society* **16** (2006): 75–94.

Wear, Andrew. "Caring for the Sick Poor in St Bartholomew's Exchange, 1580–1679." *Medical History* Supplement No. **11** (1991): 41–60.

Webb, Sidney and Beatrice Webb. *English Poor Law History, Part I: The Old Poor Law.* Orig. publ. 1927; London, 1963.

White, William. "Excavations at St Mary Spital: Burial of the 'Sick Poore' of Medieval London." In *The Medieval Hospital and Medical Practice,* ed. Barbara S. Bowers, 59–64. Aldershot, 2007.

Willen, Diane. "Women in the Public Sphere in Early Modern England." *Sixteenth Century Journal* **19** (1988): 559–75.

Willson, A. N. *A History of Collyer's School.* London, 1965.

Withington, Phil. *The Politics of Commonwealth.* Cambridge, 2005.

Woodbridge, Linda. "Jest Books, the Literature of Roguery, and the Vagrant Poor in Renaissance England." *English Literary Renaissance* **33** (2003): 201–10.

Wooding, Lucy E. C. "Charity, Community and Reformation Propaganda." *Reformation* **11** (2006): 131–69.

Wright, H. P. *The Story of the "Domus Dei" of Stamford.* London, 1890.

Wrightson, Keith and David Levine. *Poverty and Piety in an English Village.* Orig. publ. 1979; 2nd edn., Oxford, 1995.

Wrigley, E. A., R. S. Davies, J. Oeppen, and R. Schofield. *English Population History from Family Reconstitution, 1580–1837.* Cambridge, 1997.

Yates, Margaret. "Between Fact and Fiction: Henry Brinklow's *Complaynt* against Rapacious Landlords." *Agricultural History Review* **54** (2006): 22–44.

Index

References to CUP Online Apps. within the index can be found at www.cambridge.org/mcintosh/appendices, under the "Resources" tab

Lightning Source UK Ltd.
Milton Keynes UK
UKOW06f0304190515

251819UK00009B/283/P